Impossible Love

Ascher Levy's Longing for Germany

By the same Author

The Cap: or The Price of a Life

Impossible Love

Ascher Levy's Longing for Germany

ROMAN FRISTER

Translated by Alisa Jaffa

Weidenfeld and Nicolson

LONDON

First published in Great Britain in 2002
by Weidenfeld & Nicolson

First published in Germany in 1999 as
Ascher Levys Sehnsucht Nach Deutschland
by Siedler Verlag GmbH

A CIP catalogue record for this book
is available from the British Library.

ISBN 0 297 64591 9

Typeset in Adobe Caslon by
Selwood Systems, Midsomer Norton

Printed in Great Britain by Butler & Tanner Ltd,
Frome and London

Weidenfeld & Nicolson

The Orion Publishing Group Ltd
Orion House
5 Upper Saint Martin's Lane
London, WC2H 9EA

Contents

All illustrations are the private property of
Roman Frister apart from:

'Addressee unknown – Jew'
(courtesy of the Edward Bargheer House Archive, Hamburg)

'Always remember that you are a proud citizen of Prussia, entitled to equal rights. And never forget that you are a Jew. If you do, there will always be others to remind you of your origins.'

Ascher Levy to his son, Bernhard, 1858

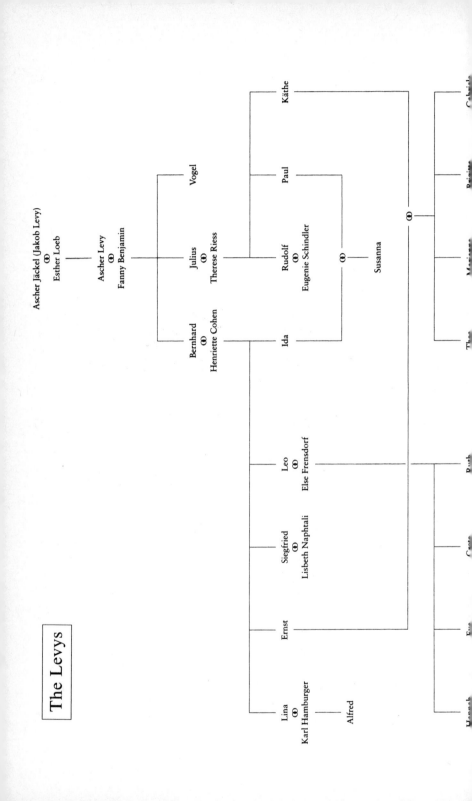

The Levys

Foreword

The key to this astonishing story was buried in an old cardboard suitcase.

On the pavement in the Jaffa flea market a junk dealer had spread out his wares. In among the brass chandeliers, shabby shoes, and old clothes, a battered cardboard case was waiting for a buyer. The top and sides were bulging from all the papers stuffed inside. There were papers covered in German gothic script, documents bearing official stamps, and yellowed photographs, some over a hundred years old. For anyone prepared to sift through them all and sort everything out, they held the key to the fascinating history of the Levy family – and also to the beginnings of the troubled love affair that bound the German Jews to their homeland.

For five generations members of the family had kept every single document and scrap of paper. These ranged from an upholsterer's bill dated 1866 for the repair of a drawing room chair in their house in the small town of Bad Polzin, to a First World War certificate awarding the Iron Cross for bravery, right down to a receipt for more than 60,000 francs deposited with a Zurich branch of the Schweizerische Bankgesellschaft before the outbreak of the Second World War.

In the severe winter of 1812, as Napoleon's defeated army withdrew from Russia, an exhausted cavalryman who had lost his horse sold the remainder of his loot: a pair of silver candlesticks, stolen somewhere along the way from Berezina. A poor Jewish pedlar named Jäckel exchanged them for a sack of potatoes. One hundred and twenty-six years later in the autumn of 1938, the German police stopped an open sports car making for the Swiss border. An attractive-looking woman in a stylish hat and a foxtail collar round her neck sat at the wheel. She handed her passport to the official. Her name was Ida Levy.

'Where to?' asked the policeman.

'To the mountains, on holiday,' she answered in a casual, matter-of-fact voice.

Her documents were in order, but the silver candlesticks and the case containing family mementos aroused suspicion. Why take such items on holiday?

Ida was taken in for questioning.

How she managed to escape the police, we shall never know. What we do know for certain is that once across the border and out of trouble, she then discovered that her brother Leo had been murdered in his own apartment in Bad Polzin by Nazi henchmen during the infamous *Kristallnacht*, the night of broken glass.

Just before the outbreak of the Second World War, the case was handed over to its rightful owners, Siegfried and Lisbeth Levy, a couple who had fled from the terrors of the Hitler regime to the picturesque holiday resort of Lugano.

A respectable lawyer, Signore Valdo Riva, had acted on behalf of the couple, settling their financial affairs prior to their expulsion from the Swiss canton of Tessin. They had found temporary asylum in Vichy France. Decades later, when I turned up without warning in Valdo Riva's luxurious office in the 300-year-old building at 7 Via Pretoria, the surprise of the by now elderly lawyer was immense. Loyalty to his clients made him reluctant to disclose any information. It was only when I showed him papers bearing his own signature, including bank documents of the Levy family, that he was convinced and prepared to co-operate.

The owners of the Hotel Windsor in Nice, where Siegfried and Lisbeth had spent their last days before embarking for the safe haven of the United States, were no less surprised when I appeared.

Florence was another place where I found myself loudly ringing a doorbell. From the entrance to the Pension Bandini on the Piazza Santo Spirito, a gloomy staircase led up to the door where in 1943 German secret agents had pounced to arrest another member of the family, the painter Rudolf Levy. A successful artist who had begun his career in the studio of Henri Matisse, he had been cut off from the rest of the family when he married a gentile. He fell into the clutches of his persecutors, who finally put an end to his life.

Further research led me to archives in Jerusalem, Berlin, and Köslin (now Polish Koszalin), after visiting Bad Polzin and other places where the Levy family had lived. As a result I discovered a daughter of the murdered Leo Levy, Hannah Slijper, who now lives in Israel. I also visited the London home of Klaus Hinrichsen, whose wife, Margarete, had found refuge there from Nazi Germany in the thirties. In Hanover I met Dr Rita Scheller, the director of the Convention of Evangelical Communities in Pomerania, who has amassed a collection on the history of the Jews of Pomerania. In addition, I spoke to people in various cities in Europe and America, who were able to provide me with important information about the Levys and other aspects of the book.

The primary source of information, the suitcase of documents, was sold to a dealer after the death of Lisbeth Levy at the age of ninety-two. This is how it came to end up in the flea market in Jaffa.

This story is based exclusively on these documents and the facts produced by further research. Yet the book is not intended to be an academic historical work. I could not employ detectives to investigate the conversations of the Levy family and others appearing in the book. So in order to maintain the form of a documentary novel, I have taken the liberty of transcribing the contents of letters and diaries into dialogue form. And in order to convey the state of mind of the protagonists of this story as well as their environment, I have drawn on contemporary newspapers, the works of other writers, and even photographs. I have invented nothing. Reality turns out to be more fascinating and yet also more terrible than any product of the imagination.

Ascher Levy.

The Long Voyage

The head steward in first class came on deck and said. 'Tea is being served in the lounge, sir.' Lloyd, the Austro-Hungarian steamship company, was careful in its choice of staff and famous for the exemplary care given to its passengers. So the steward had not forgotten the traveller standing alone by the railing ever since the SS *Ungaria* had set sail from Trieste about two hours earlier. But the passenger simply waved away the invitation and remained where he was, looking out to sea, apparently deaf to the screaming of the seagulls accompanying the ship.

Like all experienced service employees, the steward prided himself on his ability to assess people by their demeanour and appearance. Shrewdly he observed this passenger – a man of mature years, with a broad, strong back, hair combed straight back, upright bearing; his not exactly slender fingers were firmly gripping the wooden ledge of the railing. His three-quarter-length frock coat was superbly cut, doubtless by an exclusive Viennese tailor. The hairdresser responsible for trimming the man's beard and sideburns clearly knew his craft. But the practised eye of the head steward easily recognized that the impeccably dressed traveller was no man of the world. A prosperous Jew from the provinces, he guessed – and he was not mistaken.

The passenger on deck held a Prussian passport in the name of Ascher Levy. The issue of travel documents such as these had only begun a year earlier, in 1871, about a month after Germany's glorious defeat of France. The passport noted that Ascher Levy, businessman, resident in the town of Bad Polzin, was a citizen of the empire. In the suitcase containing his personal effects was a ticket for a first-class passage, along with several letters of introduction addressed to important individuals in Egypt and

Palestine, his destination. One of these letters bore the signature of Gerson Bleichröder, private banker to the 'Iron Chancellor', another that of the painter, Moritz Daniel Oppenheim. But as he turned his back on the upper deck, his thoughts were neither on his luggage nor on the events of the past few hours, but on the long journey he had endured to arrive this far.

His two travelling companions, with whom he had planned this venture over a number of years, were in the mahogany-pan-elled lounge, pungent with the aroma of fine tobacco and situated at the centre of the upper deck. Ensconced in leather armchairs taking afternoon tea were his cousin, Moritz Gottschalk Lewy,* a successful Berlin businessman, and the historian and Biblical scholar, Professor Heinrich (Zvi Hirsch) Graetz, from the Jewish Theological Seminary of Breslau. The lone passenger at the railing was not inclined to join them. His thoughts slipped back into the past, rather like the gentle surge of the sea alongside the steamer, falling back until its contours disappeared in the waves.

The ancestors of Ascher Levy had settled many years earlier in the Duchy of Posen, a territory that was the subject of constant dispute between Prussia and Poland. They had no rights, no surname, occupied the lowest social status, and by reason of their alien culture were regarded as strangers. They wore different clothes, ate different food, thought in different ways, and did not even acquire the status of so-called *Schutzjuden* – Jews who enjoyed a certain measure of protection from the ruler because their wealth or occupation were of vital importance to him. In the spirit of 'Let sleeping dogs lie' (pogroms were not uncommon in those times) they were careful not to ally themselves to either side. Although they inclined more towards the Prussians, they were careful not to reveal this openly.

They preferred to shut themselves off in their own spiritual world; this was no hard task, since essentially they were excluded from participation in public affairs. The obstacles put in their way

*One part of the family spelled its name Levy, the other, Lewy. However, the Biblical tribe is spelled Levi. All three versions are used. Moritz Gottschalk Lewy's real name was Mosche Gottschalk, but he was generally addressed as Moritz Gottschalk.

were wide-ranging – they were not allowed to purchase land, they could not employ Christians, and permission to run hostelries and inns or to lend money could only be gained with greatest difficulty. They were not allowed to marry under the age of twenty-four, and from time to time they were forbidden to settle in villages. No one had any sympathy for them. The Polish population, who were in the majority in the Duchy, were hostile to them, and with some reason, for in spite of their efforts to conceal it, everyone knew that the Jews valued German culture as a close second to their own. They read German literature, and followed events west of the frontier with intense interest. They were aware that Jews in the western territories likewise enjoyed few civil rights, but for some reason they perceived hatred of Jews in Western Europe as less hurtful than in the East.

Berisch was born on 14 June 1744, and was married at the age of twenty-one – secretly, of course, to evade the prevailing law. Towards the end of the eighteenth century he packed up his few possessions and emigrated to Pomerania. Gittel, his wife, from the Horowitz family, accompanied him. They followed in the footsteps of those members of the family who had migrated westwards before them. According to the family tree, Rabbi Yerucham, the great-great-grandfather of Berisch, had settled in Belgard as early as 1650, and was one of the founders of the Jewish community there.

So it was not surprising that Berisch and Gittel in turn made their way to Belgard. They set up home there and brought eleven children into the world. We have no information about ten of these children, as the records kept by the rulers of the day did not concern themselves with the lives of simple folk. And yet the name of Ascher Jäckel, born on 25 January 1775 in the small town of Kammin, in the Belgard district, does appear in the records. On the eighth day after his birth, when he was admitted into the Covenant of Abraham, the *mohel*, who circumcised him, predicted a life of good fortune and prosperity for him. But as an adult, like the majority of nameless Jews throughout Europe, Jäckel faced grinding poverty. He earned his living as a pedlar with no fixed roof over his head, and not even a bed of his own. He wandered from village to village, selling cloth, linen, and kitchen utensils to a suspicious, hostile world. Jäckel accepted insult and abuse – and said nothing. Humbly he accepted his fate; he was no rebel, and did not attempt to fight the status quo. He placed his hopes in his omnipresent God and awaited better times. It was only in the evenings, after he had fed his horse and put up at an inn along the wayside, that contentment would steal over him. He would count the pennies earned and dream of the day when with God's help he would get married and have sons. But above all he prayed to God to help him feel that at last he belonged, to give him the strength to feel a moral commitment to the people among whom he lived, and to set him free from the stigma of being an outsider.

Yet it seemed that this was not to be, at least not in the foreseeable future. In Germany the attitude to Jews was hostile, inflamed by the 'academic' pronouncements of philosophers and historians. Many supported the view, endorsed by those in power, that it was unnecessary to make the lives of members of the Mosaic faith any easier. Jäckel felt trapped in a maze of inflexible laws and decrees based on prejudice. Only once in his life did there seem any hope of the *mohel*'s favourable prophecy coming true after all. Napoleon Bonaparte, the French Emperor, took the countries of southern and Central Europe by storm, and subjected them to a new social order. It appeared as if nothing could stop the wheels of history. Religious territories underwent a process of secularization, and imperial cities lost their sovereignty. On 12 July 1806 the sixteen dukes of southern and western Germany established the Confederation of the Rhine, adopting Napoleon's edicts. On 1 August they seceded from the empire, and five days later Franz II abdicated his imperial powers. When in 1808 the Prussian Minister of State, Karl Freiherr vom und zum Stein, proclaimed the Prussian Town Order, which among other things granted the Jewish population some degree of civil rights, Ascher's joy knew no bounds. A few years later, on 11 March 1812, Friedrich Wilhelm III, a dyed-in-the-wool conservative ruler, signed the Prussian Edict of Emancipation, enabling the Jewish population to take Prussian nationality. There was, however, a string of conditions attached.

One result was the introduction of hereditary surnames. Ascher Jäckel adopted the name Jakob Levy, after the tribe of Levi, who according to Jewish tradition had been chosen to serve as priests in the Temple in Jerusalem in the period prior to its destruction. Ascher Jäckel, henceforth Herr Levy, was unconcerned by the fact that the new laws had been adopted reluctantly, imposed by the enemy. Quite the contrary. At long last he could breathe freely, and pursue new aspirations. By January 1812 he had completed his thirty-seventh year, and was still single. It was high time to get married. His expectations were not excessive. Ascher Jäckel Levy was well aware that rich and poor did not intermarry. When he approached the marriage broker of the Jewish community, he was not in search of a dowry, but wanted a wife who would stand by him, and bear him sons.

So when the marriage broker finally suggested marriage to Esther Löb from Arnswalde, he agreed before he had even set eyes on her. Beauty was not the bride's outstanding feature, and she brought no riches to the marriage, but she possessed sound common sense. She had a longish face, was fairly heavily built, yet looked out on the world with dark, intelligent eyes, and God had endowed her with a warm heart and a strong sense of duty. She was ten years younger than he was, and for those times was regarded as an ageing spinster, but when the couple met for the first time in her parents' home, Jäckel knew that for a man in his position this *Shidduch* would be a success. Although Esther's parents, Jehuda and Veigelche, were pedlars like him and barely eked out a living, Jehuda Löb was greatly respected in the community for his knowledge of the Torah. The more learned he was in the Holy Scriptures, the higher the esteem a Jew enjoyed from members of the community.

Esther and Jäckel were married according to Jewish law. The prevailing conditions that permitted the young couple to savour the taste of freedom and bear the surname Levy would also contribute to the improvement of their material circumstances.

There is a popular Jewish curse, 'May you live in interesting times', meaning in times of upheaval and hardship. In this instance the 'interesting times' were in fact a blessing. Jakob Levy and his young wife did not read newspapers and were not interested in distant wars. Their life revolved around the daily struggle for survival. However, occasionally there were items of news that reached even the ears of people who did not normally pay attention to world events. In the winter of 1812 a rumour spread like wildfire that the Grande Armée was on the retreat, that the affiliated Prussian regiments were scattered to the winds, and that Napoleonic soldiers were selling off treasures looted in White Russia in exchange for a scrap of warm clothing and a shot of brandy. Shrewd dealers saw the chance of easy pickings. Just before Christmas, when the Emperor allowed his troops to turn back and himself rushed to Paris in order to prevent a palace revolution, Jäckel loaded his goods on to a sledge and hitched on a pair of animals, obtained from his neighbour for 20 per cent of the profit he was hoping to make. He set out on the long journey, making straight for the column of the defeated army, in order to strike a bargain ahead of his competitors. Soon they came into view – veteran campaigners wearing medals from Austerlitz, Jena, and Wagram, now dragging themselves on frozen feet towards Prussia. Their weapons had been abandoned on the snow-covered Russian steppes; all they were carrying was loot from the last campaign. Exhausted, dressed in rags, and hungry for bread and human warmth, they were easy prey for the pitiless army of grasping dealers, lying in wait along the path of retreat. Loot changed hands almost without any haggling. A handful of beans or peas, a bandage for a wound or just an enticing kiss from a woman was sufficient to extract money, precious icons, jewels, and other valuables taken from the palaces of the Tsarist empire.

Jäckel acquired the first pair of candlesticks for a sack of potatoes, but with each deal he gained experience, and by evening of the same day a sack of potatoes bought him pieces of jewellery more valuable than anything he had seen so far. On leaving Kammin, he had had to count every penny, but after two weeks he returned home with his pockets full. But this did not make a spendthrift of him. Jäckel knew the full value of every coin – flat for holding in a tightly closed fist, and round enough to spin after a successful deal. He invested his unexpected wealth in the purchase of an inn in Belgard. The couple packed their belongings and moved to Belgard. At that time there were eight Jewish families living there, and there was no problem finding a quorum of ten adult men, a *minyan* for the *Shabbat* service. Although they wished to be citizens like those around them, Jäckel Levy and Esther, his wife, never forgot the teachings of their Jewish religion.

The inn at the northern edge of Belgard stood on the road where traffic from Köslin, the regional capital, entered town. The business was at the front of the house, where drinks were sold across a counter. It was a good location, as many coachmen would stop here to take some strong alcohol. Jäckel did not possess a licence for an inn, and he was strictly forbidden to serve drinks. But what was the harm if a coachman, a farmer, or a travelling salesman bought a bottle or two to drink elsewhere? However, the tavern owners of Belgard spotted this illegal business, and more than one of them threatened 'Levy the brandy Jew' with violence. Their threats alarmed Esther, and she was always sure to bolt the door leading to the two rooms at the back of the house. The bedroom window looked out on to the courtyard, surrounded by a high stone wall. The shutters were always kept closed, as the rear courtyard was used to store the barrels and bottles. Many people sampled Jakob's brandy, for he knew his trade, and his reputation soon spread. It was not long before the farmers from the surrounding villages streamed into the shop to drown their sorrows in the requisite drop of brandy. Jäckel himself never touched alcohol.

The records of Belgard note that on 8 December 1814 Jakob Levy was granted permission to reside in the town. In actual fact the document simply confirmed the existing circumstances, yet it was highly prized by the recipient. The business flourished and grew, and when Jäckel observed Esther sitting in the living room sewing baby clothes, this was no unwelcome surprise. Property needed heirs. The first son, named Ascher like his father, saw the light of day on 8 Cheshvan by the Jewish calendar, being 10 October 1815 according to the Gregorian calendar.

When Esther was five months pregnant, hundreds of the

town's citizens streamed into the market square to hear a proclamation brought by a herald of the King. In those times a royal herald was a rare sight, and it was only on very special occasions that the government chose this means of bringing news to the common people. On this occasion the crier was accompanied by two officers, and they sat at a table set up for the purpose in the middle of the square. In ringing tones the man read out that the commissioner for war, Simon Kremser, wished to announce the establishment of a war fund to equip the troops setting out to fight the decisive battle against Napoleon Bonaparte. The *Vossische Zeitung* had already published detailed reports of the Emperor's return. Accompanied by loyal supporters, the Emperor had escaped from the island of Elba, where he had been banished on the instructions of Prussia, England, Austria, and Russia. He had landed on the beach at Cannes, set out on his triumphant march towards Paris, once again seized power, and attacked Belgium. The newspaper reported the advance of the French Emperor, and for the first time in his life Jäckel became interested in affairs outside his home town.

Vast sums were needed to equip the army in order to halt the French attack. Gebhard Leberecht Blücher, popularly known as 'Marshal Forward March', once again stood at the head of the Prussian troops. His name made many hearts beat faster. Jäckel had never before made donations, other than minor amounts to the Jewish community for charitable purposes. This time he did not hesitate. This was the moment to prove his love of his country, and his loyalty to the throne. He took out his purse, stepped forward, and placed it on the table. One of the officers counted out the coins, praised him for his loyal citizenship, and shook him warmly by the hand. Jäckel gazed in amazement first at the officer and then at his hand. Even when settling a deal, until now most Germans had refused to shake hands with him. In full view of the assembled crowd, the officer now made out a receipt, gave it the official stamp, and handed him the document. Jäckel accepted it as if it were a gift from the King in person, and hurried home to hang it up at the end of his bed, so that it was the first thing he would see on waking. From that day on he was filled with pride whenever he glanced at it. In his eyes, this donation was like an umbilical cord attaching him to his homeland.

Late in the evening of 18 June 1815, as Jäckel sat doing his accounts, he was interrupted by loud knocking at the door of the shop. 'Closed,' he called out to the customers. The knocking turned into hammering. He could hear a babble of voices, and impatiently got up from his seat at the table to open the door. A joyful crowd of townspeople rushed in. 'We want to drink to Blücher!' they cheered, suggesting that several bottles of brandy had already passed their lips. 'Hurry, Jew,' they insisted loudly, 'hurry.'

'Come back tomorrow. I'm closed.'

He tried sending them away – but to no avail. The customers were already making for the shelves laden with beverages. 'Haven't you heard?' cried one of them. 'Napoleon is done for!'

As the bottles of brandy passed across the counter and the coins jingled in the till, Jäckel heard the news just brought by a messenger on horseback. Wellington and Blücher had been victorious in the decisive battle defeating Napoleon. The miracle had taken place outside the village of Belle Alliance near the small Belgian town of Waterloo. The outcome of the battle had been decided by the Prussian army of recruits who had led a successful flank attack on the French. Jäckel's eyes filled with tears of joy. He poured himself a sizeable drink and downed it in one go. Little did he know that this would be the last toast of his life.

With the defeat of Napoleon, the old order returned. Leaders and diplomats of the ruling powers met in Vienna to divide Europe up anew. Hard on their heels came journalists, courtiers, and well-to-do notables, attracted by the glittering life of the Austrian capital. Decisive plans often took shape in the salons of wealthy ladies – including Jewish ladies of rank – at tables laden with delicacies and to the strains of orchestral music, giving rise to the saying, 'The Congress dances, but doesn't move on.' This was somewhat exaggerated, for in the spring of 1815 diplomats in Vienna did in fact draw up a new map of Europe. Prussia was represented by Karl August, Baron von Hardenberg, and by

Wilhelm, Baron von Humboldt, ambassador in Vienna. They were humanists, in favour of social reform, and held Jews in considerable esteem. Humboldt was a regular guest at the literary salon of Henriette Herz, a celebrated Jewish hostess in Berlin, in whose house Heine, Börne, Madame de Staël, and Count Mirabeau would assemble. But when it came to negotiating the constitution of the German Confederation, which ultimately consisted of thirty-nine member states without a seat of government, the conservative representatives gained the upper hand. And when the Congress came to set out Paragraph 16 of the Act of Congress, repealing the rights that had been granted to Jews in the territories and that had continued under the influence of Napoleon, the intervention of prominent Jewish personalities did not help. Even the influence of Ludwig Börne could do nothing. The wheels of history went into reverse, and Prussia too retracted her progressive laws, which she claimed had been adopted in a 'moment of weakness'. Friedrich Wilhelm III referred to a 'liberal virus' that had overrun the state. Once again the heavy curtain of autocracy descended over Prussia. Every attempt to sue for civil rights was roundly rejected. In this respect at least, the Jews and the simple Christian folk suffered equal oppression, although their common fate in no way created a brotherly bond between them. The dissatisfaction of the people grew and with it the readiness to give vent to their bitterness and frustration. And, as so often before, the hunt was on for a scapegoat.

Ascher Levy was barely four years old when many parts of Germany were struck by a severe drought. This was the last straw. There was a widespread rumour that rain had ceased to fall as a result of a curse made by the Jews. Riots broke out, which historians later dubbed the 'hepp-hepp' riots, the cry of the insurgent masses. On 2 August 1819 the mob gave vent to their pent-up anger in Würzburg. For Maximilian, King of Bavaria, these events spelled imminent revolution, and he sent in his troops to restore order. There may have been another factor at play – Würzburg was the home of the brothers, Jakob and Salomon Hirsch, the King's private bankers. However, the soldiers' bullets could not stop events from taking their course. The 'hepp-hepp' riots spread like wildfire. On 10 August they erupted in Frankfurt, reaching Heidelburg during the Prince Ludwig Festival, arriving in Hamburg on 20 August, and two days later overrunning Belgard. Just after Esther had put her little boy to bed, strangers came hammering at the door of the shop. Jäckel got up and went to the door, quietly cursing those who would not allow him his due rest. Sometimes thirsty customers would want to buy brandy after he was officially closed, and he did not dare refuse them. But this time the visitors came for another reason. No sooner had he turned the key in the lock than a few men came rushing in, brandishing flaming torches. Before he could say a word, the shelves had already caught fire. Jäckel flew into his apartment, barricading the communicating door behind him with a heavy wooden bolt, and called out to Esther to take the child and run for her life. In no time the barrels of alcohol were ablaze, and soon nothing remained of the distillery. Although the house was built on stone foundations, the walls were wooden. The firemen were unable to control the fire. Yet no one else attempted to quench the flames, no one came to their aid, no one cared about them. The family spent the night in the nearby forest. When Jäckel looked at the charred remains of his house next morning, he realized that he had come full circle. His days of prosperity were over. He was left with nothing, back where he had started.

His wife did not weep. Somehow she had always known that their luck would not last for ever, and had almost seen the catastrophe coming. Nor did Jäckel bemoan his hard lot. God gives and God takes away. Seven fat years are followed by seven lean years. The name of Jakob Levy no longer had the least significance. It was simply the remains of a great illusion. Without the help of the rabbi of the Jewish community, he, his wife, and their little boy would have gone hungry. The rabbi found him a humble lodging and work on a farm where, as everywhere in the region, the staple crop was potatoes. Until his death in 1834 Jakob Levy served as a farm labourer. His and Esther's greatest concern was for the future of their son. She taught Ascher to read and write; under her watchful eye he learned arithmetic, studied the

Holy Scriptures, and was taken on as a trainee by Louis Stärger, owner of a successful business in Märkisch Friedland.

Louis Stärger was only a small trader, but he was extremely greedy. Dealing in spirits, he had built up a profitable enterprise. He could have been the prototype for Karl Borromäus' play *Our Company*, in which the Jew and his growing assets are derided and the protagonists are portrayed as leeches, sucking the nation dry – a leftover from the days of the 'hepp-hepp riots'. But apart from his financial greed, Stärger was an observant Jew, and this was critical for Jakob Levy, who in spite of all that had happened wanted his son to grow up in a religious household. 'Religion and faith are all we have left,' he said on the day of his son's departure. With these words in his ears, and a bundle of clothes under his arm, Ascher Levy boarded the stagecoach that travelled from Belgard to Friedland.

However, religion and faith in no way made the relationship between master and apprentice any easier, and young Ascher had a difficult life. He was given an attic room, and his working day lasted from morning prayers to sundown. At first he was given simple tasks – filling the cracks in leaking barrels and – equally important – carefully shredding tobacco for the master's pipe. But Stärger soon recognized the young man's common sense and ability, and gradually extended his range of duties. Before the year was out, he handed over the firm's bookkeeping to Ascher and let him deal with the customers. Eventually he even entrusted him with the keys to the till, when he himself went away on business trips. This did not mean that Ascher's pay went up accordingly. But the apprentice who had been promoted to employee held his tongue. He never complained or asked for more money. He knew the cruel law of supply and demand. There were dozens of young men like him waiting for an apprenticeship.

What he found far harder than the work was the loneliness. He was a stranger in the small town, with no friends or acquaintances, so his main enjoyment was going for long walks. On *Shabbat* when the business was closed, he would wander through the countryside. The green fields, the thickly wooded forests, and the murmuring rivers of Pomerania all had a secretive quality for him. The magic of the open countryside conquered his heart and intoxicated his senses. Roaming along narrow paths among shrubs with their beguiling scent, when he watched a leaf as it fell from a bough or spotted a hare hiding between the poplars, he felt a sense of elation, as if God were close at hand. His father's faith had never strayed beyond the Holy Scriptures. Jäckel's faith had always remained between the covers of these books, as rigid as the straight lines of the written text.

Ascher was different. He discovered the wondrous connection between the printed word and the work of the Creator. The dry language took on a shape, and the words filled with meaning. This revelation was far too intense to be kept to himself. The waves of emotion that he experienced needed an outlet, and Ascher entered them in the diary he had started to keep on arrival in Friedland.

It was a dialogue with himself, a substitute for conversation with a kindred soul, and he wrote with German thoroughness and Jewish feeling. He expressed almost everything that he felt or did with great precision: the everyday routine of work, exchanges with customers, the amount of spirits he sold. Had he known how to write music, he would have transcribed the twittering of the birds and the rustling of the wind in the oak groves in perfect notation. When he felt the need to talk to a like-minded person, he would withdraw to his room where, despite leaden fatigue, he would light a candle and in the flickering light write to his cousin, Moritz Gottschalk, who was working for a moneylender in Labes to learn about banking. He loved these tranquil evenings with the day's work behind him, when he could concentrate on intellectual contact with his cousin.

Little did he know at that time that one day as prosperous adults the two of them would embark on a sea voyage to Palestine together. In those early years in 1834 a first-class passage on a luxury steamship was beyond his wildest dreams. The walls of his attic room sloped inward down to the darkening square of window. His bed occupied the opposite wall, with many books on a shelf beside it. He had just read the Mishnah in a German translation, as well as Sir Walter Scott's most recent book. On the wall above the bookcase hung portraits of the King and of Maimonides. Under the window was a plain pinewood table.

Neatly arranged on it lay exercise books, tools for sharpening goose quills, and a blue inkwell. On this evening of 12 March 1834 he wrote down what was on his mind:

My dearest Moritz,

Today I have been walking in the hills in the neighbourhood of Wilkensdorf. The sky was a miracle, as if someone had scattered stardust across it. Alongside a winding path lime trees and a solitary oak threw their long shadows. I stood perfectly still and listened to the whispering of nature. It may have been for no more than a minute, but it may have been as long as an hour, I have no idea. The moon climbed from the depths of the earth up into the firmament and illuminated the surroundings. My whole body trembled. In that moment I sensed that there must be an almighty Creator who made this world surrounding me, it has to be so. I was filled with both elation and fear. I heard the clattering of the mill wheel from afar and a dog barking. I recited the psalm. You can't have forgotten it: 'When I behold the heavens, the work of Thy hands, the moon and the stars, that Thou hast made, what is man…' I went home, opened a book, but could not read, so I put out the candle. Yet before I went to bed, I made a vow – I shall always lead a Jewish life. I shall always follow my conscience. I shall always try to perform the mitzvot for God and my fellow man.

However, the everyday business world that taught him the lessons of reality was no place for such noble precepts. Many Jews seeking an entry into society and its cultural life converted to Christianity. For those who kept to their Judaism, the only way upward was in the financial world, but they stood no chance of acquiring membership to the exclusive club of 'true patriots'. Heinrich Heine had good reason to mark the opening of a Jewish hospital in Hamburg with the following words:

> A hospital for poor sick Jews
> For sons of man triply afflicted
> With threefold ailments –
> Poverty, bodily pain and Judaism!
> And of all three the last is the worst.

Yet the poet's mistake was in hoping that conversion to Christianity was the cure-all for the pains of being Jewish. Even this would not change the attitude of those opposed to the integration of Jews into the Prussian nation, as the Hamburg journalist, Dr Eduard Mayer, was quick to point out:

> Heine is a Jew, like Börne, and Saphir. Baptized or not, it makes no difference. It is not the religion of the Jews that we hate, but the many ugly qualities of these Asiatics, that do not disappear on baptism: the shamelessness and arrogance that are a common feature, their bad manners and their frivolity, the impertinent behaviour that is one of their predominant characteristics ... they belong to no nation, no state, to no community, they travel through the world like adventurers.

Many intellectuals soon joined this libellous campaign. An essay by Professor Jakob Friedrich Fries of the University of Heidelberg, which was passed from hand to hand, maintained in all seriousness that the Jews were corrupting the German character, and that the only solution to this 'problem' was the physical annihilation of Jewry. The Professor of History at the University of Berlin, Christian Friederich Rühs, saw the greatest danger in, of all people, those Jews who sought to establish a bridge between their own religion and their affiliation to the German nation. He proposed the introduction of some unmistakable form of identification, 'so that no German may be led astray by the speech and conduct of his Jewish neighbour, and have any difficulty in recognizing his foe'. The worthy professor went on to say that 'A foreign people should not enjoy the same rights as the Germans, just because they become Christians,' and he suggested the reintroduction of the tax on Jews. Another recommended that Jewish

women be locked up in houses of ill repute, and that Jewish men
be castrated and sent as forced labour to work in mines, or sold as
slaves to the British colonies. 'Perhaps,' wrote another, 'it would
be best to cleanse our land entirely of these scroungers, to drive
them out, as Pharaoh did from Egypt, or to exterminate them on
the spot.'

Although the government did not officially endorse these agitations, it did nothing to oppose them. The deceitfulness of the
Prussian court became apparent a few years later in the
Lieutenant Burg affair. Burg was an instructor at a gunners' training camp. Impressed by his junior officer's commitment and
exceptional ability, his superior put him forward for promotion to
captain. The general staff insisted that Burg should first convert
to Christianity, but Burg refused. In the course of endless
appeals, the case finally landed on the desk of Friedrich Wilhelm
III. In a letter to the commanders of the artillery, the Prussian
ruler wrote:

> I cannot elevate First Lieutenant Burg, serving at a training
> camp for gunners and sappers, to the rank of captain in the
> Prussian army. I have to know that someone of his education
> and intellectual skills acknowledges the truth and the light of
> the Christian faith. Nevertheless I should like to do justice to
> his achievement in the drafting of teaching manuals, and in
> recognition of his efforts, I enclose the sum of fifty gold thaler
> with this communication.

Since Jews were expected to convert to Christianity, only to
find that by taking this step their social status was in no way
enhanced, many opted for the golden mean – the reform of
Judaism. First, prayer books were printed in German, and no
longer in Hebrew. Some Jews went even further and insisted that
all references to Mount Sinai and belief in the coming of the
Messiah be deleted. In their opinion neither a mystical redemp-
tion nor an additional Land of the Fathers other than the
German Fatherland were now necessary. A Reform movement in
Hamburg published the following memorandum: 'We do not

await the coming of the Messiah, who will bring the Israelites to *Eretz Israel.* Such a Messiah is unwanted here, and we recognize no other Fatherland than the one where we were born, and of which we are citizens.'

Ascher Levy rejected conversion to Christianity, but the reformers did not convince him either. In discussion with Stärger, his employer, he maintained that a link had to be established between the old and the new, between yesterday and today, between the Torah of the fathers and the reality of the present day, but this in no way meant abandoning the principles of the Torah, which had sustained the people of Israel for thousands of years. Yet when asked how this was to be put into effect, he was unable to provide a solution.

At the beginning of the 1830s Germany was fragmented into many minor principalities, and every ruler was concerned to pre-serve his own sovereignty. Every electoral prince and every monarch imposed laws on his subjects and every tiny state pursued its own sole interests. The protective tariffs payable at every frontier resulted in invisible walls springing up and hin-dered the development of a common economy. Not until 1834 were these absurd tolls partially removed. Jews were the first to benefit from this. Because so many of them had relatives else-where, they were able to build up a far-reaching information network, first all over Germany and later throughout Europe, and to set up large-scale commerce in goods and finance.

The signs heralding a new age did not, however, reach as far as Pomerania, one of the most backward provinces. In other regions a new class of Jewish bankers and advisers was gradually emerg-ing, whose wealth helped them gain entry to the cream of society and even to acquire titles, for by this time financial dealing and commerce no longer held a stigma. Even junker families and landowners now engaged in financial transactions, which would hitherto have been totally inappropriate to their status. Jews were, however, still barred from public office; they could not become high-ranking officers, judges or governors, but there was no longer any law or statute to prevent them from acquiring wealth. People saluted the flag and the uniforms, the rulers and the symbols of power, but in the end everyone knew that money was more important than anything. And just as the Jews did not utter the name of God, it was not done to refer to money by name. His Royal Highness Prince Money ruled anonymously, a true grey eminence in a society in transition from feudalism to capitalism.

Money conferred a hitherto unknown feeling of security. But those with scarcely a penny in their pockets were in a desperate situation. Karl Marx, the son of a baptized Jew from Trier, had yet to publish his *Communist Manifesto* when, at the age of nineteen, Ascher Levy realized that convictions depended on your situation in life. The conclusions he arrived at were rather different to those of the prominent representatives of the Jewish proletariat. He was not concerned with the class struggle, but rather with bettering his position. It was this that would secure him a privileged position – with the aid of money, naturally enough.

But the road ahead was still a long one. On a monthly wage of seven thalers, he had to be very careful about what he spent. Luxuries were beyond his range. He contented himself with simple food, provided that it was kosher. But his mind hungered for more.

He thirsted for knowledge. Most of his money went on books, but he did not read indiscriminately, being very selective in what he chose. Gradually he discovered a new world. He embarked on imaginary voyages, on fascinating expeditions to distant lands, and began to learn about previously unknown ways of life and thought. The heroes of the novels that he read would appear in his dreams, and in his waking hours he would add new figures from fresh books. Moshe ben Maimon, also known as Maimonides, would look down on him from his portrait on the wall, and sometimes it seemed to Ascher that the rabbi regarded him with a merry twinkle in his eyes.

'My dearest Mother,' he wrote home, 'I am engrossed in the pages of the Gemara and the wonderful logic of our sages. But I am also reading serious secular literature, and I find it provides more than mere entertainment. Please do not mention this to Father, as he would not understand, and only get angry...'

Entries in his diary were written in straight and even lettering,

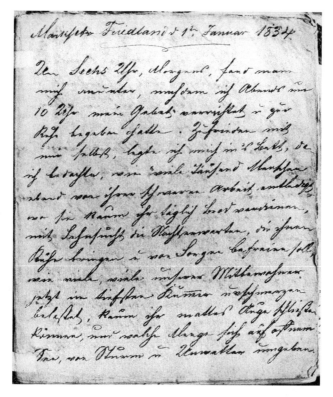

Entry in Ascher Levy's diary, dated 1 January 1834.

as stiff as Prussian soldiers, recording the latest books he had read – the historical novels of Sir Walter Scott.

'I discovered,' he notes, 'that the author had got into financial difficulties and ten years ago he was even declared bankrupt. Since then he has been writing more and more books in order to be able to lead the kind of life appropriate to his status. From this I conclude that necessity can make you inventive and creative. Maybe there is a lesson here for my own future.'

Ascher's father never did find out about his son's passion for secular literature. On Thursday, 17 April 1834, Ascher began work as usual at half past six in the morning. Stärger was standing at the door of the shop and gave him a searching look.

'Have you said your morning prayers yet?' he asked.

Ascher wondered what his employer might be leading up to at this early hour, and answered briefly: 'Of course, sir. I've just come from morning prayers. I've never missed them.'

'Good, for I have sad news for you.'

'How can something sad be good?'

'You're being cheeky, my boy,' warned Stärger.

'Please excuse me. I had no intention of being rude. I assume that it has to do with the firm of Hagen in Berlin, as the accounts are due today. Though I have had word that the old gentleman Hagen is in difficulties.'

'No, this time it has nothing to do with the business.'

'Has something happened?'

'I have received a letter from Belgard. Your father died yesterday morning. Blessed be his memory.'

Ascher stood motionless, as if turned to stone.

'I have no idea how it happened,' Stärger added. 'I didn't hear that he was ill.'

'The Lord giveth, the Lord taketh away. Blessed be the name of the Lord,' murmured Ascher.

'I suppose that you want to go home,' said Stärger. 'I am quite prepared to give you leave. You must observe the *Shivah*.'

'Thank you.'

'Not at all. You are not allowed to work during the *Shivah*. I shall pay you half your wage for the week that you are away. I am only human, after all.'

'I appreciate your goodness of heart, Herr Stärger, but I'm afraid I cannot accept your generosity. I have no savings, and I don't even possess enough to hire a horse and carriage for such a long journey, and the stagecoach is not due until the end of the week,' replied Ascher, giving his employer a questioning look.

Stärger pretended not to have understood. 'I'm sorry,' he muttered, and shrugged his shoulders.

'So am I.'

'What will you do then?'

'I shall finish the report for the tax officials. Any delay and they land us with a fine and interest.'

'Clever boy,' said Stärger smiling, and before disappearing into

his office, he added, 'and see to it that the documents are ready
for Baron von Blanckenburg. I have told him to be here at nine
o'clock.'

Baron von Blanckenburg, a member of a Prussian aristocratic
family responsible for appointing many high-ranking officers and
state officials, owned a number of villages in the area. The beautiful Wilkensdorf estate also belonged to him. The Baron held
balls, played cards, and went on long voyages, without sparing a
thought for the administration of his farms. But he had reached
the end of the road. The money he won at cards had been squan-
dered on ill-considered dealings on the volatile stock exchanges
of Frankfurt and Berlin. Failed investments now forced him to
call on the services of moneylenders. When short-term loans
became due for payment and creditors were already hammering at
the gates of his castle, he had even had to take out a mortgage on
the family estate as the only way of avoiding humiliating legal
proceedings, which would have sullied the honour of his family.
Blanckenburg became dependent on Jewish moneylenders. For a
nobleman of his rank this was an intolerable situation.

Two years earlier Louis Stärger had met every request from
this individual with demonstrative courtesy. The slightest hint or
remark had Stärger rushing to the anteroom of the Baron's property, with sweeping bows. Now it was a matter of 'Have the documents ready. I have told him to be here at nine o'clock,' and it
was taken for granted that the nobleman came to the office of the
Jew, as if both were of equal birth. Ascher Levy was about to
receive an instructive lesson on the power of money.

And indeed on the dot of nine the Baron appeared at the
office. Ascher watched as he descended from his magnificent
coach, ordering his servant to wait with the coach at a distance of
about a hundred metres. He clearly did not want anyone to find
out about his dealings with the Jew. Stärger, too, as he saw him
approach, hastily withdrew into the storeroom. Blanckenburg
entered the premises, leaned his walking stick against the
counter, and angrily demanded: 'Where are the papers?'

Ascher spread out the promissory notes in front of him.
Blanckenburg studied their contents and probed: 'Is this your work?'

Ascher lowered his gaze in embarrassment, lest the Baron be offended by the pity in his eyes.

'Yes, my lord. I prepared the papers. I hope I have not made any mistake.'

Ascher looked up and their eyes met. The Baron replaced the promissory notes on the counter in silence. A heavy odour of brandy hung in the air.

Ascher plucked up courage and said, 'Sir, you should not have invested so much in Spanish bonds.'

'And what do you know about bonds, my boy?'

'I'm learning, my lord.'

'You appear to be a credit to your teacher,' the Baron observed, with evident anger and derision in his voice.

Both knew that the Baron was about to sign away a further part of his property to Stärger. The landowner's anger was mounting and Ascher could feel the tension. The Baron could not restrain himself any longer and asked: 'What exactly have you learned?'

'I follow my employer's business dealings. He owned Spanish bonds as well. But he predicted the collapse of the stock exchange, and sold them one by one.'

'Sold them? When?'

'About a year ago, as soon as news of the death of King Ferdinand reached him. Herr Stärger explained that he did this because Spain had already built up massive debts from the high cost of maintaining its large army in Mexico, and that there was now very likely to be a war of succession. A war with Don Carlos. Queen Isabella...'

'That's enough! I didn't come here for a history lesson from you.'

Ascher said nothing.

'Filthy bastard! Stärger knew perfectly well I had invested in Spanish bonds, and he didn't say a word. He didn't warn me.'

'It was no secret, Your Highness. The newspapers were full of it.'

'He didn't warn me, the bastard. He wanted to ruin me, to plunge me into debt. He wants to seize all my property. Filthy little Jew. How was I supposed to realize the effect of public events of that kind? Why didn't I see that he had his eyes on Wilkensdorf? What will be the end of it? A Jew on the property of a junker? Merciful God, why have you allowed this Jewish pestilence to spread through our land?'

'Jews, Your Highness, have been living here for five hundred years. They were here before the Prussians, my lord. They were living in this region when it was still ruled by the Slavs. It was Watislav IV who granted us the right of residence in the district of Belgard. And that was in the fourteenth century, my lord... And as for your unsuccessful transactions, my lord, permit me to observe that shrewdness is no sin.'

'Do you have an answer for everything?'

'I try to understand the course of events, and draw my own conclusions. Does your lordship consider that wrong?'

'You are devious. Yes, cunning. Like all your race. I was warned against you, and advised to avoid you like the plague. A shame that I didn't follow that advice.'

'I am not dishonest, my lord. I have never cheated anyone,' replied Ascher.

'At your tender age, you just haven't yet had the opportunity.' The Baron took the bills, glanced at them briefly and signed. 'Now are you satisfied?'

'I'm just a simple employee,' was Ascher's response.

'Yes, that Stärger, that... He was always whining away about the dreadful fate of the Jews. How cruel we are to the Jews. It seems to me that this time he has no cause for complaint. Tell him he should put up your wage by a thaler a week. You're worth it!' he grumbled angrily.

When Stärger heard the door slam, he returned to the shop, inspected the documents, folded them up, and tucked them in his pocket. 'That's that,' he proclaimed cheerfully.

He who laughs last, laughs longest. Stärger drove to Stettin and deposited the bills of exchange with the bank as security for a major loan. On the journey home he stopped to visit his brother in Kammin and suggested he join him as a partner in a new enterprise. After just a few months the brothers opened a large

firm trading in wool. The new firm's accounts were entrusted to
Ascher, by now almost twenty years old. Sheep's wool was all the
rage on the market. The formula for success was a simple one.
The wool was bought cheaply from local farmers and sold on at
high prices to the textile manufacturers. But the industry was still
in its infancy and there were frequent crises. The banks would
only support the major corporations that operated at a large
profit, employing cheap labour, mostly women and children.
However, the Stärger brothers dealt almost exclusively with small
factories, which were frequently unable to meet their commitments and ultimately fell prey to bigger competitors. Each factory
that was obliged to close made the crisis worse. And when it
came to the point that the returns from the liquor trade could no
longer absorb the losses, the brothers were forced to declare
themselves bankrupt. There was no other work available in the
town, and so in the summer of 1835 Ascher Levy returned to
Belgard. He arrived with empty pockets and meagre prospects for
a better future. On 15 September his mother, Esther, died
penniless.

His father, Jäckel, had started out as a pedlar, and now it was
up to his son to follow suit. He loaded his wares on to a plain cart.
'Good things! Cheap things! Grab a bargain!' he called out in a
strong voice, and the peasants would come running out of their
cottages to take up the offer there and then. The work was hard,
not just because the peasants were stubborn, but in winter the cart
was difficult to pull along. It did not take Ascher Levy long to
realize that this occupation, even when he had a good day and
returned home with an empty cart, was not going to bring him
any nearer to his goal. He had to find a more profitable way, and
he did so.

In the short period between sowing and harvesting, he would
turn up at the huts of the poor knowing that they would have
spent all their money on seeds. This was his big moment. He
knocked on the peasants' doors and spread out his wares before
them. Often he would deal only with women, as the men had left
in search of work in the industrial centres. 'No money? Don't
worry. Leave it to me,' he would reassure them as they admired

his goods and stretched their hands out for them. 'Take what you like. No need to give me cash now. You can pay me in grain after the harvest.'

To calculate the equivalent value of the grain, he went by the price of the previous year's crop. The slow but steady price increase of agricultural produce ensured him a tidy profit. And then there was the additional seven per cent interest laid down by law.

He soon began to refine his approach. Instead of returning to the villages at harvest time to call in what was owed to him, and then having to find a buyer or pay out – in his view – huge amounts for the transport and storage of the grain, right there and then he would strike the next deal: in the winter the peasants would buy weaving material and linen, and would pay for these in the summer. But at sowing time they needed fresh seed. What could be simpler than to offer them their own grain for seedcorn? But how were they to pay? A little bit of land, for example, or working days in lieu, which could be passed on to the societies that were just beginning to lay railway lines.

Needless to say this was hardly the way to make himself popular. But after a few years of this kind of dealing, Ascher found himself in quite a satisfactory financial situation. When he took a walk through the streets of Belgard, older citizens would even greet him first, raising their hats and showing him respect, a marvellous and hitherto unknown experience. He had even developed something of a paunch, as befitted a bourgeois with a healthy bank account. So it came as no surprise when leading marriage brokers, some from as far afield as Stolp, Köslin, and Dramburg, approached him with enticing propositions. He well remembered the Talmudic tractate of blessings – there are three things that make up a man's reputation: a fine home, a beautiful wife, and elegant household utensils.

He heard about Fanny Benjamin through a marriage broker named Moses, from Dramburg. Moses praised the virtues of this nineteen-year-old young lady, and didn't omit to mention the dowry that the young bride would bring to her marriage. It was decided that Ascher would meet her in the house of mutual

friends in Dramburg, and would not make up his mind until he
had set eyes on her. The arrangement was instantly accepted.

   Ascher Levy had never dreamed of romantic love. For him
marriage was the precondition for fulfilling the commandment to
multiply, and beyond that a long-term investment requiring
serious reflection. His attitude to marriage stemmed from
Judaism, to which the concept of the 'eternal woman' is
unknown, and which does not regard love as an aim in itself. He
knew the Holy Scriptures almost by heart, and consequently
knew that apart from the Song of Songs, eroticism had virtually
no part in marriage and sensual lust was always presented in a
negative light. Further, he was familiar with the tractate in the
Talmud, stating that a true hero can master his desires.

   A week later he was on his way by mailcoach. There were no
real roads at the time, and the coach stopped at every village to
deliver letters and packages. Although he had set out at dawn, he
did not reach Dramburg until evening. His friends received him
warmly. The marriage broker had informed them beforehand of
the purpose of the visit, so they suggested, 'Please stay overnight
with us.'

   Ascher gladly accepted their offer. He had had enough of evil-
smelling taverns and inns where the customers would get drunk
and then abuse visiting Jewish traders. Attacks and theft were frequent occurrences. His friends provided him with a room in their
house, and in his honour, the lady of the house even heated water
for the bathtub. Once he had washed off the dirt from his travels
and put on clean clothing, he accompanied the master of the
house to the local synagogue for evening prayers. On their return
they found the table laden with tasty delicacies. As Ascher
lowered himself into an armchair he felt completely at home, and
visibly savoured the cup of tea his hostess gave him. She offered
him his favourite pastries – warm apple strudel, explaining that
the recipe came straight from Vienna. 'The Austrians know the
way to a man's heart,' laughed his hostess. But the high point of
the evening was when the young lady appeared in a magnificent
evening gown – as if by chance, Miss Fanny had dropped by,
together with her mother, to call on their neighbours.

In terms of appearance, her breasts were not as grapes on the vine, nor was her neck a tower of ivory; in short she did not step straight out of Solomon's Song of Songs. Her gown encased an ample figure with spreading hips. But when she looked up at him, Ascher Levy saw dark eyes brimming with curiosity. As her gaze rested on his paunch, he instinctively tried to pull it in. Yet from the moment Fanny crossed the threshold, he knew she was to be the lady of his heart. Her light, long hair hung down over a white lace collar, and he loved the way she nervously tossed it back from time to time.

'So you are the man,' she said softly. She did not behave as if she had no idea what was at issue. Her frankness, defying all convention, appealed to him.

'Yes, I am the man,' was his reply, conjuring up a smile from her when he added, 'provided you are the woman.'

But there were still the customary procedures associated with this kind of ritual to go through. First the women withdrew to engage in conversation, while the men discussed the current political developments. Here in Pomerania life had not changed, everything still moved at a ponderous pace. By contrast in the southern and central states of Germany liberal movements were springing up and feelings were running high. Many intellectuals were demanding a legal constitution, to curb the power of the electoral princes, and regarded this as a potential miracle cure for all state and social problems. The social power of the bourgeoisie was steadily increasing and, regarding itself as the upholder of the state, it led the campaign. The Baden Chamber was considered the stronghold of liberalism. The local press had expounded at length on the issue. Pointing to the newspaper, Ascher Levy asserted, 'We don't have the time for such nonsense, and I thank God for that.' He was not, he said, one to struggle for dramatic changes, his main concern being to improve his own situation. The master of the house nodded in agreement. Both had had their fill of past attempts at revolution, which had not had a lasting effect and had only given rise to unfounded hope.

The *shidduch* was approved, but not before Ascher Levy and Fanny's father had spoken in private. The following day they solemnly sat down together to size each other up and agree on a date when the dowry should be handed over. Herr Benjamin wished to know how much his future son-in-law was worth. Ascher had accumulated a considerable bank balance, and owned a number of estates that he had acquired in his time as a pedlar. For his part, the future bridegroom did not hesitate to make his own requirements known with regard to the dowry. The Benjamin family would be responsible for paying the bulk of the purchase price of a house for the couple to live in. Benjamin was well aware that the family was fortunate in finding Ascher Levy. At this time the total number of Jews living in Pomerania amounted to approximately 5000, and marriage brokers were hard pressed to find well-matched partners. It was no mean feat to come up with a bridegroom such as Ascher Levy, a man in the prime of life and, moreover, prosperous. No sooner had the two men finished talking and shaken hands in agreement than the marriage broker was knocking at the door and asking for payment.

Ascher was familiar with this part of the country. He had travelled throughout the area, and knew every village and tiny hamlet. Now that it came to deciding on a place to live, he chose Bad Polzin, a holiday spa famous for its curative springs. He loved the quiet of this small town, surrounded by dense forests. The landscape reminded him of the vicinity of Friedland. For many years Polzin had remained virtually unchanged, effectively since the Thirty Years' War and the days of the Great Electors. The little town nestled against a sloping hillside, and at its centre rose an impressive castle, a reminder of the former Polish rulers, who had built it on the foundation walls of an ancient monastery. The mayor, a certain Herr Schmieden, had once been a customer of Ascher's. The houses were attractively decorated, and their inhabitants earned their living in the main from providing services to the surrounding large estates, all specializing in raising seed potatoes. The remaining inhabitants let out rooms to holiday guests. Hundreds of these came every year, to take the waters at the Luisenbad spring, at the cost of one Reichsthaler and ten groschen a time. The spa was the pride of Polzin's citizenry, and was considered one of the most modern installations of its kind. When Majorin von Roschnitzka bought it from her sister in 1837 for a mere 3500 thaler, she had struck a most profitable deal.

South of Polzin lay a series of enchanting glacial lakes, the biggest of which, Lake Dratzig, was full of fish. The area around the little town was sparsely populated. There were more aspen and lime trees than people. Its outstanding beauty had given rise to the area being known as 'the Switzerland of Pomerania'. The population of Polzin at this time was about 1500 souls, of which 700 were Jews.

Although the local teacher, Itzig Hohenstein, struck Ascher Levy as a man of questionable piety, it occurred to him that once he had children, there was at least a Jewish school for them to attend here. He had not forgotten the oath he had sworn many years earlier. He had never once missed saying his morning and evening prayers, and never failed to observe the dietary laws. Yet he distanced himself from the Eastern European Jews, who refused to cut their sidelocks and wore broad-brimmed dark hats and black caftans. He took care not to stand out from the original inhabitants of Pomerania, either by his clothing or his behaviour. His German bore no trace of an accent. He spoke High German like the upper classes, and in addition he mastered the local dialect. For the humble folk, he could have been one of them, and equally he could have passed without muster in the drawing rooms of the wealthy.

He could have done, but did not. When he discovered that a two-storey house, 14 Brunnenstrasse, was for sale, he consulted a member of the von Manteuffel family, the owner of the property. He waited a full hour on the verandah of the nobleman's house, before the latter finally condescended to admit him. And when Ascher expressed his readiness to pay 1350 Reichsthaler, a sum that even a well-placed junker did not scoff at, still he was not shown into the drawing room. The purchase was concluded in a side room, used by the steward as an office. Ascher Levy was not offended. He knew his place in the social order, although he was firmly convinced that he would gradually climb the ladder, rung by rung. He was in no hurry. He was aware that it was not possible to rise more than one rung at a time, and that one had to be careful and patient. Ascher Levy was both.

The Brunnenstrasse was considered one of the best addresses in Polzin. It was just three minutes' walk from the spa gardens and the centre of the small town. There would come a time when the street would be known as Adolf Hitler Strasse. However, at the beginning of the 1840s it was not merely a good place to live, appropriate to Ascher's economic status, but it was also the right place for the offices of the firm that Ascher had long been planning to set up. Previously his chief source of income had been the purchase of grain on site, and he now decided to have this done by commercial travellers. He believed that in time this would prove a profitable move. He would no longer have to chase after customers; from now on they would have to come to him in Polzin. He was still under thirty and in the best of health. The only thing he suffered from was an excess of energy. But he was reluctant to go on these long journeys any more. He was of an age to become the father of a family. Fanny, too, was not afraid to speak her mind. She hadn't married him to be left alone in a cold bed for nights on end.

Ascher and Fanny set up home in a three-roomed apartment on the second floor of the house. On the walls of the spacious bedroom they hung the portraits of Maimonides and Friedrich Wilhelm IV, now King of Prussia since the previous year. The bedroom furniture, part of the dowry, came from Dramburg. The rest of the furniture was purchased from a local carpenter. Both shared the same taste for what was simple and modest. They were concerned with quality, not appearance and style. The only purchase that Fanny made from a well-known shop in Stettin was the velvet trimming for the curtains and fabric for the bedlinen. During their first nights together, Ascher didn't know what to admire first – the white goosedown pillows, the smooth bedcovers, or his wife's body.

The two rooms at the far end of the dark and narrow corridor were turned into a dining room and drawing room, the latter doubling as a private study for Ascher's use. On the oak desk

stood an engraved silver frame containing the receipt that his
father Jäckel had been given for his donation of twenty-five thaler
to the war fund against Napoleon Bonaparte. This document and
the portrait of the King that hung in the bedroom were evidence
of Ascher's allegiance to the fatherland. By placing them in his
own private apartments rather than in his office for any stranger
to see, he endowed his allegiance with a very private quality. Love
of the fatherland and the existing situation were totally different
issues. Ascher harboured no illusions. Deep down he was
depressingly conscious that his attachment was not reciprocated.
No matter what his feelings were for Prussia, Prussia did not
return his love.

There was just one drawer that he kept under lock and key,
even from Fanny, lest she be tempted to open it, just as Eve had
been tempted to eat an apple from the Tree of Knowledge. Here
he stored nationalist pamphlets and tracts that warned of the
'Jewish peril', calling for revenge against the crucifiers of Christ,
the murderers of the Son of God, and demanding that Prussia be
saved from the influence of those who did not believe in the spirit
of Christianity. Although he knew that this fiendish propaganda
was not directed against him in person – in Polzin he was known
as a difficult but honest man – nevertheless he could not pretend
it did not exist and influence the people around him.

On *Shabbat* after morning prayers, Ascher Levy used to meet
up with other Jewish businessmen. Not with them all, of course,
just with three of four of those on a par with him. Over a friendly
cup of tea or coffee they would give serious consideration to the
current situation. His companions were supporters of liberalism,
regarding this as a boost to their hope for greater equal rights.
Ascher, however, supported the King, for he was no believer in
revolutionary ideas. Besides, he had always been inclined to identify with a figure of authority. He would not hear a word against
the royal house, and in the heat of debate, when all logical arguments deserted him, he would passionately burst out: 'And what
have the liberals done to help with laying the railway tracks?'

The railways! The very word was magic to his ears. His cousin,
Moritz Gottschalk, had recently opened a money exchange office

in Berlin, earning a fortune on the stock exchange, and he urged him on: 'The future is in the railways, make sure you don't miss your train.' The two had been close friends since their early days, and although they could not meet often, they frequently exchanged letters. Ascher kept Moritz Gottschalk's letters in a drawer too, but one to which Fanny had access. His cousin kept up with the latest developments – the era of roads and canals, which had opened up the interior to traffic, was now succeeded by the meteoric expansion of the railways. Despite an unfortunate start, with the first railway journey from Berlin to Potsdam taking about half an hour (longer than it took by horse-drawn coach), the railways soon triumphed. Importers of iron, steel, and loco-motives from England became rich, engineers were highly paid, and landowners who permitted tracks to be laid and stations to be built on their land pocketed vast sums. Further, on the King's instructions the government began paying out a minimum divi-dend of three and a half per cent on railway shares. Ascher saw no good reason to 'miss his train' and he ordered the purchase of shares in his name for the Fürth–Nuremberg railway company. It was a profitable investment, encouraging him to invest further.

Friedrich List had become his hero, not only for producing a solution to the transportation problems that lay ahead and pro-viding a source of income along the way, but first and foremost for laying the foundations for a unified Germany. The combina-tion of profit and national consciousness appealed to Ascher. Hitherto he had been known in Polzin as 'the corn Jew', now he was mockingly named 'the railway Jew'. In actual fact the local wits had got it absolutely right. In the space of just four years more than 1000 kilometres of railway track were laid, and Ascher's investments made him the wealthiest Jew, not merely in Polzin but in the entire region of Belgard. His next investment, once again on the advice of his cousin from Berlin, was a share-holding in the Leipzig–Magdeburg railway. In the space of a few years their dividends rose from four to ten per cent, and the share price had tripled. His bank account increased beyond expectation.

However, at this point, when he now possessed a considerable fortune, Ascher came to the conclusion it was best not to put all his eggs in one basket. He continued to deal in grain, and invested a substantial part of the accrued profits in a sawmill in the village of Kollatz four kilometres away. The demand for timber was great and the vast forests of the surrounding region ensured the supply of raw material for years to come, if not for decades. The sawmill proved a wise investment that was to yield a considerable profit.

Ascher's high regard for Friedrich Wilhelm IV's conduct of the affairs of state was not simply based on the material profit he himself accrued. Barely a year after the coronation, the King was turning his attention to the Holy Land. Great Britain, Austria, and Russia had preceded him. The European major powers suspected that the ailing empire of Ibrahim Pasha would be easy game and each in their own way was rushing to claim an appropriate share of the spoils. The Prussian King suggested common patronage of the holy Christian sites, but met with refusal. The Tsar of Russia and the Austrian Emperor were not interested in taking on another partner in their dealings with the Ottoman empire. The power struggle to expand existing spheres of influence in this sinking empire was at its height. The French saw themselves as the protecting power of the Catholics. As heir to Byzantium and guardian of the Greek Orthodox in the Mediterranean region, Russia was asserting her claim. The British wanted the land passage to India secure. The Austrians disguised their seizure of influence behind a supposed cultural and religious sympathy for those individuals from Central Europe, mainly Jews, who had settled in the region. Friedrich Wilhelm IV did not waste much time before moving into action. He sent Ernst Gustav Schultz as acting consul on an official mission to Jerusalem, the city that lay closest to Ascher's heart, second only to the cities of Prussia.

Moritz Gottschalk kept him informed of these exciting developments. His cousin had meanwhile become a partner in some of the smaller enterprises of Gerson Bleichröder, an agent of Rothschild the famous banker. His letters contained vivid accounts of life in Berlin, and when describing the struggles for prestige and power that went on, Moritz stressed the importance of moving in the right circles: 'Believe it or not, but here in the capital a single invitation to a ball given by an influential lady is enough to swing the balance between poverty and wealth.' Moritz Gottschalk was not a guest at these elegant salons. But he possessed a literary talent, and the picture he painted in his letters of the social pyramids in this great city was so vivid that Ascher had the feeling of actually being present at these fascinating events. He was glad not to have to climb these pyramids himself: for to fall from such a height could have ended in catastrophe.

Compared with Berlin, Polzin was more like a calm island at the centre of a stormy ocean. On the lake in the spa gardens a few ornamental swans swam about contentedly. Here in the provinces you did not have to use your elbows as forcefully as in Berlin, where politics and greed went hand in hand. The traditional social order remained the same. Junkers were still junkers, workers did not dream of representation in parliament, and peasants knew their place. What Moritz Gottschalk wrote about having the right connections did in fact also apply to Polzin. Ascher was adept at making compliments, where needed, and he took the view that if jingling coins in the right place and at the right time was music to the ears of whoever he happened to be dealing with, he did not stay idle. Ascher knew that a coin was flat for keeping in the hand, and round to be set rolling where appropriate.

The morning of 19 October 1841 was cool but pleasant. A smell of autumn hung in the air. Ascher and Fanny were elegantly dressed as they left their house. Ascher was wearing a dark suit, a hat, and a checked waistcoat. A gold chain hung from his waistcoat pocket, disappearing at the other end into his trouser pocket. Fanny had a long black coat over her dress, the top faced in black silk. They walked slowly across to the town hall, acknowledging the greetings of passers-by with a nod, befitting people aware of their standing. Waiting for them in the mayor's office were several members of the municipal authority and other dignitaries. The town clerk was seated at a small table with a stack of documents in front him, an inkwell, quills, and the official seal of the town of Polzin.

'Welcome to the swearing-in ceremony,' proclaimed the

mayor, holding out his hand to Ascher Levy and nodding to
Fanny. The clerk indicated a seat for her among the onlookers.
Ascher did his best to hide his excitement. In reality, this ceremony did no more than confirm an existing fact. He had long
since achieved a place of honour in the little town. And yet the
imposing document spread before him by the official symbolized
a move from the past to the present, something that his father
would have dearly wished for, but had never achieved. Jäckel had
striven with all his might to put down roots in this land, and yet it
had been denied him. Ascher recalled the day he had had to leave
his parents' home, in order to go and earn his own livelihood. His
father had accompanied him to the inn from which the mailcoach
was leaving, and said to him: 'Be aware of how you behave.
People judge you not according to your actual worth, but by how
they see you. A piece of fruit has a stone and a skin. The stone –
that's you – your nature, your thoughts, your faith. But people
will judge you purely and simply by your skin. It's your skin that
gives you an appearance. It will not be a part of you, and you have
no power over it. It is like a veil that is only transparent from one
side. You can see through it, but those around you cannot. People
will only observe you according to their own perception. To them
you will always be a bloody Jew.' Ascher could hear his father's
words as if he were whispering in his ear at that very moment.

'Would you sign here, please, sir,' said the official. 'I am
pleased to inform you that the municipal authorities have granted
your application. Welcome to our community.'

This was the customary wording, as if the ceremony was in no
way special and just a simple formality.

Ascher Levy took the document, read it quickly to himself,
and then read out loud:

The municipal authorities of the royal Prussian town of Polzin
in the Province of Pomerania hereby make known and
declare that the merchant Ascher Levy, having given proof of
the necessary requirements appropriate to his request, has been
accepted as a citizen of this town. And the above mentioned
has today pronounced the following oath:

I, Ascher Levy, swear by Almighty and all-knowing God and by His Royal Highness, the King of Prussia, my most Gracious Lord, to be a humble subject, loyal and obedient, and willingly agree to yield to my superiors, conscientiously to fulfil my duties as a citizen and to work to the utmost of my ability for the good of the state and the community to which I belong, so help me God, in the name of His Son, Jesus Christ. Having sworn to execute all civic duties, the President of the Town Council hereby grants the said Ascher Levy the enjoyment and practice of all rights and favours to which a citizen resident here is entitled, on the understanding that once the civil rights have been granted, and so long as he does not show himself unworthy of them, he will defend them with all his might against any challenger.

Presented and documented in the presence of the councillors, and sealed under the town seal of Polzin, 19 October 1841.

The President of the Town Council

When Ascher had read the entire text aloud, he shook his head. 'I regret that I cannot sign.'

Mayor Schmieden raised an eyebrow. 'Herr Levy...?'

Ascher placed the document on the table, turned round to exchange a glance with Fanny, and then said quietly, 'I should like to suggest a small alteration in the wording of the civic oath.'

'An alteration?!' exclaimed the clerk in astonishment.

A look of consternation came over Schmieden's face. 'With the greatest respect, sir, it seems to me that a most regrettable misunderstanding has arisen. This wording was set out by the highest power in Prussia, and it does not befit you to change it.'

'I hope you will agree that this oath is intended for Christian citizens. However, I am of the Mosaic faith, and I cannot swear by the God of the Christians and his crucified son.'

'Other Jews have signed without raising any objection,' countered the official.

'That may well be. But even if I were to sign, what validity would there be to my oath? Just consider for a moment: would

Certificate of citizenship granted to Ascher Levy, 19 October 1841.

this oath be binding on me? What would you say if you were made to swear on the Torah? Would you be bound by such an oath?'

'That makes sense.' Schmieden indicated to the official to place the document in front of Ascher a second time. Ascher struck out the words 'in the name of His Son, Jesus Christ' and wrote a few words in Hebrew above them. The official examined the alteration, without understanding what it meant. Ascher then dipped the quill into the inkwell and signed.

'This patent of citizenship will be recorded in the town archives under the number two hundred and eighty-seven,' announced the official in a dry, monotone voice.

Those present approached Ascher and shook him by the hand. 'Heartiest welcome to our community.' Ascher smiled. Most of those offering him congratulations were customers of his and owed his firm money.

'Now you are one of us,' declared the mayor and placed his arm around Ascher's shoulders.

'I always have been. It has just taken you a long time to realize it.'

That evening there was a banquet at the Levy house. All were invited, Jews and non-Jews, important clients, friends and, naturally enough, the town dignitaries. The mayor and the members of the town council stayed away. Ascher Levy may have become one of them, but only as far as his doorstep. He felt deeply humiliated, but said nothing. Why spoil everyone's pleasure? Fanny had spent many hours in the kitchen preparing her very best dishes – kosher, it goes without saying – to bring to the table. As he sensed her disappointment, he put an arm round her shoulders and gave her a fleeting squeeze. She acknowledged the comforting gesture with a smile. Later, when Salomon, the cattle dealer, had had one too many and commented loudly on the absence of Schmieden and his colleagues, Ascher rebuked him, saying: 'That's enough! Tonight let's drink to the King.'

'To the King,' chorused the guests.

'And to his mission in the Holy Land,' added Ascher excitedly. 'God willing, the day will come when I shall travel there as a proud citizen of Prussia and a proud Jew, who does not deny his religion.'

The banquet went on well into the night. After the last of the guests had left Ascher went up to his room on the second floor and wrote in his journal: 'A few moments of happiness make up for long years of suffering.'

Next day a sign was put up above the entrance to his house in Brunnenstrasse, inscribed in clear, bold lettering:

Ascher Levy
Banker, Grain and Agricultural Merchant
Sawmill and Timber Wholesaler.

A successful business needs an heir. On 13 June 1845 their first son was born. In accordance with Jewish tradition, Ascher and Fanny decided to name the child in memory of Grandfather Rabbi Berisch. But to keep abreast of the times, they were concerned to give the name a German ring, so Berisch became Bernhard. A year later Fanny gave birth to her second son, Julius. And after two more years their sister Vogel came into the world.

Now that Ascher was a family man, had acquired property, and furthermore had been elected chairman of the small Jewish congregation, he directed all his energies into the expansion of his business. It had a good reputation, as it met all obligations promptly and the word of its owner was his bond. Of course people gossiped about him behind his back; success brings envy in tow. But people would greet him in the street, as befitted an honourable citizen. When farmers came into the office, to ask for an advance against the next harvest or to enquire about employment or loans, they never omitted to wipe their feet carefully on the mat at the entrance. Then they would stand in front of Ascher's desk, twisting their hats round in their hands, and would wait patiently until the esteemed proprietor or one of his assistants had time for them. The greater the need of the client, the deeper he would bow. But as the bows became deeper, so the loathing and hatred grew. However, they had to be careful what they said. The 'esteemed sir' would cross the room with measured steps, the glittering gold chain attached to his waistcoat buttons, hands sunk in the pockets of his black trousers. The 'esteemed sir' reflected on whether or not to grant a loan, to agree to or reject a business deal. Although in a position to rescue, the 'esteemed sir' could also destroy.

The sawmill at Kollatz was already working two shifts, a quite unusual state of affairs for sleepy Pomerania. In 1847 Ascher Levy bought a 50 per cent share of the sawmill of Gustav Möller & Successors. His partner was the Falkenheim family from Stettin, who belonged to the local gentry. When the purchase was made public, there were many who turned up their noses, for a partnership between junker and Jew was not an acceptable proposition in the province of Köslin. Many people warned Ascher against expanding too rapidly; they maintained that impatience and ambitiously high targets were bound to lead to trouble. But the orders flooded in, putting money in the till. The products of both the sawmills were transported south to the centre of the kingdom, where expanding industry called for ever greater supplies of raw materials. Industrialization very rapidly changed the existing social order. It gave rise to a new social class – the proletariat. It also had a profound effect on the traditional workshops.

Competition from major industries gradually drove the small manufacturers out of business. The employment of female and child labour severely reduced the income of the male workforce. Many men became unemployed, thereby changing the structure of traditional family networks. Dissatisfaction increased, along with a determined refusal to accept the inevitability of these developments. In London Karl Marx published *The Communist Manifesto*. The liberal movement gained influence, making Frankfurt-am-Main its centre, in contrast to conservative Berlin.

In the middle of April 1847, Ascher paid a business visit to Belgard, the town where he had been born thirty-two years earlier. His parents' home, burned down by an angry mob, had since been rebuilt. The family who lived there now made their living from letting out its rooms. Most of the occupants were Jews who had fled from Eastern Europe, making their way to the port of Stettin, from where they hoped to emigrate by ship to

America. Anyone changing their mind at the last moment from embarking on this enormous venture was helped by the landlords. They knew their way around in dealing with the authorities, who could either grant or reject a request to settle in the Kingdom of Prussia. There were many who opted to stay. None of them could guess that a hundred years later their decision would spell death for their descendants.

During Ascher's stay in Belgard, bloody hunger riots broke out west of the Bay of Stettin. As the news reached him, friends advised him to cut short his stay, lest unrest should also break out in Polzin. But Ascher would not listen to these warnings. He could not imagine that residents of his town, all of whom he knew in person, could represent a danger to his family. Being so near his parents' former home and knowing its awful fate made no difference. Ascher did not identify with the demonstrating masses. By now he was on the opposing side and sheltered behind his prosperity. However, his feeling of security was entirely unfounded. The unrest spread and the violence increased, finally reaching Polzin. Hundreds of people, workers included, headed for the neighbouring streets and stormed the market, robbing the traders and even attacking passers-by. Jentsch, the chairman of the Town Council, felt his hour of glory had come. Realizing that political capital could be made from the situation, he placed himself at the head of the insurgents. Mayor Schmieden was sick and confined to his bed, and Polzin's one and only gendarme, Johann Preiss, was powerless as he faced the assembled mob. There is no knowing how things might have turned out had it not been for the swift intervention of the head of the Kleist-Retzow region. With the aid of a hastily mustered police force he put an end to the uprising. Not long after, the district assembly allocated several tens of thousands of Reichsthaler for the purchase of Russian rye so that bread could be baked and distributed to the hungry. But a carrot and stick approach could not solve the essential problem. On Sunday, 2 April 1848, there was a renewed outbreak of violence, even worse than before, and now it was directed against the Jewish residents, first and foremost the wealthy ones. Ascher's house was the worst affected, although it was saved by the militia, who called on the local riflemen. Even so, Ascher Levy still refused to recognize the writing on the wall.

In southern Germany the hungry peasantry rose up against the taxes they were obliged to pay to the feudal lords. They refused to yield even when the army moved in. In March 1848 Friedrich Wilhelm IV ordered his cavalry to break up the demonstrations in the streets of Berlin. Moritz Gottschalk wrote: 'Think yourself lucky not to have witnessed these events. By the way, I advise you to get rid of all your shares in the railway company with the utmost haste.' But nothing would shake Ascher Levy's trust in royal justice, and he sent his cousin a long and detailed reply, saying that selling these shares at such a terrible time would be tantamount to treason against the King. His assertion of loyalty was to cost him dear, and although usually a most prudent businessman, he suffered heavy losses.

Although these were historic events, sweeping the country into uncharted territory, Ascher remained unimpressed. He regarded the summoning of the national assembly in Frankfurt's Church of St Paul as neither significant nor worthy of support, although fifteen Jewish members participated in this constitutional session. He still remained unmoved when Eduard Martin von Simson was elected parliamentary president. Simson, a baptized Jew from Königsberg, had for years been calling for a united German state under a strong and wise ruler. Twenty-eight German states supported Simson's suggested constitution. Ascher, however, remained true to his king, who in April 1849 had rejected in horror the offer of the imperial crown symbolizing a united Germany without Austria, offered to him by a delegation led by Simson. Ascher found himself in full agreement with Friedrich Wilhelm IV, who wrote:

> By the grace of God, a legitimate King is expected to accept such a head covering made of dross and rags? Can the King of Prussia who enjoys the blessing of certainly the noblest if not the oldest crown be expected to wear such an item? [...] If the thousand-year-old crown of the German nation, put away for forty-two years, is now to be handed on once more, then it will

be I and my ilk that will pass it on. And woe to him who seizes what he is not entitled to!

The crown that the King had turned down in the White Chamber of the city palace of Berlin was taken back to Frankfurt by rail. Shares on the stock market crashed in response, and the worst affected were shares in the railway companies. Despite all this, Ascher Levy was content – the King had kept the upper hand and the Frankfurt parliament fell.

At 14 Brunnenstrasse changes were gradually introduced. The old-fashioned furniture was replaced with pieces in the Biedermeier style, and gas lamps took the place of candles.

The newfangled lighting made Ascher's work easier, for he had trouble with his eyesight and had to wear spectacles. Neighbours marvelled at the round tables resting on a central broad carved pedestal, and at the armchairs upholstered in brown and gold striped velvet. The walls were covered in bright coverings of pure silk. For his birthday, Fanny bought the master of the house an enormous bookcase with glazed doors. The Holy Scriptures were neatly arranged inside, and in among the volumes of the *Talmud* there were also a number of books by Sir Walter Scott. In a corner of the drawing room stood a glass cabinet in the English style, ornamented with a fine frame, which displayed a collection of dancers in lacy costumes and characters from German fairy tales. All the figures were made of the finest, most costly porcelain. The carpenters in Kollatz produced small desks for the children, in preparation for the time when they would be ready to do homework.

It was in this comfortable, homely setting that Ascher would climb every evening into his marital bed with its pure cotton covers. Fanny would already be waiting for him. He loved telling her in lengthy detail about all the business developments. After that he would mostly sink into the deep and restful sleep of a man content with his actions. And why not? Men measure their own achievements alongside those of others. He was aware that in the centres of political action far more brilliant careers were being carved out. But in Polzin he was without rivals. His house was the finest in the neighbourhood. In the small Jewish community he was regarded as the first among equals. Despite some minor setbacks, his assets had constantly increased. And before he fell asleep, he could stretch out his hand and feel the warm body of his wife. His world was clearly defined, enclosed by a protective carapace of status, money, health and a profound belief in the will of the Creator. Obstacles, which in the past towered up like insurmountable walls, had disappeared. The future held no threat of specific dangers. He had ensured a safe and comfortable way ahead for his two little sons. They would be his heirs. From time to time he thought about how he would divide up his business affairs, leaving one son to deal with the financial affairs, and the other to take over the trade and industrial side. Bernhard would be the one to conduct the finance and Julius would specialize in directing the sawmills and the grain trade. And God willing, he would find a husband for Vogelchen, who observed the mitsvot, the laws, and could offer her an easy life of good fortune and prosperity. All this could be planned and decided. There would be no more surprises. The Levy family had put down deep roots, and no power in the world would ever uproot them.

His personal dreams were of a different order. Sometimes he would lie in bed, brooding before he fell asleep, and then the world outside his house ceased to exist. The quiet of the night descended over Polzin. His eyes wide open, his gaze would travel across the ceiling.

'What are you thinking about?' asked Fanny.

'Nothing, my dearest.'

'But...'

'I told you – about nothing.'

'Ascher,' she sighed.

'There's no need to worry.'

'All the same, I do worry.'

'But everything is all right, believe me.'

'No. Everything is not all right. There is something that you are keeping from me, I can feel it.'

'Another time perhaps, Fanny. Go to sleep. It's late.'

Ascher got up and put out the lamp. He loved being able to turn the light on and off. The gas lamp was still a novelty, and he took as much pleasure from it as a child with a new toy. The moon hung above the small town, bathing it in a pale white light. Moonlight came through the curtains. Fanny kept silent. He heard her breathing and knew that she was still awake. Could he let Fanny into the secrets of his heart? She knew him as a person who acted soberly in all things. How would she react if he told her of the obsession that had taken hold of him and would not let him go?

He wished to make a pilgrimage to Jerusalem. There he would push a scrap of paper between the stones of the Wailing Wall, with a request written on it, asking for God's help to raise his sons; he would feast his eyes on the Holy Land, and take in the same air that the prophets had breathed long ago. The idea was not a sudden impulse. He could not remember when it had first entered his mind. Possibly in his youth, perhaps during the long walks through the Wilkensdorf countryside, near Friedland, which figured as an influential experience in his life? Over the years, the heartfelt desire to put this idea into action had become ever stronger.

As day dawned, he went across to his desk and set out his yearning in a detailed letter to Moritz Gottschalk. To his surprise, his cousin did not ridicule the idea – quite the contrary. 'I agree that this is not a wise undertaking for people of our age. Let us wait until our hair has turned grey, before we set out. Together. Perhaps this journey will prove to be the pinnacle of our friendship.' And, as in his previous letters, he urged Ascher not just to think of profit, but also of his public position.

His insistent pleading fell on fertile ground, since Ascher had been turning his mind to this for some time past. As a Jew in conservative Pomerania he did not stand the slightest chance of being elected to the district assembly. However, when a vacancy arose in the town council of Polzin, he wasted no time in handing in his candidature. Did he not count for every bit as much as Peter Rohn, the coppersmith, who had been on the town council for twelve years, and had recently died?

So he thought. But others were of a different opinion. Mayor Schmieden, who for months past had been confined to his sickbed, received Ascher for a friendly chat in his home.

Patiently he listened to Ascher's declaration, nodding in confirmation of the list of donations from 'Levy, the corn Jew' to the city welfare institutions and the special fund for the park extension around the spa assembly rooms. As Ascher Levy came to the crucial point of his account, the master of the house sat up in his bed and advised him, albeit in a conciliatory tone: 'I am sorry, but this is not a good time to appoint a Jew to the town council.'

'And why not?' asked Levy, flaring up. 'Aren't there Jews in the Prussian parliament?'

'Polzin is not Berlin,' answered Schmieden. 'And since you mention parliament, you should know that news of Bismarck's speeches has reached Pomerania. He comes from this region originally, so it is little wonder that his words carry weight here. He is one of us.'

'And am I not?' asked Levy in surprise. 'After all, I was also born and raised in Pomerania. I too have sworn an oath of allegiance to the King and the Fatherland, just as he has.'

'My good sir, you are a clever man. You know very well there is a difference.'

'A difference that is essentially unacceptable.'

'Maybe. But that doesn't change reality.'

'Reality is not like mathematics, sir. Reality is subject to a process of constant change.'

'In that case, you will have to wait until your hour comes, and Bismarck changes his position.'

Ascher Levy knew only too well what the other was referring to. In the drawer that he kept locked at home lay a copy of a speech given by Bismarck on 15 July 1847 in the Prussian parliament. Ascher knew the contents by heart:

I am no enemy of the Jews, and should they be enemies of mine, I forgive them. In some instances I even love them. I have no objection to their quest for all rights, except one, namely to be admitted to public office in a Christian state. [...]

In those parts of the country where the Edict of 1812 applies, they are, to the best of my memory, deprived of no other rights than entitlement to occupy public office. This they are now challenging, and demand to become parliamentary deputies, generals, ministers, indeed in certain instances even ministers of religion or ministers of education. I fully admit, that I am full of prejudices that I took in with my mother's milk, and it would be hopeless for me to deny them. But, if I picture myself as a representative of the sacred majesty of the King, in the presence of a Jew, whom I am supposed to obey, I must confess that I should feel profoundly depressed and humiliated. The pleasure and the upright sense of honour I derive from doing my utmost to fulfil my duties towards the state would disappear. These are feelings that I share with the mass of the lower orders of the people and am not ashamed of aligning myself with them. [...] I recognize that in Berlin and generally in the larger cities the Jewish element consists almost without exception of respectable people. I further recognize that in the country such Jews are not altogether absent, and occasionally they do exist. [...] But I know of a region with a large Jewish population, where the peasants can call none of their possessions their own anywhere on the land they farm; from their bed down to the cooking fork every single item of their furnishings belongs to the Jew, the beast in the manger belongs to the Jew: [...] the corn in the field and in the barn...

No one claimed that Ascher had acquired his wealth by dishonest means, but his honesty was of no avail against Bismarck's assertions. The fact remained that when others suffered losses, many Jews ended up the winners. And even Ascher could not get round this.

Both Ascher Levy and Otto von Bismarck had first seen the light of day in Pomerania in that fateful year of 1815, as the cheering crowds were shouting, 'Napoleon is finished.' Whereas the birth of Ascher Levy had been a modest family event, that of the little Otto had been greeted with joyful proclamation. The bawling infant on the Schönhausen estate was the offspring of an old-established junker family, known for their hard-headedness. They had been living in Pomerania even before the Hohenzollern ruled there. The Levy family tree had its roots abroad, in the Orient, and was neither dazzling nor aristocratic. There was a yawning abyss between the two families and the two worlds. It took just a few words from a junker to cut the ground from under the feet of a Jew. Neither of them could have guessed that one day their paths would cross.

Ascher sought consolation in his work. It was his habit to rise early, sometimes even before dawn, and he rarely went to bed before nine at night. Contrary to the promise he had once given his wife, he was still frequently away on business. His reputation as a merchant reached far and wide, from Stettin in the west to Kolberg in the east. There was no time for the children. It was Fanny who concerned herself with the differences between Beri and Juli. By the age of four, Beri was already remarkably like her husband. He moved like his father, covered huge distances with energetic strides, spoke in a soft and reflective way, and if something was not to his taste, he would grimace just like his father. When the time came for him to attend the Jewish school in the town, he shone at mathematics and history, but also made good progress in his studies of the Holy Scriptures. The teacher was constantly praising the keenness of this pupil who did not stop at learning everything he was taught by heart, as was the custom then, but frequently tried to get to the bottom of things. 'Your son has no time for nonsense,' he was accustomed to say. Fanny, however, was afraid that the boy would grow up too quickly. 'There is nothing worse than a child without a childhood,' she maintained. Ascher just shrugged his shoulders. For his part, he was satisfied.

Juli was completely different. Although younger than his brother, he soon overtook him in height. He was slim and good-looking, and it was only his impatience that prevented him from being popular with his fellows. His school marks did not exactly delight his parents. The school and its rigid discipline was against his nature. He preferred dreaming about the swan lake in the park, and planning schoolboy pranks with the neighbours' children. Ascher hoped that in due time Juli would become more serious. But even as he grew older, he showed little interest in the family business. Money was of no importance to him, so it was hardly surprising that as the time approached to take a decision, Ascher revealed the secrets of the business only to his older son.

Unemployment in the big cities made the 1850s a difficult decade. However, the little town of Polzin experienced something of a boom. When Ascher Levy had settled there, the town had a population of approximately 1,500. Now there were 4,200 residents, about 700 of whom were Jews. There was work for everyone even though their pay was low. Ascher's factories alone employed eight staff and more than 120 workers.

The government forged ahead with major road construction works. First of these was the road to Jastrow, and since the district assembly had allocated the sum of forty-three thaler for every mile built, engineers were quick to get the project going. The Fuhrmann family beer brewery also expanded, and when in 1852 the owner, Karl Fuhrmann, decided to purchase another factory, the Sering brewery on the Bärwalder Chaussee, the obvious thing for him to do was to take up a loan from Ascher Levy of 500 Reichsthaler, to be paid off within five years at a rate of interest a full one per cent higher than the dividend Ascher had received from his shares in the railroad companies. As the Polzin cloth-makers were adversely affected by the industrialization of textile production, they decided to move with the times in order to avoid a major crisis. In the summer of 1852 work began on the building of a new spinning and cloth fulling mill, and by 5 February 1853 the factory was in operation. The first order was placed by the army, getting the factory off to a promising start.

It was at about this time that the leader of the Kleist-Retzow parliament decided to expand the use of the spa waters and to erect a hospital to be run by nuns as a secondary settlement of the Bethany mother-house in Berlin. The property was acquired for the sum of 200 Reichsthaler, and altogether the fully fitted hospital cost 23,000 thaler. When public donations were sought towards this huge sum, the Levy family gave 250 thaler. Although Ascher received a letter of thanks for this generous donation from the parliamentary head in person, he was not invited to the laying of the foundation stone. He was not entitled to stand alongside the dignitaries of the little town and the region, to greet His Majesty, King Friedrich Wilhelm IV, who attended the ceremony. He had to remain in his office and content himself with the newspaper report, which of course did not appear until the following morning:

At one o'clock in the afternoon of 29 August, His Majesty stopped in the festively decorated town, on his way to Neustettin; peals of bells announced the arrival from Belgard. As he passed through the great gate of honour erected at the entrance to the town, the King was met by a guard of riflemen, and then at the market place, where he changed horses, he was received by members of the district assembly introduced by the chairman of the regional council, and by the town authorities and those who had travelled from Schivelbein, Dramburg, and Falkenburg. He then permitted himself a few minutes' respite in the house of apothecary Bückling, where a room had been specially prepared. Thereupon his most gracious Majesty, and his retinue, and representatives of the town's officials made their way to the construction site of the great Bethany hospital, some 500 paces from the town, where in the customary fashion the ceremony of the laying of the foundation stone was conducted with the highest solemnity. Kleedehn, the preacher, received His Majesty at the construction site amid singing by the choirs of Polzin, Schivelbein, and Dramburg. The preacher gave a short, appropriate address and recited the blessing, after which His Majesty exchanged a few friendly words with him. Thereupon Freiherr von der Reck on behalf of the Bethany board thanked His Majesty for having most graciously participated in the work, thanked the head of the authorities for the fact that His Majesty had seen fit to honour the town of Polzin with his most gracious presence, and went on to express the hope that His Most Gracious Majesty would extend his protection for many years to come. It pleased the King to reply: 'I thank you!', whereupon the procession returned to town, where His Majesty was good enough to partake of refreshment prepared for him in the Bückling house, to the accompaniment of singing of the combined choirs, then to permit himself to be introduced to Gaffrey, the artist responsible for the construction of the gate of honour, and then amid thunderous cries of hurrah from all those gathered from the town and the surrounding countryside, towards two o'clock in the afternoon he set off to continue his journey to Neustettin. The satisfaction of His Majesty with his reception in Polzin, expressed in such gracious words and gestures, was immensely gratifying to the town and will remain an everlasting memory.

Ascher carefully folded up the newspaper and laid it on his desk. At lunchtime on the previous day, at the height of the festivities, when he heard the cheering of the crowd through an open window, he had taken his coat from its hanger, intending to make his way to the gate of honour, and at least catch a glance of his revered king. But at the last moment he had suppressed the impulse. Whatever would people say if they saw him mingling with the humble folk, while those far less worthy than him raised their glasses to drink to the King? He crept back into his room, and would not even open the door when Fanny came to cheer him with a cup of tea and a shot of rum.

In these days Fanny was not only a loyal wife, but a true support, in the most literal sense of the word. She was blessed with sound business sense, and Ascher readily sought her advice when he was uncertain whether a particular business venture was worthwhile. Despite his reserved nature, he opened the deepest feelings of his heart to Fanny, and when he went away on business, even just for a few days, he would write her letters in which business affairs would be mingled with expressions of tenderness. The well-judged *shidduch* had developed into an intimate relationship of mutual understanding. And now as her looks were fading, her figure spreading with the birth of three children, and the sparkle in her eyes gradually dimming, now of all times, passion welled up in him unlike anything he had previously known. Both were considering whether to bring another child into the world. Fanny wanted a large family, and Ascher wanted another heir to take Juli's place. But God did not bless them with any more children, and even Dr Jakob Wachsler, the gynaecologist from Stettin, was unable to help them.

It was Fanny's suggestion that he take time off from the firm and accept the renewed invitations of Moritz Gottschalk, who had meanwhile become a well-known figure on the stock exchange. In the early summer of 1858 Ascher decided to follow her advice, and set out for Berlin. It was his first visit to the Prussian capital. Moritz Gottschalk entertained him royally in his large house at 47 Französische Strasse. He was eager to display his wealth and his standing in the financial world to his cousin from the provinces. Every evening the cousins dined in company, mostly with Jews who had reached undreamed-of goals. Their conversations mainly revolved around people who had attained wealth and power, and who enjoyed the respect of the government, aided by connections with the upper ranks of society.

On the very first evening Ascher's cousin described with barely suppressed excitement the glittering career of Gerson Bleichröder, considered a financial genius, who had risen to the position of personal banker to Otto von Bismarck. Before being sent to St Petersburg as ambassador, Bismarck had entrusted his financial affairs to Bleichröder, and this had evidently not remained a secret. Political opponents of the future 'Iron Chancellor' saw to it that the nationalist-inclined newspapers were informed of the connection between the well-known junker and the 'Jewish gravedigger's grandson'. Rumour had it that the connection had come about on the advice of the Rothschilds, who were likewise engaged in Bismarck's investments. 'I keep up with everything that Bleichröder does,' explained Moritz Gottschalk proudly. 'I have agents who for a small consideration keep me informed in every detail of his dealings on the stock exchange. When Bleichröder buys, I buy. And if he sells, then I do the same. Believe me, it's a recipe for success. Since then, I haven't lost a single penny. Don't you want to jump on the bandwagon?'

Ascher Levy shook his head. No, he did not belong to the pan-

European world of business. Actually, his only reason for coming to Berlin was to discuss the subject closest to his heart – their intended journey to the Holy Land. But once again Moritz Gottschalk suggested postponing their departure. His complicated dealings, he explained, made it impossible for him to be away for any length of time. Observing Ascher's disappointment, he consoled him, saying: 'I haven't given up the idea.'

The displeasure Ascher felt at this was directed not at his cousin, but at the world in which he moved, a world where men were prisoners of their material aspirations. When he had first struggled for his own place in this world, such considerations were alien to him. It was only now that he became aware of them, as he spoke to Moritz Gottschalk, and he felt a growing distaste for the frenetic pace of the capital, where the one and only thing that counted seemed to be the profit motive, leaving no place for human emotions. Alongside the issues that concerned the public at large and the topics of conversation in the salons of the wealthy, Ascher's business successes paled in significance, making them seem of little worth. Polzin appeared even more provincial and the firm he was so proud to have founded and built up single-handedly suddenly appeared tiny and unimportant.

He came near to stammering as he informed Moritz Gottschalk that he had invested thousands of thaler in a railway company that was laying railway tracks from Stargard to Köslin, so that within two years Polzin would be linked to the leading towns of Pomerania. He went on to tell his cousin of his intention to acquire more forest land to secure the source of raw material for his sawmill at Kollatz. He calculated that, even with the cost of felling the timber, this investment would have paid off within only six years. In Pomerania both land and labour were still cheap. If this transaction turned out well, he also planned to purchase the sawmill at Gross Linichen near Dramburg. This would make him the most important Jewish businessman in the whole of the Köslin area. But it was obvious to him that his plans were of little interest to his cousin. 'We may be flesh and blood, but our pulses beat at a different rate,' said Ascher sadly, as he took his leave after ten days.

On his return Bernhard's bar mitzvah took place. One *Shabbat* soon after Beri's thirteenth birthday, he was received into the *minyan* of the adult community and called up for the reading of the Torah. Ascher's heart filled with fatherly pride as he heard his son's melodious voice chant the verses in fluent Hebrew. As they left the synagogue, he embraced him and said: 'Always remember that you are a proud citizen of Prussia, entitled to equal rights. And never forget that you are a Jew. If you do, there will always be others to remind you of your origins.'

Five more good years passed. Early one morning Bernhard was called to the office, before the arrival of the first customers. With due propriety, he knocked on the door. His father was sitting at a large desk, piled high with papers. 'Sit down,' he said, indicating the chair opposite. Bernhard sat down, and waited for what was to come. He had never been summoned to his father's office before, and was wondering what the reason was. One and then two minutes passed in silence. Ascher Levy's fingers drummed on the desk. Bernhard folded his arms and waited.

'I expect you can imagine why I have called you in,' said Ascher.

'I have no idea, Papa.'

'We must give your future serious thought.'

Inwardly Bernhard grinned. The 'we' was merely a token polite form. The only person reflecting on his future was his father. He leaned forward, and obediently replied: 'I will do as you wish.'

'I have been thinking about this for a long time,' Ascher continued, still drumming away with his fingers. 'At first, I wanted to send you to Berlin. My cousin generously offered to help you, and you could have lived with him and learned banking. However, certain considerations led me to change my mind. My business affairs here are expanding and diversifying...'

'...and you need someone at your side.'

Ascher made a satisfied noise. 'Right. You've guessed.'

'Would you like to assign a particular task to me, Papa?'

'Your brother shows no interest whatsoever in the business, which is a source of great sadness to me. Someone will have to take over the firm, when I decide to stop working.'

'Stop working? At your age?'

'I make my plans years ahead. It will take quite a while before you master all the complex business affairs.'

'I can be patient.'

'Then start by learning the basics.'

'I'll do anything you ask me to do.'

'You won't be treated as the boss's son, you will start right at the bottom, like any other apprentice.'

'I didn't expect anything else, Papa.'

'I intend to expand into property. I shall appoint an employee to manage this side of the business and you are to learn from him. Keep your eyes and ears open. You will be dealing with important landowners. Don't show me up. Be unyielding, but honest.'

'What you mean is that I should just be myself, isn't it?'

Ascher smiled contentedly. 'Yes, that's what I meant.'

'And when do I start?'

'Today.'

Before Bernhard was able to go away on business and do deals on behalf of the firm, he had to spend a full year learning all the aspects of bookkeeping. Ascher attached great importance to his son's having a clear picture of everything that went on in the business; above all, he should know how to read the balance sheets just as accurately as the Holy Scriptures. Not until Bernhard had mastered these requirements to the satisfaction of his father was he allowed to go on business trips, which ranged from the southern lakes to the Baltic coast in the north, in search of good timber forests, or to draw up contracts for felling timber or the purchase of forest land.

Bernhard's skill at coping in every situation, his friendliness and politeness soon made him a valued business partner. Ascher followed the progress of his son with pride. After three years he considered changing the name of the firm to 'Ascher Levy and Son', but rejected the idea when Fanny objected forcefully, saying, 'You can't do that to Juli, the child would be deeply upset.' But Julius had long since left childhood behind. At twenty years of age, much to the chagrin of Ascher, he was still not earning a living. Fanny was equally troubled by this, but she did not have a solution, either.

Ascher continued to correspond with Moritz Gottschalk and they wrote to each other at least once a month. In the autumn of 1869 Ascher invited his cousin to attend a joyous occasion. Still unmarried at the age of twenty-one, Vogel had at last been found a suitable marriage partner. A widower by the name of Hirsch Hirschfeld was a prosperous relative from the small town of Neuwedel. Ascher and Fanny made a generous settlement when they sat down with the marriage broker. Vogel was given a sum large enough to purchase a new and spacious house, as the widower already had four children and the couple intended to have more of their own. In addition, in the customary way she also received clothing and linen, as well as all the items necessary for setting up a household. This was not simply prompted by parental generosity; at the time a dowry was considered part of a woman's inheritance, and consequently was the clearest indication of Ascher's financial status. Furthermore, Ascher decided to celebrate the event by setting up a special fund to benefit the youth of Polzin. Even before the bride had left for her new home, a document was drafted at the town hall setting out the administration of this new foundation:

1. A scholarship to be awarded to an industrious student, who must be born in Polzin, and who specializes in the sciences or commerce. Once the accrued capital reaches the sum of 1500 Reichsthaler, half the interest to be distributed to assist the poor.
2. The Town Council to administer the fund. No fee will be paid for this.
3. The administrative office to be located on the first floor of the huge newly built Town Hall on the market square.
4. The sum donated for the foundation is hereby deposited in the municipal savings bank. The deposit account book number 6184 to be placed in the chief security depot of the municipality, to which there are two keys. The main key to the safe to be held by the depositor.

'Forgive me for asking, Herr Levy, but would you not wish to add a clause permitting you and your heirs to determine who should receive the scholarship and the assistance?' asked Mayor Schmieden.

'No, the town council will set up an official committee, that will decide,' replied Ascher and turned towards the door.

Placing his hand on Ascher's arm, the mayor stopped him and said, 'Just a minute, Herr Levy, I can't let you off so easily. What if this committee decided in favour a young man who is not of the Mosaic faith? And would you wish to assist the poor lying in the Christian Bethany Hospital?'

'It is you who makes the distinction between Jew and non-Jew. In my eyes, there is no distinction, Mr Mayor.'

'Could you be giving us a lesson in tolerance?'

'God forbid! But truth be told, there are those who might benefit from such a lesson. Of course, I did not have you in mind, Mr Mayor.'

The wedding canopy for Vogel and Hirsch was erected in the synagogue on the Grosse Muehlenweg. The only guests invited to the celebration were family members and close friends. Having once been bitten, Ascher deliberately omitted to invite the mayor and the local dignitaries. He could not have borne a second public humiliation. As he and Fanny drew up the guest list, he poured his heart out to her. 'Here am I, a citizen with equal rights. My money doesn't smell, and yet they still whisper behind my back that I stink of garlic. Our house isn't good enough for the land-lords and the gentry, and we're not considered worthy to be graced by their presence. I've heard them calling me "moneybags" behind my back...'

At the top of the guest list was Moritz Gottschalk, and he was duly the first to arrive, wrapped in a sable fur and laden with pre-sents. He had become stout and was greying at the temples. 'Good living has made me fat, and sorrow has turned me grey,' he said, laughing heartily, as the cousins withdrew to a quiet corner after the festivities, and took up the conversation broken off nearly twelve years earlier. Gottschalk had brought a lot of exciting news from the capital. Every event he described was

'wonderful', 'amazing' or 'inspiring'. Naturally enough, the heady
events centred on the balls thrown by Gerson Bleichröder, his
idol. He lingered lovingly over details of luxurious receptions,
where exquisite French wines were served along with other delicacies, and went into every detail of the orchestras hired to enter-
tain the dancing guests, who naturally enough were all noblemen
and for the most part decision-making members of the government. Had Ascher not known that his cousin had never crossed
the threshold of the Bleichröder establishment, he might have
been tempted to believe that Moritz Gottschalk had been there in
person. In reality the source of the information was the gossip
columns of the *Vossische Zeitung* newspaper and the Berlin
tabloids, which were tireless in their reports of the goings-on in
the house of the richest man in all Brandenburg. Moritz
Gottschalk had even gone so far as to cut out a picture from one
of these newspapers, showing the huge building in the
Behrenstrasse where Bleichröder lived and had his offices, and he
presented it to Ascher as if it were a valuable painting by a famous
artist. 'This is where these balls take place, and here is where he
receives his clients,' he whispered, as if it were a well-guarded
secret. 'Did you know that even the Jew-hating Richard Wagner
has most of his financial affairs managed by him?'

'It would never have occurred to me. How do you know?'
Ascher inquired.

A mysterious smile crossed Moritz's face. 'No one has any
secrets from me. I've told you before: without the right access to
information, you'll never be wealthy.'

'I don't want to be wealthy. I'm happy as I am.'

'It hasn't escaped me that you don't want for anything,' Moritz
Gottschalk said in a playful way.

'God has not deserted me,' replied Ascher in all seriousness.
'And now that my little Vogel has found her place in the world,
my good fortune is complete.'

'You don't want to get rich, but you certainly don't want to lose
anything, do you?'

'Why do we have to talk about money all the time? Today is a
day for rejoicing and ...'

Moritz Gottschalk cut him short: 'It might interest you to know that the house of Bleichröder and that of Oppenheim are selling their French and Spanish interests on the quiet. Surely you remember that I bought French securities in your name to the value of two thousand thaler? I've sold mine.'

'I may know something about cereals, timber, and provincial banking, but very little about international politics. But you may remember that I learned my first lesson in this area when I was nineteen years old and was apprenticed to Louis Stärger. I seem to remember writing to you about it at the time. The outcome of the war of the Spanish succession meant that Spain got into financial difficulties then. As a result, a Prussian nobleman, whose financial affairs were in the hands of Louis Stärger, lost almost everything he had. This taught me to take losses in my stride. How much will I lose if I sell?'

'Nothing. You can still sell at a reasonable price, and even make a small profit. I remember the story of Stärger and the junker all too well. Well, in 1834 Isabella won the upper hand, although not for long. Now a group of officers and politicians who call themselves progressives have seized power in Spain. But they wish to appear legitimate and are casting around for a suitable candidate to occupy the vacant throne – a man of straw, who looks as if he is ruling, but in reality will carry out their instructions. In my view the charade will soon begin, and market prices will fall.'

Moritz Gottschalk was right in his predictions. In less than a year rebellion broke out and the throne was offered to Prince Leopold of the house of Hohenzollern-Sigmaringen. Given the turbulence that had beset his brother Karl in his struggle for the Rumanian crown, Leopold was in no great hurry to accept the tempting offer. The candidacy of this prince, related as he was to the royal house of Prussia, was not at all to the liking of the French government. They regarded it as an immediate threat to French interests. Initially their displeasure simply affected diplomatic relations. But as the decisive moment approached the Emperor Napoleon III peeled off his velvet gloves, and on 6 July 1870 sent a warning to Berlin and Madrid, saying that France would not tolerate a ruler with hostile intentions at her southern frontier. Bismarck's response was equally unequivocal – Prussia gave Prince Leopold its wholehearted support. The exchange of diplomatic couriers between the two governments resounded like the clash of drawn swords. Hostile exchanges flew to and fro like snowballs, eventually unleashing a roaring avalanche that buried relations between the protagonists. On 19 July war broke out.

Ascher Levy sat in his office, hunched over the newspaper headlines announcing the outbreak of war. Suddenly there was a knock at the door. Ascher, who disliked being disturbed first thing in the morning, said abruptly: 'Enter.'

In the doorway stood Julius, also with a newspaper in his hand.

'Two newspapers in the same house?' snapped Ascher. 'What extravagance!'

Julius ignored his father's comment. 'Hear me out, please, before you get angry,' he pleaded.

'What is it now?'

'I've decided to enlist as a volunteer.'

'Have you gone completely *meshuggeh*?' replied Ascher, aghast.

'It's you who is always referring to love of the fatherland, Papa. You're the one who's always talking about loyalty to Prussia.'

'But that didn't mean ...'

'Well, that's how it is. This time I'm serious – me, the idle good-for-nothing. And I'm not rushing into this. I've been thinking about it all night long.'

'That never results in a sensible outcome.'

'That's hardly relevant at the moment, Father.'

Ascher let the newspaper fall to his knees, and looked up at his son. Facing him stood Julius as he had never before known him: erect, confident, and decisive. He suppressed a comment on Julius's impudence and nodded, as if in agreement with him. In direct contrast to his usual reasoning, he felt a certain pride, and yet relief as well, that it was not Bernhard standing there in front of him.

'There are other ways of serving the fatherland,' he countered in a quiet tone.

'I have chosen mine.'

'I won't stand in your way,' replied Ascher. 'But you must also get your mother's consent.'

Fanny's tears were to no avail. Two days later Julius caught the train to Belgard, to the nearest barracks where medical examinations were being held. The departmental officers were astounded at this young man wishing to serve in the Prussian army. By now doctors, paymasters, and quartermasters of the Mosaic faith were no longer a rarity, but for a Jew to volunteer for the front, let alone in a rifle brigade in the front line, was new to them. Some 12,000 Jews in Prussia, Bavaria, Saxony, and Baden had in fact volunteered to serve in the army, but news of this had not reached Belgard. The medical board found Julius fit to bear arms, and a month later Lance Corporal Julius Levy was at the front, on the banks of the river Maas. His first letter home was written from there, saying in a brief and matter-of-fact way that he was healthy, happy, and proud.

On 2 September 1870 at one-thirty in the afternoon, the official on duty at the Berlin telegraph office received a telegram addressed to Queen Augusta that read:

> Surrender at Sedan has just been concluded with General Wimpffen, who took over command from the wounded General MacMahon, and the entire army has been taken prisoner. The Emperor in person surrendered to me, since he was not in command, and leaves everything to the regent in Paris. I shall decide where he is to stay, as soon as I have spoken to him at a meeting that will take place immediately. What an outcome by the Grace of God! Wilhelm.

'What an outcome by the Grace of God!' proclaimed a huge banner at the Brandenburg Gate on the very same evening. The closing words of the telegram soon became a catchphrase that passed from mouth to mouth in Prussia with intoxicating effect. 'Victory, victory! Long live the King!' cried the crowds that had gathered in the market place of Polzin. Lamps were lit; people raised their glasses and sang military songs. For a moment all quarrels and disputes were forgotten; Germany was never as united as in the days following the Battle of Sedan.

Although this first battle decided the outcome of the war, the hostilities were not at an end. Michael Harward, a British historian, wrote at the time: 'A tragic chain of unfortunate events dragged France into the war, militarily unprepared and without allies.' In simple words Julius Levy sent home the news: 'My dearest parents, the first victory is won. I am the happiest of all men, to be given the opportunity of making my own contribution to the victory. The things I have seen are incomprehensible. And yet it is a wonderful feeling to be present at the pulse of events, it is a great thing to belong among the citizens of the Prussian kingdom at this time...'

Whereas the Prussian artillery was the best in the world, the same could not be said for the postal service. Every morning Fanny waited impatiently in front of the house for the postman to call. Even before he had emptied out the business letters from his postbag, he would shrug his shoulders apologetically, saying: 'No, no news.' The letter from Lance Corporal Julius Levy lay in some office of the royal military mail, between France and Polzin. For weeks the family were left without news.

Outwardly life went on as normal in the house in the Brunnenstrasse and business carried on as usual. In the evenings when the family gathered in the dining room, Fanny was requested to stop her sobbing. Bernhard preferred to keep his eyes down, to avoid his mother's gaze. Ascher did not speak. None of them dared to utter what was on their minds. The cook served the evening meal, and they ate in silence.

One evening when they had already withdrawn to their bedroom, and Ascher was putting out the light, Fanny plucked up her courage and asked: 'What do you think, will he come back?'

'If something had happened to him, we would have heard about it long ago. Bad news travels fast.'

'But what do your instincts tell you?'

'I prefer to listen to the voice of logic, Fanny.'

'You and your logic...'

Taking her head between his hands, he drew it protectively to his chest. 'Don't say that,' he comforted her. 'My heart also tells me everything is all right.'

'I can hear it.'

'You see? As long as it's still beating, you have no need to worry.'

'I know, and yet... Why doesn't he write?'

'You know Juli. He has never had any family feeling.'

'I hope you're right. But still...'

'Fanny, I'm tired.'

'I know, forgive me. Go to sleep. You have a heavy day ahead of you.'

She had always stood by him in times of joy and sorrow, but now she could not find the strength to do so. The weekends were the hardest time, for that was when the family gathered to celebrate *Shabbat*. One seat at the table remained empty. In vain Fanny tried to hide her reddened eyes below her bonnet, her hands trembling as she lit the candles and recited the blessing: 'Blessed art Thou, O Lord our God, King of the universe, who has sanctified us by your commandments and commanded us to kindle the lights of the Sabbath.' The candles stood in the very same antique silver candlesticks that Ascher's father, Jäckel, had bought from a French soldier on the retreat from Russia, barely sixty years earlier. Since then they had adorned the table on every *Shabbat*. It had never occurred to Fanny that probably no one had ever been killed or robbed on account of them. But now all this was a possibility. And as Ascher lifted the white cloth covering the *challah*, the traditional white bread, to divide it, her thoughts were with her son away at war.

The nightmare lasted for weeks. Every morning she prayed to God, and the postman, that her pleas would at last be answered. And then finally at the beginning of February 1871, the moment arrived. Franz, the postman, came hurrying towards her, waving the brown envelope in the distance. With trembling hands she tore it open and instantly recognized the familiar handwriting. In bold, upright characters, Julius described his experiences in detail.

He was out of danger. His unit had been transferred away
from the field of action, to Versailles, the very centre of government. Lance Corporal Levy was saluting the leading figures of
the nation, who had at last arrived to hammer out the conditions
of surrender. Bismarck and Moltke passed through his camp, and
even Gerson Bleichröder and Henckel von Donnersmarck came
speeding past in a magnificent military carriage. What was the
Jewish banker doing in the headquarters of the winning side?
Julius had no idea. His father smiled as he read the letter. The
reason for Bleichröder's presence was no secret. Bleichröder
himself had seen to it that his mission was public knowledge. He
was responsible for making sure that at least a part of the war
reparations – two billion gold francs – were paid over with all due
haste. The London branch of the Rothschilds stood surety for
this transaction. In the end the French agreed to a payment of
approximately five billion gold francs in the hope that this would
enable them to keep Strasbourg and the Alsace. However, the
outcome was that they not only had to take on the burden of this
vast sum, but they also had to accept the loss of these territories.

From Versailles, the correspondent of the *Frankfurter Zeitung*
newspaper reported that talks had taken place between Bismarck
and Adolphe Thiers, the future President of France. According to
this report, the French statesman had complained about the enor-
mity of the reparations. Had the payment of this money begun as
far back as the time of Christ, he asserted, a sum so big would still
not be repaid. To this Bismarck countered: 'I have thought about
that. That is why I have brought a banker with me who began
making payments at the time of the Creation.' Bleichröder and the
Prussian politicians were experienced in calling in debts. On 2
February the *Kölnische Zeitung* (the Cologne newspaper) had published an article in praise of the Jewish banker and the Minister of
Finance. What the press had not yet uncovered was the private
war that Bleichröder was waging against his rivals. He had not
wanted any other bankers present at Versailles, as they would certainly have attempted to secure a share of the spoils from this leg-
endary sum. Worse still, they would have tried to dispute that the
success had been his alone.

The people were drunk with victory, the financiers and the politicians were lusting for money. The war against France had brought Germany what numerous statesmen had sought to achieve over many decades – the unification of the German kingdoms, dukedoms, and Hanseatic towns. The leading status of Bismarck's government and the Kingdom of Prussia was beyond question. The way now lay open to a united empire – without Austria – and Bismarck seized the day. The German empire was proclaimed, not, it has to be said, at the Palace of Sanssouci, but on hostile territory, now conquered and one hour away from the Arc de Triomphe in Paris. On 18 January 1871 princes and senators, politicians and members of the army, in splendid coloured uniforms with richly ornamented swords, assembled in the magnificent Hall of Mirrors at Versailles to witness the historic event, and to observe with their own eyes as Wilhelm I was crowned Kaiser and received the crown that his predecessor had rejected with horror. What an outcome, by the grace of God!

The *Kreuzzeitung* was not a newspaper that was read in the Levy house in Polzin, nor was any other nationalist newspaper. But his acquaintances saw to it that Ascher was kept informed of the articles reporting the mission of 'Bismarck's money Jew'. They would often pass him the gutter press rags, which blamed the Jews for all manner of offences. Ascher stuffed them in the drawer where over the years he had been keeping similar publications locked away. It was clear to him that this time anti-Semitism was serving as an instrument to attack the Chancellor's policies. And still it was painful, deeply painful, since for Ascher the Chancellor was the personification of love of the fatherland. It hurt to read the abusive tirades against Bismarck, where 'enslaved to the Jew' was among the more moderate expressions.

Angrily, Fanny asked: 'What on earth are you reading this rubbish for?'

'The customers bring them in.'

'Does that mean you have to read them? Just throw them in the waste-paper basket!'

'My love, do you really think we can escape reality that way?'

'Such things aren't aimed at people like you,' she insisted.

'What do these power struggles have to do with us? Just because Jews like Bleichröder drag us through the mud along with themselves? You are loyal to Prussia, and your son is in uniform.'

'Bleichröder is just as loyal as I am,' he replied and indicated that the conversation was at an end.

Letters from France were arriving more and more often. For Fanny and Ascher they brought a ray of light to their everyday existence. Julius had seen the sea of flags, the gala uniforms, and the victory parade on its way to Paris. He had overheard important discussions and was breathing the same air as princes and the King, now crowned as Kaiser. He described the firework displays in his letters, unaware of the mess the rockets left behind. 'My dear parents, I am the happiest of all men. Yesterday I was put on duty in the vicinity of the Hall of Mirrors, and was able to follow part of the grandiose ceremony. A great hour in my life.'

It was also a great hour for Prussia. Germany was blessed with unification, with five billion gold francs in war reparations, a Kaiser, and the territories of Alsace and Lorraine, which had also been wrested from the French. Bismarck received the title of Grand Prince. Bleichröder returned to the offices of his bank in Berlin with the Iron Cross, Second Class dangling from a white ribbon edged with black – a high honour for the architects of the victory, which had not been won on the battlefield.

At the end of March, on a day when the snow was beginning to melt, there was a knock at the door of the Levy home. On the doorstep stood Julius Levy, soldier, decorated with the Iron Cross, Second Class, on a black ribbon edged with white, an honour awarded only to courageous soldiers.

His mother did not even notice the medal. She flung her arms round Julius's neck and burst into tears. Now there was no need to hold them back any longer. The employees rose to their feet and applauded. Ascher too embraced Julius and, glancing at the Iron Cross, said: 'I'm proud of you, my son.'

Industry, too, had benefited from the war. Prussia now faced the realization of a dream – to outstrip England in industrialization. The reparation payments enabled the government to pay off its domestic debts in full, with a handsome sum left over in the coffers of the Imperial Bank. It was the age of investment and industrial progress. New opportunities were open to both skilful and ruthless entrepreneurs, and even Pomerania woke from its slumber. Astute businessmen secured contracts for supplying the army. In many areas demand exceeded supply.

Ascher Levy's grain depots were emptied in no time and the workforce at his two timber works were unable to keep up with the orders, even though they were working several shifts. His biggest customers now were the Jewish brothers, Georg and Moritz Behrend. These two had set up a cellulose factory two years earlier in Köslin and required colossal quantities of raw material. Moritz proved to be a shrewd and prudent businessman, but his brother Georg was careless with the firm's money, spending on risky investments, and a large part of the profits went on amusement and betting. There were times when Ascher Levy had to wait months for payment of timber that had been supplied, as the Behrend firm's account with the Ritterliche Bank in Stettin was not always covered.

When their debts yet again reached excessive proportions, Ascher seriously considered breaking off relations with the factory in Köslin. But his son, Bernhard, urged him not to do so. For the Behrend family owned shares in another company that also produced cellulose and paper. Also, the Behrend brothers had rapidly established themselves as the sole purchasers of timber and consequently had been able to dictate the prices. Bernhard repeatedly stressed the fact that the main suppliers of the Behrends was still the Varzin estate, which since 1867 had belonged to Otto von Bismarck. 'If Bismarck has confidence in them, why shouldn't we?' he insisted. Ascher asked Moritz Gottschalk for advice. His cousin agreed with Bernhard, adding the latest tidbit of gossip: 'Rumour has it in Berlin that it was the four hundred thousand thaler awarded to Bismarck in recognition of his success that enabled him to purchase Varzin. It's almost certain that the Chancellor acquired the estate on the advice of King Wilhelm, and that he paid a half a million thaler for it. It's worth it. There are seven villages on the estate, which includes more than twenty-two thousand acres of woodland.'

Once again Bernhard was sent to the north of the area, in order to purchase anything he could lay his hands on. Ascher's agent in Stettin was instructed to purchase a block of shares in a newly-formed company. Its founder was a banker named Charles Strousberg, who had initiated the laying of railway tracks in Rumania. Strousberg's consortium promised shareholders a dividend of seven per cent, three per cent more than any other railway company. Ascher's earlier investments in railway construction in East Prussia, prompted by this same businessman, had already brought in healthy returns. Yet the further he expanded his position in business and the higher the yield, the more he had the feeling that this was no coincidence, and that the hand of the Almighty was steering his destiny. He became increasingly devout, with results that were soon felt. As chief contributor to the funds of the Jewish school, he insisted on the dismissal of Hohenstein, the teacher, who in his opinion was laying too much emphasis on secular subjects while neglecting religious teaching. The favourable attitudes of the other parents were not much help to Hohenstein. He was obliged to hand in his resignation. Ascher's letters to Moritz Gottschalk contained repeated references to his longing for *Eretz Israel*, 'the spiritual homeland of all Jews', and urged that 'the matter be taken up with Professor Graetz'.

In September 1871 the three men met at Bad Kissingen. It was no accident that Moritz Gottschalk had chosen this particular place. The spa of Bad Kissingen with its curative waters had become fashionable and was attracting famous people in society. Members of the imperial family, Bismarck, and even Hans Bleichröder, Gerson's wayward son, could be found walking in the spa park. At their first meeting, Heinrich Graetz, professor at the Jewish Theological Seminary in Breslau and one of its leading scholars, was compelled to admit that he could not raise the necessary funds for this expensive journey to Palestine. Moritz Gottschalk and Ascher were quick to reassure him that the two of them would divide the cost of his travel expenses. At all costs they wanted him as their travelling companion, for they feared that without him they would not achieve the aim of the journey, namely a study of how the Jewish settlement, the *Yishuv*, was faring in *Eretz Israel*.

The desirability of the *Yishuv* was a topic being hotly debated in many parts of Germany at this time. Whereas the Reform movements were keen on strengthening the *Yishuv* in Palestine, the Orthodox, on the other hand, regarded any attempt to change living conditions in Jerusalem as an instant threat to the principles of religion and tradition. They maintained that a battle between the new and the old would be disastrous for the tiny *Yishuv* and that *Eretz Israel* was not suitable for 'educated people with a little Jewishness'; in other words, for dissenters. Professor Graetz was actively engaged in the dispute, which was being pursued in two papers, the *Israelite*, the organ of the ultra-Orthodox, and the *Orient*, a literary, academic weekly. His opinion carried great weight. He was known both as a historian and as a philosopher.

As the three were walking through the Kurpark, Ascher unexpectedly said: 'Please don't mock me for this comparison, but I feel like Moses with the Tablets of the Law.'

'I don't quite understand, my dear friend,' replied Graetz.

'Where are your stone tablets?' joked Moritz Gottschalk.

'You can hardly call this a desert,' added Graetz, with a sweeping movement of his arm. 'Look around, we happen to be in one of the most beautiful parks in Germany.'

'What I meant ... I wanted to make a simple point. Our feeling for the Holy Land is so profound, so genuine, so tangible, and yet so abstract. I have never set eyes on it.'

'Well, of course, that's the reason we are all here. The time has come. We're going!' said Moritz Gottschalk decisively. 'All we need is the will, the time, and the money. Thank God, we have all three.'

'All these years, we've been writing to each other about it, and dreaming of making the pilgrimage to *Eretz Israel*. Now I find it really hard to believe that the time is near. For you the journey may just satisfy your curiosity. For me it is a necessity, to complete my life's work.'

'Well then, when do we set off?' asked the Professor.

Moritz Gottschalk suggested the following February.

Professor Graetz nodded. 'I have just completed the eleventh volume of my *History of the Jews from the Earliest Times to the Present*. So I'm ready.'

'Any departure date suits me, the sooner the better,' Ascher replied. 'Then we shan't have to pray *"B'Shanah haBa'a BeYerushalayim"* – "Next Year in Jerusalem" any longer.'

They had just a few months to prepare. Moritz Gottschalk made use of his Berlin contacts to obtain from people in high places letters of introduction to the European consulates in Jerusalem. He took particular pride in a document signed by Gerson Bleichröder addressed to Ismail Pasha, the kadi of Egypt, requesting that 'his illustrious acquaintance be given every possible assistance'. Much to Bismarck's disappointment, Bleichröder supported the initiative of a French company that had undertaken the building of the Suez Canal. The banker had purchased shares in the company on a massive scale, and had consequently made a name for himself at the court of the Egyptian viceroy. Ascher Levy equipped himself with maps of the Mediterranean territories and plotted their intended route. Fanny observed her husband's mounting excitement with some concern. She was uneasy at the thought of this voyage, and feared the dangers that awaited him in that wild and distant land.

Julius was now out of uniform and had joined the business. On the advice of his father, he accompanied his brother on business trips, participated in negotiations with clients, and looked after the bookkeeping. The brothers were keen not to miss a single opportunity. But this sphere, where everything depended on the calculation of profit or loss, was not for Julius. When a charming young Jewish lady by the name of Theresa Riess fell in love with the valiant soldier, he felt flattered and asked for her hand. Ascher was annoyed. The relationship had developed behind his back, without the aid of a marriage broker, and no financial arrangements had been reached between the parents of the bride and groom.

'Where will you live?' he asked his son, as if Polzin would not be a suitable place.

'Theresa's parents own a factory in Danzig.'

'What kind of factory is it?'

'A tannery.'

'A stinking tannery,' said Ascher and turned up his nose.

'But bearable,' grinned Julius. 'They're prepared to build us a house.'

'Under the terms of my will I have left one half of my fortune to your mother, and one quarter each to you and Bernhard. You can take your share of the liquid assets and the shares now. God be with you. I shall continue to be in charge of the business together with Bernhard.'

'Don't you want to meet your future daughter-in-law, Papa?'

'Yes, certainly. Ask her to come for *Shabbat*,' Ascher replied reluctantly, and turned back to his affairs.

Before the end of the year he stepped up his correspondence with Moritz Gottschalk and Heinrich Graetz. In January 1872 an enormous package arrived in Polzin, containing eleven leather-bound volumes of *History of the Jews from the Earliest Times to the Present*. The personal dedication on the first page ended with the words, 'It's time to set off.' Ascher invited his relatives and friends to come and visit. Even Vogel in an advanced state of pregnancy arrived from Neuwedel. Julius and Theresa Riess came from Danzig and Moritz Gottschalk from Berlin.

Ascher lowered himself into his armchair, placed a volume of Graetz's book on his knees, and opened the proceedings with a blessing: 'Blessed art Thou, O Lord, King of the Universe, who has preserved us, kept us alive, and brought us to this season.'

'Amen,' replied everyone in unison.

'I have invited you all here to drink to two important events in my life. A great honour has just been bestowed on me – I have been made a member of the town council. I intend to perform my duties to the best of my ability and my conscience in the public interest. But before I take up this office, I shall fulfil a dream that has possessed me for more than ten years. I shall shortly make the pilgrimage to the holy city of Jerusalem, in the company of my cousin Moritz Gottschalk and Professor Graetz. God willing, we shall bring the message of the solidarity of our people to the

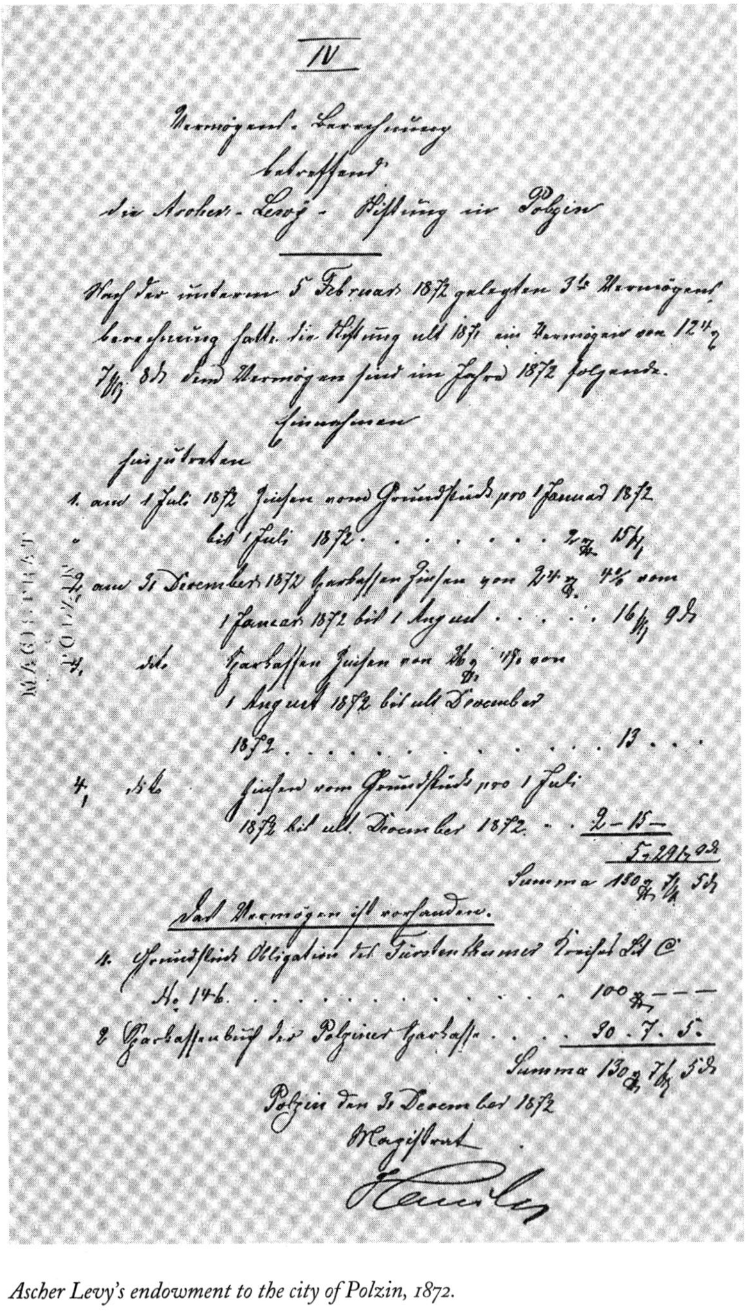

IV

Vermögens-Berechnung
betreffend
die Ascher-Levy-Stiftung in Polzin

Nach der unterm 5 Februar 1872 gelegten 3ten Vermögensberechnung hatte die Stiftung ult 1871 ein Vermögen von 124 Thl 7 Sgr 8 d. Dem Vermögen sind im Jahre 1872 folgende

Einnahmen

hinzugetreten

1. am 1 Juli 1872 Zinsen vom Grundstück pro 1 Januar 1872 bis 1 Juli 1872 . . . . 2 Thl 15 Sgr
2. am 31 December 1872 Sparkassen Zinsen von 24 Thl 4% vom 1 Januar 1872 bis 1 August . . . . . 16 Sgr 9 d
3. dito Sparkassen Zinsen von 26 Thl 4% von 1 August 1872 bis ult December 1872 . . . . 13 . . .
4. dito Zinsen vom Grundstück pro 1 Juli 1872 bis ult. December 1872 . . 2 - 15 -

5 - 29 - 9 d

Summa 130 Thl 7 Sgr 5 d

Das Vermögen ist vorhanden.

1. Grundstück Obligation des [illegible] Lit C No. 146 . . . . 100 Thl - - -
2. Sparkassenbuch der Polziner Sparkasse . . . 30 . 7 . 5 .

Summa 130 Thl 7 Sgr 5 d

Polzin den 31 December 1872

Magistrat

MAGISTRAT POLZIN

Ascher Levy's endowment to the city of Polzin, 1872.

Jewish settlement in Palestine, while stressing that we see no conflict between our love of the land of our forefathers and the love for our fatherland. But before we raise our glasses I should like to remind you of a document that is of immense importance to us all.'

He read:

Decree: concerning the equal rights of religious denominations within the civil and national framework. [...] We, Wilhelm, by Grace of God, King of Prussia, pursuant to the assent of the Bundesrat and the Reichstag issue the following command:

All remaining deprivations of civil and state rights on the grounds of differences in religious beliefs are hereby abolished. In particular, the entitlement to participate in local and state assemblies and to occupy public office shall be unrelated to religious belief.

Hereby confirmed by our personal signature and accompanying parliamentary seal. Proclaimed: Schloss Babelsberg, 3 July 1869.

Waving the paper from which he had been reading in the air, Ascher added: 'These are not hollow words, for they also apply to the composition of the town council, and represent the guarantee for fundamental change.'

Those present burst into applause, and Ascher nodded in thanks. 'And to conclude, please will you now listen to a few lines from Professor Graetz, taken from the foreword to the eleventh volume of his work.'

Again, he read:

I am more fortunate than my predecessors, and have been able to conclude [*The History of the Jews*] on a positive note. The Jewish people has at last found not only justice and freedom in civilized lands, but has also gained a certain recognition. It has been granted unrestricted space to develop its strengths, not as a favour, but as a well-earned right, following the thousandfold injuries suffered on a scale that hardly any other people on earth has had to endure, and in recognition of surprising achievements of world importance, which likewise are almost without equal.

Dream and Reality

The dream came true. Ascher was standing at the stern of a ship, now on the high seas. The date was 20 February 1872. At this time of year darkness fell very early. A grey mist dropped over the sea, and soon everything was veiled in darkness. A fresh breeze blew. Ascher shivered, not from cold, but from excitement. He could feel the vibration of the ship's timbers under his feet. He listened to the sound of the ship's propellers, rhythmically ploughing through the sea. The SS *Ungaria* was running southwards at a speed of eight knots. The travel agent in Trieste had solemnly assured them that they would arrive in Egypt within four days, at the very latest, provided everything went according to plan. First they were going to stay a few days in Alexandria, then pick up a small Russian coastal steamer for Port Said, and from there on to Jaffa.

Never had Ascher felt the nearness of God as much as in these moments, while his gaze swept across the horizon, where the sea and the sky fused into a black curtain. Somewhere beyond this black curtain lay the Holy Land, the source of his Jewish existence and the destination of his prayers. And at the same time, he had never before been so proud to be a citizen of the greatest and mightiest empire in Europe, the state that was the foundation of his human existence and to which all his dealings and efforts were directed. That evening, with the bustle of Berlin and the tranquillity of Polzin thousands of miles away, the contradictory aspects of the empire and Palestine became blurred in his mind, and a notion took over that a firm bridge could be constructed to link the two, that religion and love of the fatherland could exist alongside one another. Packed in his luggage was the document informing him of his admission to the town council, official confirmation of his equal rights as citizen of the German empire.

'Sir, the evening meal is about to be served.' The steward's words brought him back to reality. Ascher muttered his thanks, and slowly descended the narrow companionway to the first-class lounge. There were about twenty people gathered in the smoke-filled room. They were drinking Ceylon tea from wafer-thin porcelain teacups, and were engaged in animated conversation. Professor Graetz and Moritz Gottschalk, absorbed in a game of chess, did not notice Ascher's arrival. On the carpet in between the tables, children of the passengers were building castles with coloured wooden bricks.

Most of the men travelling on the ship were English and Italian, and were going out as reinforcements for the team oper-ating the newly-built Suez Canal. A few years earlier Jewish bankers in Berlin had tried to interest their clients in this project. Ascher had not been tempted. In his view, Ferdinand, Vicomte de Lesseps' enterprise was a risky venture. He preferred to con-tinue investing in the railways. In 1869 when the canal was offi-cially opened with a glittering ceremony, the shares shot up sevenfold in value, and Fanny wanted to know whether he didn't regret not having bought any.

'Absolutely not,' Ascher had replied. 'No German citizen should help the French gain a stronghold in the Levant. That's not what we sent Julius to the front for.'

'We sent ... ?' his wife let out in surprise.

'Well, all right,' he muttered. 'He went of his own accord. But that doesn't alter the facts.' Then he read aloud what the *Vossische Zeitung* newspaper had written about the opening ceremony, about the fifteen-year-old dancers from a Parisian ballet ensem-ble, who were certainly all very pretty but couldn't dance, and a singer who had enthralled the Cairo public, admittedly not with her somewhat mediocre singing but more by her ample bosom, which tended to slip out of her décolletage.

'Disgusting,' he commented, adding, 'Pity that the Crown Prince was obliged to be present at such an embarrassing occasion.'

Regardless of the ballet-dancers, the Suez Canal brought

about changes for trade agreements and shipping in this part of the world, and with its opening the eastern part of the Mediterannean awoke to new life.

Ascher Levy stood at the doorway of the lounge and observed those present. They were immaculately dressed, and their behaviour was likewise impeccable. In a corner, a pianist was playing melodies from *Aida*, emphasizing the link between the passengers and the canal. They appreciated the allusion and rewarded him with a round of applause. Levy took advantage of the interval, and wove his way between the tables.

'We were beginning to think you preferred the company of the seagulls,' said Moritz Gottschalk. He pushed the chessboard aside, and motioned to the waiter to bring another cup of tea.

'Oh, no, they're far too noisy for me.'

'I prefer Verdi as well,' smiled Graetz and suggested a hand of skat.

The waiter brought a pot of tea, and removed the chess game. Moritz Gottschalk took a pack of cards, shuffled, and dealt them out with a practised hand. The pianist had sat down at the grand piano again, and the lounge filled with the melodious strains of Franz von Suppé.

'Takes me back to Vienna,' sighed Graetz.

'Not a place I miss,' said Ascher drily. 'I don't think I could live in Vienna.'

'I could,' remarked Moritz Gottschalk.

'You, Moritz?' exclaimed Ascher in surprise. 'I thought Berlin was the only place for you.'

'We had a good time there, didn't we?'

'Entertainment and existence are two separate things. You go to the circus for entertainment, but you would hardly want to live in one.'

Professor Graetz looked at them over his cards. 'How can you possibly compare the two?' he asked, almost offended.

'Both are equally frivolous.'

'I didn't realize you were so puritanical, my friend.'

'My cousin loves order. In his world, everyone has their fixed place,' Moritz Gottschalk butted in, with a hint of mockery.

'Well, what about you? Aren't you in favour of regulated order? Have you turned into a revolutionary?'

'No, but Vienna is a city open to the world. I didn't feel out of place there. In Berlin...yes, I'm not ashamed to admit, there are times when I feel like a stranger in my own town. Even if I were the richest man in town, with all that money I still couldn't buy the goodwill of the people there. When we were poor, we were considered a nuisance. Now they claim that we have got rich at their expense, that we have too much power and infect the "purity" of their society. Whatever we do, they will always regard us as an inferior and harmful race. Even those who bow to us and do business with us, they hate us. We hardly amount to more than one per cent of the population of Berlin. But draw up a list of all the entrepreneurs, bankers, and industrialists in the city, and half of them would be Jews. Many find that situation intolerable. What about you, Ascher? Aren't you the richest man in Polzin? And? Are you quite sure that they don't curse you behind your back? In Vienna that wouldn't happen. But why argue? You're just embarrassed. I can well understand. From Polzin to Vienna...must have been quite a shock to the system.'

Ascher said nothing. He had to admit that defensiveness had prompted his aggressive tone. Vienna had struck him as seductively magical, and for that very reason it was dangerous. He was and always would be a man from the provinces. The splendid frock coat, made to measure by a fashionable Viennese tailor, in no way changed his outlook on the world. Berlin, capital of the German empire, stood unalterably at the centre of this world. Even if he didn't feel at home there, and was bound to accept what his cousin said about it, nevertheless in his eyes this city symbolized the might of the empire and all its values.

In the past decade Berlin had expanded with breathtaking speed. It now had 852,000 inhabitants and, following the victory over France, most of them believed they were living at the hub of a new world, where history was being made. Ascher did not judge the attractions of the city by its external appearance. Did he love Fanny any the less just because her face had grown lined? It was certainly true that Berlin had become ugly. A ring of workers' districts had encircled the city like a rusty hoop. And the newly rich who built houses in the smart parts of town did not always distinguish themselves in terms of good taste. Factory chimneys belched smoke into the skies. But does a city necessarily have to look like a work of art? A current success in the satirical cabarets of Berlin was a piece entitled 'Berlin – world centre'. Sarcastic critics had dubbed it 'Berlin – money centre'. For Ascher Levy the criticism and ridicule were unfounded. On the contrary, he regarded the close connection between power and wealth a desirable virtue. Without the union of financial strength and solid standards there could be no progress. This was the basis of his contempt for Austria, whose army had been defeated by Prussia in 1866; he considered it a liberal, tolerant but lightweight state, unable to offer resistance to its enemies. From the moment he set foot on the overcrowded railway platform, Vienna struck him like a baroque stage-set for a comic operetta. Even though the ethnic mix of Austrians, Jews, Hungarians, Serbs, Croats, Czechs, and Poles might be the melting pot of European intelligence, in his eyes it hardly amounted to a consolidated nation.

Dr Leopold Kompert, a friend of Professor Heinrich Graetz, had taken them on a guided tour of Vienna, through the 'lace-work jungle' as he chose to describe his city. They had spent the morning in the museums, sampled the famous coffee with whipped cream at one of the coffee houses on the Kärntnerstrasse, and equipped themselves for the voyage ahead at the department store owned by Jakob Ruthberger. They had then dined with their host, and discussed the nature of modern Judaism, a subject close to all their hearts. Kompert's *Tales from the Ghetto* (*Aus dem Ghetto*) had been severely criticized by the Orthodox Jews. The conversation ranged from Kompert's provocative stories to the fundamental issue of religion versus nationalism.

Ascher had followed the polemic of the different strands in Judaism for many years. Yet he was amazed to discover how enormous the gap really was between the conservatives and the reformers, and the unremitting struggle that raged between them. Like Graetz and Moritz Gottschalk he was influenced equally by the writings of the Orthodox Rabbi Ezriel Hildesheimer of

Berlin's *Adass Yisroel* community, and by those of the Reform movement. Fortunately Ascher could bridge the old and the new. 'How can you be a Prussian patriot as well as an observant Jew?' many acquaintances repeatedly asked, for the most part Christians. Even his own wife, Fanny, had once asked, 'How can you reconcile your love for Germany with your love of *Eretz Israel*?' His simple reply to these sceptics was: 'The implied reproach does not escape me. But this dual loyalty is really not a problem for me. Prussian nationalism protects my body, Jewish nationalism is a part of my soul, my spiritual compass. That's all there is to it.'

After one week in Vienna, Ascher, Moritz Gottschalk, and Heinrich Graetz made their way by train to Trieste. Kompert accompanied them to the railway station. He had already been to Palestine, and was familiar with local customs. Just before the guard gave the signal for the steam engine to depart, Kompert called out to them, 'And don't forget the magic word that opens all doors in the Ottoman empire – baksheesh!'

The travellers stayed only two days looking round the busy port of Trieste. In the studio of the local portrait photographer, Signore Boccalino, Ascher Levy had himself photographed wearing his new frock coat, and sent the picture to his loved ones back in Polzin. Fanny was not a little surprised to see her husband seated in a chair in a full-length frock coat, fastened only by the top button. A black velvet stripe ran the length of his flannel trousers, and he held a pair of deerskin gloves in his left hand. Fanny placed the photo in a small case, where she kept family mementos, and would never have dreamed that the same photo would turn up a hundred years later on the flea market in Jaffa.

The first place they stopped at was Alexandria. True to Lloyds' reputation, the SS *Ungaria* arrived on schedule, and its crates were unloaded on the quayside. Porters swarmed around the passengers. Their cries in Arabic, Italian, and French mingled in deafening Oriental confusion. Beyond the harbour, the travellers were greeted by a totally different scene. Magnificent carriages sped along the city avenues past apathetic camels. Elegant ladies dressed in the latest Parisian fashions sheltered from the sun

Ascher Levy, photographed in Trieste, 1872.

under brightly coloured silk parasols. Alongside them, local
women walked enveloped in black from top to toe, their faces
veiled. Overwhelmed by these impressions, Ascher withdrew to
his hotel room and wrote to Fanny:

Alexandria, 29 February 1872

My dear, beloved wife,
    No sooner had I sent my letter from Corfu than the very
fears expressed in it were realized. We dropped anchor in the
roads, whereupon we were immediately surrounded by such a

swarm of small craft and Greeks that our clothes were virtually torn from our bodies. I fled to the upper deck to escape, and watched the spectacle from there. In so doing (until eleven in the evening) I must have caught cold, so that later the same night my head and teeth were aching, but with the heaving rolling of the sea, this turned to seasickness. Practically all the other passengers aboard, apart from Dr Graetz and most of the English, were affected in the same way for the next two days. Yesterday it was a little better, so that I was able to drag myself to the foredeck, and the effect of the lovely sunshine, like we have in June, was such that by midday I was able to take a cup of bouillon and half an orange. At four in the afternoon, we had our first sight of Alexandria, where we arrived towards six, and disembarked an hour later. No one who has not witnessed this scrambling, jostling, shouting, cheering, fighting, this babel of languages, can have the remotest idea of what it was like. Making our way by water, foot, donkey, and carriage we finally arrived with all our things at the Hotel de Trieste, not without incident, despite the distribution of baksheesh.

Today we called on the Consul, who was not there in person, but we were received very warmly by his secretary. In the morning we attended to a number of business matters, and in the afternoon we took a drive through the city, and saw Pompey's Column, Cleopatra's Needles, the Maimudiye Canal, and a number of gardens. The vegetation is as far advanced as it would be with us in July and August; the leaves on the trees have already lost their spring freshness, the maize is ripening, and the roses have bloomed once and are now showing their second flush of buds. We couldn't find any kosher restaurants, and were invited to eat at the home of a gentleman called Shalom Aboth. The details of our onward journey are still uncertain; we should like to see Cairo and the Pyramids, but that means giving up eight days of the little time we have. Tonight after supper, we shall be taken to the German Club, where we will find out the exact departure times of the various ships, and make up our minds whether to take the Russian steamer to Jaffa the day after tomorrow, or whether to visit Cairo...

The next day the three travellers dined at the home of a certain Mr Menashe, a Jewish businessman also known as 'the Egyptian Rothschild'. Ascher's diary had the following entry:

> Here is a man after my own heart. His enormous wealth does not make him forget his faith. The impressive balls he hosts are famous throughout the land of the Pyramids. Prominent guests visit his magnificent house, feast on the delicacies of his cuisine, and everything is strictly kosher. Even His Excellency the Khadif Ismail in person undertook a special journey from Cairo to attend one of these balls. The customs here are quite different from ours. In a large room, Mr Menashe bade us be seated on Persian carpets and scattered cushions. This is probably what a Turkish harem looks like, or is my imagination running away with me? As ever, the exotic dishes (strictly kosher) were served by Arab servants, wearing turbans – each course served separately on silver platters, and the cutlery, believe it or not, of pure gold! Our friend, Professor Graetz commented: 'Here we have European Asia and Asian Europe.' How very aptly put. Of course we also visited synagogues, and saw the provisions made for the community of five thousand souls. The Jews of European origin more or less keep to their inherited way of life, but the Sephardis, well, they really are part of the Orient. Finally, I cannot help stressing the following: in this city, where Maimonides once dined, there is not a single kosher restaurant to be found...

While Ascher's body and soul were basking in the Alexandrian sun, in Pomerania it was cold enough to freeze the breath of the inhabitants. People swore that even in the time of their forefathers there had never been such a severe winter. When Ascher's letter arrived, Bernhard was just getting ready to set out on a business trip. Fanny's attempts to discourage him from going had been useless, and even the pleas of the coachman, afraid of the snow-covered roads, had fallen on deaf ears. The heavy snowfalls had brought the railways to a standstill, so, undeterred, Bernhard decided to go by sleigh and replace the small carriage horses with four massive, powerful creatures that could weather the cold.

During his father's absence Bernhard had been conducting the business like a modern commander on the battlefield. He did not issue instructions from his base in Polzin, but was constantly on the move – a true revolution in the administration of the business. Bernhard possessed great powers of persuasion and took the view that dealing with clients and authorities face to face was preferable to correspondence, even to letters composed by his most competent members of staff.

This time his destination was faraway Glogau. The information network set up by his father was extremely efficient, and he had discovered that farmers in the Glogau region were selling their cattle. The effect of the intense cold had made the price of cattle feed soar, and the farmers could no longer afford to provide adequately for their animals. As the coachman harnessed the horses to the front of the sleigh, he wrapped himself up in woollen blankets, pulled his cap down over his face, and looked up at the sky. The clouds were leaden grey, and he crossed himself. Bernhard was encased in sheepskins. 'There's no need to worry,' he reassured Fanny and the employees, who had stepped outside the house to bid him farewell. 'I'll be back in a week – and I won't be empty-handed.'

'Hey-up,' the coachman cried out and spurred on the horses with a crack of his whip. Fanny remained motionless until the sleigh had disappeared from sight. It was only when she had gone back into the house that she became aware that the cold had frozen her right to the bone.

Good as his word, Bernhard did not return empty-handed. But even before he met the middlemen who were to take him to those selling their cattle, he was presented with an offer of an entirely different nature. The local marriage broker had come knocking at the door of his hotel room with a proposal, in the form of Henriette, a daughter of the Cohen family. He was obviously abreast of the times, for instead of making a long speech, he pulled out a photograph of the intended bride to show to Bernhard. Gazing out at him from the picture was a pretty young woman. Her features were distinctly Semitic, radiating gentleness and gravity. Her black hair was pinned up like a crown; she had heavy eyebrows, and her dark eyes and flaring nostrils signalled a passion for life. Skilled at his trade, the marriage broker realized at a glance that the young woman had conquered Bernhard's heart. He took the photograph and slipped it back in his pocket. At this point Bernhard offered him a chair and the elderly man sat down heavily. In a leisurely fashion he enumerated all the points in Henriette's favour – that she was of sound health, came from a good family, her forefathers included rabbis well known in the principality of Posen and, no less important, her family was prosperous. Had Bernhard not been obliged to rush off with all speed to the villages, he would have been tempted to call on the Cohen house in the very same week. But business came first, and so he agreed that he would visit Henriette in the near future.

The severity of the snowstorms that had paralysed life in the north of the region had affected the postal service. Bernhard and Fanny had informed Ascher about what was going on, but their letters lay stranded in the Polzin post office. So the three men left Alexandria without any news from home. They were not unduly worried, for their immediate concern was the crossing on the *Oleg*, a small Russian steamship that regularly shuttled between the ports of the eastern Mediterranean. The Professor's attempts to secure a ship of the Egyptian royal household had been unsuccessful. And now the captain of the *Oleg* was telling them that all the cabins were already reserved by Russian Orthodox pilgrims, making their way to the Holy Land for Easter. The Russian government was at pains to increase the flow of pilgrims, and to extend their presence in Jerusalem. To this end the Tsar was acquiring property there and having churches and monasteries built. They tried Dr Kompert's advice, which proved wonderfully effective – baksheesh opened the doors to two of the best cabins on the ship, immediately next to the captain's quarters.

On 2 March, the ship weighed anchor. It first put in at Port Said and, after two further days' sailing through calm waters, arrived at the shores of Jaffa. On the afternoon of the 4 March 1872 they set eyes on the gateway to the Promised Land. Their first impression was somewhat dreary. *Eretz Israel* had no appropriate harbour. Sheer cliffs protected the entry to Jaffa, and only small boats could tie up to piers sunk into the beach. Ships the size of the *Oleg* had to drop anchor several hundred metres from the breakwater and drift on the waves, as they waited for dock workers who would convey the passengers ashore in little sailing dinghies, which could easily navigate the cliffs and pass through to the shallow waters of the landing stages. There, officials of the Ottoman empire would be waiting for the passengers, and its bureaucracy would take over. The inspection of travel documents and customs control took for ever. Once again baksheesh proved to be the magic word. While the pilgrims were still arguing and haggling with the customs officials, Ascher Levy and his two companions were already entering the only hotel in Jaffa with a Jewish proprietor.

It was a bitter disappointment. Ascher Levy had imagined Jaffa surrounded by green fields, with the scent of golden oranges wafting though the air. For him Jaffa was the port to which King Solomon had brought cedarwood from the Lebanon for the building of the Temple; it was the town where Simon the tanner had once lived and received Saint Peter. It was on one of the rooftops of this town that Peter had had a vision, which prompted him from that moment on to eat *treife* (non-kosher food) and do missionary work among the Jews. However, the sight that met Ascher's eyes from the roof of the hotel in no way corresponded to what he had imagined; he saw instead an ugly, dirty, Oriental town. On the way from the harbour to the hotel he had already been stripped of any illusions. They had struggled through narrow alleys that had no pavements, past dilapidated houses and street traders' stalls. Beggars emerged from dark recesses and molested them. Barefoot children begged for alms, muttering incomprehensible words. In the central square was a colourful, noisy market. Men in long, wide caftans, which must have once been white, sat on low stools in front of miserable-looking coffee houses, slurping sweet tea or muddy coffee from tiny cups, playing backgammon or staring listlessly into the sky. The braying donkeys and mules relieving themselves did not seem to bother anyone. Ascher had the greatest difficulty imagining how 250 Jewish families could fit in here.

The next day Ascher, Moritz Gottschalk, and Graetz visited the tiny community of German Templars that had settled in Jaffa about two years earlier. There they met a few French people who were likewise on their way to Jerusalem. They decided to make up a caravan together; this would lower the cost and add to their safety. It appeared that bands of marauding Bedouins lay in wait in the hills going up to Jerusalem. The hotel proprietor offered them the services of his Arab servant, as a dragoman.

'What is a dragoman?' asked Ascher Levy.

'Without a dragoman you cannot get about in *Eretz Israel*,' explained the hotel owner. 'It's the official term for interpreter at the foreign consulates. A dragoman speaks perfect Turkish as well as one or two European languages. He is familiar with the customs of the country, knows how to find his way through the maze of Ottoman laws, and can serve as intermediary with the government officials that you will encounter in every little town and village. Without their permission you will not be able to continue your travels. Only the dragoman, who knows these people in person, knows the going rate for such permissions. The dragoman's pay is based on his skill in dealing with these matters. My servant is not exactly cheap, but he is worth every piastre.'

'Fine. Please have him called,' Ascher agreed. When the Arab appeared, he asked him his name.

'I am known as Gamad.'

'Dwarf?' Ascher said in surprise, for he understood the Hebrew word.

'Yes, because of my height,' replied the servant, keeping a perfectly straight face. Gamad was almost six feet six inches tall, which even by today's standards is very tall, but at that time was considered gigantic.

In March 1872 Gamad demonstrated his skills with the travel preparations. He even managed to get hold of a cook familiar with kosher cooking. On his advice two kavasses were also hired – guards armed with firearms and swords.

The party wanted to cover the sixty-five-kilometre stretch between Jaffa and Jerusalem in two days. The Sultan had had the road built linking the two towns when he learned that the

Emperor Franz-Joseph intended to attend the opening ceremony of the Suez Canal, followed by a pilgrimage to Jerusalem and its holy sites. The Emperor had come and gone, and the road had remained. The travellers set out around ten in the morning, and by sunset they had reached Ramallah. They stopped at the Catholic monastery there, where they were given large, clean rooms, and there was even a kitchen where their cook could prepare them a meal. The dragoman urged them to have an early night, as the caravan intended to set off again by five the following morning. The difficult ascent through the hills on the way up to Jerusalem would take a long time, and to attempt this part of the journey after dark was considered dangerous. They spent a peaceful night and set off next morning somewhat later than intended, and it was not until the afternoon that they had their first sight of the walls of the Holy City. Ascher Levy reined in his horse and dismounted. He went to the side of the road, bending low in the direction of the city, and gazed at it in silence.

'Are you praying?' asked Moritz Gottschalk.

'I'm trying to, but I simply can't find the right words.'

That evening he wrote to Fanny from the hotel:

> We left Ramallah half an hour later than intended. We formed an impressive caravan, consisting of seventeen horses, mules and donkeys, and ten riders, including several Frenchmen and someone from Württemberg. After a number of hours we reached the Sharon Valley, and then the route led us through a high flat plateau, and finally to the Judean hills. There we stopped at half past ten and had breakfast in an Arab tent. This consisted of a cup of black coffee and roast chicken. After an hour's rest, we continued on foot for two hours, uphill all the way between tall, barren cliffs, with occasional vegetation of fresh green leaves, indicating cultivation at an earlier period. Now and again we came across miserable hamlets lying among olive groves and a few cornfields. We continued uphill, until we arrived in a valley, and stopped at Kalanseer to eat our lunch of coffee, bread with sheep's butter, and eggs. We left

there at three o'clock, and riding at a furious pace, spurred on by longing to see *Yerushalayim*, we arrived at the Jaffa Gate at half past five. After a short rest, we were still in time to take a short walk through the immediate neighbourhood. We are staying on Mount Zion, overlooking the Tower of David, but at my instigation we shall move elsewhere tomorrow. In the morning I shall go and see if there is a letter from my loved ones waiting for me. Till then...

Ascher did not tell his loved ones everything. There were certain thoughts and impressions that he kept to himself, hidden in his journal. Staying in Jerusalem was a powerful spiritual experience for him. And yet was this how he had imagined the capital of his spiritual homeland? Although the city was an abstract and metaphysical concept to him, and only a historic location of religious significance, he could not ignore what he saw before him. Could this really be the city extolled and promised in the Holy Scriptures? He couldn't bring himself to share this thought with Moritz Gottschalk and Professor Graetz. His two companions were firm in sticking to the intended aim of their visit – in particular they wished to experience daily life, and to this end they repeatedly sought out the Jewish Quarter inside the city walls, where a small Jewish minority lived cheek by jowl. The people there were subjected to ill-treatment by the Muslim population and by the Ottoman officials; they lived in constant poverty and studied the Torah, engaging in endless discussions about it. Although the living conditions of the Jews dwelling outside the city walls were better, they could hardly be described as satisfactory by European standards.

Eretz Israel was one of the most backward provinces of the declining Ottoman empire. To compare Prussia, which was fizzing with life, with sleepy Palestine was somewhat depressing. Although Ascher had heard and read a lot about life in the four holy cities of Jerusalem, Sefat, Tiberias, and Hebron, the reality was very different from these descriptions. When Ascher used to put money in the collection box of the synagogue in Stettin in memory of Meir Ba'al Hanes, the '*wunderrabbi*' (the miracle-working rabbi), which would then be traditionally passed on to the Jewish community in *Eretz Israel*, or if he contributed directly to the *Yishuv*, he did so in fulfilment of an important religious commandment, a mitzvah. But now he was beginning to fear that by doing so he had supported something fundamentally pointless.

About nine thousand Jews, almost half the population of Jerusalem, did not follow any productive occupation. Apart from a few people, who were engaged in some form of independent work, and a few dozen small traders, the rest spent their time zealously studying the Holy Scriptures and devoted their lives to the service of God. Their generous brethren in the Diaspora made themselves responsible for their upkeep – the money poured in mainly from England, France, and Prussia. With the establishment of the Reform movement in Hamburg, Berlin, and Dresden, there were attempts to collect funds for modern educational institutions as well, which failed due to vehement opposition from the Orthodox. Some years earlier Ascher Levy had made a donation towards the building of a German hospital for lepers, and could now see for himself whether it actually existed. In his view the funds he had transferred to the Jewish welfare committee were a complete waste of money. Much earlier, in 1809, the rabbis in Jerusalem had set up a committee intended to organize fund-raising and distribution and to put an end to the campaigns conducted along partisan lines by the different *Kolelim* or communities. An internal, complicated, and carefully drawn-up agreement set out the guidelines for the distribution of these funds: who was to receive how much and in what form and at what time. Those in charge of these funds effectively dominated the *Yishuv*.

Prompted by a sense of their own importance, the members of the committee ruled with an iron hand, and woe betide anyone who dared to rebel or oppose them!

These people did not take kindly to the arrival of the small band of travellers from Germany. Graetz, Ascher Levy, and Moritz Gottschalk were known to favour progressive educational establishments and to support the settlement of Eastern European Jews in *Eretz Israel* by helping those newcomers who took the pursuit of a productive living just as seriously as the religious commandments. Nevertheless on the first evening of their stay in Jerusalem, the travellers were summoned to pay a courtesy visit to the leading rabbi, Avraham Ashkenazi, the *Chacham Bashi*.

A *Chacham Bashi* had many functions: he was the acknowledged representative of the Jewish community and enjoyed the support of the *Kaimakam*, the Ottoman governor of Jerusalem. Despite his elevated status, the *Chacham Bashi* went out to greet his guests at the gate. Ascher Levy was surprised to see his magnificent ankle-length official robe of lustrous black fabric edged with silver threads and gold lace collar. A fez crowned the sage's small head. His arms, folded across his chest in greeting, emerged from wide, dangling sleeves.

'*Bruchim HaBaim* – Welcome to the Holy City of Jerusalem,' he said and invited them to step inside. Wine and light refreshments were served. While they were sampling these, the *Chacham Bashi* described the poverty of the community in his charge. The cause of their impoverished circumstances, in his opinion, lay in the miserliness of the Jews living in the Diaspora.

'The rich and mighty of European Jewry must be more generous. Have you forgotten that your donations are not alms?'

'Well, what are they?' asked Ascher.

'The words of the Torah command us to return to *Eretz Israel*. If a Jew is unable to fulfil this mitzvah, he is obliged to give money for those who do so in his place. That is entirely logical, isn't it?'

The travellers had already heard from various inhabitants of Jerusalem about the Orthodox customs and their curious logic. They had spent the first evening with an old acquaintance, Dr Benjamin London. News of their arrival had already spread and uninvited guests had streamed to the home of the doctor to express their anger: 'The members of the committee apply double standards.' 'Unfortunately they are often far worse than the Ottoman officials.' 'There is no appropriate public control over the distribution of the funds.' 'They are stuck in the Middle Ages.'

The doctor had tried to pacify them, pleading: 'Please leave my guests in peace.' When they still refused to leave Graetz and his two companions alone, he added in a conciliatory manner, 'As you can see, the Jewish leadership here refuses to move with the spirit of the times, but that's still no excuse for harsh words and exaggeration.'

Dr London had adopted this form of understatement from the English community in Jerusalem, with which he had close contact. Not only did the representatives of the *Yishuv* in *Eretz Israel* refuse to move with the times, they adopted extreme measures to prevent other members of the *Yishuv* from doing so. In their eyes, any form of productive activity constituted a departure from the true path, namely service in the name of God. The learning of a trade or a foreign language, for example, was strictly prohibited, let alone a secular education.

The guests told of bitter experiences: 'Anyone who does not conform is totally excluded.' 'If you reject the views of the president of the community, you are literally left without any means of support. But please don't quote me, for if the slightest suspicion should fall on me, then even the consuls wouldn't be able to help me.'

The consuls in Jerusalem enjoyed a special status and particular privileges. Their protection extended to the religious communities, and they safeguarded those who had come from Europe from attacks by the Ottoman regime. Ascher Levy had made the acquaintance of Baron von Alten, the German Consul, several years earlier when the diplomat had been on home leave. He had met him in his cousin's house on the occasion of a dinner in honour of Rabbi Hildesheimer. Ezriel Hildesheimer was the founder of the *Jüdische Presse*, the only Jewish newspaper to promote the settlement of German Jews in *Eretz Israel* at that time. Ascher Levy had no time for this idea, for in his opinion the Jews of Eastern Europe who did not recognize their countries of origin as their homeland were the ones who should settle in Palestine. He had soon found common cause with the consul. Von Alten had used his vacation to find out more about those organizations that supported the *Yishuv* in *Eretz Israel* and their activities. Levy, who had refused to give a single penny for the founding of this newspaper, had, however, pledged a generous sum for a Jewish hospital that was to be set up in the foreseeable future, near to the Jewish orphanages in Jerusalem.

'When you come to Jerusalem, you will see for yourself what we have done with your money,' Alten had said to him.

'God willing,' Ascher had replied.

The consul's goodwill towards the Jews did not only stem from his love of the land of Israel. The major powers were competing to expand their spheres of influence in the Holy Land. Their institutions, particularly the consulates, were of prime importance in the current political penetration of the Turkish Mediterranean area. And in this struggle for influence and power, the subjects represented an important factor. The only reason that the Ottoman empire was still in existence was that each of the great powers refused to yield supremacy to any one of the others.

That England had been the country to beat Prussia in laying down railway lines and the first of all the European states to set foot in Palestine had been a thorn in the flesh of Ascher Levy. Delegations of British missionaries active in Palestine were exerting enormous pressure on the Foreign Office in London, and were demanding protection from interference by Ottoman officials. A British consulate had been set up in Jerusalem in 1839. Not to be outdone, Friedrich Wilhelm IV, the Prussian King, had appointed his own consul in Jerusalem in 1840, a year after taking power, and on 20 May 1842, Ernst Gustav Schultz, a specialist in Oriental affairs, had taken up his position. The French, who had unsuccessfully tried to gain a foothold in the region 130 years before, returned in 1843; the Americans in 1844; and the Austrians in 1849. The main operation of the Russians was the setting up of a shipping company in Jaffa, one of whose activities was military espionage, but officially it existed to look after the thousands of Russian Orthodox pilgrims. The French and the Austrians acted as protectors for the Catholics. The British and Prussian consulates were responsible for the Protestants.

Two years before Consul Schultz took up office, the King of Prussia and Queen Victoria had signed an agreement for the opening of an Anglican episcopacy in Jerusalem. This bilateral agreement stipulated that the bishops would be appointed jointly and the expenses would be shared. In furtherance of these expansionist policies, the Prussian consulate was most concerned to see to the well-being of the Jews of European origin in every respect. As a specialist in Oriental studies, with his mastery of Hebrew and Arabic, Schultz had already distinguished himself by practical aid to the Talmud schools that existed in the city.

Dr Georg Rosen, likewise an Oriental scholar, was one of the few Prussians to have befriended the representative of the Jewish community in Stettin. He had even married a Jewish girl from Pomerania. On the strength of his affinity for Palestine, he supported the missionary institutions and helped a group of German Templars (a Protestant sect founded in Württemberg in the 1860s) to settle there. Initially they set up virtually unnoticed in abandoned houses in Jaffa, for at this time the attention of Europe was focused on the opening of the Suez Canal. Dr Rosen had been astute in his assessment of these people – they were ideally suited to activate the expansion of German culture in the Levant. Over the years the Templars became the pioneers of German settlement in the Holy Land. It was not until the beginning of the Second World War, when the British Mandate viewed them as the fifth column of the Nazi regime, that they were driven from their settlements. The men were interned in prison camps, mostly in Australia, and the women and children were exchanged for British citizens who for one reason or another were stuck in Occupied Europe.

Rosen's successor was Baron von Alten. The new consul inherited a well-run Prussian consulate (which in 1871 became the Consulate of the German Reich) as well as about twelve hundred charges, of which no more than two hundred were in fact German citizens. The consul acted as guardian for the others. The more protégés a foreign mission was responsible for, the greater was its influence, and at this time the German and Austrian consulates, each of whom felt equally responsible for the *Yishuv*, were competing for influence over the population. A festive service in the Ahavat Zion ('Love of Zion') synagogue in celebration of Prussia's victory over France had shown von Alten the strength of his position in the circle of Jerusalem's Jews.

And now von Alten and Ascher Levy were shaking hands like two old friends.

'I am sorry that we didn't succeed in building the hospital as planned,' were the consul's opening words. He added, 'I passed your donation of one hundred thaler to a special fund, devoted to the setting up of German–Jewish schools. I do hope that is not contrary to your wishes?'

'No, quite the contrary,' replied Levy. 'I have only just found out about the difficulties encountered by those wishing to promote the education of Jewish youngsters here. Any form of support for their efforts seems entirely appropriate to me.'

'It's no easy task. Opposition from the Orthodox quarter...'

'I am aware of these problems, your lordship, but they do not frighten me. Today I learned that under-age girls are being forced to marry at the age of fourteen or fifteen. How backward! And this by order of the Orthodox rabbis or the synagogue board. Things cannot continue in this way.'

'And what do you intend to do about it, Herr Levy?'

'We should combine our efforts. You as German Consul, and I as a citizen of the Reich.'

'What do you have in mind?'

'Both I and my travelling companions have decided to contribute to changes in living conditions in the city.'

'In that respect, we certainly agree. But you should know, Herr Levy, that although we have been working for thirty years in the city of Jerusalem, until now we have not succeeded in finding anyone inside the Orthodox community with whom we could enter into dialogue.'

'The Orthodox are useless in pursuing the interests of the Reich here in the Levant. Most of them have nothing in common with us, for they come either from Muslim countries or from Eastern Europe.'

'I am aware of that. But what is your idea of a solution?'

'Progressive schooling. There is no progress without education. No society can exist without productive work. I do not honour God any less than the leading rabbi, Ashkenazi. But you cannot shut yourself away in the ivory tower of the Torah. You must look reality and life straight in the eye.'

'The Jerusalem rabbis consider such remarks sheer blasphemy.'

'As I well know. These disputes are going on in Germany too. But is that a reason to give up?'

'Well, what do you suggest?'

'I intend to found a modern orphanage. Rabbi Hildesheimer of Berlin has promised us his support.'

'I have met him. A charming, wise man.'

'We shall insist that the young people will be educated along the lines of Jewish tradition. But in addition to studying the Torah, they will also be taught German and Hebrew. They will be introduced to European culture and be trained in some form of occupation, so that they will not be dependent on the system of *chalukah*.'

'You go right to the heart of the problem,' remarked von Alten.

'Can we count on your support?'

'Certainly.'

'Thank you. I knew you would not let us down. I shall inform Professor Graetz and Moritz Gottschalk of your agreement right away.'

'But don't think that my support will sweep away all obstacles.'

'I don't have any illusions on that score, my lord.'

'Past experience does not bode well.'

'I know.'

'My Austrian colleague has had his fingers burned. I expect you remember the affair of the Lämel School? This was the woman who spent a fortune setting up a modern school on Viennese lines, and was largely cursed and shunned for her pains.'

'One thing after another. We shall try to learn from other people's mistakes. And what is more, Rabbi Hildesheimer is not Frankl.'

In the 1850s Elisa Herz, née Lämel, a well-to-do Austrian Jewish woman, had the revolutionary idea of setting up of a home for poor children in Jerusalem, where they could receive a secular education. She dispatched her friend, the author Ludwig August Frankl, to *Eretz Israel* with the necessary finance and a detailed plan of action. At the same time a secret communication from the Viennese foreign ministry was sent by diplomatic post to the Austrian consulate in Palestine, with express instructions to give Herr Frankl every assistance in carrying out his mission. This was seen as part of the political efforts to extend Austria's sphere of influence in the Ottoman empire. However, it was not the Ottoman authorities but the representatives of the Orthodox community who brought the plan down. Frankl, not an observant Jew, was declared persona non grata and was slighted and shunned. As the Jerusalem rabbis had threatened to impose a ban on anyone supporting Frau Lämel's education project, the original plan could not be carried out.

Ascher Levy, Moritz Gottschalk Lewy, and Heinrich Graetz had been aware of this defeat, even before they had set out from Berlin. They agreed that their plans would not succeed without the moral support and active help of a recognized religious authority. It was for this reason that they had approached Rabbi Ezriel Hildesheimer, who was respected in Orthodox circles.

On the third evening of their stay in Jerusalem, Professor Graetz invited Jacob Valero for a chat. Valero was the representative who looked after the poor in Jerusalem and was responsible for the distribution of donated funds. Approximately fifty thousand francs passed through his hands every year, and control of these finances made him a powerful figure. Graetz and the two cousins outlined their idea for an orphanage, giving him the express assurance that religious and traditional education would come foremost in their scheme. However, the official refused to be persuaded. Like the *Chacham Bashi*, he rejected the plan outright.

'You are intent on destroying what we have built up over the course of generations. But you will not succeed.'

'We shall see,' replied Ascher.

Ascher Levy continued to avoid any references to these difficulties and disputes in his letters to his wife and son. He restricted himself to accounts of fascinating experiences, enlivened with descriptions of anything exotic that he encountered. But at home in Polzin the truth soon began to filter out. At first there were just coded references in reports in the Jewish press in Holland and Germany, but then these were followed by more detailed articles, throwing doubt on the value of the initiatives undertaken by Graetz and the two cousins. Fanny's feminine intuition soon sensed that these were warning signs of a brewing storm, and she became afraid. She feared that her husband would be drawn into the whirlpool of public polemic, which he so detested. But she too said nothing on this subject in her letters, which mainly consisted of reports of day-to-day events, as well as singing the praises of Bernhard and his devotion to work.

After five days in Jerusalem the travellers took their leave of Baron von Alten, and promised to return after visiting the south and Galilee. They mounted their horses and set off for Hebron. As before, Gamad was their guide and headed the caravan, Ascher was second, followed by Moritz Gottschalk and Graetz. Bringing up the rear were the muleteers and the two kavasses. Although everything had gone smoothly until now, Gamad had still insisted on the two guards, as there was always the chance of being attacked by robbers. Graetz was in some doubt as to the ability and even the readiness of the guards to protect them if need arose. Their weapons consisted of just two rifles, which had evidently seen service way back in the time of the Napoleonic wars. However, on their visit to the Cave of Machpela, when the little group was surrounded by countless Arab beggars, the kavasses proved their worth. The cave was said to be the burial place of the forefathers and mothers of Judaism, Abraham, Sarah, Rebecca, and Jacob. Contrary to his expectations, Ascher Levy was not overcome by any great feeling of reverence, as he had been when visiting other holy sites. His laconic entry in his diary reads: 'All we saw was a hole in the wall.' On the evening of the following day, he sat down as usual to write a letter to Polzin:

Tuesday, 12 March

Great rejoicing today in Israel and Judah, for your longed-for letter has just arrived per express from *Yerushalayim*. I cannot tell you how glad I was to hear that you, my dear Fanny, are in good health, and also sleeping well. I have been very concerned these last days to have news from home, and would surely have been more so, had it not been for the fact that every square of earth here has a classical history, with thousands of associations that occupy one's thoughts.

... We are going to have to cut short our intended route, as Professor Graetz and Moritz are worn out from all the horse-riding, though I could easily go on another two to three hours a day. So we shall not be getting to Damascus.

Today we set off early on foot from Hebron towards Abraham's Oak, mounted our horses (my mare is called Rosi) at eight o'clock and after a short break we arrived here at one o'clock, where we are camping again by Solomon's Pools. We had barely taken an hour's rest and drunk coffee when we heard the tinkling of little bells coming from across the hills, and a caravan of horses and mules approached us. They halted and began to unload and eventually pitched their tents, which together with ours amounted to twenty in all, including two luxury tents, flying the English flag. My dear, we also have two tents flying the German flag, and one of them is fitted out with every comfort, three beds with soft pillows and mattresses, a washstand for each of us, six chairs, and a table in the middle, covered with a cloth. The tent itself is fourteen metres in diameter, made of double-thickness canvas, coloured on the inside. Picture for yourself this tent city, with long paper lanterns hanging between the tents and to the side some 100 to 150 horses and mules, grazing and making an orchestra of sounds...

The travellers spent the weekend back in Jerusalem. They visited many religious and social institutions, and each visit reinforced their feelings that 'things cannot go on like this'. Ascher Levy and his companions simply could not understand why most of the Sephardi Jews, predominantly from North Africa, were able to sustain themselves by manual work, whereas the majority of the Ashkenazi Jews from Eastern Europe regarded any activity other than the study of the Holy Scriptures as an unpardonable sin. There was extreme poverty in both communities, but in the Ashkenazi community social decay was an additional factor. Von Alten related that eighteen years earlier the British Consul, James Finn, had attempted to involve Jews in the planning of streets, and to enlist them to work in the quarries and at stonemasonry. After a brief initial success – several hundred had taken up the offer – the rabbis had stepped in and issued a prohibition. Fear of being put under a ban had driven the last Jewish workers to give up. Other attempts to increase the output of the *Yishuv* who had 'turned away from the Torah' had been similarly unacceptable. But past failures, including that of Karl Neter, who following his visit to Palestine in 1868 had spent four years trying to shake the Jewish communities in Germany and France out of their torpor, did not deter the three travellers. They recorded every detail and collected every conceivable scrap of evidence that might prove useful in the future.

They celebrated the festival of Purim in Tiberias on the shores of Lake Kinnereth. From there Ascher wrote to Fanny:

My dear, good wife,
    You must not take it amiss that I have not fulfilled my intention to write to you daily for the past three days. The day of our departure last Wednesday it rained so heavily that we were soaked to the skin, and would have remained thus, had not the sun come out soon after. By the evening everything inside the tent was wet as well, and yesterday, when the weather was magnificent, I had stomach pains on arrival, but I am feeling completely well again now. Our journey over the last days has continued to be interesting. Right behind Samaria we entered the Valley of Dothan, where Joseph was sold by his brethren. After we had passed through this area of pasture, we stopped for lunch in a ruin below a village, and spent the night at Jenin, which we left early yesterday. We then reached the Valley of Jezreel, which we crossed in a day. Ahead of us in the distance was Mount Hermon, to the right of the mountains of Gilboa. It was here that the prophetess Deborah slew Sisra

with *barak* [the Hebrew for 'lightning flash'], and Saul and his
sons fell in the battle against the Philistines and David sang
the immortal verses. Here too King Jehosophat was killed in
battle, and King Yeshayahu was wounded in the war against
the Assyrians; here Napoleon I with 16,000 men defeated the
entire Turkish army, not to mention the blood spilled in this
place by the Saracens and the Crusaders. The earth must be so
red as a result or the fertility such that despite utter neglect the
grass grows high. It is a great shame that in this wonderful
climate such fertile soil should lie fallow. The few fields sown
with barley, wheat, and millet are proof of the fertility of the
soil.

At four o'clock we arrived at the foot of Mount Tabor, and
since, as I mentioned, I was not feeling very well, Professor
Graetz and Moritz climbed it without me, and returned by
moonlight. Today we made an early start, rode through a
wood, if crippled oaks are worthy of such a name, around
Mount Tabor, which revealed a new panorama. As soon as we
left the wood, a deep, beautiful valley opened up before us as in
a dream, enclosed by the hills of Galilee to the north, overlooked by the snow-covered peak of Mount Hermon. We took
a short midday break in the deep grass between briers, which
afforded little shade from the burning heat of the sun. We
soon started off again, and after a one-hour ride and one hour
on foot, we arrived here. We are camping below a ruined wall,
destroyed in the last earthquake, with Lake Kinneret before us
and to our right the town of Tiberias with its domes and
minarets – in actual fact a miserable dump of a place. We shall
spend the night in tents, but will dine in the town. We still
intend to go and bathe in the lake today.

Sunday, 24 March, Purim. We were quite prepared to see
something unusual take place here. The little town, a cluster
of houses huddled together in crooked, winding streets, full of
dirt and rubbish, contains 2000 Jews out of a population of
3000, and at present is host to the three Europeans, who are
visiting its synagogues, seminaries and rabbis, and bringing
news. Yesterday we were visited by the nobility, assembled a

minyan, and I read the *Megillah*. We heard trumpets, pipes, rifle shots and watched the show. Refreshed by coffee and cake, we then took a boat trip on the lake to the hot springs, the tombs and various strange places, and returned towards five in the afternoon, exhausted by the intense heat. In the evening a *Purimspiel* [Purim play] was performed for us. We intend to travel on from Tiberias for two days towards Haifa, where we have arranged to spend the night at the German Colony founded by the people from Württemberg, who live there. On 29 March we shall board the ship in the afternoon and leave Palestine. Adieu, land of my sufferings, land of my yearning, but adieu, also, land of my hopes. And to you too, dear Fanny, my own promised land, adieu for today. Another three weeks and I hope to embrace you, and find you well and in good health. Greetings to all friends and acquaintances from your Ascher.

The crossing from Haifa to Trieste again took them by way of Alexandria and passed without incident. The three used the time to discuss the content of the memorandum they intended to publish on their return. They decided that Moritz Gottschalk should draw up a kind of appeal to be distributed initially among the circle of interested persons, and after that it should be published in the Jewish press throughout the Reich. The friends also agreed to meet in Berlin before its publication, to work out the final wording. On reaching Trieste they went their separate ways. Heinrich Graetz travelled to Breslau, Moritz Gottschalk to Berlin, while Ascher had decided to stop for a week in Venice. After this short holiday, he travelled right through Austria and Germany on his return to Posen. He was most concerned to get to know his son's fiancée there, or strictly speaking, to assess his future relatives and their status. Transport between the two major cities was by express trains, which Ascher enjoyed on two counts: first as a comfortable journey, and second as the product of his investments.

At the end of April, Ascher set out once again, this time to Berlin to meet his two travelling companions. Moritz Gottschalk invited the professor and his cousin to his new home at 4 Lennéstrasse. On the table stood a bottle of Rakoczy, of which the professor was particularly fond, and the latter thanked his host for this thoughtful touch. 'I am generous in small things,' answered Moritz Gottschalk with a smile as he poured the wine. They clinked glasses, and leaned back in their ample leather armchairs. For a short while no one said anything.

Finally Graetz broke the silence: 'You're both familiar with the saying – You must visit a country to discover its true face. And there is no escape from this truth.'

'Certainly,' replied Moritz Gottschalk. 'I hope that it will be evident in the memorandum that I have put together.'

'You've already finished it?' asked Graetz in amazement. 'How did you manage to do it so quickly?'

'If it weren't ready, I shouldn't have invited you. But before I hand over to you what I have written, I must tell you that I'm afraid this text may destroy many people's image of the Holy Land. Friends will weep and enemies gloat.'

'Concealment is more harmful than the truth,' said Ascher with conviction. 'It is our duty to do what we can to change the way things are.'

'All the same, it might be better if this report, which I have written in all our names, were perhaps just dropped. I wouldn't be upset. We could just approach a number of influential friends and acquaintances. Meet them individually, appeal to their con-sciences, and try to persuade them to give money for the establishment of a secular orphanage.'

'No, Moritz Gottschalk,' countered Graetz. 'Secretive, furtive action doesn't help us at all. Jericho cannot be taken without tearing down the walls.'

'So we go ahead and publish the memorandum, no matter what may happen?'

Ascher summed up: 'Without any ifs or buts.'

'Are you certain, Professor, that Rabbi Hildesheimer will still approve of our plans?'

'I have spoken to him. He supports the welfare initiative, but...'

'He has his doubts, correct?' interrupted Moritz Gottschalk.

'Correct. But why argue, before we have even read the text?' objected Graetz, and asked to see the memorandum.

At the beginning of May the memorandum went into print. By the middle of the month several dozen copies were sent out to selected individuals. The three had set out the objective of their journey in the foreword:

> In the month of March of this year, the undersigned travelled through a large part of Palestine. It was not originally our intention to ascertain the living conditions of our co-religionists, as we were simply following the tug of our hearts to see the land of our fathers. But the circumstances forced themselves upon us; we could not close our eyes or our minds to the material and spiritual destitution. As a result, we set out to meet people from the most diverse circles and confer with them about the underlying causes of the situation, and to suggest that by removing these causes it might be possible to alleviate these social ills. The *Chacham Bashi*, the official rabbi in chief of Jerusalem, as well as the German and Austrian Consuls General and a number of other people were in remarkable agreement in what they told us in confidence. We set out our observations and experiences in this memorandum, and go on to make suggestions for the relief of these ills.

They attached statistical data about the Jewish population, and the system of distribution of funds as well as its effects. An entire chapter was devoted to describing the poor state of health of the city dwellers, the root causes of which were set out in unusually harsh terms.

> This debility, combined with poverty, is the result of one deep-rooted evil, namely the marrying of young children to one another. As a rule, boys between the ages of thirteen and fifteen are still being wedded to girls between twelve and fourteen. It amounts to nothing less than child murder. For if the young mother and her offspring survive the birth, the children from such a union are afflicted with lifelong physical infirmity

and mental weakness. A generation such as this is dependent on charity from birth. There is no hiding the truth: this appalling situation occurs only in the Jewish population [...]

However, there is a further reason for impoverishment, namely the way in which the incoming charitable donations are distributed. Jerusalem has not one, not two, but fourteen separate communities, which are self-contained, and none of which has anything to do with any of the others...

Every communal group has its own president [...] The funds donated by a particular country or group in a region from which the community originated are sent to this individual on the tacit understanding that the money should be distributed only to people within that particular community. The president is entitled to retain a commission for himself [...] from the total transmitted. The rabbis also receive a commission. So, for example, money collected by Russian and Galician Chassidim will be distributed only to *Chabad* members, charity from Hungary will be restricted to the Hungarian community, and the remaining communities will not receive a cent of the money [...] Members of the Hod group are considered well off, as they amount to no more than forty-seven souls, and money for them is raised throughout Holland and Germany. The Hungarians are in a similarly advantageous situation. By contrast the amount that reaches the Jews of Spanish origin per capita is minute, as there are so many of them, and they rely on funds from the Jews in Turkey, and even then a portion is still creamed off for the *Chachamim* and board members. The position of the Maghrebi Jews, immigrants from Tunisia and Morocco, is worse still, as they receive very little from their homeland – they constitute the pariahs of the Jerusalem population. [...] Many of them live in what amount to hovels – where large numbers of people are crammed together, a pitiful sight! It is perfectly obvious that if the funds flowing into Palestine from Europe, America, and Asia were evenly distributed, regardless of the different groups, each individual would receive a far greater share, and the poverty among the most disadvantaged would be alleviated.

There is a further, quite contrary perspective, which renders the distribution even more unjust. In civilized countries it is generally considered shameful to accept charity, and publicly at that, and people will stoop to doing so only if forced by direst need. By contrast, the Jewish population of Palestine consider it an honour to be remembered by donations, or to take part in the receipt of *chalukah* [...] The Jewish population in no way regards these donations as alms, but as a reward merited by each individual for living in the Holy Land and studying the Talmud or the *Kabbalah* there. Moreover the donations are by no means intended for the poor, but are first and foremost for those devoting themselves to the Talmud. Most of the men, regardless of how little they understand of the Talmud, regard themselves as rabbis or *chachamim* [...] and accept a share of the donations as a well-earned right. [...] The fact that widows and orphans are also granted a share is regarded as magnani-mous, but it forces the rest of the community to give up part of their entitlement. This explains why we were taken aback by the fact that capitalists and house-owners claim a share of the funds and are virtually accepting alms. Out of consideration we shall not mention any names. [...] Given this state of affairs it is reasonable to suppose that the most helpless, the widows and the orphans, come off badly when the funds are shared out.

The effects of this paradoxical outlook and unjust distribu-tion of funds are distressing. Jewish orphans in need, or actual-ly going hungry, allow themselves to be taken into the English and German missions, where they are received with out-stretched arms, simply in order to satisfy their hunger. At present there are forty young Jewish boys in the mission school in Jerusalem, being prepared for baptism. We were unable to ascertain how many Jewish girls there are in Christian educa-tional institutions. What also happens is that poor fathers or mothers sell their children to the missionaries...

There must be an end to the concealment of this terrible state of affairs, which promotes demoralization and idleness. Since the vast majority of the male population lives on charity and has no form of occupation, they have no idea what to do with their time. Most of them claim to be Talmud scholars, but in fact spend little time on the Talmud, and hang about the streets, listening out for any scrap of news. Gossiping, boasting, scandal-mongering, slandering each other, and other evil vices are what such idleness leads to.

The authors followed this by listing a number of suggestions intended to improve the grim state of affairs:

The donations should strictly be used for:
1. Those entirely without means, widows, orphans, the old and the impoverished;
2. Those truly functioning as rabbis, Talmud teachers and students; and finally,
3. Artisans and industrious persons, who despite their best efforts cannot feed themselves.
4. The fragmentation into separate communities must cease, at least as far as charitable funds are concerned. Anyone in need of support should receive it regardless of which communal group he belongs to. [...]
5. All young men under the age of eighteen and girls under the age of sixteen who marry shall be debarred for all time from receiving assistance. [...] Likewise those who keep their children away from school up to a certain age shall be excluded, and finally those who hand over their children to the missionary institutions.

As if these accusations and suggested changes were not enough, Graetz, Ascher, and Moritz Gottschalk further called for a public vote to elect the community leader. Before any candidates could put themselves forward, they would have to agree to waive their share of the charitable funds. In conclusion, they stressed the necessity to build orphanages, where in addition to learning *Tanach*, the Hebrew language and the Talmud, the children would also be taught reading, writing, arithmetic and geography. This document, published in the year 5632 according to the Jewish calendar and in May 1872 according to the Gregorian calendar, was signed: 'Dr Heinrich Graetz, professor, Breslau;

Ascher Levy, merchant, Polzin in Pomerania, and M. Gottschalk Lewy, merchant, Berlin'. Two months later an official organization was formed to build a progressive orphanage in Jerusalem.

The memorandum was only intended for a selected circle and was sent to scholars and potential donors with a request for funds in support of the struggle to improve the existing circumstances. It soon leaked out beyond this circle of individuals; someone had passed on extracts to the press, and the text was translated into Hebrew and Yiddish. This prompted harsh criticism, spreading from one town to another, and from state to state. European Jewry was incensed and angry, feelings ran high, with resurgence of the old conflicts between the Orthodox and Reform. Both sides brandished the memorandum like a banner. Accusations and slander were parried like swords in a duel – clashes resounded on all sides. The fieriest reactions came from Jerusalem and the heartlands of Eastern European Jewry. Many of the accusations were levelled not only against the three authors of the publication, but also against Rabbi Ezriel Hildesheimer, who had initially welcomed the Association for the Education of Jewish Orphans in Palestine.

Although privately still in favour of the project, Hildesheimer decided to withdraw from the public dispute, which had unleashed a veritable storm of indignation. This put the newly founded association in a difficult position. The Orthodox proclaimed a ban on the three men, who were attacked in the press and were regarded by the silent majority as traitors to the community. Their only support came from Jewish intellectuals in Germany and England. In this overheated atmosphere it was virtually impossible to raise the necessary funds for the project. It was to be more than a decade before they were able to realize their plans. For eight long years the three stood in the crossfire of public criticism, which was an entirely new experience for Ascher and Moritz Gottschalk. Heinrich Graetz, who had previously brought down the wrath of Orthodox circles on himself, was able to cope with the situation. But Moritz Gottschalk had to endure the loss of many long-standing clients, not only Jews but non-

Jews as well, as a result of his attitude to the *Yishuv* in *Eretz Israel*. Ascher Levy withdrew to his little town in Pomerania, but even this sleepy province was no refuge from unpleasant slander. Beside the usual business papers, there was now a growing pile of newspaper cuttings on his desk, copies of articles and readers' letters, libellous pamphlets, and furious letters.

Suddenly the Levy house found itself at the centre of the dispute. After every synagogue service, the members of the little Polzin congregation would be arguing with increasing vehemence about the significance of Ascher's actions. As the press reports grew more negative, Ascher's Jewish neighbours became more vociferous. They accused him of betraying all the guiding principles that they had followed for generations. But Ascher remained unmoved. Just as he had never seen any contradiction between his religious beliefs and his loyalty and allegiance first to Prussia, and then to the Reich, equally he did not consider that there was any conflict between his love for Jerusalem – his spiritual home – and his struggle for improved living conditions in Palestine. At first he responded to his critics, sometimes with restraint, and on occasion indignantly, but each of his replies provoked fresh reactions, and he soon came to realize that this would continue endlessly; he would never succeed in convincing his enemies. The arguments swept logic aside, and in the end emotion gained the upper hand. Both supporters and opponents of the progressive orphanage were driven by the same inner wishes and the same love for Zion, and so in this battle the end ultimately justified the means.

One day the raging dispute literally reached Ascher's doorway. By now it was autumn, a season that Ascher loved. As he returned home from a long walk in the nearby woods, he found Bernhard waiting for him in front of the house. He was leaning against the doorpost and seemed embarrassed, as if there were something he was trying to hide.

'Has something happened?'

'No, Papa, nothing,' replied Bernhard and leaned even closer against the door.

'Are you going to let me in?'

Reluctantly Bernhard moved, and Ascher's gaze landed on the words that someone had painted across the door. 'Death to the destroyer of Israel!' he read aloud, as slowly as a child just learning to read. Bernhard was about to say something, but was silenced by a furious gesture from his father. Over and over again he read the words, as if he was having difficulty in understanding them. At last he said quietly, 'Call Victoria to get rid of this filth.'

Bernhard was about to do as he was bidden, but before he could do so, his father laid his hand on his shoulder. He stood there motionless. A full minute passed without a word being spoken, until Ascher finally removed his hand and went into the house. Bernhard listened as his footsteps took him upstairs. Fanny was in the middle of changing the bed linen. The marital bed, in which they had slept ever since their wedding, was very intimate territory, and the maid Victoria was not permitted so much as to touch it. As Ascher appeared in the doorway, Fanny looked up at him in surprise. He was as white as a sheet.

'Aren't you feeling well?' she asked in concern.

'It seems as if I have drawn my own home into a civil war,' he said. 'I am most terribly sorry.'

Fanny let go of the bed linen. Their eyes met, and for the first time in his life Ascher lowered his gaze in front of his wife.

'Maybe I have been wrong,' he sighed. 'Someone has daubed our door with abuse.'

'My dear, I love you for your strengths and your weaknesses,' she said simply and stretched out her hand to him. Ascher took it and squeezed it. Fanny stroked his cheek. 'Besides, haven't you always said that we are just tools in the hands of the Creator?'

Ascher looked at her as if he had suddenly discovered a totally new side to her. 'How lucky I am to have you,' he said with a catch in his voice, and left the room.

Business continued as usual in the offices of the company. Compared with events in Europe the dispute over the building of an orphanage in Jerusalem seemed of little importance. The world was advancing as never before, Germany was now a major power, the chimneys of the expanding industries were spewing smoke, and many new railroad tracks were being laid. And yet Ascher and

The company headquarters and family home in Brunnenstrasse, Bad Polzin.

Moritz Gottschalk spied the first clouds on the horizon. Contrary to his principle of investing only in German enterprises, for the first time in his life Ascher had finally taken the decision to sell some of his German railway stock in order to invest the money in Russian shares for the new railway line from Kursk to Charkov. The transaction proved profitable; within five years the value of the shares had risen by eight per cent, and over this period they yielded a handsome dividend of three to four per cent per annum. When even key German industries, such as the Laura steel works and the Hibernia coal mines, one of Bleichröder's ventures, got into financial difficulties, no one could dispute the fact that Ascher had acted prudently.

But even though these international deals were making large profits for Ascher Levy, his heart continued to be in his Pomeranian business. Here he had his finger on the pulse of events; he was familiar with the territory and could give good advice. The sawmills were working round the clock. Bernhard was continually being sent off to locate forest owners compelled to sell part of their woodlands at low prices because of financial hardship. The landowners in particular had allowed themselves to be carried away by the dream of the industrial revolution. They had overextended themselves in buying shares, and were now hard pushed to meet their commitments. Maintenance of the estates required constant high expenditure, but the new, extravagantly ostentatious lifestyle of the nobility also had its price. In the space of two years, the Levy family had become one of the biggest – if not the biggest – leaseholders of the entire Belgard region, and they were almost self-sufficient in supplying their sawmills with raw materials.

Ascher was not in the least surprised that Bernhard was travelling ever more often to the principality of Posen. It was already some time since his son had informed his parents of his most successful 'acquisition' – Henriette Cohen. The betrothal period was coming to an end, and it was now time to bring the woman of his heart to Polzin and begin a new chapter in his life. Ascher, who had stopped at Glogau on his way back from Venice and befriended the bride's parents, joyfully gave the couple his blessing. The Cohens wanted the wedding canopy to be put up in their home, and so the wedding took place in Glogau. Several hundred guests honoured the young couple by their presence. Professor Graetz had made the effort to come from Breslau. Moritz Gottschalk had taken it upon himself to invite Gerson Bleichröder on the family's behalf, but the banker had contented himself by simply sending a telegram of congratulations. The mayor of Polzin likewise just sent a telegram. After the wedding, Henriette packed her things. Then came the farewells – people waving, mother's tears, brotherly advice, sighing sisters, and finally the piercing shriek of the steam locomotive…

A fine apartment awaited the couple in Polzin. Julius had paid the rent for a whole year: 'instead of a conventional present, if you have no objection, big brother,' he wrote from Danzig, with apologies that illness had prevented him from coming to Glogau.

'Quite the contrary, little brother,' Bernhard wrote back. 'And if, God willing, we have a child in a year's time, we have no objection to your giving him a similar present, because he is very likely to be living with us...!'

There is a saying that the apple does not fall far from the tree. However, there must have been a strong wind blowing when Bernhard was born, making the apple fall quite some distance away. Ascher Levy had always known how to maintain his romantic feelings within his business persona. Although the emotional surges of his youth had subsided over the years, he was always inclined to remain emotional. Coldness and indifference were only a front with him. Bernhard, however, was made of entirely different stuff. His composed behaviour towards his family and those around him was not just a shell to protect an inner softness. He was by nature a sober and introspective person. His emotional life remained a mystery, and even Henriette was compelled to admit in her letters home that she had 'never cracked this nut'. But she was not a particularly demonstrative woman either. Behind the grace and frankness that had so impressed Bernhard on their first meeting, other qualities lay hidden that were a match for those of her husband, and in this respect at least they were a perfect couple. Both regarded 'cracking the nut' more as an intellectual challenge than a matter of the heart. He withdrew into business affairs, and listened to her advice, but essentially the two of them – quite unlike Ascher and Fanny – lived alongside each other without a deep spiritual bond.

However, their sober everyday existence certainly had no adverse effect on the intimacy of their physical relations. Within a very short time Henriette had given birth to three boys and two girls. A governess from the area was employed for the children. Bernhard and Henriette saw to it that they did not run wild all over the house and disturb their peace. A detailed daily timetable was drawn up for each child. Whereas Ascher Levy had adapted to Prussian order and discipline, Bernhard had grown up with it.

His life was strictly compartmentalized – rights and duties, good and evil, day and night. Everything had its fixed place, with no allowance for anything that did not fit into this scheme.

Ascher Levy had had to fight his way up the ladder of success from the very bottom and had gained his social position by dogged persistence. To start with he had to struggle to make a living, then to get the house, and afterwards establish himself in Polzin society, followed by expansion of the firm as well as gaining a place on the town council. For years after he had been appointed, he would announce his arrival at meetings in a loud voice, saying, 'Here I am.' It was as if he wished to emphasize not only his physical presence, but another, clearly far more important fact: that he had covered a vast distance – he had come, so to speak, from another planet, characterized by poverty, strangeness, and humiliation. His ethical success was for him an additional source of pride. At the age of nineteen he had sworn to lead a Jewish life, and he had not broken this oath. His journey to *Eretz Israel* had strengthened his commitment to Judaism even further. It was no longer simply a matter of a spiritual tie to the Holy Land, but rather a very specific connection to specific people in a specific geographic location. But beyond his commitment to Zion, this obligation had been a problem all his life; he had continually struggled with the moral issues of Jewish conscience and the prescribed rules of conduct.

Bernhard had not experienced these tribulations. He took his place in society for granted. He felt no surge of satisfaction when the farmers and labourers in the little town raised their caps to him or when he was greeted by the Prussian gentry. These things were as normal to him as water, air, and money. Ascher had always striven towards higher goals. Bernhard, however, lived his life as if he had already reached the top. Ascher had tried to conquer the earth's gravity. But Bernhard strode with such assurance that he was not even aware of his inability to fly. The legacy of earlier generations weighed heavily on Ascher's shoulders. His close links to the past made it possible for him to live the life of a man with roots, even though his freedom of action was severely curtailed as a result. The leap into the world of big business had

Bernhard Levy.

been a very real leap. Ascher used to say, 'My sons will be the ones to take the next step,' when Beri and Juli were still at primary school.

But Bernhard did not possess the endurance of a long-distance runner. He preferred to remain where he was. As a result he was spared the problems and tensions faced by his co-religionists, striving for 'a place at the centre' of the sophisticated echelons of society in the Reich. Polzin offered far fewer challenges. Success lay within one's grasp, and as one knew who one's enemies were, the weapons of engagement remained the conventional ones. Everything was familiar, clear, and obvious. Bernhard loved his home town.

While the Reich was undergoing the turmoil of the industrial revolution, in Polzin it was as if time stood still. People simply grew older, and ivy crept up the houses of the local dignitaries. The few changes that occurred did not rouse the provincial town from its torpor. A large spa building was officially opened in the park, and in the summer months there were many guests who visited it. They at least brought a breath of the big wide world with them. In winter Polzin was like a sleepy island surrounded by an ocean of snow. The big cities far to the east and west were developing at a roaring pace, so fast that often people could no longer control it. In the jungle of the big city, new laws prevailed, both written and unwritten. Moritz Gottschalk wrote to his cousin, 'Anyone who treads water has lost; whoever is unsuccessful has lost his right to exist; and anyone growing old in poverty has lost his dignity. A grim world. But it's the one we live in.'

What counted most of all in this new world was speed, shrewdness, cunning, and adaptability. Bismarck's banker, Gerson Bleichröder, was given a title. As is well known in any such case of noblesse oblige, privilege carries with it obligations. Prominent society figures were only too happy to be invited to his residence in the Behrendstrasse. But the ostentatious display of wealth and power by influential Jews such as Bleichröder was not without consequence. A head of social and political steam built up in Berlin.

The German Reich had attained a position of enormous power, but its internal divisions were becoming ever deeper, more far-ranging, and more disturbing. Jewish emancipation had opened the floodgates. Jews became active and revealed their own abilities, in the words of Henrich Graetz, 'not because of the goodwill of the goyim, but as a result of their own long suffering'. At the same time a cultural struggle was raging between the Catholics and the Protestants. Each side feared the loss of its supremacy and material influence. The junkers relinquished their property but not their pride, and rose up against the plutocracy.

Henriette Levy, née Cohen.

The artisans were ousted by industrialization. Those on the
winning side financially were alarmed by the 'red peril' of social-
ism. The workers, on the other hand, were organizing themselves
against capitalist exploitation, but this left them without protection from unemployment. This world of turmoil, brimming with
hatred and despair, was crying out for a readily identifiable scapegoat, which could be pointed at with an accusing finger. It was
not slow to be found.

Anti-Semitism had always existed in Germany. In the past
Jews had been persecuted for their betrayal of Christ. Their hands
were allegedly stained with the blood of Jesus, and every

generation had been made to suffer anew for this sin in the dim and distant past. Now that the Jews had virtually acquired equal civil rights and had fought their way to the upper strata of society by their own skills, it did not take long for their Christian fellow citizens to see this as a danger to the nation and the empire, a threat to the values of German culture, and a seizure of positions previously reserved exclusively for the Christians. The descendants of old-established aristocratic families or members of the Prussian – and now the new German – nation could not come to terms with the fact that the Jews, who only yesterday were seen as small-time crooks, were the rising chiefs of industry and even the political advisers of tomorrow. A Jew who dealt in money, incessantly plotting intrigues and pulling the strings behind the scenes, became the epitome of everything that upset the traditional, the natural social order, and it was only right and proper for his place to be outside society.

These attacks were not confined to the Jews alone. Anyone associated with them – regardless of status – was regarded as 'infected'. It was enough for the political opponents of the Chancellor to recall the latter's connections with the Rothschilds and the Bleichröders for him to be instantly guilty of assisting 'the Jewish seizure of the Fatherland'. The expression 'Jewish money' now became a term of abuse – effectively a curse.

But the emerging industrial state simply could not manage without it. The Jew-haters could not find a way out of this vicious circle, and their dependency fired their hatred. In 1879 Wilhelm Marr's *Jewry's Conquest of the Teutonic World* was published. This tract ran into twelve editions in less than a year. The author warned his readers: 'You are admitting foreign rulers into your parliaments, you are promoting them to law-givers and judges, you are turning them into dictators over the state financial order, you have handed the press over to them [...] The Jewish race is spreading its genius like wildfire to defeat you as if this were only right, and you have deserved it a thousand times over.' In less than a year Marr had found wealthy sponsors to finance his newspaper *German Guard*, in which he proposed the setting up of an organization to be called the Anti-Jewish Union. It is also worth pointing out that Marr was the first to employ the term 'anti-Semitism' as a political slogan.

These events so enraged Moritz Gottschalk that he wrote to his cousin in Polzin, 'They cannot stand me, but they cannot live without me. Business is booming but so is hostility. With every thousand I make in profit, I gain a thousand new enemies. I should like to retreat, and creep off to a quiet corner and take a rest. Would the Polzin rest home have a place for me?'

Polzin was neither a rest home nor a paradise for Jews. But Pomerania had on the whole been spared these rabble-rousing agitations, since the region lagged behind in industrial terms, and had produced no bankers or industrialists of the Mosaic persuasion. North Prussian society was conservative. Social democracy and national liberalism, the driving progressive forces, found little support here. Hatred of the Jews had become something one could live with. Ascher Levy did not flaunt his wealth, he did not drive in a splendid carriage, and he did not give magnificent balls in the Bleichröder style. He did not seek a title, he kept out of politics – with the one exception of his place on the town council, and he had long since given up any attempt at social contact with his Christian neighbours. He kept his personal contacts to a minimum, and in this way avoided unnecessary distress. It was only in matters of business that he was unyielding and insistent. He considered arguments in this area a natural ingredient in the fight for survival – common to both Jews and their enemies alike.

When Ascher turned sixty-two, he became aware that his vision was deteriorating progressively. He found it difficult to read, at first only by gaslight, but gradually even by daylight. Moritz Gottschalk put him in touch with a well-known Berlin eye specialist. Although the diagnosis was obvious, the specialist was unable to help him. Ascher was suffering from glaucoma, for which there was no cure. First he suffered from burning and pressure in both eyes, later from intense headaches, and ultimately from non-specific pains all over his body. Sedatives and painkillers had no effect. He stopped studying the account books, and it became more and more difficult for him to find his way about without help. His increasing loss of vision affected his mood, for he had always been able to move around freely. Sometimes he did not leave his room for days on end, even to go downstairs. Fanny sat by his side. When he asked her to, she would read to him from the Holy Scriptures, or from the newspaper. But mostly he simply wanted her near him. They would sit together without speaking, and their silence conveyed more intimacy than any conversation. Officially Ascher was still head of the firm but, given the circumstances, Bernhard had taken over in practical terms.

In October 1877 the director general of the bank in Stettin that administered the bulk of the firm's funds died in mysterious circumstances. There was a persistent rumour that the bank's books were not in order. Ascher could not tackle the long journey to Stettin, and in any case he would not have been able to read the copies of the transactions undertaken on his behalf by the bank. Bernhard had to go there on his own. It was a complicated and very delicate affair. A complaint from the firm would have made public the size of their business, which both were keen to avoid. Ascher warned his son: 'You will have to be very circumspect. Given the prevailing atmosphere it would be fatal to reveal everything. As it is, the junkers who have been driven out are calling us leeches. You know the way they speak.'

'Don't worry, Papa. You can rely on me.'

In the event Bernhard came to a satisfactory arrangement with the directors of the bank. Reliable surety was found for the firm's money and confidentiality regarding the business was retained.

Ascher was reassured by his son's performance. From now on he withdrew even more to his room, and effectively left his son in control.

According to the tax authorities, in 1877 the firm of 'Ascher Levy, Banker, Grain and Agricultural Merchant, Sawmill and Timber Wholesaler' was the biggest and most prosperous enterprise in the region of Belgard. Ascher continued to take decisions regarding investment, but Bernhard was in charge of all other affairs. However, it was not always easy to draw a dividing line between the two spheres of activity. Bernhard felt as if he were seated on a spirited horse, with someone else holding the reins.

At times it was difficult for him to get a definitive answer from his father. Ascher had become somewhat sluggish in his movements and his thoughts, and he tended to put things off.

'This is no way to run a business,' Bernhard said to his mother. 'Couldn't you speak to him?'

'That would need someone more heartless than me.'

'Do you happen to have me in mind, Mama?'

Fanny shrugged her shoulders. 'Take it as you will, Beri.'

'When it comes down to it, I am the one doing all the business, apart from the banking transactions.'

'And isn't that enough for you?'

'Please don't misunderstand me. I have no intention of taking over the firm, and it wouldn't occur to me to encroach on Papa's rights. But a firm cannot advance if decisions are not taken at the right time. We own a successful, highly dynamic enterprise, which needs rapid decision-making.'

'If that's the case, what do you intend to do?'

'What we need is order, Mama. The employees in the office also need a guiding hand. They have to know who is ...'

'Who is the boss?'

'That's not all. The customers also need to know who they are dealing with.'

'The customers are used to dealing with Papa.'

'They've grown old, just like Father. They have sons, and he too has a son. One generation steps back, and the next takes over.'

'Patience, Beri. Your father is still alive.'

'You don't understand me.'

'I understand you very well. Better perhaps than you think. You're impatient, Beri, but I have no objection to your speaking to him. He will understand.'

Bernhard shook his head. 'He won't understand, he'll be angry. But I have no choice.'

That evening he went through the balance sheets of the firm. He sat bent over the accounts until midnight, analysing the long columns of debit and credit, and he summarized them on one sheet of paper. The enterprise was solid. This business year, they had made a profit of about seven per cent after tax, and they had approximately half a million marks in the bank, mostly invested in bonds and shares. The properties owned by the Levy firm amounted to a value of 830,000 Reichsmarks, in addition to which there was the income from leases. As the family was sitting at breakfast the following morning, Bernhard handed his father his summary.

'What's this?' asked Ascher, screwing up his eyes.

Bernhard read the figures out to him. Ascher smiled. 'You're not telling me anything I don't know. You've forgotten to include the investments I made through Moritz. The agents of the Bleichröder bank are responsible for those.'

'I've been made a tempting offer – part of a forest near to Köslin. Oak, some pinewood, and a lot of top-quality maple, hard as rock. All of it ready for felling.'

'And the price?'

'A *metzieh* – a real snip. The owners are in financial straits.'

'Do we need to pay cash?'

'Of course. You know how things are done today. Pay cash and you get a discount.'

'I know, but I don't believe we have that much in liquid assets.'

'No problem, Papa. We can arrange the finance.'

'It's not a good time to take out credit,' replied his father.

'I wouldn't go to the banks.'

'What then? Are we supposed to print the notes ourselves?'

'There's a much easier way, Papa.'

'What do you mean?'

'The railway shares. The stock market price is steady, but the dividend has dropped. Scarcely more than three per cent. In my opinion, it's time to get rid of them.'

'I didn't buy them to speculate. It's long-term investment. And it's proved worth it over the years.'

'I'm looking ahead, Papa. And besides, you yourself speculated with these shares.'

'I bought shares in Russian railway companies,' said Ascher, somewhat put out.

'Quite so. But right now rumour has it that there may well be a war between Russia and England. You've read about it in the papers.'

'You forget that I can't read the papers any longer.'

'I'm sorry, Papa. I didn't mean to upset you. But even if there isn't a war, the rumours alone will make the share price drop. And by the way, what about the shares that Moritz has? Are they also Russian?'

'No.'

'Well, what do you think?'

It was probably the first time that Ascher saw his son not just following his instructions, but putting forward ideas of his own against him. But although the idea as such was not at all to his liking, he was delighted to see this other side of Bernhard. He moved to his last point.

'Selling German shares at this of all times is not being loyal to the fatherland.'

Bernhard raised his eyebrows in surprise. 'You're trying to talk your way out of this, Papa,' he sighed. 'Since when did you mix business with sentiment?'

'I've never forgotten that I am a German subject.'

'You know, Papa, that reminds me of something. When I was in Stettin on account of the bank scandal, I talked to the director generals. One of them brought up all manner of accusations against the Jews. In order to disguise their own wrongdoing they tried to push me up against the wall and to imply that I had no patriotic feelings. I answered them by saying: "Sir, I may be of the Mosaic faith, but first and foremost I am a German." And do you know what he replied?'

'Is it important?'

'He said in a poisonous tone: "Here in the Reich, we are Prussians, Bavarians, Saxons, Württemburgers, or what you will. You Jews, you always maintain that you are Germans. For me that is the best proof that you belong to no other people than to the Jewish people..." Those were his words.'

'That has nothing to do with discussing shares.'

'Of course not. But we've already decided the question of the shares.'

'Decided? Who decided anything?'

'You and I. In the end you don't doubt the logic of what I set out for you, Papa. First we'll sell our shares in the Charkov railway line. They will fetch a good price. And I would be only too pleased to get rid of the bundle of shares in the textile industry. It's hanging about like a lump of lead in the bank, doing absolutely nothing. The sooner we get rid of them the better. Those shares are falling by the minute. Although I'm not sure we'll find a buyer for them.'

'How much money do you need?'

'I need fifty thousand right away, and another fifty thousand at the end of the year. Ten thousand for the sawmill at Kollatz, as it's already working to capacity and we have to enlarge it. It wouldn't do any harm either to refurbish Gross Linichen, but that can wait until next year, when we have more orders. The rest is needed for the leasing of forests near to Köslin. If we don't hurry, the Behrend brothers will snatch them away. They are like dogs with their noses to the ground all the time, sniffing out profitable business. They're good at that, Papa, very good indeed. Especially Moritz. Georg is an adventurer, not worth a cent. I'm astonished that Bismarck should have chosen him of all people to buy the Fuchsmühle with. They say that the factory is in debt to the Berlin Chamber of Commerce, and that the cellulose produced there is of such poor quality that he has to sell it below manufacturing cost. If we can still sign the lease this month, we shall be able to make a good profit from the large-scale production of timber beams.'

'For laying down railway tracks?'

'Papa, all you think of is railways. No. I'm hoping for a contract to supply colliery props. Coal is a product much in demand today. Wooden props to support the galleries in the mines. That would be an absolute winner.'

The discussion had worn Ascher out. The pressure in his eyes affected his concentration. 'Go ahead. Do what you think right,' he said, indicating that he wished to put an end to the conversation.

Bernhard went over to him and planted a kiss on his cheek. 'Thank you, Papa. I knew we wouldn't quarrel.'

That evening when they were in their bedroom, Ascher took

Fanny's hand. He ran his fingers over it, as if it was new to him, and sighed: 'When sons become adults, fathers grow old.'

Fanny looked at him in astonishment.

The timber trade had been conducted for centuries along the same lines and was chiefly in the hands of the Prussian junker families. As a rule the woodcutters came from Posen, one of the largest principalities in northern Poland. The Polish peasants were a good and cheap labour force. They spoke no German, had no civil rights, and were altogether without the means to organize themselves. Nor could they hope for support from the German labour unions, who did not care about them or their working conditions. The junkers' attitude was to exploit them to the full. This cheap labour force, combined with the abundant forests in East Prussia and Pomerania, were such a huge source of profit for the junkers that they never gave a thought to forest management.

By the middle of the nineteenth century, as the pace of industrialization grew in Central Europe, the demand for timber had soared. The coal and steel mines had the most need for wood, but railway tracks, bridge building, and derricks also all relied on it. In the 1860s demand was at its peak. The Polish workers, competent and cheap as ever, continued felling, but eventually delivery bottlenecks arose. There were too few sawmills to meet the orders. The raw timber began piling up, and customers had to wait weeks, sometimes months, for their supplies. Bernhard had been quick to realize that whoever could control this bottleneck would also dominate the market. If the sawmills bought less timber, the price of the raw material dropped. If the sawmills fell behind with their deliveries, the price for sawn timber rose.

Time was pressing, as there were tempting contracts with the big industrial corporation Hibernia on the horizon. Moritz Gottschalk, Bleichröder's agent at the time, was acting as middleman in this deal. The Hibernia mines were in urgent need of support props and were buying up everything available. Any moment the contract might be given to the firm of Levy. Bernhard was all the more surprised when Moritz Gottschalk informed him that he was coming to Polzin to discuss the matter. No sooner had the visitor stepped off the train than he announced: 'Bad news, I'm afraid. There's not going to be a contract with Hibernia.'

'We can drop the price,' said Bernhard hurriedly.

'It's not a question of the price,' explained Moritz Gottschalk. 'It's a far more complicated matter – politics are involved.'

'What has the one got to do with the other?'

Moritz Gottschalk frowned. 'Bismarck gave a speech in parliament this week calling for a new tax on the timber industry.'

'I read the speech. He stated in parliament that only idiots would continue to cut down trees without considering their intended use. And that given the current circumstances, the forests would soon resemble a desert. He is only looking after his own interests, but as far as I'm concerned that's quite all right. We're both in the same boat.'

'You and Bismarck? That's a bit of an overstatement, isn't it?'

'I'm not fighting him for the office of Chancellor. We're both just timber merchants.'

'That's exactly the problem.'

'I don't understand.'

'You soon will. The Bismarck family owns vast tracts of forest in Pomerania. And any number of sawmills. Our esteemed Chancellor may well be hungry for power to govern, but he also thirsts for money. If the tariff is introduced, the price of timber will rise, and the sawmills will have to meet the cost. However, as someone well placed, and who moreover dominates production, he can absorb the fluctuations in cost without doing himself any harm.'

'I've already gone into this, my dear uncle, and I'm now in competition,' said Bernhard confidently.

They entered the office. The employees rose to their feet and bowed. Moritz Gottschalk opened the door to Ascher's room.

'Where is your father?' he asked.

'He's not at his best.'

'Perhaps he should hear this too,' suggested Moritz Gottschalk.

'What else is there to hear?'

'I haven't finished, Beri. There is another obstacle.'

'You take too gloomy a view.'

'I haven't yet told you the main thing. Bismarck is our rival for the Hibernia contracts.'

'So what? Well, we shall be rivals, then,' Bernhard burst out. 'Let us compete the way that decent business people do. Why ever not? We have every right to do so. Or don't we?'

'No,' said Moritz Gottschalk.

Bernhard looked at him in astonishment. Then he said in a quiet, even voice, stressing every word: 'Do you mean to say that Hibernia will turn down our offer even if it is more favourable?'

'Do you know who sits on the Hibernia board of directors?'

'Yes, Bleichröder. Or rather Herr von Bleichröder, as he now is.'

'Do you still not understand?'

'Otto von Bismarck and Gerson Bleichröder against Ascher and Bernhard Levy…I'm afraid you're right, Moritz. We don't stand much of a chance.'

'It's not a question of standing much of a chance. You don't stand any chance at all.'

'What's that you're talking about? Nobody told me you'd already arrived.' Ascher Levy came down the stairs. Bernhard stood up, to give his father a seat. The cousins embraced and kissed one another. 'How was the journey?'

'Absolutely fine. Now that there's a direct connection from Berlin to Belgard, it's a real pleasure. Not like the trip on horseback from Jerusalem to Tiberias,' joked Moritz Gottschalk.

Ascher sat down heavily in the chair. Moritz Gottschalk repeated his report. Ascher frowned. Bernhard hastened to reassure him, saying: 'No need to worry, Father. We have plenty of contracts. Hibernia? Well, yes, Hibernia would have been the jewel in the crown. But the Liège mine operators and the two North African companies are virtually begging for supplies from us. Transport costs will be high, of course, but we shall still make a handsome profit. Absolutely no need to worry.'

'Juli fought against the French, and you want to do business with them? No, the house of Levy will not have anything to do with these Frogs.'

'You're mixing business with politics again, Father.'

'No, not with politics, but with my conscience. There are limits.'

'All right, I won't insist.' Bernhard quickly backed down, but added with a hint of mockery: 'Though I don't suppose my lords Bismarck and Bleichröder would show the same restraint as you do.'

In the end it was not the Levys but the Varzin sawmills that got the Hibernia contract. The fact that the Levy firm did not get it was no great loss, as there were plenty of other orders, including those from companies in England and Wales. It was not long before the two sawmills could no longer keep pace with the contracts. Bernhard invested 150,000 marks on a partnership in another sawmill in the neighbourhood of Köslin, very near to the forests on which they had recently taken out a lease.

Ever since Germany's famous victory over France, Bismarck had been planning to nationalize the railways. The way in which ownership was fragmented between the individual *Länder* of the German empire and private companies was a thorn in his flesh, for not all the companies had been run efficiently, thereby undermining investment in extending the lines. Under pressure from him, parliament voted for the setting up of an Extraordinary Railway Ministry. Established in 1873, the responsibility of this Reich Railway Ministry was initially to standardize the cost of transportation and co-ordinate the timetables, which would be followed by nationalization. Bismarck wanted a national railway network, controlled from Berlin, which could bring economic advantage to the Reich in peacetime, and provide rapid troop transportation in time of war. His experiences in 1866 and 1871 had made him and the general staff aware of the importance of the railways for strategic planning.

Much to Bismarck's disappointment, however, things moved very sluggishly, due to both opposing economic interests and political rivalries. And yet the merest whisper of nationalization was enough to speed up the process. There was speculation on the stock exchange. Nationalization of the private railways could only be achieved through purchase of these shares, and those who sold them at the right time made a profit. On the advice of Moritz Gottschalk, who by reason of his connection with the Bleichröder firm had an advantage over other speculators, within a few months Bernhard bought and sold a huge amount of shares in the Berlin–Stettin railway line, as well as in the Rechte-Oderufer Railway. These two transactions brought a net profit of 20,000 marks in less than a year. Now that Ascher was finally convinced of his son's capability, he turned all his attention to the matter of the orphanage. Although he had spent over 10,000 marks on it and Moritz Gottschalk had solemnly sworn to match every 1000 Ascher had given with donations of his own, they were nowhere near the necessary sum.

At the beginning of July 1882 Ascher Levy travelled to Berlin to consult a famous eye specialist. He seized the opportunity to speed up the building of the orphanage. During the train journey he remembered how ten years earlier he had stopped in Vienna for a week on his way to *Eretz Israel*. One evening, accompanied by Dr Kompert, they had gone to a place halfway between a pub and a cabaret, where to the great delight of the public, the performers had sung a refrain that went: 'There's just one and only robbers' lair, and Berlin is its name …' He had been furious – how could these easygoing, lax Austrians be so tactless as to make fun of the Prussian capital, with its barracks and poor districts? The Berlin of the seventies had been transformed, and to outward appearance at least it had become a cosmopolitan capital. The first streetcar by Siemens and Halske ran in the suburb of Lichterfelde. By now there were numerous coffee houses in the Parisian style, where the intellectuals gathered. The huge government building radiated power, and luxurious private residences were springing up like mushrooms. Moritz Gottschalk's own house was also new and furnished throughout in the latest style.

Including their own donations, so far the cousins had collected 30,000 marks for the orphanage, but they needed almost twice that amount. They had been offered a suitable house for rent in Jerusalem. But the outlook was quite dismal. They needed enough money for renovation, furnishing, and for teachers, at least some of whom were to come from Germany. Moritz

Gottschalk suggested enlisting two of the leading Jewish bankers, Gerson Bleichröder and Abraham Oppenheim, to help with the fund-raising. There was keen rivalry between the two millionaires as to which of them was the greater benefactor. Not for them discreet charitable gifts, as prescribed by Jewish tradition. The donors wanted due mention in the press, so that people should learn of their generosity. Oppenheim supported the setting up of museums and theatres. Bleichröder helped build hospitals, offered a generous donation to a synagogue in Ostende, and made a gift to a pastor collecting money for the construction of a Protestant church in Berlin. The donations amounted to hundreds of thousands. Would the two patrons be prepared to stump up 20,000 marks for a Jewish orphanage in the Holy City?

Abraham Oppenheim declined, since he was already involved with a similar project. The initiative of Professor Graetz and the two cousins had also provoked opposition to such an ambitious project. This was from Orthodox fanatics who had decided to build their own orphanage – a strictly Orthodox institution without any secular tuition. The rival project was under the auspices of potential donors such as Moses Joshua Judah Leib Diskin, who had forestalled Ascher and Moritz Gottschalk. According to one source Oppenheim had pledged support for this venture, and for this reason he was unable to meet the cousins' request. All hopes now rested on Bleichröder.

The official dispute about the nature of education in Palestine and the fact that Moritz Gottschalk was one of the initiators and investors in the progressive orphanage had made his name known beyond the financial world of this politically influential magnate. Despite this social position and his wealth, Moritz Gottschalk was still a nobody in comparison with the rich and highly-placed Bleichröder. Professor Graetz and the parliamentarian, Ludwig Bamberger, were regular guests in Moritz Gottschalk's home, and he was proud of his acquaintance with Rabbi Ezriel Hildesheimer. Bleichröder, by contrast, was among the Chancellor's house guests; the Emperor received him at court; he corresponded with Disraeli in London and King Leopold II of the Belgians. Champagne flowed in his home for ambassadors and princes, politicians and generals. There were many who pleaded in vain for just one invitation to the exquisite social gatherings given at least once a month by Bleichröder. His home remained closed to officers and members of the lower aristocracy. The most strenuous efforts were needed before he declared himself prepared to receive the cousins for a private talk – a brief and matter-of-fact meeting, as his private secretary indicated beforehand.

A liveried servant led them into the offices of the bank, another bade them be seated at a table. Beside it was a crystal mirror that made the sparsely furnished hall appear even larger. Light streamed through the glass roof as if in a huge greenhouse. On the wall a portrait of the head of the firm in a richly ornamented gold frame gazed out at them. Brown and grey marble squares formed straight lines on the floor. They waited in silence over tea, served in wafer-thin porcelain cups by a third employee, until a young lackey appeared in the doorway, announcing in a loud voice: 'Baron von Bleichröder!'

Gerson Bleichröder adored ceremony. In measured steps he advanced towards them. Pince-nez with thick lenses rested on his nose. Somewhat sparse mutton-chop whiskers contrasted strangely with his closely shaved chin. He held out a ringed hand to Moritz Gottschalk and said with a smile, 'Warmest welcome! I've heard a great deal about your tilting at windmills.'

Moritz Gottschalk got to his feet and bowed low. 'My lord, I should like to introduce you to Herr Ascher Levy from Polzin.'

Bleichröder nodded. 'I'm pleased to meet you. Please, gentlemen, do sit down. It seems to me that I've heard of you, too. Doesn't your firm have business connections with the Behrend brothers?'

'That is so, my lord.'

The banker muttered a few indistinct words. The servant, who had positioned himself behind him, immediately stretched out his hand to move the padded chair towards him. Bleichröder lowered himself heavily, seating himself directly under the portrait, in which he appeared more energetic and less pale than in reality. In Berlin rumour had it that the painting, the work of the well-known artist, Franz von Lenbach, had cost 30,000 marks, whereas Lenbach had only charged Bismarck 5000. When questioned on this, Lenbach allegedly said that it had been a far greater pleasure to paint the Chancellor of Germany than a Jewish banker.

Ascher had been prepared for a cool and distant conversation. But Bleichröder dispensed with all formality and he suddenly struck Ascher as a warm and understanding person. To his amazement, his host, who usually maintained a certain reservation towards Jewish affairs, was extremely well informed. He knew about the dispute regarding the situation in Jerusalem that had been unleashed by their publication, as well as the motives of those in favour and those against.

'I give generously to the Alliance Israélite, and make no secret of it,' he said. 'The attention I attract on account of my involvement in the affairs of the Reich is quite enough for me. I don't wish to get entangled in the quarrels you have provoked. Provide the cartoonists with even more material? No thank you... I don't want to get drawn into pointless discussions. But if I understand correctly, it's not my name but my money you're interested in, isn't it?'

'Your name carries more weight than money,' Moritz Gottschalk hastened to remark politely.

'Only when I'm standing surety for loans,' smiled the banker. 'But why are we wasting time, bandying words about. I think very highly of the work of Professor Graetz and, of course, of your efforts as well. How much do you need?'

'Twenty thousand,' said Moritz Gottschalk.

'You shall have it, but on one condition only – the matter must be kept secret. I shall make the appropriate payment today. The money will be transferred to an account at the Rothschild bank in Frankfurt, and then passed on to the public charity that you have set up. I do not wish the gift to be traced back to me. The donation will be made anonymously.'

'I thank you with all my heart, Herr Baron,' said Ascher with emotion. Bleichröder nodded and got up. The three shook hands. A gleam of sunlight was reflected in Bleichröder's pupils. The banker took a pair of spectacles with dark lenses from the pocket of his frock coat and put them on in place of the pince-nez. Plucking up courage, Ascher said: 'We appear to be fellow sufferers.'

'What? You too?' asked Bleichröder in surprise and gave the servant a sign to leave them alone.

It transpired that the banker had developed glaucoma several years earlier. The doctors had not kept it from him that in time he would become totally blind. 'You see, gentlemen, there are some things that money cannot buy,' he said without rancour and asked Ascher: 'Have you consulted any doctors in Berlin?'

'I've been examined by Dr Evers.'

'I know him. An excellent doctor. There was a time when I was interested in only two things – finance and politics. Now there is a third subject – medicine. I know the best doctors in Prussia and Vienna. Shall I tell you a secret, Herr Levy? They cannot help me.'

'I am so sorry.'

'Do not pity me. Look after yourself. You and you alone. Sometimes I ask myself, what is better – to be healthy and poor, or rich and sick. I don't know the answer. But if we have to be ill, I suppose it is probably better to be able to afford the right doctors, isn't it?' Bleichröder patted him on the shoulder, as if they were old friends. 'What do you occupy yourself with, Herr Levy, apart from the timber trade?'

'At the moment, with the orphanage. My son has taken over the business, and I am very satisfied with the way he is running it. Apart from that, my one remaining small pleasure is the buying and selling of shares. Shares of the railway companies.'

'I believe in the future of the railways,' said Bleichröder. 'Especially now that they are going to be nationalized. The state will issue shares in the railways, and anyone who believes in the future of Prussia should also put trust in Prussia's credit. This is not advice from a banker; after all you are not one of my clients; simply regard it as a comment from a loyal citizen of Prussia. As a banker, I would tell you that there is absolutely no reason to restrict yourself to home ground. Finance and trade are international, and in the Orient, too, it is not simply a matter of charitable affairs. Baron Hirsch has donated millions for the Eastern European Jews. How do you think he earned them. Let me tell you: from the railways that he built and runs in the Orient. Yes, indeed, the Orient is still fertile ground for prudent investors. I have found out that Baron Hirsch is at this moment planning a railway line from Vienna to the Ottoman empire, all the way to Baghdad. Believe me, Herr Levy, this is a venture where the Bleichröder bank will not stay on the sidelines. My intuition has never let me down before. And the satisfaction. The satisfaction! In the end it is not just a matter of profit, but also of participation in political intrigue on a vast scale. You feel that you have influence. Do you know that feeling? No? You just don't know what you are missing. I follow what is happening, and see to my sorrow how England is taking over Egypt. First it was Disraeli who took charge of the Canal. Now Gladstone and the French are sending troops to Alexandria. The Austrians are setting their sights on the Balkan peninsula. The lions are fighting over the spoils. And where are we? Where is Germany? The railways lead us straight into the Ottoman empire. First come the railway tracks, then the German goods, and then political influence. An opportunity that we cannot afford to miss. What do you think, Herr Levy?'

Ascher was somewhat taken aback by Bleichröder's enthusiastic outburst. 'I agree with you entirely, my lord,' he said.

'If you are interested, get in touch with us. We shall save you a place on this train.'

'Thank you. But I am not sure whether I shall really take advantage of your generous offer.'

'Why not?' asked Bleichröder in surprise. 'Far bigger people than you have the pleasure of doing business with my bank.'

'That's just it, Herr Baron. We are a small firm, we're not made for the big, wide world. I would always feel like a hanger-on in the end compartment, like a blind passenger, to be left behind at any moment in some far-off station.'

'That is a matter of principle.' Bleichröder tapped him on the shoulder once more. 'But think about it – do you prefer to be leader of a pack of foxes, or the weakest in a pride of lions?'

The conversation was at an end.

Bleichröder did not carry out his plans in the Orient. Instead by a strange coincidence Ascher Levy's grandson was to be actively involved in laying the Hejaz railway track from Baghdad to Mecca. At the time of this conversation, however, that grandson was not yet six years old.

The 'anonymous' donation from Frankfurt enabled the orphanage to be opened. A year later the first twelve pupils were admitted, which filled Ascher Levy with satisfaction.

'I feel my life has had some purpose, after all,' he said to his son.

'I'm not wasting my life, either,' was Bernhard's response.

A Place in the Sun

Twice a week Polzin's traders and market women would gather on the market square, selling vegetables, fruit, and meat, and on these days the town would come alive. The small cobbled square was surrounded by two-storey houses. The largest of these was the Preussischer Hof, a hotel mainly for visitors who did not come for the medicinal springs and therefore did not stay at the Luisenbad or any of the other buildings that had sprung up to accommodate the spa guests. On the north side of the square was the town hall and middle-class houses faced the hotel. Local dignitaries and the wealthy had settled some time ago on the Bismarck Promenade and on the other streets near the Kurpark. The houses on the market square had reddish-orange, steep brick roofs in accordance with Prussian building regulations, and the flowers blooming in the window boxes were nearly all red and pink geraniums.

Long ago a fountain had been installed in the middle of the square, but by now every household had running water. The fountain taps were rusty and tarnished, and the whole structure looked like a cast-iron memorial. In other small provincial towns of Pomerania the citizens had supported the erection of imposing monuments. Their heads held proudly aloft, kings, princes, and knights sat in splendour, astride stone or bronze steeds. But the Polzin town council had so far not been in any hurry to spare money from the civic coffers for a similar project. Of all people, it had been Ascher Levy who had suggested putting up a bronze statue to commemorate the thirtieth anniversary of Friedrich Wilhelm IV's visit, in place of the redundant fountain. 'I am prepared,' he had informed the other members at a meeting of the town council, 'to meet half the cost.' The generous offer was turned down. In the name of the full assembly, Herr Bauch, the new mayor, had replied that they should be content with the memorial put up in 1872 in memory of the sons of the town who had fallen in the war against France. A statue for the King would have to be imposing and magnificent, as befitted a great ruler, but the depleted town funds did not permit high expenditure of that order. Ascher seemed satisfied with this reply. But Bernhard was convinced that the real reason for the rejection was that the donation would have come from the purse of a Jewish citizen.

So things remained as they were, with the one exception that a beer cellar opened in the market square, which soon became the workers' favourite haunt. Here the Polzin townspeople would discuss historical events over a jug of foaming beer. Members of the Levy family kept away. Whereas the local traders, employees and business people would escape from their homes for an hour to drown their troubles together at the pub, Bernhard would never seek their company if something worried him; quite the reverse. This unyielding, buttoned-up man would retreat into his own shell for an 'abstention hour', as Henriette was accustomed to say in her dry humorous way.

In October 1888 Ascher Levy celebrated his seventy-third birthday. He had finally retired officially from running the firm when he turned seventy. Nowadays only complicated financial problems continued to be brought to him. His vision had deteriorated even more and, as Bleichröder had predicted, no doctor, however good, was able to help him. Along with his diminishing sight, his physical health was also getting worse. Yet, he was finally coming to terms with the new situation, and now took part in the life around him with renewed interest. A ladder with three steps had been built for him at the Kollatz sawmill, which he used to help him mount his horse. Fanny's pleading that he should travel by carriage had fallen on deaf ears. 'Have you forgotten that I rode from Jerusalem to Tiberias on horseback, and nothing happened?' was Ascher's constant reply. 'And quite apart from that, the world looks far better on horseback.'

On his birthday the landscape was tinged with hues of orange, red, and brown. Rain had not yet set in, and the air was clear and dry. Ascher leaned back and reflected on his life's harvest. As soon as the guests had left, his son informed him of several new potentially profitable deals. The grandchildren were growing, developing, and studying diligently. Moreover, the political situation conveyed a feeling of stability and strength. The Reich had risen to be a major power. The political focus had moved from the periphery of Europe to the centre. The far-sighted Chancellor, Otto von Bismarck, had manoeuvred Great Britain, France, Austria, and even Russia into a situation where it was hard for them to ally themselves against the new Germany. The map of the Fatherland now included overseas colonies. Citizens of the Reich had long since become familiar with names such as Togo, Cameroon, and East Africa. It was gratifying to be part of this new reality. Ascher Levy meticulously saved every newspaper cutting that reported the process of the consolidation of the Reich. However, when Ascher was offered articles from the *Reichsglocke* or the *Kreuzzeitung*, two nationalist and anti-Semitic newspapers prophesying the downfall of Germany at the hands of the unholy alliance between plutocrats, politicians, and Jews, he simply waved them away. 'I'm afraid my eyesight is too weak, and my wife has no time to read to me just now.'

His daily routine followed an ordered pattern. On weekdays, he would go out for a ride on horseback, usually in the mornings, accompanied at Fanny's insistence by an employee who would ride in silence alongside him. On his return he would take breakfast with his wife: three boiled eggs, bread fried in vegetable fat with kosher goose-liver pâté, and coffee. As a rule, Bernhard would join them at the breakfast table and wonder in amazement at his father's hearty appetite. For his part, he would restrict himself to a cup of tea and a piece of dry toast with home-made strawberry jam.

These mealtimes were leisurely affairs, often lasting until midday. The conversation at table tended to range over family affairs, and in this peaceful atmosphere father and son only seldom touched on politics. When Bernhard finally turned to business matters, Ascher would drink a glass of mineral water mixed with milk to make it more digestible, as he maintained. He would cross the room several times, then lower himself into his armchair and wait for Fanny to collect the bundle of newspapers from the office and read the most important news items to him. He always wanted to be kept up to date, and subscribed not only to the *Polzin and Belgard Regional News* but also to the leading Berlin and Frankfurt papers. If Fanny attempted to skip reports that might have upset him, he could immediately tell from the change in her voice.

In the afternoons he would usually take a nap on the sofa, and at four-thirty on the dot, half an hour before the office closed, he would make his way downstairs to the ground floor for a quick word with the employees: 'Just so they don't forget who started the firm.' As he entered the office, they would all jump to their feet and greet him in unison, as if he were a high-ranking officer come to inspect his troops. They were all perfectly aware that Bernhard was now head of the firm, and that his signature alone was binding. He conducted negotiations with clients and received important visitors, and for some years now he had had the last word in all financial matters. But he had never made Ascher feel that he was excluded from the business. Bernhard held his father in high respect, and valued his experience and advice, even if he did not always share his opinion.

On Sunday evenings Bernhard would appear in his parents' drawing room. He had already suggested on numerous occasions that they should give up their − in his view − old-fashioned and unsuitable living quarters, and move into the modern and spacious ground-floor apartment in the house that he occupied with Henriette and the five children. But Ascher and Fanny would not hear of it.

'Good evening,' he said. 'I hope I'm not disturbing you.'

Fanny had made herself comfortable on the sofa in one corner, and was working at some lace-making. Ascher sat bent over a book bound in black. He had a magnifying glass in his left hand. On the round table stood a gas lamp, which gave out a bluish light.

'Good evening, Beri,' replied Ascher. 'D'you know what is curious about the prayer for *Rosh Chodesh*? The strange thing is that we ask God to make the new month come to us for good and for blessing, for joy and for gladness, for salvation and consolation, for support and for sustenance, for life and for peace. All those requests have a positive content, only two refer to negatives. Look at what is written here.' Ascher adjusted his thick-lensed glasses and read aloud: '"A life without sin or shame." That's what it says. Do you know why?'

Fanny got to her feet, went over to kiss her son on the cheek, turned up the light of the lamp, and went back to her corner.

'Well, Beri, do you know the answer?' Ascher insisted.

Bernhard nodded. Just like his father, he loved to interpret the meaning of the lines.

'Well, my son?'

'I think that the text is trying to make a clear distinction between good and evil. And in this way the values are given a concrete form.'

'Right. That is absolutely right. But your explanation is too simple.'

'Why make it complicated, if it can be put simply, Papa.'

'I have thought long and hard about the formulation of this prayer,' Ascher expanded his thoughts. 'It seems to me that this is far more than a simple matter of making a distinction between good and evil. I think that the origin rests on another fact – it may be possible to exist without peace and rich nourishment. But someone wishing to live as a free citizen in his country cannot live a life of sin and shame. I have read this prayer over and over again and thought back to times gone by, to my father and my grandfather, of blessed memory. How hard it was for them! They had to live in a hostile environment, which wanted to reject them. It wasn't easy to live as a Jew, without sin and shame, humiliation and submission. How admirable these people were, however pitiful they may have seemed. What enormous strength lay hidden in Rabbi Berisch's stooped back, what fire in his heart…' Ascher gave a sigh. 'A pity that he cannot see us here and now, equals among equals.'

'You're upsetting yourself, Papa.'

'I'm not ashamed to do so. In my view, this is one of the prayers that gives us encouragement.'

Bernhard smiled. 'Emotions, emotions. Not that I disparage them. Oh no, but...'

'No buts, my son.'

'Not everything is black or white; there are also shades of grey, aren't there?'

'I have never been one to compromise.'

'Nor I,' Bernhard hurriedly stressed. 'But there is a difference between compromise and flexibility.'

'These are terms from your commercial viewpoint, Beri. They do not apply in the spiritual sphere. I'm actually not sorry to have felt guilt on occasion, for it was just this that brought me nearer to morality. Without this feeling of imperfection, would I have been impelled to search for greater perfection? Bit by bit you realize that it takes an entire lifetime. Meanwhile, I have learned to devote my curiosity even to those things that are not of immediate use. I have understood that this is the only way to discover what is otherwise concealed and which one only benefits from later.'

'I accept your words like the revelation on Mount Sinai.' Bernhard sat down in an armchair facing his father and stretched out his legs, placing them on a dark green velvet-covered footstool.

Fanny put down the piece of lace she had been making in a corner of the sofa and stood up. 'I expect you're going to move on from philosophical reflections to more down-to-earth matters,' she said. 'You won't have any objections if I bring you some tea and apple strudel.' Before either of them could answer, she had already disappeared into the kitchen. Apple strudel made with flaky pastry was the entire family's favourite.

'Your mother is a wise woman,' said Ascher.

'And I am a wise child to have chosen the right parents,' joked Bernhard, adding, 'and moreover business partners.'

'What do you mean by that?' asked Ascher with suspicion.

'Does the name von Blanckenburg mean anything to you?'

'Certainly. A junker family from the Stargard region. I believe the eldest in the family, Karl Julius, died a few years ago. He moved to Erfurt, if my memory doesn't deceive me. When I was young, I worked for a Jewish trader who had business dealing with the Blanckenburgs. In your terms that was back in prehistoric times.'

'Yes, in the thirties, when you worked for Stärger.'

'I don't remember ever telling you ...'

'It wasn't you who told me, Papa. It was Herr von Blanckenburg. I mean his son, Eugen. The family now lives in Dresden, but he spends most of his time in east Prussia.'

'I don't understand ...'

'You will in a minute, Papa. Eugen studied chemistry in Heidelberg. He now lives in Königsberg, where he runs a factory producing red phosphorus and other chemicals. We met by chance at the bank in Stettin. Then we wrote to each other a few times. Now we're thinking of following up an idea. We intend to go into business together.'

'The Blanckenburgs and the Levys?'

'No, the Levys and the Blanckenburgs.'

'Go into business together?'

'Yes. Is there anything wrong with that?'

'I was only asking.' Ascher kept his gaze fixed on his son.

Bernhard drew a few papers from his pocket, studied them in detail and said: 'I think I've found a way of making our sawmills work more profitably. You remember the poplar and birch forests we bought two years ago?'

'Of course I remember. In my opinion that was a dubious investment. We paid a high price, and the timber is unsuitable for railway sleepers. Or for mines ...'

'That's quite true, Papa. But the timber is exactly right for producing matchsticks.'

'Matchsticks?' gasped Ascher. 'What on earth do we have to do with matchsticks?'

'Blanckenburg produces phosphorus and other explosive material. We can produce vast quantities of matchsticks. Two and two make four, don't they?'

'Your command of mathematics is impressive, Beri. But what does that have to do with the production of matchsticks?'

'The plan of action is very simple. The government retains its monopoly and also subjects the consumer price of the matchsticks to the principle of cost-plus. Our friend Bismarck has exacted from parliament a fixed tariff for timber. However, chemical products are not subject to price control. Let's assume that we set up a joint-stock company for the manufacture of matchsticks. The company would not be registered in our name. It would obtain the chemicals from Herr Blanckenburg in East Prussia, and pay rather more than the usual market price. This would neither be dishonest nor a crime. But it would be a means of artificially pushing up the production costs. As a result we could permit ourselves to fix a higher price for the consumer, keeping to the principle of cost-plus. An appropriate contract with the government would bring us alongside the royal monopoly. Are you listening, Papa?'

'I'm all ears.'

'Sounds good, doesn't it? I've made enquiries as to what equipment we need. The Swedes have an excellent machine for making matchsticks. A highly lucrative investment.'

'But what guarantee do we have of getting a contract with the royal monopoly?'

'The Blanckenburgs have connections in Berlin.'

Ascher seemed unsatisfied. 'We would have a huge wastage in the production of the matches. The lion's share of the profit would go to the partner.'

'I've also taken that into consideration, Papa. You're absolutely right as far as the wood shavings are concerned. We would have about fifty per cent waste. But we wouldn't be selling it at a relatively low price to cellulose producers. The Behrend brothers will have to find other suppliers. We would use the refuse to fire the boilers, so that we should have a cost-effective fuel to operate the sawmills. I've discussed this with Kutschke, the engineer at Kollatz. He thinks it's an excellent idea.'

'If you carry on like this, you'll end up by inventing a perpetual motion machine.'

Bernhard laughed, but then became serious. 'Admittedly, the arrangement would have to be confidential, to ensure our share of the profit. But to tell the truth, Papa, I'm looking much further ahead. Why shouldn't we rid ourselves of dependence on the

Blanckenburgs? Given time, we would have gained the experience to set up a rival chemical company. Not in east Prussia, but
here, near to the sawmills. That would save on transportation and
dominate all the areas of production. Then we would be able to
say to Herr Blanckenburg: "Terribly sorry, but..."'

'I don't like the sound of it, Beri. Have you forgotten what I
was just saying about sin and shame?'

'Papa,' Bernhard straightened up and raised his voice slightly.
'It's not as if I'm going to pull a fast one on my partner. I don't
cheat and I don't have a trump hidden up my sleeve. This is all
above board, and let the best man win. It has nothing to do with
sin and shame.'

The door opened and Fanny entered with a tray. 'I hope you've
finished,' she said and began cutting the strudel.

The two men fell silent. Ascher stared into his teacup. Then
he looked up, his brow furrowed as he gazed at his son. Strange,
how things turn out, he brooded. There sat Beri, his oldest and
most beloved son, and yet all the same, he was something of a
mystery to him. His own flesh and blood, but cast in an utterly
different mould. He felt a sudden urge to take Bernhard's hand in
his own, to restore intimacy between them. But he did not do so.
Fanny, yes, Fanny would have understood the impulse, but Beri?
He was no longer a child. A mature man of forty-three sat facing
him, with a neat, blond moustache and beard. Most members of
the Levy family were blond and blue-eyed, in defiance of anti-
Semitic ethnographers, who asserted that Jewish features were
totally different. Ever since the birth of Beri, Ascher had had the
deepest love for him, yet he had never slackened his hold on him,
and had never given in to him as a child. He had never openly
showed his love, had never embraced him or given his feelings
free rein. When the essential character of his son, Julius, revealed
itself, it became clear to Ascher that it would be Bernhard who
would continue in his footsteps. And now he could not reconcile
Bernhard's proposal to his own outlook on life. Perhaps it wasn't
really a question of fraud, perhaps this was the way that business
was done these days, and yet – no, he simply could not approve of
this procedure. He muttered something to himself.

Fanny asked him in concern: 'Did you say something? Are you all right?'

'Oh, yes, my dearest. I'm all right.'

On 16 August 1889 the contract with Eugen von Blanckenburg was signed in the chambers of Rengler, the Stettin notary, who acted on behalf of the major landowners. His partner met his obligations, and scarcely two months passed before the New Prussian Timber Company received all the necessary certification from the royal monopoly. They could go into production. The Swedish equipment arrived at the beginning of December, and was immediately installed in the Köslin sawmill. 'We shall light the candles on the Christmas tree with matches of our own production,' declared von Blanckenburg happily. Bernhard agreed and did not forget to send his partner a tree cut from his own forests.

The new collaboration took time to work out, but the rest of the family's business continued as usual. The firm's finances were on solid ground, and whereas other enterprises found themselves in difficulties, the Levys were spared any upheavals. 'We are like Noah's Ark, that did not fear the flood,' Bernhard had once said, to which Ascher had replied in characteristic fashion, 'It wasn't Noah's wisdom that saved the people and the animals, but the will of God.'

The weaker Ascher's eyesight became, the more he tended to withdraw into his own world, although he did not sever all connections with the world outside.

Above all, where *Eretz Israel* was concerned he was unwavering. Now that Ascher was no longer active in the firm, he spent at least one month a year at Bad Kissingen, where he met up with Heinrich Graetz and Moritz Gottschalk. Sometimes Gerson Bleichröder joined them as well. Bleichröder, who had been so concerned with his reputation and social position, had opened up to Ascher, of all people. Their disability had drawn them together, and a curious relationship developed between the great banker and the provincial merchant, even if it could hardly be described as true friendship.

Bleichröder spoke to Ascher about being widowed (his wife

Emma had died in 1881) and about his disappointment at the way his children had turned out. His efforts to secure his younger son, James, the rank of officer had at least succeeded. As a result of friends putting in a word on his behalf at the royal court, his older son had been made an officer in the cavalry. But his associating with women of bad reputation had led to a dishonourable discharge. Else, his one adored daughter, had first married Baron Bernhard von Uechtritz, but despite a dowry of 2.5 million marks, the marriage soon ended in divorce. Two years later Else had married again, this time in Berlin's Church of the Holy Trinity. For a tradition-conscious Jew like Bleichröder, this had been a severe blow.

But Ascher was less concerned with the sorrows of the banker than with the fact that the Jerusalem orphanage project was still hanging by a thread. Two teachers, who had been sent to Palestine from Germany, had had a ban imposed on them by leaders of the Orthodox community, and had had to return home. It proved virtually impossible to find replacements. Both camps, the Orthodox as well as the advocates of progressive thinking, had entrenched themselves, and there seemed to be no way out of this painful dispute. The hopes of the three authors of the memorandum, which was to effect a change in the distribution of charitable donations, had been dashed. Admittedly the network of schools built up in the Holy Land in recent years by the Alliance Israélite represented a glimmer of hope, but there was a snag. As tuition in these schools was in French, and French was their prevailing culture, the French consulate had extended its patronage to these schools. Ascher Levy wanted a school that focused on the German language and Prussian culture. France's official policy in Muslim countries was based on an overtly anti-Semitic attitude, and the expansion of French influence angered Ascher Levy every bit as much as the intransigence of his opponents.

The so-called Jewish question also continued to occupy Europe and the Reich. The past decade had plainly demonstrated that the legal introduction of equal rights for the Jews had opened the floodgates. Even if it was only a very narrow upper level of

Jewish society that had managed to advance their careers in economic and cultural fields, in banking and financial affairs, in the press and in academic circles, these were the very areas that especially attracted public notice. With the economic crisis that followed the establishment of the Reich, it was the Jewish bankers who were pilloried by an infuriated public. Moreover the anti-Semites not only targeted those Jews who were wealthy, but also attacked the Jewish socialists, who supported workers' rights.

At Bad Kissingen along the spa promenade, Heinrich Graetz, the Jew, and Heinrich von Treitschke, the anti-Semite, would politely raise their top hats when they passed each other. But in the political arena, customs were rather different. Bismarck was caught in the crossfire of his critics, for there were many who associated the Chancellor's policies with the social advancement of certain Jewish circles. In the wake of the social upheaval accompanying the establishment of the Reich and its advancing industrialization, a dangerous alliance developed between the conservative powers and the embittered losers. At the beginning of the eighties, anti-Semitic riots broke out in Neustettin, just a few kilometres away from the residence of the Bismarck family. There were some who asserted that this geographical proximity was no coincidence. The local synagogue was destroyed by fire. A rumour was put about that the Jews had started the fire themselves, in order to collect a hefty amount from the insurance. Had it not been for intervention on the part of Bismarck, similar acts of violence might have broken out throughout the Reich. Bismarck regarded these outbreaks as the powers of darkness attacking what in his eyes were the holiest of all values – property and possessions. In reaction to the events at Neustettin his government issued a prohibition on anti-Semitic assemblies and speeches in Pomerania and West Prussia.

As the rabble went on the rampage through the countryside armed with knives, pitchforks, and clubs, in the cities respected individuals emerged in the political arena to lend the anti-Semitic agitations a political flavour. One of these was a regular visitor to Bad Kissingen – Professor Heinrich von Treitschke, originally a national liberal, but later an independent member of the

Reichstag and one of the leading historians at the University of Berlin. It was he who coined the phrase: 'The Jews are our misfortune.' His journalistic activities made anti-Semitism as acceptable in intellectual circles as the writings of Richard Wagner had done, who up to the time of his death in 1883 had demanded that 'German society should be cleansed of the Jewish plague'. When in 1887 Konrad Hilton, the hotelier, refused to accept a Jewish banker by the name of Josef Seligmann as a guest in his Hotel Grand Union in the United States town of Saratoga, there was rejoicing by like-minded Germans, saying, 'You see? We're not the only ones...'

Yet compared with the pogroms in Eastern Europe, the German form of anti-Semitism appeared somewhat harmless. Thousands of refugees were fleeing from the Tsarist empire and the Russian-occupied territories in search of a safe haven in the west. In 1884 *Chovevei Zion* societies were springing up in Russia. This movement pursued the notion that the people of Israel dispersed in the Diaspora should return to settle in their Biblical homeland. The *Chovevei Zion* were chiefly active in Russia, but were spreading to Central and Western Europe, the United States, and Australia. They were committed not only to the consolidation of existing settlements, but also to the setting up of new settlements in *Eretz Israel*, and they fought for national recognition and for the revival of the Hebrew language.

The refugees from the Tsarist empire, disparagingly referred to as *Ostjuden* (eastern Jews) by the German Jews, terrified the Jewish bourgeoisie of the German Reich. Both the well established and those aspiring to such a state were disturbed by these poor people, who stood out because of their alien appearance. They knew that German society's rejection of these refugees could well rebound on them; after all, to anti-Semites all Jews are alike, but the usual prejudices would be even more likely to attach to these conspicuously foreign-looking Eastern Europeans. Concern about the immigrants prompted Heinrich Graetz and his two friends, Moritz Gottschalk and Ascher Levy, to support the *Chovevei Zion* movement. In their view the movement's efforts were beneficial on two important counts. On the one hand, no one in the Reich would have to deal with the festering problem of this undesirable group of people, and on the other, these immigrants would swell the productive element in the Jewish community of the Holy Land.

But within a few months Heinrich Graetz distanced himself from the agenda of the *Chovevei Zion*. Ascher and Moritz Gottschalk immediately followed suit. In the end, Ascher Levy withdrew his support from the movement because the idea of national rebirth ran contrary to his own outlook. This Jewish nationalism undermined the bridge he had built between his Judaism and his Prussian nationality. His Judaism excluded the concept of nationalism, and consequently spared him the dilemma of dual loyalty and the additional insistent question – 'Ascher Levy, son of Jäckel, who in fact are you? Are you German first, and Jew second? Or are you first and foremost a Jew, and only then a German?' This, God forbid, would inevitably have meant having to make a clear and complete separation between the two. 'We must hold fast to what we really believe in,' wrote Ascher Levy to Graetz. 'We simply cannot support any suicidal action. My conscience is clear, and that is the main thing. These new movements are good for those fleeing from the terrors of Eastern European rule, but they are in direct opposition to the guiding principles of German Jewry. What we need in our fatherland is not a national solution, but absolute equal rights.'

The fact that Ascher Levy withdrew his support from the *Chovevei Zion* obviously in no way changed the new realities, and the spectre of nationalist Zionism – with the concrete aim of creating a Jewish state – could no longer be banished. In Berlin the Young Israel Society soon came into existence, led not by an activist from Russia, but by a German Jewish student by the name of Heinrich Loewe. But the real slap in the face for Ascher came on a grey winter's day at the end of January 1896, less than a year before his death. At Fanny's insistence Ascher now hardly ever left the well-heated house. His doctors had warned that just the slightest chill could seriously endanger his frail health. 'Don't forget you are eighty-one,' Bernhard was constantly reminding him. When the frost had made the streams and the lake in the

Polzin park freeze over, and the cold had penetrated his bones to the marrow, his family no longer needed to beg him to stay indoors. He preferred to make himself comfortable in his armchair, a woollen rug over his legs, and would frequently nod off. On this particular occasion a loud argument roused him from his slumber. He recognized the voices of his wife and his son. The door flew open and his son stormed in. His cheeks were aflame from agitation and the severe cold.

'I begged him not to disturb you now,' Fanny excused herself.

'I simply couldn't wait, Papa. I got here as quickly as I could...'

'More haste, less speed,' said his father. 'What's happened?'

'Does the name Theodor Herzl mean anything to you, Papa?'

'Certainly it does. He's the crazy journalist from Vienna. Kompert has told me about him in his letters. In Vienna they avoid him like the plague.'

'And rightly so, Papa. The man will be our undoing.'

'Now what has he been up to?'

'Been up to is putting it mildly. He has... but why should I be the one to tell you? We've had an express letter from Moritz. Read it for yourself.' Bernhard handed his father a large envelope.

'Where is my magnifying glass?'

Fanny handed it to him. Bernhard wanted to say something more, but Ascher stopped him with an impatient gesture. He buried himself in the letter. In it his cousin informed him of the contents of a pamphlet written by Theodor Herzl entitled 'The Jewish State – a modern attempt to solve the Jewish question'. Moritz Gottschalk wrote:

The man has written some poor pieces in the past, but what he now suggests in all seriousness strikes me as more dreadful than any of his previous work. Much to my distress it is in no way encouraging. His suggestion of a Jewish state has come like a bolt out of the blue here. You will probably dismiss the idea with a shrug of your shoulders – I know those shoulder shrugs of yours. But the matter is far too serious to leave it at that. Herzl has drawn up a plan to resettle our co-religionists in *Eretz Israel* and to this end has made contact with a variety of personalities all over Europe. It seems that he does not understand the extent of this madness and its almost inevitable consequences. A Jewish state! Can you imagine how Vienna and Berlin will react? It amounts to pouring oil on the fire of the anti-Semites and the enemies of emancipation. One hundred years of persistent effort could be lost at a stroke!

We have investigated the affair, and must admit that Herr Herzl has put together a detailed work on the subject which he has submitted for publication to a number of the major publishing houses. Luckily for us, all of them turned it down in disgust, and so long as he does not find a publisher among the ranks of our enemies, he has no chance of spreading his doctrine of salvation. This has apparently made him decide to publish just an abstract of his pearls of wisdom, and the *Jewish Chronicle* in London has agreed for unfathomable reasons to serve as his platform. But who can guarantee that this entrée won't be followed by a main course? As ever, I considered it right to let you have the translation of this article right away, so that you can acquaint yourself with the affair and, if you wish, respond. I have found out that the *Allgemeine Zeitung* is prepared to publish readers' letters. However, a number of our friends are of the opinion that it is best to keep absolutely silent on the matter. What do you think? ...

Ascher let the letter drop from his hand. The expression on his face registered grave anxiety. Bernhard waited for him to react, but when his father had remained silent for some time, he could not bear it any longer, and burst out: 'Can you make any sense of this, Papa?'

'It's the beginning of a *danse macabre*.'

Ascher heaved a sigh. 'Theodore Herzl...Kompert told me that he eats pork, rides on *Shabbat*, and even puts up a tree for his children at Christmas. And this man of all people is proposing the foundation of a Jewish state!'

'A foolish idea.'

'The idea as such is not at all important. Perhaps it isn't even that stupid. After all, don't we support the immigration of

Eastern European Jews to Palestine? But from now on we shall be told that our fatherland is Palestine. Wagner will rise up out of his grave and compose an opera about the Jews of the Reich who have found their place at last.'

Moritz Gottschalk had hoped that Herzl's proposal could just be hushed up. German citizens of the Mosaic persuasion, their organizations, and their newspapers exerted the full weight of their influence to remove national Zionism from the agenda. But all their efforts came to nothing. Theodor Herzl's proposal grew from a snowball to an avalanche, and nothing could halt it. On 29 August 1897, a fine summer's day, the first Zionist Congress met in the Swiss city of Basel. Two hundred and eight delegates from sixteen countries filled the chamber of the city casino, to give support to the 'foolish idea' and translate it into action. When Kaiser Wilhelm II visited the Holy Land in November 1898, he received the founders and spokesmen of national Zionism for talks in his camp, right outside the city walls of Jerusalem. Before the visit he had already promised to present the Zionist movement in a favourable light to the Turkish Sultan, Abdul Hamid II, and he raised hopes for a Protectorate of the German Reich. However, influenced by his Foreign Minister Bernhard von Bülow, who allied himself with Jewish bankers, intellectuals, and journalists in vehemently rejecting the notion of a Jewish state, he did not live up to his promise and ceased to support the proposal. Nonetheless history took its course. Half a century on, the General Assembly of the United Nations voted for the establishment of the State of Israel. Herzl acquired the unofficial title of 'State Visionary' and every Jewish child knows about him today. Ascher Levy was spared the burden of these experiences. On 3 March 1897, a Wednesday, at about seven in the evening, he passed away.

Fanny was just preparing supper. The employees had already left. Bernhard locked the downstairs offices and left in turn. The evening hush descended over the house in the Brunnenstrasse. Ascher had nodded off in his armchair. As the wall clock struck the hour, Fanny entered the drawing room with a tray.

'I've made you roast meat with sauerkraut, just as you asked,' she said and set the dishes down on the table. Ascher did not reply. She went across to him, to wake him. Recently he had been falling asleep as soon as he sat down for a rest. But this time his arm swung loosely over the arm of the chair when she gently touched him. A shudder of apprehension ran through her. Fanny felt his forehead, then fell to her knees beside him and brushed her lips across his hand. It was cold. Fanny knew immediately what had happened. Her mind went strangely blank. Finally she stood up and very softly said to herself, 'I always knew this was bound to happen.'

Dr Willi Stutz was Polzin's only doctor. The portly fifty-year-old bachelor had worked for years as a ship's doctor, and had reached an advanced age before deciding to settle down in one place. His family owned a small estate in the neighbourhood of Polzin, which had probably determined his choice of this sleepy little town in Pomerania. Gossips wagged their tongues, telling dubious tales about him, chiefly about the many women he had allegedly seduced and abandoned all over the world. But when it came down to it, no one really knew anything about his past. He himself never commented, either to confirm or deny the rumours, which amused him hugely. He was a pleasant man by nature who quickly made friends with people, and his work as a doctor assured him a good livelihood.

That evening, Dr Stutz was sitting as usual in the beer cellar in the market square. When he was called to the Levys, he asked the servant who came to fetch him, 'What's the hurry? I know old man Levy. He's like a machine that sometimes creaks, but never breaks down entirely.' But when he arrived at the house in the Brunnenstrasse, he immediately realized that this time things were different. 'I am very sorry, Frau Levy. No medicine in the world can help him now.'

Fanny, Bernhard, and Henriette stood there as if turned to stone. The ticking of the clock was the only sound in the room. At last Bernhard broke the silence and in his customary serious way, he asked in a matter-of-fact voice: 'Do you know the cause of death, Doctor?'

'That's easy,' replied Dr Stutz. 'The good Lord has called him away.'

The emotion that had choked Fanny's throat only now gave way, and she broke out into loud weeping. Henriette attempted to comfort her. Dr Stutz closed his bag, took his hat, and said to Bernhard, 'As there is nothing more I can do to help now, I shall leave. Please come to my surgery tomorrow, and I shall then make out the death certificate. The fee is two marks fifty pfennig.'

After the *Shiva*, all the members of the family assembled for the reading of the will. Distant cousins who had never kept in close contact with the deceased, and aunts whose existence Fanny had completely forgotten, all arrived. Naturally, Julius also appeared. The last time he had seen his parents was five years earlier. At the time he had arranged a celebration for them in Danzig on the occasion of their golden wedding anniversary. Now he arrived by train by way of Kolberg with his eighteen-year-old daughter, and his two grown-up sons, twenty-one-year-old Rudolf, and Paul, who was a year younger.

Bernhard sat down at the head of the table. To his right sat Fanny. On his other side was a man whom none of the guests had ever seen before. 'My father drew up a will and instructed me to read it when the time came,' said Bernhard and placed a large sealed packet in front of him. 'I believe it is worth mentioning that the date on which we are gathered here is the seventh day of the month Adar, the date on which our teacher Moses was born and died. This date lends our assembly a significance that far exceeds the customary reading of a will. I have asked notary Stolpe from Stettin to be here, as he has been responsible for the family's affairs for many years. His presence lends this family gathering an official character.'

The grey-haired notary nodded, and Bernhard broke open the seal of the envelope. In a dry, monotonous tone he read aloud his father's testament:

We must never forget where we come from and in which direction we should look. Our life merely represents one link in the eternal chain of Judaism, and even when our life ends, we continue to exist as if nothing had happened to us. Herein lies the secret of Judaism, perhaps even the secret of all humanity.

It is for this reason that I do not wish my dear ones to mourn my death. I hope to appear before the Supreme Judge and render account for my deeds, while my soul is pure of many of the sins that often occur in our society. To this end it is important for me to know that after my death the firm will continue to be run along the same lines as it has been since it was established, and that my successor will always put honesty before prosperity, just as profit must be placed ahead of expenditure.

Ascher left the firm, together with all the various financial investments and items of property, to Bernhard. Fanny inherited the house in the Brunnenstrasse. Bernhard was obliged to secure a good income from the finances of the firm for Fanny until the day of her death. The Association for the Education of Jewish Orphans in Palestine received 10,000 marks, but only on condition that the money was not used to further Zionist aims, but solely for educational purposes. To his son Julius he left the sum of 75,000 marks, to be paid in equal amounts over three years. Ascher had further stipulated where this money was to come from. 'Before the firm is transferred to my eldest son, Bernhard, the partnership with Eugen, Baron von Blanckenburg is to be dissolved whereby a just, lawful and equal division of the ownership of the matchstick factory must be guaranteed.' Each of his five grandchildren from Bernhard and Henriette's marriage was left 5,000 marks. One thousand Marks went to the municipal scholarship funds, and further small amounts to distant relatives.

The guests departed in the evening. Bernhard accompanied them to the station. It was only a few years since Polzin had been linked to other towns in Pomerania. Anyone travelling to Stettin, Danzig, or Berlin still had to change, but connection to the national network made life a lot easier for the townspeople and had given Ascher great pleasure.

Right up to the end he had been obsessed with the railways, even after he had ceased to invest in them. When Fanny went through his papers after his death, she was astonished to find an old bundle of shares in the Strousberg company.

Strousberg, a baptized Jew from East Prussia, had made a fortune from the railways, and only one of his major projects had turned out to be a complete failure. In the sixties he had set up a company and issued shares in order to acquire the concession to put new railway lines in operation in Rumania. Strousberg brought in the capital. In return the Rumanian government had committed itself to pay out a regular dividend of seven per cent. Technical and bureaucratic hurdles caused endless delays in putting the line into operation, so that the share price fell to half its initial value. The shareholders, mostly small investors from Silesia, Berlin, and Munich, felt they had been swindled. When the Rumanians finally announced that they were unable to meet the guarantees issued for the dividend distribution, the value of the shares went into free fall.

Ascher Levy had also bought these shares, on the advice of Gerson Bleichröder. 'This is no investment, this is a mitzvah,' had been the banker's encouragement at the time. Rumanian Jews were suffering from the discriminatory policies of the government. Bleichröder had thought that in return for assistance in putting the line into operation, the politicians responsible would moderate their anti-Semitism. The hope was soon shattered. As mentioned, the Rumanians refused to make the payments owing to the shareholders. Even when in May 1878 Germany terminated the existing trade agreement in order to put pressure on the state – German Jews living in Rumania were also affected by the discrimination – the Rumanians still did not give way. At the time of Ascher Levy's death the Strousberg shares were not worth the paper on which they were printed. Ascher had lost about 5,000 marks at the time. He had not spoken of this to a single soul. Even Bernhard did not know about it.

When Fanny found the share certificates, a thoughtful smile flitted across her face. It was really not like him, she thought to herself, to stuff these worthless shares right at the bottom of a drawer, as if he was trying to hide his failure. She tore the shares into shreds and threw them into the waste-paper basket.

Bernhard and his brother Julius stood on the railway platform. The train going south was late. Until the reading of Ascher's will, contact between the brothers had amounted to no more than occasional correspondence. They only met every few years on family occasions, and even then they found little in common to talk about. Now their father's death had brought them closer together.

Julius placed an arm around Bernhard's shoulder and sighed: 'I had the strangest feeling as I was standing by his grave today. It was as if a chapter has been closed, an era has come to an end, and we are moving from one world to another.'

'The Levys will never change,' replied Bernhard.

'I know. And yet ... The good old days are always in the past.'

'There are also good times ahead.'

'D'you know what I envy about you?'

Bernhard threw his brother a searching glance.

'I envy you your self-assurance, Beri, your calmness. I am always worried. It always seems to me as if tomorrow has unpleasant surprises in store. I worry about the future of my children and of my business. Where do you find this absolute certainty that everything you do is right and good, appropriate and just and ...'

'A defendant is innocent until proved guilty, isn't that so?'

Julius changed the subject. 'You will look after Mama, won't you?'

'Do you doubt it?'

'No, no. I just wanted to mention it.'

'Don't waste your breath,' Bernhard advised him. Julius detected his brother's somewhat superior tone, but let it go at that.

Bernhard's gaze wandered along the platform. Beside an iron column stood his daughter Ida with his nephew Paul, who was stockily built and with a hint of stoutness to come. He was wearing a broad-brimmed hat. Ida had shot up, and was slender and graceful. She had only just turned fourteen, but already displayed feminine charm. Julius followed his brother's gaze.

'Paul finishes his engineering studies in a year's time,' he said lightly.

'Ida attends a boarding school in Berlin. She is still very young,' he added, equally casually, and went on to ask, 'What is Paul going to specialize in?'

'Railway line construction.'

'That would have pleased our father, blessed be his memory.'

'He knew about it. If truth be told, it was actually his express wish. When I left home, he gave me my share of the firm in cash. When Paul finished high school, he promised me he would leave me a handsome sum if I guided Paul's choice of profession in this direction.'

Bernhard said nothing. He had always known that his father had constantly had a hand in all family affairs. But he was surprised to learn that his father had had some secrets that he had not known about. For an instant he was offended. He was about to say something, but at the last moment he held back.

His nephew Rudolf came hurrying towards them, set two suitcases down on the platform and gasped for breath.

'We would have left without you, if the train hadn't been late.'

'I do apologize.'

Julius turned to his brother. 'He's always late and permanently impatient – quite unlike the rest of the Levys.'

'I believe there are two factors involved,' was Bernhard's telling reply. 'In my opinion nature and nurture are what make up a person.'

Rudolf clasped his hands behind his back and slowly made his way over to the little station building. He stood in front of the railway timetable, tracing his finger across the columns of figures. Unlike Paul, he was tall and slim, and very handsome.

'How old is he?'

'Twenty-one.'

'I've heard that he is keen on painting.'

'Keen?' grinned Julius. 'Colours, landscapes, and shapes are all that he sees. I wanted him to study at university like Paul, but it was like talking to a brick wall. He left high school without taking the final exams. He may appear gentle and fragile, but he is a stubborn boy who has always known how to get his own way. Meanwhile we have reached a compromise. He is apprenticed to a cabinetmaker. It's a craft that involves creativity, and he will still be able to earn a living from it.'

'It all depends on the parents, Juli.'

'Well, we believe that a child has the right to choose his own path.'

'Even if it's a crooked path?'

'That's a relative term, Beri. In the end, it's the destination that counts, not the means of getting there.'

'I hope you see to it that they marry Jews, according to the family tradition.'

Julius said nothing. Rudolf, who was still standing in front of the timetable, had his back to his father. In a low voice Julius said, 'Marriage doesn't interest him, Beri.'

'Yes, yes, I understand – these artists. The bohemian life. But he will change his mind. That comes with age.'

'You don't understand, Beri.' Julius's face clouded over. 'He ... how shall I put it ... he's not attracted to women.'

'Don't worry. Some young people are late developers.'

'I'm afraid that in this case that doesn't apply.'

Only now did Bernhard understand what his brother was trying to tell him. 'Surely you don't mean ...'

Julius nodded. 'Yes, Beri. There are some things that even the strictest parents can't control. Nature is stronger than we are.'

'The train's coming,' called Paul and reached for the suitcases.

In less than a minute the train had arrived at the station. There was no time to continue the conversation. The brothers shook hands.

'From now on we'll definitely keep in touch,' Bernhard promised.

'Definitely,' replied Julius as he got into a second-class carriage. The Levy family never travelled first class. Paul found an empty compartment. The stationmaster waved a little red flag. The guard gave a blast on his whistle, and the train began to move. Paul removed his hat and brandished it in the air. Ida waved a white-gloved hand. Suddenly Paul's hat slipped from his hand, fell, and rolled on to the platform. Paul's disconcerted expression made Ida burst out into peals of childish laughter, which mingled with the hiss of the locomotive. The station filled with a dense cloud of smoke, and the rear lights of the last wagon looked like two red eyes, which gradually disappeared in a black cloud.

'Let's go home,' said Bernhard and took his daughter by the hand. The stationmaster bent down to pick up the hat and waved it at them. But Bernhard took no notice of the official and strode out of the station. The stationmaster called out after them comfortingly, 'Never mind, Miss Ida! You'll meet again.'

Ida was the youngest of the five children, and Bernhard still treated her like the baby of the family. A year after she was born, it transpired that Henriette could not have any more children. Bernhard sent her to the best gynaecologists in Stettin and Berlin. She underwent treatment in a number of health resorts, but all to no effect.

Lina was the oldest daughter. After her came the three sons – Ernst, Siegfried, and Leo. Ernst was for 'earnest', Siegfried for 'victory' (as in *sieg*), and Leo for 'lion'. Bernhard's planning in both his business and his family life was highly meticulous. He considered himself fortunate in having a wife like Henriette, for she too took the view that life was far too important to leave things to chance. Both parents had planned their children's future from the time they were still playing with dolls and tin soldiers. The individual desires of the children and their personal inclinations simply did not enter the equation.

Ernst was sent to Berlin to study law at the university. Bernhard expected him to be the first representative of the house of Levy who would work in a Prussian institution. Maybe he would be a privy councillor in a ministry, possibly even ending up as a judge, thereby taking advantage of opportunities now open to Jews in the new Reich, without having to convert to Christianity. Bernhard was concerned to match the material status of the family with public recognition. But being a prudent and rational person, he had also built in a fall-back position. 'Even if for some reason he doesn't attain the right position, he will always be able to earn his living as a lawyer,' he told Henriette.

Siegfried was born on 10 June 1875. He developed into someone who knew how to enjoy life. But his father saw him as his predestined successor. Leo, too, who was more serious-minded than Siegfried and would have been inclined to follow some form of study, was destined to enter the business. The boys had been prepared for this role from a very early age. Whereas other children read fairy tales, they would sit facing their father on narrow, uncomfortable chairs, listening to him tell of the magic of the business world.

Siegfried had no liking for these 'information evenings' and would drift off into his own dream world. Leo, on the other hand, soaked up his father's every word like a sponge. The business terms of the financial sphere soon became a fixed part of his childhood vocabulary, and besides learning his tables he also learned bookkeeping. By the time he had grown up he was not only able to distinguish between sacred and secular, but also between profit and loss.

At times Henriette distanced herself from her husband's methods, although essentially she too favoured a strict upbringing. On those occasions she would say, 'You're robbing them of their childhood.' Then Bernhard would take the wind out of her sails by agreeing: 'You're right, you're absolutely right,' while beaming with delight, because Leo was a creature after his own heart and was destined to follow in his footsteps.

When Leo had to shave for the first time, Bernhard judged the boy old enough to step into the family business. Siegfried, on the other hand, still didn't know his way around the business at the age of twenty-four. For this reason Bernhard decided in April 1899 to send him to England to continue his training with the firm of Linck Moeller & Co. at 144 Leadenhall Street in London. Linck Moeller specialized in the timber trade, and its structure closely resembled that of the Levy firm in Polzin. The business connection between the two dated back to the days when Ascher Levy had refused to do business with France. At that time the Levys had turned to England. Linck Moeller had no objection to taking Siegfried on for a time in order to expand his horizon as a businessman. However, Bernhard clearly did not rely on the English partners alone, and wrote Siegfried detailed daily letters packed with advice and instructions. He went so far as to suggest that Siegfried should buy himself an inch ruler. He wanted Siegfried to sound out the market, as his father had read in one of the papers that there was a shortage of wood for pit props in England, a commodity that the family firm could supply in unlimited quantities: 'And be sure to enquire what the customs duty would be on this kind of trade.' Moreover, Bernhard drummed it into his son that he was a German subject, and that he should not forget for an instant that he would be regarded as a representative and an example, 'for the English will judge us all by your behaviour'. And of course he insisted that his pleasure-loving son observe a Jewish way of life. He was to go to pray at synagogue, to draw strength from the values of his religion, to avoid non-kosher food, and to keep the *Shabbat*. 'I know that this is not easy to do if you are living among goyim, but he who turns away from the Torah and tradition, loses himself and ends up by striding towards a void.'

But the twenty-four-year-old knew all too well where he was heading. The English capital fascinated the young man from the Pomeranian provinces. He soon found his way from the gloomy offices in Leadenhall Street to the more lively haunts of London, which naturally enough took its toll on his work. The directors of the firm refrained from complaining to Bernhard. When, six months later in October 1899, the time came for Siegried to return to Polzin, Linck Moeller sent a briefly worded testimonial: 'Mr Siegfried Levy entered our employment at the end of April 1899, and leaves us now to return home. His main task was correspondence, and he discharged his duties satisfactorily.'

This was anything but an enthusiastic reference, and Bernhard knew only too well what the few lines indicated.

'It would appear that you hardly excelled at your work,' observed Bernhard drily after he had read the report.

'But I didn't disgrace you, either,' Siegfried burst out. 'I kept *Shabbat*, I ate kosher, I behaved as a citizen of the Reich should, and I even bought an inch ruler.'

'And you are just as impudent as ever.'

'I am consistent by nature, Papa. Isn't that worth something in your eyes?'

'I expect you would like to take one or two days' rest.'

'No, Papa. I am ready to return to work whenever you wish.'

'Right. First go and say hallo to your mother. Then come to the office. Leo will tell you what there is to do.'

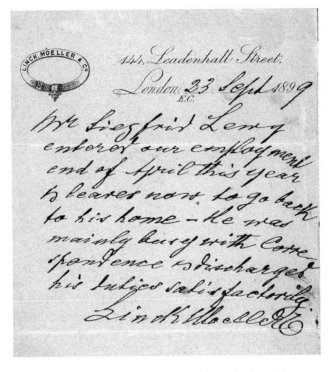

Testimonial of Siegfried's employment with Linck Moeller & Co.,
September, 1899.

'As you wish, Papa,' said Siegfried in a sudden rush of obedi-
ence. He took his things and left the office. Bernhard's searching
gaze followed him to the door. Siegfried could feel it like a
painful stab in the back.

Apart from this cool reception, a pleasant surprise awaited him
in Polzin. During his absence his father had acquired some rooms
in a large building on the Bismarck Promenade. The building
had formerly been a convalescent home, and was designed
accordingly. On each storey there were long corridors with rooms
leading off them, so that every room had a separate entrance.
Bernhard had engaged plumbers and decorators who were converting the rooms into an apartment for the family. The offices
remained in the old house in the Brunnenstrasse, with the upper
storey turned into more offices, for by now the firm had thirteen

employees and apprentices. A modest apartment had been installed on the top floor for the head bookkeeper and his wife.

The new apartment of the Levy family was furnished simply, with no display of wealth. The most important ornaments were the two silver candlesticks, reminders of the Napoleonic wars when Jäckel had acquired them. The Levy family was not really interested in the fine arts, and there were no paintings in their apartment. Here and there were framed tapestries that Fanny had worked in tiny cross-stitch from printed patterns. In the drawing room, above a chest with many drawers containing cutlery, table napkins, and tablecloths, hung two etchings – the portait of Maimonides and a portrait of Wilhelm II.

Their everyday housekeeping was equally modest. Bernhard kept meticulous accounts of all expenditure. When Henriette's friends whispered or even spoke openly about Bernhard's miserliness, Henriette coolly responded by saying she had no intention of throwing money about in Polzin. Bernhard spent money on other things. Since he no longer travelled so much on business trips he had a telephone line installed, only the second one in Polzin. The first one had been installed by the mayor. Admittedly the connection sometimes left something to be desired. On occasion one of the employees would have to wind the handle for several minutes before the voice of the operator could be heard. All the same, this black box represented a huge step forward. A telephone connection to the bank in Stettin and the matchstick factory was important. Indeed, the factory had not yet closed, as Ascher had stipulated. Bernhard realized that at some stage he would have to implement this clause of the will, and his mother reminded him of it from time to time. But so long as she did not exert inordinate pressure on him, he continued to postpone taking action. It was making good money, so he was reluctant to give it up. Of course the firm was in a healthy position, even without the matchstick factory.

The grain trade brought in a healthy profit, and the sawmills were working without a loss. But Bernhard's real passion was for financial affairs. Unlike his father, he had not bought shares in the railway companies or in industry. He simply lacked the patience to wait for years on end until investments began to make a profit. Instead he took advantage of the bank's offer of credit facilities at a favourable rate, which were reserved for privileged customers like his firm, and he worked with these resources – he made loans to other merchants who were obliged to work with liquid funds, and profited from the difference in the rates of interest. These were delicate operations, which called not just for a huge measure of discretion but also for weighing up all manner of risks. Bernhard knew his business and all went well.

With a mix of humour and respect, his staff called him 'Multiplication Maestro'. He read balance sheets the way others devour detective thrillers. The most complicated calculations left him undaunted. Even New Year's Eve found him sitting in his study poring over columns of figures. Siegfried entered the room and said in astonishment, 'The twentieth century begins tonight, Papa, and here you are almost in the dark, as if it were just any ordinary evening.'

Bernhard did not even look up. He shrugged his shoulders slightly, saying, 'Thank you, I also have a calendar.'

The twentieth century appeared promising. In Polzin it was celebrated with a beer festival in the beer cellar in the market square. A brass band did itself proud, wine and spirits enlivened the atmosphere, and at midnight glasses were raised to the Kaiser, who promised the Reich a glowing future, 'a place in the sun' in the words of a flowery catchphrase. Ten years earlier he had dismissed Bismarck from the office of Chancellor and proclaimed his 'personal regime'. The old Chancellor, who had been an invaluable support to Wilhelm's predecessors, had retired to his estate of Friedrichsruh in the forest of Saxony and had died there in 1898, embittered and cut off from political events. Bleichröder had passed away five years earlier. The generation of Ascher and Moritz Gottschalk was over.

Outwardly Germany appeared stronger than ever; Wilhelm II wanted the Reich to be a great power, and had commissioned the secretary of state of the Reich Naval Office, Alfred von Tirpitz, to build up a powerful fleet. The notorious fleet programme was set into motion. The shipyards of Hamburg and Stettin were working at full stretch, and people basked in a reassuring feeling of military superiority. The masses cheered as the Kaiser announced in public: 'It is the soldier and the army, and not the parliamentary majorities and their decisions, that have bonded the German Reich together.'

The policy of German armament was viewed with great concern. Without Bismarck, who had juggled a policy based on the balance of power in Europe, the Kaiser could not appease the fears of the British Admiralty. Admiral John Arbuthnot, Lord Fisher of Kilverstone, coined the famous phrase, 'We have to Copenhagen the German fleet,' a reference to the successful destruction of the Danish fleet in a surprise attack by Nelson in 1801. Great Britain was not prepared to tolerate a second European naval power other than herself. But the Germans were not afraid of the English. The 'French danger' also seemed to have dispersed. Tsarist Russia would soon suffer a decisive defeat in the war against Japan, and thereafter would only overcome her internal problems with the greatest difficulty. Austria was facing a new crisis in the Balkans, this time in Serbia. The Reich felt safe, and soared to exaggerated fantasies of its own might: '*Deutschland, Deutschland, über alles.*'

No one wanted to acknowledge the ominous portents of the coming horrors of the twentieth century. The bloody suppression of the Boxer Rebellion by the European powers displayed a hitherto unknown degree of cruelty. South Africa, where the Boer War was raging, became the site of the world's first concentration camp. Prompted by German naval policy, a dynamic of armament spread throughout Europe, which ultimately led to the First World War. Hints of social unrest were evident in the German Reich as well. In the crisis of industrial expansion, it had become evident that the nation was by no means as united as it outwardly appeared. Individual social groupings drifted further and further apart, and while the Kaiser continued to rely on the traditional aristocracy, an increasingly expanding industrial class was pulling in the opposite direction.

The potential for conflict was still concealed by successes. The German nation had only just united; it felt invincible and had some brilliant economic achievements to show. At the World

Exhibition in Paris the visiting crowds stared in amazement at the gigantic machines of Siemens, Mannesmann, and Krupp. At about the same time a German Jew by the name of Tietz opened a large department store in Berlin, creating an entirely new set of guidelines for the retail trade. Albert Ballin, another German Jew and a leading Hamburg shipowner, became a confidant and Privy Councillor of the Kaiser. Rumour had it that Ballin was to be made a minister, but at the very last moment the Kaiser changed his mind – His Majesty simply could not come to terms with the idea of having a member of the Mosaic persuasion in his cabinet.

Ballin had first tried his luck in textile dyes and in the coal industry, but without success. He would probably have remained unknown and without influence had it not been for a very simple idea; the establishment of a travel agency for the tens of thousands of Jewish refugees seeking to escape the pogroms in Eastern Europe by making their way to America. These impoverished people from Russia, Rumania, Lithuania, and Poland brought him untold wealth and public recognition. His ships waited for the fugitives in the harbours of Hamburg and Stettin to take them across the ocean. Some of this stream of refugees passed through Pomerania and, as had happened earlier, some of them chose to stay in Europe.

Bernhard Levy viewed this with distaste. When one of these stranded individuals knocked at his door seeking work, he would drive him away. He ordered his staff in writing that they should in no event take on refugees from Eastern Europe or persons who were not citizens of the Reich. He refused to give money to the relevant welfare organization or to support an appeal by the liberal Jews for the Germanization of refugees. Like his father, he too found the Eastern European Jews an alien and disturbing element; they were likely to fuel the existing virulent anti-Semitism; they would probably promote Theodor Herzl's Zionist movement; and finally they could thoroughly undermine the 'delight [he] derived from his love of the fatherland'.

'I don't feel any common destiny with the refugees from Poland or Russia,' he once said to his son Leo. 'They don't speak our language, they don't think like we do. In their countries of origin they were never citizens with rights and duties, as we are. This is why they are completely incapable of understanding our close connection to the Reich and our loyalty to the Kaiser.'

And he expressly set out to his son Siegfried the reasons why money should in no case be given to support refugees who did not want to travel on to America:

'We have our own problems. We must first and foremost devote ourselves to those born in Germany, who breathe the German air and have grown up with the culture that is dear to our hearts. They too are in need. No, not in material terms. Those I have in mind are people your age, our sons, who are fighting for their place in society and are prepared to abandon Judaism in order to find it. In this respect, I am following the path trodden by my father, your grandfather. I am prepared to give generously for their education.'

'Sometimes I get the feeling, Papa, that you are too generous with your donations.'

Bernhard did not answer. He went over to his bookshelves, took down a volume of the Talmud, and asked, 'Have you ever read this?'

Siegfried said nothing.

'Of course not. A pointless question. My love of the Holy Scriptures was passed on to me by my father. But it seems that I'm the last link in this chain. You're not interested in what is really important. Leo has also distanced himself from our spiritual heritage.'

Bernhard leafed through the book, found the text he was looking for, and immersed himself in it. Then he shut the book, so that just one finger stuck out from between the pages, and began to recite: '"Ten strong things have been created in the world: a rock is strong, but iron can cut through it; iron is strong, but fire can melt it; water is strong, but the clouds carry it; the clouds are strong, but the wind scatters them; the wind is strong, but the body can bear it; the body is strong, but fear can break it; fear is strong, but wine can dispel it; wine is strong, but sleep drives it away; but death is stronger than them all and yet it is written: *Charity keeps death at bay*."'

When he had finished, he looked at his son. A faint smile hovered around Siegfried's lips. 'Very impressive,' he said, and added hurriedly, 'but a bit old hat.'

Bernhard pursed his lips. Siegfried was his offspring, but once again the apple had fallen far from the tree. There were times when he asked himself where he had gone wrong. There was one simple reason why he couldn't find an answer – Bernhard was of the firm opinion that he had never done anything wrong. No one around him had ever dared to contradict his views. It was only Siegfried's behaviour that sometimes caused him to focus his thoughts on the subject. But then he would return to matters in hand, which was far more comfortable than troubling himself with questions that threatened to undermine his self-image.

In his reserved, quiet, and practical way, Leo presented him with fewer difficulties. Leo had inherited many of his father's qualities, especially his ambition and determination, but also his stubbornness. His obstinacy had shown itself for the first time when Bernhard had asked him to study law as Ernst had done, and if not law then economics. When Bernhard called him to discuss the matter seriously, Leo protested strongly against the plan: 'I'm sorry, Papa. I'm afraid studying law or economics simply doesn't interest me.'

'Times have changed, Leo. Nowadays a firm with various interests like ours simply cannot be run without specialist training.'

'I'm not interested in being a timber merchant or running sawmills.'

'Do you want the firm to come to an end, when I die?'

'Really, Papa...you're still young. Your life is still ahead of you. And apart from that, I have two brothers and two sisters.'

Bernhard had not expected to be met with opposition. He wanted to bring the full weight of his authority to bear and impose his will on Leo, when Henriette entered the conversation. 'You're like Sigi. Law and economics are not to your taste. Well, what are you actually interested in?'

'Chemistry,' replied Leo.

'Chemistry?' asked Bernhard in astonishment. 'That's news to me.'

'But not to me, Papa. You've never taken any interest in what interests me, and you've never listened to me either. I've always been interested in chemistry. The problem is that the matter simply hasn't been important enough for you.'

'Don't be impertinent to your father.'

'I'm not being impertinent, Mama. You have taught me always to be truthful. And this is the absolute truth.'

'And what do you propose to do as a chemist? Do you intend to work as an employee in some company?'

'What would be so terrible about that? I would have a laboratory, and occupy myself with experiments.'

'A scientist in the Levy family,' mocked Bernhard and looked across at his wife.

But Henriette remained serious. 'You know, Leo, we are people who like to investigate everything thoroughly. I hope your father will agree with me. Perhaps studying chemistry is not such a bad idea. We might be able to reach a compromise between the family's interests and your own.'

'What are you up to?' asked Bernhard cautiously, as if afraid of being caught in a trap.

'You'll see in a minute. Let's assume we finance Leo's studies... Just a moment, don't get excited, Beri... So, we shall enable him to learn the profession that he wants. But we shall regard this as a business deal. We shall be making an investment, from which we can also profit.'

'I don't quite follow you, Mama,' Leo hastened to say.

'Be patient. I suggest we permit the chemistry studies. In return, Leo, you must undertake to return to Polzin and work in the firm. Wouldn't that be fair?'

'The firm doesn't need a chemist, it needs a businessman,' protested Bernhard. 'We shan't build a laboratory here to discover the philosopher's stone.'

'I have a practical solution,' said Leo. 'We could work with other stones. In the sand dunes at Gramentz there are limestone deposits. The area is no good for agriculture or afforestation and is in state ownership. We could lease it at an advantageous rate. It's an ideal site for a lime factory. And whether I build this factory or do some other work in our business is surely immaterial.'

Bernhard stared first at his son and then at his wife. 'Have you two been plotting behind my back?' he asked more in surprise than anger.

Leo grinned. 'It's a good solution, don't you think, Papa?'

Bernhard did not reply for a few seconds. Then he went across to Leo, embraced him and murmured, 'God bless you. I hope we've done a good deal.'

In the middle of that summer, Leo left Polzin. He had been accepted at the University of Heidelberg and very soon became one of its outstanding students. When he returned home after completing his studies, he not only brought the title of doctor with him, but also a surprise by the name of Else Frensdorf.

Else, the daughter of a respected and old-established religious Jewish family from Hanover, used to spend her holidays with relatives in Stettin. Leo often visited this coastal town too. On one of these visits he had met Else at the home of Louis and Anna Lewy. Louis was the nephew of Moritz Gottschalk, and his house on the Friedrich-Karl Strasse, a broad avenue lined with shady trees, was the meeting place for all members of the family scattered throughout the whole of Prussia. Louis earned his living from selling workmen's clothing, made by women outworkers. His wife Anna, a small, resolute woman full of energy, worked as a teacher. In addition she was an esteemed singer of secular songs, and as head of the Jewish women's guild she also devoted time to charitable work. Bernhard knew about the couple's way of life, and when he discovered that Anna had been involved in this *shidduch*, he gave his future daughter-in-law a joyful welcome. He bought more rooms in the house on Bismarck Promenade where the family lived, and gave them to the couple as a wedding present.

The Levy family now occupied an entire storey, a dozen rooms in all. Right up to the thirties, when the history of the family on German soil was to come to an end, that floor of the building was to be the home of all the Polzin Levys. Over the years the storey changed; walls were knocked down and others put up; balconies and toilets were added to meet the requirements of the ever-increasing family. But the rooms bought for Leo and Else stood empty for a long time, as Leo did not marry Else until 1913, when he reached the age of thirty.

Five years earlier Ernst had married Käthe Levy, daughter of his uncle Julius. The couple went on honeymoon to Paris, an extravagance that would have been out of the question a generation earlier. Käthe's brother Rudolf was their guide in the city. He had moved to France as long ago as 1903, where he tried to make it as an artist. After bidding him farewell, they did not return to Polzin, but settled in Berlin. There Ernst completed his training and temporarily joined a law firm as junior partner, his ultimate ambition being judicial office.

Soon after, Lina married Karl Wilhelm Hamburger. And then it was the turn of the youngest daughter. Ida had been educated in Berlin at a Jewish boarding school for girls from good homes. She had been accepted into the capital's way of life, much to her parents' disapproval. Ida adored huge cartwheel hats adorned with flowers, fashionable clothes, and glittering trinkets. When out of sight of the family and teachers at the boarding school, she would wear a lot of make-up and perfume. Friends wrote to Polzin saying she had been seen at a Parisian-style nightclub, known as the meeting place for writers, poets, artists, and other 'dubious' types. 'This shady dive is under constant police observation, and is certainly no place for a young woman from a good home,' they reported. Bernhard and Henriette were alarmed. Small wonder that they decided it was high time for Ida to be married.

It was no accident that Paul was their choice. Since the incident on the platform at Polzin on the day when Ascher's will had been read, the cousins had corresponded. As Ida grew older, the correspondence increasingly took on the nature of a dialogue between man and wife. Bernhard travelled to see his brother in Danzig to obtain his agreement to the *shidduch*.

Paul had completed his engineering studies and a brilliant career was predicted. The German Reich still had an eye on the Orient and was attempting to acquire a sizeable piece of the weakened Ottoman empire. Major entrepreneurs and concerns were interested in extending the railway line so that Muslim pilgrims could travel from Damascus to Mecca and Medina. Paul was shortly due to set off for Syria with a group of engineers and construction workers.

Julius hesitated. 'This is the chance of a lifetime for a young engineer, and I want him to take advantage of it.'

'Marriage to Ida is also a once in a lifetime opportunity,' answered Bernhard. The brothers grinned at each other.

Julius was still doubtful. 'I'm afraid that life in the Syrian desert and the Arabian peninsula as an engineer's wife would hardly be to Ida's taste. I've heard she is a woman who – how shall I put it – appreciates the comforts and good things in life.'

'You of all people know that members of the Levy family are tough and resilient.'

'Even daughters of the Levys?'

'She will obey and time will do the rest. We ourselves didn't marry our wives for romantic considerations.'

'Speak for yourself, Beri.'

'Right, I'd forgotten. And still ...'

'Doesn't the blood relationship worry you?' asked Julius. 'First my daughter Käthe marries your son Ernst, and now Ida and one of my sons?'

'So long as we don't mix milk and meat, I don't see that there's any problem.'

'The *halachah* permits marriage between first cousins. And while we're on the subject, Henriette told me that even kings and princes don't refrain from marriage between blood relations. Virtually all the royal houses of Europe are related to each other.'

'You've convinced me,' laughed Julius. 'Paul and Ida shall live like royalty.'

The brothers sealed the *shidduch* with a handshake. After supper they sat down together to sort out the financial details. It was not until the following morning that Julius asked for his son's opinion. Paul regarded the offer as an order he dared not refuse.

In the same year, 1908, Ida brought Lisbeth Naphtali, her friend at the boarding school, home for a weekend. Lisbeth, from

Ida Levy, Danzig, 1902.

Schweidnitz in Lower Silesia, was six years younger than Siegfried, and very mature for her age. She was not particularly pretty, but her qualities corresponded to what Bernhard considered suitable in a wife. He saw her as a woman with a practical outlook on life, whose down-to-earth attitude would compensate for Siegfried's irresponsible nature, and without hesitation he gave the couple his blessing. The ceremony took place on 9 June 1908, and the couple decided to live in Stettin.

Now that all the children had settled down, Bernhard turned

his entire attention to further expanding the firm. Leo was made
'travelling executive'. To qualify for running the firm he had to go
through a hard school. He was constantly travelling on business,
from town to town, village to village, and forest to forest. 'That's
the way I started. Believe me, it's the best way,' Bernhard
explained to him. Leo carried out his duties to his father's satisfaction. But he hardened visibly. He never openly spoke his
mind, and did not even complain to Else. She understood her
husband, and knew exactly how hard he found making business
deals. Every fibre in his body was tuned to research, and he
wanted nothing more than to decode the mysteries of chemistry.
But imprisoned in his father's business, he bottled himself up,
and gave less and less of himself away. He lost the knack of
making social contact with the people around him. Later on this
even affected his children. Although this process unfolded before
Else's eyes, she could see no way of changing anything. She was a
clever woman with a strong sense of family, and so she did everything in her power to empathize with her husband's situation
rather than challenge him. Leo appreciated her immensely. Both
were concerned to keep their partnership on an even keel. It was a
quiet life without excitement, everything planned down to the
last detail and somewhat uninspired, but for all that there were no
marital crises or upheavals.

At the beginning of the twentieth century Polzin was a town
of 6000 inhabitants, with forty Jewish families. These, however,
kept themselves at a certain distance from the Levy family, lest
the townspeople identify them with the 'exploiters'. This made
little difference to Bernhard and his sons. In any case their wealth
and social position created something of a gulf between them and
the other Jews of the town. They only met on *Shabbat* and festivals, especially on Seder night at Pesach, when Bernhard tended
to invite Polzin's Jewish dignitaries.

In the meantime Leo and Siegfried had also both been named
as signatories for the firm. When Siegfried married Lisbeth,
Bernhard signed over one third of the value of the enterprise to
him. On the morning after the wedding, to his surprise Siegfried
came to him with a business proposition. He wanted to add his

wife's dowry to the business, thereby raising his share to 50 per cent. Bernhard agreed, and in this way his youngest son became an equal partner. When Leo then started his own family five years later, Bernhard likewise arranged to hand over one third of the business to him, so that he himself retained a 16.7 per cent share. Each of the girls received a dowry in cash. Once he had distributed his assets according to his wishes, he turned to public activities. First he was voted on to the town council, and took over his late father's seat. In addition he contributed to Jewish charitable organizations, provided they did not support Zionism.

The German Jews continued to be fragmented, incapable of presenting a united front even against the common enemy of anti-Semitism. The Zionists proposed a state solution with *Eretz Israel*. But the members of the *Centralverein deutscher Staatsbürger jüdischen Glaubens* (Central Organization of German Citizens of the Jewish Faith) preferred the path of assimilation, integration into general public life, and adaptation to German culture, while still observing the basic values of the Jewish religion. The publications of the two rival camps, *Die Allgemeine Zeitung* and *Die Jüdische Rundschau*, attacked each other so violently that on occasion the anti-Semites used the articles published in these Jewish newspapers as weapons to further their own cause. Anti-Jewish polemic had become a useful tool in political intrigue. The centrist and right-wing parties complained loudly about the alleged 'takeover' by Jews of various branches of industry and the professions, and they fought against this dangerous expansion. Supporters of the anti-Zionist Jewish camp reacted vehemently to the danger of being once again thrown on to the scrapheap. It was not just a threat to their material existence or their civic rights; any hindrance to Jews active in public office, the law, or medicine threatened to destroy the very foundations on which their life was based. Many individuals were of course affected. When Ernst left the chambers where he had been a partner to set up on his own, he wished to function as a notary, too. However, the Prussian Minister of Justice spoke out to limit the number of notaries of the Mosaic faith. When news of this reached Polzin, Bernhard wrote to his son in Berlin as follows:

My dear Ernst!

I have heard about the struggle of the Jewish lawyers against the justice department. The action of the justice minister cannot be simply ignored, for this matter is of vital importance to us. For fifty years we have fought to open up the gates of the Jewish ghetto, and now that they stand open and we wish to emerge, it will not do for them to tell us, 'We are terribly sorry, but all places are taken.' Quite recently the appointment of a Jewish female teacher was rejected on the grounds that Christian parents would object to having their children taught by this teacher. I know her personally and I know that she is a better and more loyal German citizen than many a Christian German. Here in Polzin, too, from time to time we can sense there is a feeling that we occupy too many important positions in relation to our proportion of the population. This is an utterly reprehensible attitude, and we must fight it to the best of our ability. We receive no extra rights because of our religion, but we cannot allow any infringement of the rights to which we are legally entitled. For our part, we don't keep a tally on the aristocratic citizens who have risen to high rank in the army, so there is no reason why anyone should prescribe the percentage of German Jews in the legal profession in this way. Civic duties, love of the Fatherland and loyalty to the crown are not measured in percentages. So long as our consciences are clear as subjects of this state, it is imperative that we are entitled to equal rights and duties. I expect you never to waver from these principles, and to act accordingly, with God's help.

With my best wishes to Käthe,

Your Papa

Bernhard was not naive, and was well aware that even the most eloquent words were a poor substitute for positive action. His outlook on things prompted him to support the national liberal party with substantial financial donations. The national liberals represented the educated and property-owning citizens, and sought to bring together the old moneyed class, the junker, with the new rising factory owners. He loathed the social democrats, although in domestic politics they adopted a tolerant line towards all religions, even Jews. However, their objectives were contrary to all the principles that he stood for. He was prosperous, believed in the historic mission of Germany, and hated everything that inclined to the left. His donations to the national liberal party did not remain secret, and set the townspeople against him. The citizens of Pomerania had been conservative from time immemorial, and their votes were equally spread between the central party and the German conservative party. The latter stood for putting an end to foreign immigration to the Reich, limiting the number of Jews in public office, and preventing them from becoming army officers, and the party even wanted to close down Jewish newspapers. Siegfried did not conceal his disapproval. 'Grandfather never got involved in politics. He knew that you had to keep out of it, because it's bad for business,' he maintained.

It was still early in the morning, before the staff had arrived at work. Bernhard was already seated in discussion with his two sons. The offices opened at eight o'clock, but the family started their working day at seven, sometimes even earlier. Today they were discussing an important business deal that had fallen through because a superior official in the Post and Telegraph Office had refused to let the firm make a tender for the supply of telegraph poles. The previous day Siegfried had travelled to Köslin in order to speak to the man who had made the decision, and to ask him what it was all about.

'At first I thought that he was keeping us out of the tender because we are a Jewish enterprise,' he reported. 'I invited him to eat in a restaurant, and we spoke quite openly. I got the impression that his reason for turning us down was your support for the national liberals. The man comes from a junker family and is a dyed-in-the-wool conservative.'

Bernhard placed his head between his hands, his elbows resting on the table, and reflected. Suddenly he asked: 'Did you say you invited him for lunch?'

'Yes, a good meal helps to sort out problems.'

'And you dined with him?'

The family, from left to right:
  Lisbeth's brother and mother, Lisbeth, Siegfried, Rudolf and Käthe.
  Seated: Lisbeth's father, her brother Oskar and Ernst Levy.

'Certainly,' answered Siegfried and immediately regretted that he had not guarded his tongue. His father had set him a trap, and now it was too late to retract.

In a level but razor-sharp tone Bernhard said: 'That means you ate *treife*.'

'I had no alternative, Papa.'

'You ate *treife* and yet you have the audacity to reproach me.'

'You know that as a rule I am very careful about keeping *kashrut*.'

'That's not true, Sigi. Back in London you were already breaking the dietary laws. Mr Moeller informed me of it at the time and asked what he should do about it. To this day I regret that I refrained from intervening.'

'That meal was intended to help the business. Your actions don't.'

'It's better to offend people than to break the holy commandments of Judaism.'

'Your views are extremely old-fashioned, Papa. And maybe...'

'And maybe?' asked Bernhard with a warning tone in his voice.

'And maybe the business world is not for you any more,' said

Siegfried, completing his sentence. The hint was a reference to Bernhard's share in the business, which was now minimal.

Leo had said nothing so far. Now he jumped to his father's defence. 'Just watch what you say,' he said. 'It wouldn't hurt to think before you open your mouth.'

Siegfried tried to pacify him. But Leo had no intention of letting the matter drop. For him too, Jewish observance was more important than any business deal. He was not prepared to betray it at any time. 'Dishonesty to God equals dishonesty to one's family,' he stated drily.

'Are you accusing me of dishonesty?' asked Siegried furiously.

'You're clever enough to get the implication,' replied Leo, 'and now please excuse me. I have an appointment.'

'I have an appointment too.' Siegfried was now in a rush. 'Goodbye, Papa. I hope you can forgive me. I didn't mean to upset you.'

The sons left the office and the sound of their footsteps faded away. Bernhard stood up and went across to the window. Grey clouds were gathering and there was no one about in the street outside.

Nothing more was said about the morning's incident. Both Bernhard and his two sons behaved as if nothing had happened. In order to keep the peace in the house Bernhard and Siegfried avoided struggles about status and open conflict. And then came an event in Siegfried's marriage that made his father forget any resentment he may have felt.

When they had been married for about a year, Lisbeth announced to Siegfried: 'I believe I'm pregnant.'

Henriette, who was immediately told the happy news, advised her daughter-in-law to make an appointment with Dr Stutz. When the doctor had given her a thorough examination, he suggested that she should go for a further investigation to a gynaecologist in Stettin.

'Is something wrong, Doctor?' Lisbeth asked anxiously.

'Oh no, but you know, my medical experience has chiefly been with sailors on board ship, and none of them was ever pregnant. What you need is a specialist.'

Lisbeth Levy, née Naphtali, and Siegfried Levy.

Siegfried and Lisbeth lost no time. Siegfried had arranged a meeting with his legal adviser, Dr Marcuse and a gynaecologist's appointment was made for Lisbeth. The doctor examined her thoroughly, after which he announced that she should prepare a cradle and nappies, as she was already three months pregnant. Lisbeth was overjoyed. She rushed off to tell her husband the happy news. In her haste, she tripped on the stairs and fell. Several passers-by helped her up. But a piercing pain forced her to sit down again. The neighbours called the doctor down, who led her back to the consulting rooms. Even before he could examine her, a bloodstain spread across the couch. 'I'm afraid you have lost the child,' he said quietly and instructed his nurse to have her admitted to a hospital.

After this Lisbeth consulted one specialist after another. The doctors examined her and shook their heads. She took medicinal baths, implored the heavens with her prayers, and asked other women in the same situation for advice, but all to no avail. On 31 July 1914, after visiting yet another specialist in Berlin, she was finally compelled to accept the bitter truth. Any further attempts would be futile; she would never be able to have children. Siegfried came to collect her from the doctor's consulting rooms. They took the tram to the railway station, as they wanted to catch the fast train from Berlin to Polzin, and only change once at Köslin.

All the places in second class were already reserved so they had to travel first class. The seats were soft and upholstered in a brown and black striped fabric. Lisbeth and Siegfried sat by the window without speaking. The train left the station and passed through seemingly endless broad agricultural land. Siegfried watched the telegraph poles racing past. Lisbeth had opened a book, but the letters on the page swam before her eyes. After a while she let it slip to her knees. The silence depressed her. 'What are you thinking about?'

'Me? Oh, nothing. I'm just looking at the scenery.'

'That was our last hope, wasn't it?'

'I've stopped worrying about it, Lisbeth. It is in God's hands.'

'You're talking like your father,' she retorted indignantly. 'The doctors can't help me, nor can praying.'

'It really doesn't matter.'

'You're not telling the truth.'

'And why should I lie?'

'To comfort me. But you can't hide what a blow it is for you. What is the point of life, if one cannot bring children into the world?'

'There are other ways we can give meaning to our lives.'

'Do you know what I've been thinking about?'

'No.'

'It struck me that Ernst and Leo only have daughters. So there will be no heirs to the house of Levy. Imagine what that means! Our line will come to a dead end. You are busy expanding the business and seeing to deals, as if that were the most important thing in the world. But when the time comes for us to take our leave, there will be no one to switch the light on in the offices.'

'All in good time.'

'We have to think about it now, Siegfried, at this very moment. You cannot live without looking into the future. You

Lisbeth Levy. *Siegfried Levy.*

can't move on without planning. I don't know how we're going to tell Bernhard and Henriette. It will be a heavy blow for your father.'

'Yes,' sighed Siegfried. 'He's expecting us to give him a grandchild, an heir.'

'You see, we cannot ignore the issue. The house of Levy without a male heir, that's like an uprooted oak. This is a death sentence.'

A ticket inspector in a dark uniform entered the compartment and asked for their tickets. He left with a military-style greeting, and slid the door shut behind him. The clattering of the wheels filled the compartment. Lisbeth and Siegfried fell silent once more. The train continued on its way across the plain.

Bernhard and Henriette were waiting for them on the tiny station platform at Polzin. Lisbeth had already prepared what she was going to say to her father-in-law, knowing that her intended words would lay all hopes to rest. But Bernhard did not let her speak. They had not even left the carriage when he called out to them in agitation: 'Have you heard the latest news? The Kaiser has asked Russia to stop mobilization. If the Tsar does not agree, there will be war.'

About a month earlier, on 28 June, Serbian nationalists had made an attempt on the life of Franz Ferdinand, the heir to the Austrian throne. The royal house of Austro-Hungary had decided to exploit the situation and annex Serbia, as they had done with Bosnia and Herzegovina five years earlier. On 6 July, Wilhelm II had given Franz Joseph, the Austro-Hungarian Kaiser, his assurance that in the case of Russian intervention, he could could count on his loyal support. On 23 July the Austrians had delivered an ultimatum to Serbia. This was rejected by Serbia two days later, and on 29 July Belgrade was shelled. On 30 July both Russia and Austria issued orders for general mobilization. The next day in an unusually sharply worded letter Wilhelm II ordered Tsar Nicholas II in St Petersburg to cease mobilization immediately. Events rapidly overtook one another, and none of the European politicians seemed able to halt the avalanche. Four years earlier, Bismarck had stated that any act of stupidity in the Balkans would be enough to unleash the next war. This prophecy was to be all too terribly fulfilled.

The Narrow Rickety Bridge

It was 1 August, a *Shabbat* and a bright summer's day. It was about midday when Ernst telephoned to report that the whole of Berlin was in a state of commotion. 'Crowds of people have gathered at the palace. It looks to me as if there is no avoiding war now,' he said, the agitation in his voice unmistakable.

The family sat down together for the midday meal. Henriette had prepared cabbage soup, roast meat with dumplings, gravy, and mashed potatoes. There was also Lisbeth's favourite, cauliflower coated with breadcrumbs. As the stewed fruit was being served, the clock struck one. Everyone looked across at the clock, for this was the moment the German ultimatum expired. Had the Tsar put a stop to general mobilization?

At this time Norman Angell's *The Great Illusion* was hugely popular. A copy of it in German translation was on Leo's bookshelf. The author sought to prove that in view of the equal strength of the major powers all-out war served no purpose to anyone in Europe, and that both the winners and the losers would suffer equal losses. The book was translated into fifteen languages and rapidly became regarded as a sort of 'Optimists' Bible'. But the world powers had obviously not been sufficiently convinced by it. Nicholas II's response to the German ultimatum was an insulting silence. In the early afternoon the German Ambassador in St Petersburg received a telegram in code, instructing him to deliver the declaration of war on the stroke of five. Two hours later the news was conveyed to the Russian Foreign Minister, Sergei D. Sassonov.

'I hate the Slavs,' the Kaiser declared openly in Berlin. 'I know that it is a sin to hate your neighbour, but I cannot suppress this loathing.' Regardless of his strong dislike of the Slavs, the Kaiser also ordered the opening of the western front. According to existing plans the first countries to be occupied would be Luxembourg and Belgium. At five o'clock the general chief of staff, Helmuth von Moltke, informed all his senior command that he had been given the order for general mobilization. Top-secret war plans were taken out of hiding. The first element to be involved was the now-completed entire railway network. When the time came, more than 10,000 trains were to be put in action to transport the troops to the battlefields.

When *Shabbat* was over Bernhard and his sons went to the synagogue to offer up a special prayer in support of the Kaiser. Polzin did not have its own rabbi. Prayers were always led by the person most familiar with the ritual. At one time this had been Ascher Levy; now the task had fallen to Bernhard. Almost all the men in the Jewish community of Polzin had come to the synagogue, apart from a few refugees from Eastern Europe who had settled near the town but had not yet been absorbed into the community.

To begin with Bernhard recalled the traditional significance of this particular day – *Tisha b'Av*: 'After leaving Egypt six tragic events befell the Jewish people on this date. Our forefathers were not allowed to enter *Eretz Israel*, because the advance scouts had sinned; the Temple in Jerusalem was twice destroyed; Beitar, the last outpost of the *Bar Kochba* rebellion, fell; the city was destroyed by Titus, son of Vespasian; and furthermore the date recalled the expulsion of the Jews from Spain.' Bernhard paused and allowed his gaze to wander over those at prayer, before raising an admonishing forefinger. 'But now let us not dwell any longer on the past. We, the Jews of the German empire, have an invincible home and a country from which we are not expelled. At this fateful hour our home and our fatherland are close to our hearts, and to emphasize this fact, I wish to recite the following prayer.'

Bernhard put on his spectacles and began to read aloud in a resounding voice from the text, which he knew by heart word for word.

'Prayer for our King, our people, and our country. Our Father!

Our King! We ask you to fight our wanton enemies and punish them for their arrogance. Destroy them if they act against us, subjugate our opponents, and may they be overcome with fear and trembling. Weaken their power, thwart their plans, so that they and their forces are doomed. There are many that oppose us but we shall emerge victorious, for you, O God, are our Shield and our Redeemer, and will allow no sword again to penetrate our land. For what does the strength of military might amount to in your eyes? You can make it disappear in the blink of an eye. All that we long for is peace and goodwill, and all that we fight for is our continued existence. Your will be done, O Lord, for whatever You do is good, and in You alone we trust. God of heaven and truth, You will avert all harm from us, and every foe will offer us peace, if You, O God, are with us.

'O Lord, shelter and protect us, save and strengthen our Kaiser and King, Wilhelm II, grant him power and esteem, and let him succeed in his actions, make him subjugate his enemies, so that he may return with his army to our land crowned with victory, in peace and joy, in fame and glory, Amen.'

The assembled worshippers loudly echoed the concluding word. The service over, they emerged into the street, talking excitedly. All were in high spirits.

That night Julius telephoned from Danzig: 'Hallo, Beri,' he shouted down the mouthpiece, 'we're back to the days of Sedan! What? Rudi and Paul have already been called up. What about your boys?'

'My sons are being conscripted at the end of the week,' replied Bernhard.

'Are they pleased?' shouted Julius over the crackling on the line.

'Like everyone, they are subjects of the Kaiser.'

'I hope it won't go on too long.'

'No doubt about that, Julius. Three months. Half a year at the very most. By then our enemies will be beaten and will be begging for peace.'

'On bended knees, Beri, on bended knees.'

There was a click. The line had gone dead. Bernhard looked at the mouthpiece in surprise, and hung it back in its place.

Siegfried and Lisbeth had gone back to their apartment. 'You see, Lisbeth,' said her husband, 'all of a sudden personal problems fade in importance.'

His wife shook her head: 'I don't see any connection. Will I be able to have children if we bring the Russians to their knees, march through Paris in the hour of victory, or add the British colonies in Africa to the Reich? All that will happen is that I shall be left here alone – after all, you will also have to go off and fight.'

But unlike the other members of the family, Siegfried did not dream of glorious victories. Not at all keen on serving in the army and possibly dying for the fatherland, he preferred the pleasures of civilian life to glittering honours and heroic medals. Consequently he was delighted when the recruiting board found him unfit for service. A shadow on his lung showed up unmistakably on an X-ray, saving him from call-up. So Bernhard's two sons went very different ways – Siegfried returned home to run the family business, whereas Leo, who was to be conscripted a month later, immediately went to the tailor in town to have a uniform made to measure.

Most young men in Prussia dreamed of being in uniform, preferably as an officer. However, with a few rare exceptions, this military rank was still unattainable for men of the Mosaic faith. Even a career in the judiciary or public service was like walking a tightrope at a very great height. Only the strongest, most talented, and most determined were successful. Those with the rank of officer, on the other hand, formed an impenetrable club, and Jews stood as much chance of getting in as an elephant passing through the eye of a needle. Little had changed since the wars against Austria in 1866 and against France in 1870. Yet many Jews believed that their situation must have improved in the military field. After all, they had struck roots in the empire, imbibed German culture and even promoted it, and essentially they had assimilated. The day after the outbreak of war, the organizations, unions, and associations of the Jews of the German empire published leaflets and appeals, proclaiming in glowing patriotic terms: 'We are all behind the Kaiser!'

On Tuesday, 4 August, representatives of all faiths and the

parliamentary delegates gathered at the Kaiser's palace in Berlin, to declare their wholehearted support in all political matters. Wilhelm II, who appeared before the delegation in gala uniform, was profoundly moved. He wore a steel helmet adorned with a golden eagle with wings outspread for flight – the beatings of its wings could almost be heard. The Kaiser leaned on an ancient sword, and said in characteristic tones of pathos: 'Parties are of no significance to me now. Henceforth I know you all as Germans, and in proof of this, to show that you are all firmly determined to hold together and stand by me through thick and thin, and submit to suffering and even death, without distinction of rank or religion, I command the representatives of the parties to step forward and shake hands under oath.'

The front page of the *Belgard and Polzin District Paper* carried the following sentimental verse to herald the solemn oath:

> Hail to Thee, our Kaiser.
> You spoke the word.
> Henceforth I know you all as Germans!
> You taught us to step before God
> And pray in humility.
> Hail to Thee, our Kaiser!
> Fly the flags!
> Let the sound
> Of cheering resound. Let us sing;
> Hail to Thee, our Kaiser!
> In this war
> From battle to triumph!

Even if the Kaiser now 'saw only Germans' the finer social distinctions persisted. To begin with, both conscripts and volunteers from Polzin were quartered in the same barracks. From there they marched through the streets of the town. Onlookers waved their hats and showered them with flowers. The townspeople formed a guard of honour for the men marching past and chanted battle songs. All were swept along by joy and enthusiasm. Admittedly, Jews were obliged to march at the rear. Leo had protested, but in vain. 'It has nothing to do with being snubbed,' the staff sergeant had retorted brusquely, 'after all, someone has to be at the rear. So why not you?!'

One of the delegates who had assembled before the Kaiser on Tuesday 4 August was the university professor, Max Rothmann. His eighteen-year-old son, who had volunteered, was to fall at the front less than three months later, whereupon Rothmann, true patriot that he was, requested that his youngest son be accepted in the cadet school. This was in line with the family tradition, for the grandfather had already served the Kaiser with distinction in three wars. But the German army had no desire for Jewish cadets. A written appeal to the Minister of War was rejected, and a request for a personal interview brought the following impersonal reply, written by a junior official: 'Since the Ministry of War is obliged to uphold its earlier decision, a conversation in person would be pointless, therefore your Honour is requested not to pursue the matter any further...'

Two days earlier the chief of staff, General von Moltke, had likewise given a negative response to Rothmann's request:

Dear Professor,

I thank you for your letter, from which I am returning the enclosures. I regret that I am unable to help you, since the decision rests with the War Ministry alone. May destiny decree that we emerge from this war, to which all members of this nation are committing their lives shoulder to shoulder, with the conviction above all else that we are all Germans. Please accept my condolences but also my congratulations at the heroic death of your son, who sealed his loyalty to the Fatherland with his heart's blood.

Most sincerely yours,

Moltke, Senior General

Obviously the Levy family knew nothing of the Rothmann affair. The correspondence between the respected professor and the governmental ministries and the army was made public only after the war was over, by which time it was already known that nearly one hundred thousand German Jews had been in uniform, and seventy-eight per cent of the Jewish soldiers had fought at the front.

At the beginning of the war in the summer of 1914 the Schneidemühle barracks were still adorned with cheerful banners. The local schoolchildren sent the soldiers euphoric letters, and their mothers baked cakes, iced with chocolate inscriptions that read 'For the brave fighters'. Their basic training had been meant to last a month, but was cut to two weeks. 'You must hurry to the front, otherwise you'll miss the victory. France will soon fall, and in six months the Russian bear will surrender,' boasted the camp commander at the last roll-call.

And once again they marched through the streets of the town, this time in full regalia. 'God is with us' was emblazoned on their outfits. 'Long live the Kaiser!' a woman screamed hysterically and threw herself at the broad chest of a young lieutenant leading the troops to the railway station. The military train stood waiting at the platform. Someone had scrawled on it in chalk, 'Paris, here we come!'

The evening before the outbreak of war Rudolf Levy had left his studio in Montmartre and travelled from Paris to Danzig to enlist. He was assigned to a fighting unit, and served as a driver for Infantry Division 117 on the western front. From there he wrote to Danzig in the summer of 1915:

Dear Father,

I send you birthday greetings, which I hope will arrive in time ... You probably know that since 30 June I have been down here near Lens, in a tiny village that has been shot to pieces ... We are on night duty as the roads are under observation by the enemy during daylight. I sit in the vehicle of the convoy officer, and am of some importance as I have a good sense of orientation, and am good at finding the way. I have turned out to be a brilliant driver, have a military driving licence, and sometimes go at a speed of eighty kilometres per hour, no cigarettes allowed while doing so ... You get used to the whistling of the shells, and it's hardly possible to imagine any places that

haven't been completely devastated. Every day the French
(now it's probably the English) are shooting from the infamous
Loretto Height towards Souchez, Angres, and Liévin.
Travelling along these roads is of course extremely difficult
because of the rubble all around and the potholes left by
shelling, but nothing has happened to me so far...

Four months later, when the fighting around Artois was over,
he informed his sister Käthe with a touch of irony:

'Thank you very much for your congratulations on the Iron
Cross, which has adorned this hero's breast these last two weeks.'

And towards the end of the war he wrote to his brother-in-law
Ernst in Berlin:

'I am still in my grandiose position at GenKdo XIV RF
Combat Group Queant and the fight for Buleivart is still on, as
you will have read. How much longer can this go on? It is all so
terribly boring, at times enough to make me despair. Even a
strong belief in Judaism does not help. And yet there is much for
me to do, munitions transport, troop movements, etc...'

Now the life of the Levy family in Polzin followed a very different rhythm. Time was no longer measured in hours, days, and
weeks, but by the arrival of the forces' post. 'That was before we
heard from Leo' or 'That happened between the note from
Rudolf and Leo's letter'. Unlike in 1871, this time the postal
service was regular, and communication was maintained between
the front and those at home without interruption. Newspapers
were also delivered on time in Polzin.

Bernhard made a point of going to synagogue every day. On
his way home after morning prayers he would pick up the post
and a copy of the *Vossische Zeitung*, and the local paper was delivered by the postman at nine o'clock. During breakfast Bernhard
read aloud the reports of the senior military command and the
most important news from the battlefields. These readings
became a custom, almost a family ritual, which gave them all the
feeling of being closer to the events at the front. At first the optimistic prophecies turned out to be well founded. In the east the
Russian 'steamroller' was halted by General von Hindenburg. In

the west, 1.5 million German soldiers advanced on to foreign soil. Each of them was armed with the latest equipment, weighing about thirty kilograms: a rifle and ammunition, a spare pair of shoes, a spade for digging in, and a rucksack containing a first-aid box, iron rations, and a sealed hip flask containing brandy. Express instructions were issued for the hip flasks to stay firmly corked, to be opened only at the order of an officer. The seals were inspected daily. The rows of infantry advancing like a human wall were followed by the heavy armour that was to be decisive in the battle – cannons developed for years under strictest secrecy in the Austrian Skoda and the German Krupp factories: 305-millimetre howitzers with an enormous range. Each one of these huge guns could fire 900-kilogram shells over a distance of fourteen kilometres, and it took 200 soldiers to operate a single piece of artillery.

Drunk with this demonstration of military might, the Germans rejoiced when neutral Belgium was occupied. No one wanted to know about the ill treatment of the civilian population there. The fortifications at Liège fell in the space of ten days. These had been planned as defensive installations at the end of the previous century by the great architect, Henri Brialmont. One month after the war began, a German division marched into a small French town by the name of Sedan.

Rudolf wrote to his uncle Bernhard:

Rudolf Levy with Pascin, c. 1910.

I feel as if I am following in the actual footsteps made by my father. He was here in this exact spot on 2 September 1871, forty-three years ago to the day. My heart swells with boundless joy. The French are shelling us day and night, but I have got used to the noise and sleep well. It is only when the noise stops and it is suddenly quiet that I wake up with a start and wonder what has happened. What a life! I am a driver of a patrol unit. My duties are essential and fascinating, a pity that I am not allowed to go into any details. The roads here are bad, full of shell holes and bomb craters, but if all goes well, we shall soon be celebrating a second Versailles here, or so we are promised.

With love
Your Rudi

But all did not go well. The assault ground to a halt. The army dug in; mobile warfare turned into leaden and wearisome entrenched battles. Hundreds of thousands of soldiers spent months in trenches behind barbed-wire fences among minefields, exposed to constant artillery fire. The months dragged on like an eternity, during which each side waited for a favourable time to launch an offensive. In February 1916 the order came: Verdun. The German attack began on 21 February and ended in December. Approximately 1 million men – German, French, and English – paid with their lives for this unprecedented campaign, which was intended to set the faltering advance in motion once more. But even this gigantic number of deaths made no difference to the strategy, and the military stalemate continued despite the growing list of fatalities.

The impasse and the countless casualties at the front may have depressed Leo, but they did not demoralize him. His unit was positioned in a small town in north-eastern France. The commanders had entrusted him with the provision of supplies for a brigade of Bavarian reservists, a task that took up all his time and distracted him. In the evening hours of a grey autumn day, as the voices outside fell silent and the storehouse emptied, he sat at a small table and wrote a few lines to his little daughter Hannah.

When he had left Polzin, Else had placed a bar of Lindt hazelnut chocolate in his bulging knapsack: 'So you'll have something sweet even when you're far from home,' she had said and kissed him on the cheek. As a student Leo had chosen to write his letters home in the form of rhymes, to the amusement of one and all. Later on he had dropped the verses in favour of business prose. But here of all places, in a grey reservists' camp near to the front, the muse came to him. In slanting, spiky handwriting he wrote:

> This chocolate bar so yummy
> Was packed for me by Mummy
> When two long years ago
> Off to the war I did go.
> The letter I received did tell
> My Hannah's been a good gel
> And for children who are well behaved
> A bar of Lindt chocolate is saved.
> And for Mummy there is this
> A loving, tender *Yontef* kiss.
> May you all find the coming year
> Sweet and good and free of fear.

Leo read through the rhyme, which came from the heart, and had to laugh at its naivety. He wrapped the chocolate bar – now somewhat the worse for wear from all the toing and froing – in paper and tied it with a thin piece of string. Just as he had finished, Captain Tuch, the officer responsible for provisions, entered the depot. 'Good evening,' he said, greeting Leo in a most unmilitary fashion. Leo sprang to his feet to salute, but the officer motioned him to sit down. 'It's late now. Let's ignore the official formalities for the moment.' For an officer, this was a remarkable way to begin.

Leo hastily swept the little packet from the table. The officer smiled as he observed Leo's embarrassment. He sat down facing Leo and placed a briefcase bulging with all sorts of documents on the table in front of him. Then, clearing his throat, he said, 'Your

Leo Levy, 1915.

name is Dr Leo Levy, isn't it?' Leo nodded, wondering what could possibly be behind this question, for after all the officer knew his name. Captain Tuch leafed through the papers and asked: 'What is your religion, Dr Levy?'

'I am of the Mosaic faith.'

'That means you are Jewish?'

Leo covered his embarrassment with a smile. 'It is not the same thing, Captain,' he replied. 'Even if the facts obviously depend on the present way of looking at the world, I regard myself as a German of the Mosaic faith.'

The captain wrote down his reply. 'I understand,' he said, following the text on the paper with his pencil. 'How old are you, Dr Levy?'

'I was thirty-three in September.'

'A good age for a man.'

'Everything is relative,' mumbled Leo, who still could not understand what this was all about.

'Yes, yes of course ... And what is your position in the army?'

'But you know perfectly well, I am responsible for the Division's supplies. May one ask what is the purpose of these strange questions?'

'Orders, my good man. Staff orders.'

Leo gave his captain a puzzled look. The latter could not hide his embarrassment.

'I want you to know, Dr Levy, that this business is not my doing. I am just a soldier, carrying out an order – dutifully and precisely, as we are all bound to do.'

'Am I guilty of some misconduct, Captain?'

'Good heavens, no! You are one of the finest soldiers in the Division. I shan't forget to put that on the questionnaire.' Tuch put the papers in order. But before he got up, he again said emphatically: 'Please believe me, I find this whole affair quite distasteful. Only pen-pushers who have never come within a thousand miles of action could possibly dream up something like this...'

'I don't understand.'

'Let me explain. The War Office has ordered a census of Jewish soldiers.'

'In what way are we different from others in uniform?'

'I've already told you – I only carry out orders. I leave it to you to interpret, Doctor. Good night.'

The explanation was quite simple, and Leo had no difficulty in understanding it. The civilian population was dissatisfied with the progress of the war. In part the criticism – although in somewhat disguised terms – was directed at the chiefs of staff. No one dared to criticize the Kaiser and the influential generals openly, but privately the accusation of 'Failure!' was going the rounds. The War Office and the top brass desperately needed a scapegoat: someone who could be accused in order to distract public opinion from what was actually going on.

It is not known which official or officer on the general staff came up with the idea of once again wheeling out the age-old scarecrow of anti-Semitism. In any case the public at large was to be bombarded with statistical data in order to prove that the members of the Mosaic faith were not pulling their weight towards the war effort, compared with other subjects of the Reich. The order for the census was issued in October 1916. Contemporary documents, preserved in the archives, bear the signature of Major General von Wrisberg, the director of the War Office in Berlin. However, it is hardly likely that this initiative could have been the work of one single official, no matter how high his rank. When the order became known, arousing the indignation of some of the general public and activists in the Jewish community, Wrisberg hastened to calm people's feelings by making this announcement in a session of the parliamentary Reichstag:

'This measure was adopted with the sole purpose of collecting written evidence in order that we may examine complaints that have been raised in the army against Jews. [...] The census is intended to provide information to the War Office alone. It will supply documents, enabling us to check complaints about attempts by Jews to avoid military service...'

From August 1916 all governmental business had been concentrated in the hands of the military, and effectively they were the actual rulers. In January 1917 Chancellor Theobald von Bethmann Hollweg made one last effort to maintain 'the humane character of the war', by refusing to grant the U-boat fleet a free hand. Members of parliament did not support his stand. The Reichstag threatened to withdraw their support from him, if he did not give in to the demands of the army.

The request for unlimited U-boat action was intended to break through the sea blockade imposed by the neighbouring states of the Reich, which hung like a yoke over the German economy and was exerting a stranglehold. Sections of industry vital to the war were being paralysed, causing bottlenecks in the provision of essential products, including bread, sugar, meat, oil, cotton, and fuel.

The *Belgard Polzin and District Newspaper* appeared twice a week, on Wednesday and Saturday. It was of great interest to Bernhard as it included the official food prices. Anyone who did not keep to them was severely punished. At the beginning of 1915 a ton of potatoes had still cost fifty-five marks; by March the price had risen to ninety marks. A kilo of rye flour had shot up from thirty-six pfennigs in January 1915 to sixty-two pfennigs in December. The prices of all other goods rose accordingly. In August 1916 the district paper printed a communication from the regional parliament:

'It can be safely assumed that the sum of one billion in gold is still in the hands of private individuals. This money is to be handed over immediately to the Reichsbank!'

When Bernhard collected the paper on that morning from the Polzin post office, he was surprised to see that someone had circled this announcement in red. It was quite obvious to him that this was no accident. Someone was trying to accuse him, but who? A simple post office worker envious of his wealth or some highly placed individual wishing to draw attentions to his views? His conscience was clear. He did not possess any gold coins or bars. He had never broken the law. He had always sold his produce at the official fixed prices, even if it meant a loss. He provided the tax authorities with meticulously accurate information about the property and assets of the business, and the business accounts were also submitted to strict inspection. But Bernhard was no fool. He realized that the truth was irrelevant and that there was no way of convincing people of his honesty. However, at this moment, his greatest concern was how he could hide the paper from Henriette. He folded it up and stuffed it in the bottom of the same drawer where his father used to keep papers of this kind. And like his father, Bernhard also kept the drawer locked.

Two years after the outbreak of the Great War it became clear to many that the brilliant tactical manoeuvrings of the general staff had not encompassed the organization of reinforcements and supplies on a long-term basis. This failure may have been because they were convinced it would be a short-term military conflict. It is also possible that they were so blinded by their sophisticated plan of attack that they simply forgot about the needs of the civilian population. Now the generals insisted on being allowed to implement to the full the freedom of action granted them by the Reichstag. This meant using maximum U-boat capacity to gain access for vital supplies.

In the autumn of 1916 the leaders of the German economy recognized the devastating truth: their industrial might, which had astounded the public at the World Fair with magic machines and gigantic cannons that now, sixteen years later, bombarded the city of Paris, was facing total paralysis. The well-known industrialist Walther Rathenau, president of the AEG Works, was asked to produce a plan that would switch the entire production of the empire on to a war footing. Although he had never shared the views of this man, who was in favour of total assimilation and considered conversion to Christianity as the solution of the 'Jewish question', Bernhard accepted this news as an endorsement of his own ideas. Now the skills of prosperous Jews were in demand, matching the contribution of the soldiers of the Mosaic faith. But even major entrepreneurs could not wave a magic wand when their hands were empty. In the whole of great and arrogant Germany, where celebrated engineers were capable of manufacturing locomotives, diesel engines, and advanced electrical appliances, where the best coal in Europe was mined, excellent steel produced, and a mighty army of four million soldiers had been assembled, there was not a loaf of bread nor a sack of potatoes left for the civilian population – even though the vast lands of the Ukraine, the breadbasket of Europe, were now in German hands. The brilliant minds that had developed piston engines, seamless pipes, zeppelins, and synthetic fuel, and had patented dozens of other amazing inventions, now had to work out a means of food rationing. The U-boat war did not bring any relief to the German people but introduced another enemy, for German torpedoes induced the USA to enter the war.

The Germans had predicted a very different outcome for the campaign that ended with the Battle of the Marne. The bitterness of the civilian population grew day by day. Against this background, it was quite likely that the statistics of Ernst von

Wrisberg could appease and placate the rising feelings of the public. But even this weapon proved a disappointment to its author. Although a selected band of statisticians pored for months over the pages of figures, the results of the census were never published, as the data did not support the intentions of the War Office. When von Wrisberg finally retired, he published his memoirs, which included details of the census.

Independent historians later disputed the accuracy of these figures. There is no doubt that at the time of the census, many Jews had been transferred out of their fighting units at the front so that the statistics could be made to serve their purpose. However, it emerged that in the autumn of 1916 some 63,000 soldiers of the Mosaic faith were serving in the army of the Reich; of these only 5,000 were in the rear; 27,500 were at the front; and 30,000 were with the occupation forces. In percentage terms these figures equalled those of the Christians in uniform.

Leo sent the bar of chocolate to his little daughter, but did not disclose his state of mind in the letter to his family. The discriminatory census had been a bitter blow for him, robbing him of his belief that at least in battle there was no discrimination. Rudolf, who wore his Iron Cross with pride, preferred to remain silent about this distressing experience. However, of course, it did not stay secret. The Jewish communities and their organizations protested, Orthodox as well as Reform. Siegfried Levy, on business in Berlin, was stirred by a copy of the *Frankfurter Zeitung* of 24 November, bought at the railway station.

> The Association against Anti-Semitism held its annual general meeting yesterday. The chairman, Dr Gothein, emphasized that the hope of maintaining a truce between the religious confessions had regrettably not been fulfilled. The Association would not be redundant after the war, he declared, but would have to continue its fight. In his lecture on the role of the Jews in the war, the speaker observed that it should be known that some progress had been made. Over one thousand five hundred Jewish soldiers had been made officers, half of these

Certificate awarding Leo Levy decoration for military service, '2nd Class with Crown', January 1915.

in Prussia and most of the rest in Bavaria. Yet this number was insignificant compared with those Jews who are eligible. What the Jews achieved in the army was best shown by the fact that more than eighty have been awarded the Iron Cross, First Class; over eight thousand have received the Iron Cross, Second Class; and some the *Pour le mérite*. It is regrettable that the War Office, in the face of anti-Semitic agitation, has ordered an easily misconstrued decree to produce statistics about Jews. The pattern of these statistics is a model of how not to go about it. The object was to confront unjustified attacks on the military command, but they failed to realize that this decree would affect Jews and all their comrades in the field who defend justice. In judging the Jews in this war, it should not be forgotten what so many chemists, engineers, and financiers of the Jewish persuasion have contributed.

Just as Bernhard had done, Siegfried folded up the newspaper, but he stuffed it deep into the pocket of his winter coat. The railway compartment was not heated. The cold gnawed first at his toes, and gradually crept through his entire body. His suitcase, which he had placed in the luggage rack above his seat, contained sandwiches of goose-liver pâté and a thermos flask of hot tea. Siegfried examined the faces of his fellow passengers – tired people, huddled in silence. To feed on rolls soaked in goose fat in front of their weary eyes would have amounted to sheer insensitivity. Siegfried did without the goose-liver sandwiches and the hot tea, and instead rubbed his hands together to drive off the cold.

At home in Polzin things continued much as usual, and the larder was overflowing. Shortages of food and other essential items did not affect the Levy family. The farms on their estates supplied the best meat and fresh vegetables. Henriette saw to it that family relations in Stettin, Berlin, and Danzig received regular food parcels, for in the cities rationing had a marked effect. At first she had also sent her sons at the front all manner of delicacies, but Leo and Ernst had both asked her to stop. Their comrades had hardly been able to believe their eyes. Anyone with plenty of food in times of scarcity easily made themselves unpopular. From then on Bernhard ordered the produce being sent from the farms to be packed in large wooden boxes clearly marked 'Agricultural implements'. When the family sat down to eat, the doors would be locked to keep uninvited visitors away.

The business was not adversely affected by the war either. Siegfried travelled to Berlin at least once a month to negotiate with government officials over delivery of timber. In order to keep pace with the orders, the sawmills were working round the clock. In addition, the family invested increasingly in agricultural land. As a result of general mobilization the Pomeranian farmers could barely keep their fields tended. There were no young men in the villages – they were all in uniform serving at the front. And as most of the farms were in debt anyway, their situation became worse day by day. Some of the landowners sold their fields that were lying fallow to the highest bidders. And as the prices fell, Bernhard seized the opportunity with both hands. Sometimes it was enough for him to pay a small amount in cash and take over the debts of a farm. His landed property was constantly growing. In his prayers Bernhard thanked his Creator for rewarding his family for their steadfast loyalty to their faith and to their fatherland.

The winter passed. But the spring brought no improvement to the general economic situation. In May 1917, Bernhard and Henriette travelled to Bad Kissingen for a rest, just as if there were no war.

Siegfried bought up the shares of their former business partners, Gustav Möller & Successors, in Köslin as well as in Stettin. It had been Lisbeth's idea. She had been wanting to move to the big city for a long time. In her eyes Polzin was a godforsaken town lacking any kind of style. She loathed the Polzin business with its provincial character. She had nothing in common with the Jews of Polzin and the doors of the nobility remained closed to her. She had been invited on two occasions to functions given by Hermann-Konrad, Graf von Kleist. But business matters of the firm had gained her entrance to the aristocratic estate in Gross Dubberow, not her social standing. Most of all she increasingly had the feeling that the understanding shown her by the family simply stemmed from pity because she could not have children. Whether or not this was imaginary, she wished to cease being in such close contact with her mother-in-law and sister-in-law. Bernhard was the only one for whom she felt warmth and respect. He understood her inner conflicts and the effects of the miscarriage on her state of mind.

'I'm unhappy,' she once said in a moment of weakness, laying her head on Bernhard's shoulder, just like a little girl.

'It's been almost two years now,' he replied, gently stroking her head. 'Try to understand, time heals all wounds.'

'You simply cannot imagine how I suffer. A woman who cannot be a mother. After all, you were brought up in the Jewish tradition. In your eyes I am surely an inferior creature. You know that any orthodox rabbi could have forced me to divorce, if Sigi had wanted to.'

'Don't talk nonsense, Lisbeth. Siegfried will never leave you. Divorce is unheard of in our family, and always will be. And quite apart from that, a person's worth is not judged by whether or not they can conceive and give birth. Sometimes we feel desperately sad and at other times we may be overjoyed. There's no reason for our state of mind to depend on the function of our organs.'

'All the same I can't get any peace. I don't like the way people look at me. And I can't bear it when they pretend to be friendly, when they don't really mean it.'

'That's your own subjective reaction, and is quite unfounded.'

'That doesn't make it any easier. I happen to be an emotional creature.'

'Maybe you are right in your own way. After all, happiness means something different to each of us. But there is one idea that often helps me.'

'And that is?'

'You have to try to build a bridge between your expectations and what is possible. Siegfried would put it very simply – you can't change the way you are and, what's more, you shouldn't try.' Bernhard gave a laugh, but immediately became serious again. 'No, no, Lisi, I'm not making fun of you. I understand your problem and all its implications. Striving for more is an important spur for the advancement of mankind. But in our private lives, why not pause from time to time and reflect, and try to match our striving to exist-ing means and possibilities. What unnecessary pain we inflict on ourselves when we try to reach the unattainable! We must let sound common sense prevail. And prayer can also help. Yes, Lisi, prayer. It can fill the void between what we long for and what we are given.'

'That's no comfort to me. I wish I could believe in the Creator like you do. I often get a cold feeling around my heart as if it were empty and did not belong to me.'

Siegfried was only too pleased to move to Stettin. On one of his business trips he rented a spacious apartment, and even went ahead and bought furniture for the four rooms. But an unexpected development caused the couple to delay their move. In the summer of 1917 Lisbeth's sister-in-law, Ida, returned home from Damascus without warning. She brought a splendid daughter with her, and assured everyone that Paul would soon follow. Paul's contract with the company building the Hejaz railway line in the Ottoman empire had expired, and he didn't intend to renew it, at least according to Ida. But when for no obvious reason he failed to appear, she finally came out with the admission that her marriage with Paul was at an end. As long as they were both living in far-off Damascus, and contact with the family in Polzin had been limited to occasional letters, the incompatibility between the two had not been evident. Now that Ida had sought refuge in Polzin, the truth emerged. The marriage had never been happy right from the start. From her early years Ida had dreamed of the allure of the wide world, offering only exquisite surprises and exciting temptations. She had not found these as Paul's wife. His world revolved around Damascus, the deserts of Syria and the Arabian Gulf, and the challenges offered by his profession. They had no interests in common. Ida was now convinced of the need to divorce and build a new life for herself. No one knew what Paul had in mind.

In Polzin Lisbeth was the only one to befriend Ida. She understood Ida's longing for a different way of life all too well. Fortunately for her – unlike Ida – she was married to a man who shared her outlook. But Ida did not reciprocate the affection shown her by her brother and sister-in-law. Her reaction to the failed marriage was to smother herself in luxury. The trunks she had brought back were filled with an extravagant wardrobe. Every day she appeared in a new dress, each more elegant than the last, and left a trail of strong French perfume in her wake. She wore brightly coloured hats trimmed with silk flowers, or black head coverings with broad brims that hid her beautiful face. Her flamboyant appearance became the talk of Polzin, so that Henriette soon felt obliged to speak to her about it.

'Isn't this all a bit overdone when there is a war on?'

'But Mama,' said Ida in genuine surprise, 'do you really believe I am supposed to go about looking less feminine, just because men are killing each other?'

'How can you even say such a thing! Ernst and Leo are fighting at the front.'

'It wasn't me that sent them off to war.'

Henriette became angry. 'It's all very well for you,' she said, 'you were both far from home. Your husband didn't have to serve the fatherland, and you didn't go through the agony of worrying whether he would come back or not. Or perhaps it wouldn't have bothered you anyway?' she added bitterly.

'The future will show who has been serving their fatherland better. Have you forgotten, Mama? Before we left for Syria, it was you who said that that was the most patriotic duty we could fulfil. I wanted to live in Danzig. You and Paul were the ones who persuaded me to go out there with him. Maybe you've forgotten that, but I haven't. I remember every single word.'

Indeed, his decision to go to Syria had not just been a professional challenge and an opportunity to advance his personal career. With the idealism of youth, Paul Levy had regarded it as a duty in the service of the nation. When he had introduced himself to Meissner, the senior engineer who had come to Berlin to recruit new staff, Meissner had explained to Paul the political significance of the project. 'Pasha Meissner', as he was known in Turkey, had already supervised the laying of railway tracks in the European part of the Ottoman empire, and since 1900 he had been regarded as one of the foremost engineers building the Hejaz line. This was to link Damascus with Mecca, the holiest city of Islam, and make travelling easier for the thousands of Muslim pilgrims, for whom the long and arduous journey had until now taken up to forty days.

In the view of the Kaiser this offered a favourable opportunity for German investors and engineers and it was at the same time a powerful instrument for extending the influence of the German empire in the Middle East.

The idea of a railway connecting Europe to Asia was not new. As early as 1837 Sir Francis R. Chesney had seen it as an effective strategy for securing British rule in India on a long-term basis. Some twenty years later the British had secured the desired concession. But with the construction of the Suez Canal the sea link became more important to them than the land route to the Red Sea coast, and so in 1888 the German banks were able to take over the coveted concession. In Wilhelm II's view, the railway was the right means of transport for distributing German goods to the Middle East, intending them to be followed up by German culture and eventually political power and influence. Politicians and the military were pressing for a German outpost in the Middle East as a bridgehead, which at a given time would serve against the expansionist aims of the British. The first stretch of track was completed in 1893, and from then on it was possible to travel from Berlin direct to Baghdad by train. The Hejaz railway was simply an extension of this route. Then Sultan Abdul Hamid issued a decree that from 1 May 1900 the funds required for the construction were to be drawn on. Ten German engineers were asked to take over the project. Some, such as the Prussian Imperial Colonel Auler or Infantry General Colmar, Freiherr von der Goltz, were given high-ranking positions in the Ottoman army and were even made pashas.

A fine apartment had been put at Paul and Ida's disposal, near the Kadesh-Ish-Sherif railway station, from where the trains ran southwards. Even before their arrival in Damascus, a stretch of several hundred kilometres had already been laid. The German empire was not just involved in laying the track but with supplying the trains as well. Twenty-nine locomotives were assembled by Krauss in Munich and by Hohenzollern in Düsseldorf. Even the railway carriages came from Germany. There was one special one fitted out as a mosque.

The project was plagued with complications. The trains had to stop every twenty-five kilometres in order to take on water from

sources specially drilled alongside the railway line. Supplies for
the railway line and the construction team presented problems,
which no other project had had to face. The work of the engineers was made even more difficult because non-Muslim engineers
were forbidden to go south beyond the Mad'im Lasiah line:
staying near the holy sites could have led to their murder. There
was a shortage of labourers, so approximately five thousand soldiers of the 5th Corps were detailed to work on the construction.
Furthermore, the division of authority between civilian management and the military supreme command led to numerous mis-
understandings and held up the work. However, the railway soon
proved its usefulness. In the summer of 1908, when a revolt broke
out in the Arabian Gulf, the Turkish commander-in-chief was
the first to make use of the Hejaz railway. It carried twenty-eight
regiments to Ma'an, from where they continued on foot to the
port of Akaba on the Red Sea. There they were shipped to
Hodeida. This was the time when laborious negotiations were
being conducted with the English over the purchase of the
railway track between Haifa and Damascus. In the end this
stretch was bought by a German consortium for 925,000
Reichmarks, so that the empire could now use the port in
Palestine to import raw materials.

Paul Levy was not involved in political decisions and intrigues.
His task was to see to it that the railway worked efficiently.

At times he was stationed a long way from Damascus, where
of necessity Ida had had to spend long periods on her own, with
servants who spoke no German and neighbours who avoided
contact with foreigners. Paul was allowed to leave his posting for
short visits three times a week by slow train. However, he did not
always take advantage of this opportunity to go home to Ida. He
had very quickly made a name for himself as an expert on the
route, and was in charge of a small group who had extended the
network by 522 kilometres in the space of only four years, between
1904 and 1907. In one of his letters to his father Julius in Danzig,
Paul had compared this adventure with Ascher Levy's journey to
Palestine, given the difference that there was still no sign of civi-
lization in the desert. The areas they were working in were

completely barren. Besides the engineer, the group consisted of two officers of the Pioneer Corps, a doctor, ten soldiers responsible for transport, and twenty riders, who were supposed to protect the group from bands of marauding Bedouins. Provisions were carried by mules, with water in goatskins on the backs of camels. Meanwhile Ida had had to come to terms with an alien environment that was alarming and unwelcoming, and all she dreamed of was getting back as soon as possible to the sophisticated world of European culture.

But life in the small provincial town of Polzin, her parental home, obviously did not come up to her expectations. She distanced herself from the family, and withdrew to her room where she would bury herself in books sent to her by friends and relatives in Stettin. It was only when letters from Leo, Ernst, or Rudolf arrived that she showed any interest. Bernhard would always read these letters when all the family was gathered around the table for the evening meal. Reading them aloud became a kind of family ritual.

The letters were fairly trivial, largely because of army censorship. The sons were careful not to refer to events at the front, and avoided any kind of political comment. In any case news of any significance came not from the front but from politics. Campaign advances had come to a standstill, and trench warfare had become a continuing, nerve-racking nightmare. As disillusionment grew at the military situation, disputes on the political home front began to intensify and even reached Polzin. The beer cellar in the market square became a debating club, where alcohol and news from Berlin became an explosive mixture.

Bernhard had forbidden political discussion of any kind in his office, in the sawmills, and on the estates. 'I pay you to work. If you want to gossip, then go to the Reichstag,' he would say angrily if he caught anyone disregarding his rule. He didn't even wish to talk about what was in the papers with Siegfried. 'The politicians wreck everything of value,' he seethed. On every occasion he would repeat that the social democrats were responsible for each disaster. Siegfried was familiar with his father's views, and did not even attempt to contradict him. Their conversations

were mainly concerned with their common business undertakings.

It was only at times when Bernhard found himself alone that
he permitted himself to face facts. These were difficult moments.
It was hard for him to question the views that he proclaimed so
vehemently to those around him. He did not let Henriette know
that he sometimes felt like a traitor to the cause. After all, the
foundation of his whole life rested on what he considered sacred
principles. So he kept his confusion to himself, even though he
could not altogether disregard the unpleasant reality.

In the summer of 1917 the Reich Chancellor von Bethmann
Hollweg was removed from office by the military and the
Reichstag, because he had opposed the peace formula of 'no
annexations and no indemnities' favoured by most of parliament.
For the first time the centre-left majority of the Reichstag agreed
to a kind of coalition, and dropped a bombshell: an offer of peace
talks. Everyone had long since realized that the original aims of
the war were no longer valid. The coalition preceded Hindenburg
and Ludendorff by only one year, but at this time such a proposal
caused a tremendous uproar. But even the new Chancellor Georg
Michaelis firmly supported the principle that when supposed
'facts' no longer conform with reality, then the situation must be
changed. This was all the more important in view of the outbreak
of the bloody civil war in Russia, which might yet make military
victory a possibility.

The following year began with a wave of strikes. Embittered
and disillusioned, the workers hungered for bread and peace.
Victory was a forgotten dream, and hopes for generous war reparations – three times as high as those paid by the French at the
end of the previous war – were clearly untenable.

At the beginning of March 1918 a peace treaty was imposed on
Soviet Russia at Brest-Litovsk. However, it proved so unstable
that German troops remained tied down in the east. Fighting also
continued on the western front, with even greater intensity. In
the spring of 1918 the German military high command attempted
to revive trench warfare, and began a major offensive. The soldiers were ordered out of their trenches five times. Five times

they had to retreat. In the middle of July the Allies launched a major counter-offensive. With that, the reserve camp of Leo Levy's unit was completely destroyed. He went to inspect the buildings hit by artillery fire and watched in horror as medical orderlies carried the dead and the wounded from the scene of battle. His anger at the French, the British, and the Americans mounted.

'We shall still carry out a counter-offensive,' he burst out in the presence of Captain Tuch, who had come to see the losses and the damage with his own eyes. And so they stood there, among slabs of concrete that had collapsed under the weight of the bombardment, surrounded by bomb craters, watching the stretcher-bearers carry away the casualties.

'What makes you so sure, Herr Doctor?' asked Tuch. 'Aren't you affected by this terrible sight?'

'I believe in the Creator and in historic justice.'

'Don't you think the enemy also believes in the Creator and historic justice? Or do you happen to have a different God from us?'

Leo threw him an astonished look. 'I don't quite understand,' he said. 'Aren't you convinced of the justice of the war we're fighting?'

'There are no just or unjust wars, Herr Doctor. There are only wars that are either won, or end in defeat. The victor is always in the right, and the loser in the wrong.'

'That isn't exactly a moral view, Captain.'

'Moral – in war?' laughed Tuch. 'Are you searching for water in the desert?'

'I have never seen you so depressed.'

'Take a look around you, Herr Doctor. Does what you see here lift your spirits?'

'It's part of reality.'

'And a herald of disaster.'

'That sounds as if you're giving up.'

'It's the general opinion.'

'No, we stand for victory.'

Captain Tuch looked at him in amazement. Then he lowered

his voice. 'I have seen a copy of a secret document. A report from the supreme command. Can you guess what it contains?'

Leo said nothing.

'The document maintains,' said Tuch, 'that it is no longer possible to win this war.'

On 14 August 1918, four years and fourteen days after the out-break of war, the supreme command had assembled at Spa to discuss the situation. This little Belgian town, about twenty kilo-metres south of Liège, was the first place to have fallen to the German army, giving rise at the time to hopes for a sweeping and rapid victory. Now the generals were no longer under any illusion. The victorious Allied counter-offensive in the west was soon fol-lowed by the collapse of the south-eastern and southern fronts. But it was to take almost another six weeks before General Quartermaster Ludendorff summoned up the strength to inform the political leadership that the war was lost, and that there was no other way out but to propose an armistice to the enemy. The military abandoned all responsibility, leaving it to parliament to come to a decision and start peace negotiations. The reformist majority in the Reichstag – the social democrats, progressive lib-erals, and centrists – the outsiders in the empire, were now to be the ones to avert the worst of the crisis. From this moment onwards the situation was overtaken by events. On 3 November, revolution broke out. On 9 November the Chancellor, Prince Max von Baden, handed over power to Friedrich Ebert, leader of the social democrats. On the same day Kaiser Wilhelm II abdi-cated and went into exile in the Netherlands. On 11 November the Germans were compelled to accept the armistice on terms dictated by the enemy, and even before the snows had melted the Weimar Republic was proclaimed.

The commanders had failed on the battlefield. But blame for the defeat was heaped on the politicians, and so it was that a civilian, the centre-left Matthias Erzberger, accompanied by only two offi-cers from the high command, was obliged to take the onerous path to the railway carriage placed close to the entente's base, near Compiègne. Maréchal Foch, who received them, displayed none of the traditional niceties of French courtesy. 'There will be no negotiations of any kind,' he announced. 'Germany has lost the war, and will pay the price.' Seventy-two hours later Erzberger signed.

The price, ultimately set out in the 1920 Treaty of Versailles, was high. Germany lost Alsace-Lorraine to France, and the major part of Posen, West Prussia, and parts of Upper Silesia went to Poland. Danzig was declared a free city and Memelland was added to Lithuania; Denmark was given North Schleswig. The industrial region of Eupen-Malmedy went to Belgium; the Saar with its rich coal deposits was placed under the protection of the League of Nations for fifteen years and was occupied by the French. The highly industrialized Ruhr region was worst affected. All the colonies were taken over by the Allies; the senior high command was dissolved and the size of the army reduced to 100,000 men, whose weaponry and arms were severely restricted; tank, gas, air, and U-boat munitions were totally prohibited. Furthermore, in 1921 reparation payments were finally set at 132 billion gold marks, an amount that with the best will in the world Germany could not have paid.

Even though these details were not yet known when the armistice was signed, Germany's dream of great power had evaporated, without the military men involved being made to accept their responsibility. The public perception was that the army had fought, but the politicians had betrayed them and sold out their country. The fact that there were Jews among them did not make things any better.

For Bernhard news of the crushing end to the war was a severe blow. God had not listened to the prayer he had uttered on the day the war broke out. The Kaiser had fled, the country had collapsed. The pillars supporting his philosophy of life had been shattered. And as if that were not enough, the masses in Munich and Berlin were waving red banners and shouting revolutionary slogans. Bernhard did not support the liberals and hated the social democrats, but when it came to the communists, he was absolutely terrified.

'Maybe it's better to take the money from the bank, and keep it at home in the safe,' he debated with Siegfried.

'I already did so two weeks ago,' replied his son, winking at his father. 'I withdrew about half of the cash deposits and all the bonds. I didn't want to close the accounts, as that would certainly have created alarm.'

Bernhard nodded, and suppressed a remark. On any other occasion he would have reprimanded his son for acting without consulting him. This time he preferred to say nothing, for essentially he was reassured that their money was safe and he had not had to have anything to do with it.

Henriette began to be concerned about her husband, for Bernhard was becoming increasingly withdrawn. The fact that Wilhem II had gone into exile in the Netherlands hit him almost like a personal insult. One evening he surprised his wife by saying, 'Our time, my dear, is over.'

Henriette looked up. 'We have to adapt to new times, Beri,' she said.

'Oh no. It seems to me that this is a bridge we cannot cross. I don't belong in this new world.'

'Ernst and Leo will soon be home, and everything will become clear.'

Bernhard sighed. 'Sometimes I ask myself what kind of reality they will return home to. To the Germany of Karl Liebknecht and Rosa Luxemburg? The Spartacus followers have branded us in a way that the people won't forget too easily. And now the republic, democracy, this crushing defeat...I've no idea how much further we shall sink, but of one thing I'm certain – we, the Jews, we will have to pay for it.'

'You're exaggerating. Everything will be back to what it used to be. You always used to like quoting *Kohelet*. D'you remember – "one people is destroyed and another rises up; but the earth always remains"?'

A smile hovered over Bernhard's lips. 'You know what I love most about you?'

'You've never told me.'

'The way you're able to adjust to things the way they are. Your adaptability...Perhaps that's why our marriage has been such a success. We've lived under the same roof for so many years, and sometimes even feel really close. Isn't that a success?'

Henriette put aside her embroidery and, moving closer to him, reached out for his hand. It was rough and cold. 'You worry too much, Beri,' she said. 'Shall I make you a cup of tea?'

'You always try to solve the problems of the world with a cup of tea and a slice of apple strudel.'

'You just told me that so far I haven't done so badly.'

Ernst was discharged from the army at the end of November and returned to Berlin. He too recoiled from those in favour of the republic, people like Philipp Scheidemann and Konstantin Fehrenbach. Nevertheless he was confident that nothing now stood in the way of his attaining judicial office.

He wrote to his father in Polzin:

I have now returned to being a lawyer. There is no shortage of work, so I don't have to worry about earning a living, and the future seems secure for the two girls. And yet, like you, I find it hard to digest the fact that the Kaiser's throne remains empty, and will be no more than a museum piece from now on. Maybe the day will come when he will return to his rightful place, for it simply cannot be that Germany should be ruled by ministers who argue about what this 'New Germany', as they call it, should be like and what path it should follow. There are disturbances in the city, with demonstrations almost every day for or against something or other, so that sometimes it seems to me that they are madmen escaped from the cages of our zoo. I frequently feel as if I am living in a lunatic asylum. The day the Kaiser abdicated there was a lot of bloodshed here, but on the very same day the champagne flowed at a reception in honour of Ernst Lubitsch. He was showing his film of *Carmen* with Pola Negri. They say she is the star of tomorrow. There are those who say that tomorrow's real star is Rosa Luxemburg. But there are times when on the quiet I ask myself – will there be a tomorrow? Many of our friends here predict a communist state. I comfort myself with the thought that the German

people will at last find the strength and enough common sense
to overcome this crisis. If not I may live to regret that I didn't
die in the war...

In the middle of January 1919 the communist Spartacus uprising in Berlin came to an unexpected end. Gustav Noske, the
right-wing social democrat, who as a member of the people's representative committee had taken over the military department,
brought the uprising to a bloody end to stop the revolution.
'Somebody has to be the bloodhound,' he proclaimed. 'I do not
shun my duty!'

Noske stood for a straightforward materialistic form of social-
ism without ideological trimmings. In his youth he had dreamed
of being a forester, but his parents could not afford the training
fees and so he took up basket-weaving. In his view rising up from
the lower classes was in itself the fulfilment of the socialist idea.
'Karl Liebknecht wanted to be Germany's Lenin,' he said, raising
his glass when he learned of the gruesome murder of the leader of
the Spartacus movement. He did not perceive the danger
looming from the right.

The struggle for power between the opposing camps escalated,
and street battles became a daily occurrence in Berlin at this time.
Rosa Luxemburg and Karl Liebknecht had been horribly murdered. Fighting in the capital took place with no holds barred.
Tens of thousands of soldiers had returned home to unemployment, and those disabled in the war went begging in the streets.
Assembly points were set up in various public places in the city
for the volunteer corps, for all those who could not fit into the
democratic social order and its institutions. It was at this point
that an influenza epidemic broke out in the city. There were not
enough beds for the sick in the public hospitals, and very few
people could afford private medical assistance. Against this background, the wealthy and those who had profited from shady
wartime business deals adopted an ostentatious lifestyle. This was
the chaos into which the republic was born. Because of the
unrest, the politicians avoided Berlin and retreated to Weimar to
work out a lasting constitution away from the daily clashes.

Many opponents of the new state ridiculed the fact that the birth of the republic had not even taken place in its capital.

Leo, who had been brought up in the spirit of Prussian order, had absolutely no understanding for this turmoil. He received his discharge papers about three months before the republic was proclaimed. His farewell from the unit was brief. Captain Tuch shook him warmly by the hand and said: 'We have spent four years together. Just a short episode in terms of history, but for a human life what a sheer unconscionable waste.' Leo did not reply. His own view was very different. And so he packed his things, including a medal with a crown, the highest awarded for military service, and a letter of commendation from the Infantry General Fasbender.

He arrived in Polzin the evening before Christmas. The family had prepared a festive reception in his honour. Henriette had cooked all his favourite dishes, and the door of the house was decorated with brightly coloured paper flowers and a banner with the garlanded words, 'Welcome Home'. Hannah, aged four and a half, and Eva, a year younger, were to recite a poem they had learned by heart for their father's return. Only Siegfried stayed in the office to draw up the annual balance sheet, for he wished to impress his brother and to show him immediately on his return how well the business had been doing during his absence.

Bernhard and two employees went to the railway station to bring his returning son back to the house. As the stationmaster recognized Bernhard, he brought his hand up to his red cap in a smart salute. By mid-afternoon it was already getting dark. The snow had melted and turned into slush. It was an unpleasant, rainy day. The three sat down in the unheated waiting room. Outside on the forecourt the coachman, chewing tobacco, stood in the drizzle. The stationmaster apologized: 'There is a delay of one hour and thirty-one minutes. I am sorry, I'm afraid even the trains aren't what they used to be.'

'My son has had a four-year delay, but I'm not complaining,' replied Bernhard. It wasn't plain whether he was being cynical or spoke in earnest.

Leo eventually stepped down from a third-class compartment. He was carrying a shabby case in his left hand and a knapsack full to bursting point on his shoulder. Father and son gave each other a fleeting embrace.

'You hardly look as if you're coming back from the war,' were Bernhard's opening words and only then did he enquire about how Leo was feeling.

'Physically, I am in good shape,' said Leo without further explanation.

On the way home in the coach, Bernhard placed his hand on his son's shoulder, a hesitant form of embrace. 'We have prepared a royal welcome for you, with apple strudel and poems,' he said. 'Mama cannot wait to see you.'

Leo remained silent. The carriage drove through the familiar streets, but he did not give them a glance. He sat there bolt upright, in best military posture, without a word. It was only as they approached the house that he broke his silence and quietly said, 'I hope you won't be cross with me, but I am desperately tired. All I want to do now is sleep.'

The war had left its mark, but the Levys had at least survived without material losses. After Leo had slept for almost two days, the brothers sat down together in the old office in the Brunnenstrasse to take stock. 'Papa is a devil of a fellow,' remarked Siegfried as he spread out on the table the sheets that recorded the transactions of the firm on the grain market. Their assets amounted to about three million marks, a prodigious sum for a provincial business. It was securely invested in bonds and property, and only a small proportion had been paid into the old-established bank in Stettin. In the light of day the Levys were as rich as Croesus! But they kept to their modest lifestyle, characteristic of citizens of a small provincial town. No new furniture had been bought, the women dressed simply, and the children were not given excessive pocket money. The household was run on thrifty lines. Siegfried's suggestion of buying a car had been dismissed by Bernhard as 'completely crazy'.

This idea had actually come from Siegfried's cousin Rudolf. Rudolf had returned to paint and canvas, now at the Munich

Academy of Fine Arts, but his wartime experience with cars had left its mark. His letters to his relatives in Polzin succeeded in firing Siegfried with his own passion. But Bernhard wanted nothing to do with this 'fiendish invention'. He had nothing against cars as such, for in spite of his age and his conservative principles, Bernhard had always remained open to practical suggestions. His strict refusal was based rather on his disapproval of Rudolf. While the war was on he had heard that Rudolf had been consorting with dubious individuals. Now he discovered that his nephew had befriended a Christian girl and that the couple intended to marry. For him there was no greater sin than betraying one's religion and one's origins. Judaism was fundamental to his philosophy of life. Like Jäckel and Ascher he had succeeded in creating a bridge between his Jewish religion and his German nationality. He was well aware that it was a narrow and rickety bridge, and he was afraid of tremors that might bring the fragile structure crashing down.

Religious values had held good over the generations as the moral foundation in European societies had gradually diminished as a result of the French revolution. Already by the late nineteenth century modern man was defining his identity less and less in terms of religion. Secular issues were steadily replacing these tenets. Bernhard found it immensely difficult to become accustomed to this new orientation of universal values. The warning of his father, Ascher Levy, commenting on Theodor Herzl, still echoed in his ears: 'This is the beginning of the *danse macabre*...'

And now the *danse macabre* was in full spate. Bernhard protested against it with all his might: 'A man who relies only on himself, and does not appeal to his belief in God, is a creature in danger of losing his moral foundation. And as we have no right to exist without a moral basis, this kind of progress is tantamount to suicide,' he wrote to Ernst in Berlin. At that time he was still unaware that Ernst had overstepped the limits. When Bernhard visited Ernst, he discovered to his horror that his son and daughter-in-law no longer observed the dietary laws. So during the time he spent with them, all he ate was hard-boiled eggs. He had hesitated whether to reprimand them or to keep silent. Then he

was afraid that he did not have the strength for that kind of argument, and in the end decided against a moralizing sermon.
'Without a doubt keeping silent was weakness on my part, and a
serious mistake,' he wrote to Henriette. He was very much aware
that big movements begin with short steps, and for him this first
step would inevitably lead to a sheer precipice.

In the meantime Siegfried and Lisbeth had moved into their
five-roomed rented apartment on the second floor of a house in
the Friedrich-Karl Strasse, a quiet residential district of Stettin.
This household had likewise abandoned the traditional Jewish
way of life. When Siegfried and Lisbeth had taken leave of the
family in Polzin, Bernhard had handed them the portrait of
Maimonides. 'Hang it up in your drawing room,' he had bidden
her, adding, 'If you wonder about where we come from, take a
look at him, so that you don't forget where we belong.' Siegfried
had pressed a kiss on his father's cheek and taken the old picture.
Lisbeth wrapped it in brown paper, where it remained up to the
day when they had to flee from Germany.

In the spring of 1920, Ida also went away, first to Berlin, and
then from there to Cologne. The large house was visibly empty-
ing. Bernhard's heart was heavy. 'Wealth is no substitute for
family,' he said sadly to his wife.

Henriette attempted to comfort him. 'After all, we still have
Leo with us.'

One evening as they were sitting in the drawing room as they
usually did, with Henriette knitting and Bernhard immersed in
books, he remarked unexpectedly: 'The children and grandchildren are scattered like the Jewish people after the destruction of
the Temple. And once we have gone, there will be no Levy family
left.'

Several days later, on 19 May 1920, Henriette woke up in the
early hours of the morning. She had a strange feeling. At first she
thought she had had a nightmare, one of those dreams that last
just a few seconds, and although one cannot remember the contents, they stay as a heavy presence for hours after waking. The
sun's rays were coming through the window, and she could hear
the milkman's footsteps on the steps outside. That meant it must

be half past six. She raised her head, to listen for the everyday sounds of the morning. Suddenly she realized why she had been feeling so strange – she could not hear the heavy sounds of her husband's breathing.

From the day they were married on 1 September 1874 they had shared this enormous bed, which stood in their bedroom like an ancient wooden ship at anchor. She had brought five children into the world in this bed and – because of its great size – had also been able to preserve a certain private space in it. Once she had made fun of it, saying it reminded her of the majestic installations of the nobility, where man and wife sat at opposite ends of the dining table, and could only communicate through the mediation of their servants.

Now she sat up and, propped on one elbow, she leaned across to her husband. Bernhard had his back to her. Gently she touched his nightshirt, but even before she could stretch her hand out to feel his forehead, she knew it was cold. The doctor could do nothing but fill out the death certificate. For cause of death, he entered 'natural'.

At midday the body was taken away. Henriette gazed after it with dry eyes. She kept her pain and grief buried. To her great surprise she suddenly realized that Bernhard's large and hefty body appeared to have shrunk, and she asked herself whether this was because the soul had departed from its shell.

All the aspects of respect and luxury that Bernhard Levy had rejected in his lifetime were now accorded to him at his burial. Everyone in Polzin society attended the funeral, which had been postponed until the following day, so that family members from out of town could also attend. The local newspaper devoted an entire page to the event. The mayor appeared in his official robes and delivered a eulogy at the graveside of the long-standing member of the town council. He walked immediately behind the members of the family as they followed the body. Behind him were the business partners, the director of the Stettin bank, and representatives of the workers from the family's sawmills, factories, and estates. Black beribboned floral tributes arrived – from the charitable organizations that Bernhard had supported for

many years; from the regional administration of the railway, the
Levy business being one of its best customers; from the law
chambers of Dr Heinrich Marcuse and associates, which had for
years represented the interests of the firm; from the Association
for the Education of Jewish Orphans in Palestine, which
Bernhard had ceased to support, but which obviously wished to
be remembered in anticipation of a bequest; from the volunteer
fire brigade, to which he had donated a ladder two years ago for
their fire engine; and from friends, as well as from enemies
seeking reconciliation. Three dusty automobiles arrived from
Stettin, bringing Rabbi Moses Vermus and a delegation, including the cantor Garbarski, who chanted some prayers in a soft,
velvety voice. Anna Lewy, in whose house Siegfried and Lisbeth
had first met, had also made the journey. At the gate of the small
Jewish cemetery stood the uniformed chauffeurs and coachmen
beside the long line of cars and carriages that had brought the
mourners. In this way the full extent of the importance and also
the power of the Levy family was revealed at the funeral, although
Bernhard had never sought the limelight, preferring rather to stay
sheltered in the shadows.

After the funeral Leo gave instructions that the offices should
remain closed for the duration of the *Shiva*. All business activities
ceased, and family members gathered in the Levy home for the
week of official mourning. Leo read out loud from the book of
the Sanhedrin on the subject of burial and mourning, until he was
asked to stop and talk about other things.

After the *Shiva* was over, once again the family solicitor
arrived from Stettin. He first sought out Henriette and spent
quite a long time with her. Then he went to Leo and Siegfried in
their office and placed a sealed envelope in front of them, saying,
'I have brought your father's will with me. He drew it up eight
days before he died, and asked for it to be opened in your presence after the *Shiva*. I suggest that we meet this afternoon at five
in the apartment of the older Frau Levy.'

This time Henriette had not baked her famous apple strudel.
She had left the cook to prepare tea and sandwiches.

Dr Marcuse cleared his throat and everyone fell silent. 'Ladies and gentlemen, I should like to have your attention,' he said in a sombre tone, opening the envelope and removing several sheets of paper, which were covered in closely written lines. Then he slowly read out the contents, giving extra emphasis to the names, amounts, and conditions:

My last will!

1. My dear wife Henriette to whom I have been happily married since 1 September 1874, in addition to the contents of the domestic household, shall receive a legacy of 400,000 marks within three months of my death, this being predominantly from the mortgages in my name and from the securities on the Berlin stock exchange. She is to have free disposal for her lifetime over this capital and interests, however I wish her to take advantage of advice and assistance from our son, Leo and, should he be indisposed, then from our son, Siegfried. Further, my wife is to have the right to live in the same rooms that we now occupy. After the death of my wife, this capital is to be divided equally among my five children.

2. I name as my heirs my five children, Lina, Ernst, Siegfried, Leo, and Ida, with the proviso that the sums given as dowries, loans, and assistance shall not be added, but subtracted from the legacies.

3. A capital sum of 50,000 marks shall, at the discretion of the majority among my five sons and sons-in-law, be paid out within six months, distributed in amounts they deem appropriate to general Jewish and charitable Jewish organizations or to the poor.

4. A further 10,000 marks shall, likewise at the discretion of the majority of my sons and sons-in-law, be divided among those Jewish associations etc. that have until now received annual contributions from me.

There followed a series of complicated instructions mainly concerning a fund to be set up for his granddaughters. However, payment was to be made only on condition that they remained

§ 1

1. Lina
2. Ernst
3. Siegfried   } Levy
4. Leo
5. Ida

Bernhard's will.

Jewish, married Jews, and promised to raise their children as Jews as well. Rudolph Levy was also made the subject of his uncle's stricture:

8. My nephew Rudolph Levy, currently resident in Munich, shall receive a legacy of 5000 marks on condition that his wife converts to Judaism. Five per cent of this capital is to be paid out half-yearly from the time that this condition is met, and when he reaches the age of sixty the remainder is to be paid out in cash.

9. Given the current economic and political circumstances on the one hand and the resulting condition of my business interests, it is impossible to make binding arrangements at the moment, should there be disagreements between my children. However, my wish as their father is that my sons Siegfried and Leo should continue the business established by my late father and managed in the same way by me, and that they should keep it going in the same old way... and to enable my wish to be carried out, my other three children should accommodate them to the highest possible degree.

However, in the event that against my wishes it turns out that a mutual understanding over the succession to the business cannot be reached, then I expressly insist that the firm be of necessity liquidated, without the agreement of Siegfried and Leo, by winding up within four years, beginning on 1 September after my death. In assessing the value of the factories, the machinery and the land on which they stand, Siegfried and Leo are to have the option of purchase.

Should Siegfried and Leo be unable to agree over any question in conducting the business, it shall be decided by the majority vote of my sons and sons-in-law, with the result that one of the two shall be the director of the business.

The will ended with the memorable paragraph:

Together with my wife, I have always lived according to the precepts of Jewish teaching, and have also not forgotten those in need. My children have been raised in the same way. God's blessing has obviously fallen on our children and their descendants, as well as on us, on my business dealings, and my undertakings. I urge my children to live their lives by the same principles and to teach these to their children. If one of my descendants should abandon Judaism for any egoistic reasons, they shall be permanently excluded from the community of the family. I wish that the blessing of heaven, which I hope will continue to shine on my family, turn away from this degenerate descendant. I request that my children and their descendants, both the boys and the girls on reaching their sixteenth year, be informed of this, and continue to be so.

The lawyer came to the end, and placed the sheets of paper on the table. 'Are all the terms clear and understood?' he asked. Total silence reigned in the room. Only Henriette, who had not shed a single tear during the entire week of mourning, now broke out into inconsolable weeping.

The Writing on the Wall

'I am so pleased to greet you as our guest,' said Curt von
Bleichröder, extending his hand to Siegfried Levy. 'Our grand-
fathers were successful business partners. Both of them were men
of great vision, although they both suffered from eye disease.'

The young banker gave a dry laugh. He had a habit of coming
out with such improvised puns. Siegfried made no response. His
only reason for being there was that a man in his position could
not afford to turn down an invitation from one of the most
important bankers, even if he personally could not stand
Bleichröder. Although Siegfried had very liberal views, he found
it hard to come to terms with the fact that Curt, like all
Bleichröder's other descendants, had abandoned Judaism and had
become a Protestant. In this respect he had exactly the same
outlook as his late father. When the latter had learned that all
Bleichröder's sons had converted to Christianity, he had sworn
never to set foot again in the Behrenstrasse house. What now
made Siegfried incandescent with rage was the news that his host
had joined the 'Steel Helmets' (*Stahlhelm*).* But since he had
finally made up his mind after much hesitation to accept this
invitation, Siegfried was resolved to be pedantic to a degree in
observing the rules of the game, and not display his abhorrence.
Bleichröder, who did not suspect anything, led Siegfried to a

*In January 1942 Curt von Bleichröder appealed against being deported to a con-
centration camp since he was a 'half Jew' and on the grounds of his services to
the Nazis as a member of the *Stahlhelm* (a right-wing paramilitary veterans'
organization). Adolf Eichmann, SS Obersturmbannführer responsible for
deportations, who was working on his case, agreed to have him sent to the 'Old
People's Ghetto' instead. Curt von Bleichröder, knowing this meant
Theresienstadt, fled to Switzerland. His sister, Baroness von Campe, was
deported to the Riga concentration camp.

group of people seated at the far end of the large room. As they approached, a man of about forty rose to his feet, taking a good look at them through his gold-rimmed pince-nez. A second man was also present, but he remained seated.

'Let me introduce you,' said the host, 'Herr Otto Spangler, Privy Councillor in the Ministry of Finance, and Paul Schwabach Junior, head of our bank.'

Those present shook hands. Siegfried sat down uneasily. He felt extremely uncomfortable. No doubt his mother would also have been unhappy at this meeting. But Henriette had died in January 1922, about two years after her husband. Against a background of the oppressive reparation payments that Germany was having to pay the victors, and the resulting mood of crisis and defeat, her funeral had been a very simple affair without any fuss. Less than a month later, the unexpected invitation had arrived from Berlin. Actually, it should have been Leo, in his capacity as director of the firm, who should have attended, but he had refused to meet the banker 'whose conduct would have been tantamount to a slap in the face for our father, of blessed memory'. Siegfried argued in his pragmatic fashion: 'After all, we have nothing to lose; there could even be something in it for us.' So he decided to travel to Berlin himself. His brother was furious, and Siegfried tried to pacify him with the mocking words, 'I've never heard that conversion to Christianity is an infectious disease.'

And yet Bernhard's fears had been perfectly justified, for keeping to his traditional observance was not easy. Bernhard had seen this coming, and had attempted to enforce his wishes by means of his will. Leo shared his father's fears. Since he had become the head of the Polzin Levy family, he had insisted on turning the house into a fortress, defying all outside influence. Out of the approximately one dozen remaining Jewish households in the town, only two or three still kept a kosher kitchen. By now it was a problem to find the necessary *minyan* for *Shabbat* prayers. But the Levy household continued to observe the dietary laws, as in Bernhard's and Ascher's time. But as the family members moved further away from Polzin, they distanced themselves from their origins. As Leo frequently stayed in Berlin on business, he very soon came to realize, as Bernhard had before him, that in the home of his brother Ernst, milk and meat were no longer kept separate, and that his brother and his family travelled by tram on the *Shabbat* and on festivals. His sisters Lina and Ida no longer lit the candles on Friday evening. Ida was now divorced from Paul, although she had waited until after the death of her parents, to avoid hurting them. And when his cousin Rudolf had married a goya, the entire Polzin family had refused to attend the wedding ceremony in protest. Siegfried had been the only one who had not hesitated to congratulate Rudolf by telephone. Although Siegfried never abandoned Judaism, he too neglected the mitzvot. When he came to Polzin on a visit, he tried to adapt to the way of life there, mainly in order to avoid upsetting Leo. But in his own home in Stettin, he and Lisbeth also lived a fairly unobservant life.

Siegfried differed from the other members of the family both in terms of character and looks. He was an optimistic individual, who appreciated the small comforts of life and enjoyed lively company. He had acquired a second apartment at 25 Badenallee in the Charlottenburg district of Berlin, and rapidly discovered the advantages of the capital. All the same, Leo expressed his reproach in a friendly way: 'If my brother devoted himself as eagerly to the study of the Talmud as he does to restaurant menus, he would long since have become a scholar.' But the Holy Scriptures played no part in Siegfried's home. Lisbeth devoured romantic novels, while Siegfried preferred the stock exchange reports, which he found just as absorbing. He rapidly acquired a remarkable familiarity with complicated financial transactions, and many entrusted him with their money to double or treble their profits. Malicious gossips later maintained that he had converted this capital into pounds sterling and deposited it in an English bank at the beginning of the inflation, only withdrawing it when the mark hit rock bottom; they also asserted that he had feathered his nest in this way at the expense of those who had entrusted him with their money. Although Siegfried and Lisbeth emphatically denied these allegations, there were many who wondered how this man had come by his fortune.

When the invitation from young Bleichröder reached Polzin, Siegfried had hoped for an opportunity of making a profitable investment. But what he heard as he sat opposite the banker exceeded his wildest dreams.

'I suggest that we turn to business right away,' said Curt von Bleichröder. The Privy Councillor nodded.

'I'm all ears,' announced Siegfried and spread his arms, as if he wished to embrace the whole world.

'How many sawmills do you own at present?' asked Spangler.

Siegfried began to list them: 'We own the sawmills at Kollatz, Gross Linichen, and Gustav Möller & Successors in Köslin. Apart from which we have an interest in a number of other concerns, including the Neuhof sawmills. The Neu Buslar estate and the limeworks in Gramentz belong to the family. The limeworks have long been leased. We hold the major share in all the partnerships.'

'I thought as much. The Levys can be relied on,' remarked Bleichröder contentedly.

'It's no secret. We have invested our wealth as widely as possible.' Siegfried looked at the banker, adding, 'That is the Levy family tradition.'

'And yet it appears you can hardly keep up with delivery schedules.'

'That's true, the orders are very healthy. They are working three shifts in the factories, and even so we can hardly keep up. At present we are specializing in telephone and telegraph poles. It makes you think that everyone is suddenly dying to make telephone calls and send telegrams.'

'Gentlemen, let us get to the point.' Privy Councillor Spangler lowered his voice. 'Are you aware where these deliveries are going?'

'Certainly. The goods wagons are going straight to France. Our government gives the money, France receives the goods. I assume this is a part of the vast sum we have to pay the Frogs.'

Bleichröder raised a warning finger. 'I must warn you that this conversation is highly confidential.'

'That goes without saying,' the Privy Councillor said in

confirmation. 'Previous talks with Herr von Bleichröder have informed me that the Levy family are completely trustworthy.'

'Our family has proved its loyalty to the fatherland for more than four generations.'

'And there is nothing better than combining service to the fatherland with business that can make a healthy profit. After all, only those with a livelihood pay taxes.' Bleichröder gave out a dry laugh.

Privy Councillor Spangler ignored the last remark and continued, 'This affair is of vital importance, but also extremely delicate. In the event that we do not meet our obligations, the French are threatening us with political sanctions. We are anxious to avoid direct confrontation. In brief, we wish you to double your output. I shall be responsible for making the necessary contractual alterations.'

'Double the output? But I have just explained to you, we are already stretched to full capacity.'

'Why not modernize the works? And why don't you purchase another sawmill or possibly even two?'

'This is hardly the right time to break into our financial reserves for investment purposes. You must surely agree with me on that; after all, you are from the Finance Ministry. Inflation is racing ahead. A year ago the exchange rate for a single US dollar was one hundred and sixty marks. Now it stands at seven thousand, and I wouldn't be at all surprised if it didn't rise to seventy thousand by the end of the year.'

'The higher the inflation, the bigger your profit.'

'I beg your pardon?' asked Siegfried in astonishment.

'Obviously I don't intend you to finance this yourself,' the Privy Councillor went on to explain. 'The government is prepared to grant you credit at very advantageous rates.'

'And our bank would guarantee repayment of the debt,' Bleichröder promptly added.

'You simply cannot turn down an offer like this. You will be offered any sum necessary for expanding your production. After a period of five years you will pay back the credit at the nominal value, what's more in cash, which by that time will be as good as worthless. Everyone in the know is aware that inflation is a paradise for prudent businessmen.'

'I am familiar with the fate that befell Adam and Eve,' said Siegfried coolly.

'You have eaten the wrong tree,' countered Bleichröder. 'But then, it's you who are the tree expert, if I'm not mistaken?'

'That's my speciality.'

'Well then, I suggest we go into my office to set out the details and sign the contract.'

The men got to their feet. For a moment Bleichröder stood beside Siegfried, grasped his arm and whispered, 'Er, to avoid any future misunderstanding – I think, you understand, that the bank fees involved will have to be guaranteed by a loan, tied to the actual value of the sawmills, including the plant you will need to purchase.'

'I haven't come across that before.'

'Basically the very notion of credit is new to you, isn't it?'

'Correct.'

'And I didn't get the impression that you were discouraged by these conditions.'

'I understand. All the same, please allow me to consult my brother in Polzin. We run the firm as equal partners. Under no circumstances would I take such an important decision without first obtaining his opinion.'

'We don't have much time at our disposal.'

'I shall let you have an answer tomorrow.'

'That will be fine, Herr Levy. I wish you every success. It is a great pleasure for me to do business with a man who knows his job.'

The agreement with the Polzin firm of Levy, as well as dozens of similar arrangements with other sawmills throughout Germany, did lead to a lasting improvement in relations with the French government. Germany was collapsing under the weight of the reparation payments. The government pleaded for a part of the enormous debt to be waived. However, the French were of the opinion that deliveries were being deliberately slowed down,

in order to achieve a moratorium. Hundreds of thousands of telephone poles that were due to be delivered to France in 1922 did
not arrive on time, and this was the proverbial straw that broke
the camel's back. The French threatened reprisals.

With additional stoppages in coal deliveries, the French prime
minister, Raymond Poincaré, ordered his army to occupy the
Ruhr. The German workers responded with a general strike. In
an armed encounter at the Krupp works in Essen, thirteen
workers were shot by the soldiers. The local population reacted
with a series of acts of sabotage. But even these underground
tactics did nothing to change the facts – the industrial heart of
Germany had been lost, and collapse was inevitable.

Siegfried returned to Polzin with a transfer sum enabling a
large-scale expansion of the timber business. The brothers immediately bought another sawmill in the neighbourhood of Köslin.
When Privy Councillor Spangler handed over to Siegfried the
credit amounting to 100,500,000 marks, the sum was equivalent
to $260,000. On 20 November 1922 the credit was deleted from
the ledgers of the Levy firm – deleted in cash, as the bookkeeper
observed. With the aid of the Bleichröder bank, it was reim-
bursed to the state at full value, plus the legally fixed interest rate.
At this point the debts including the interest amounted to just
seventy dollars and eighty-five cents!

Was all this a calculated manoeuvre? In his book published in
the 1950s, *The Rise and Fall of the Third Reich*, William L. Shirer
puts forward the view that the German currency was quite deliberately brought down, initially to dispose of the huge state debt of
100 billion marks resulting from the cost of the war, and later to
shrug off the reparation payments.

Inflation raced ahead beyond all expectations. By the end of
1923 the exchange rate for the dollar had reached 25 million
marks. After that the exchange rates soared to wildly absurd
dimensions. Inflation impoverished many smaller investors, and
ruined the middle classes. Major industries and bankers paid off
debts unrelated to foreign currency in worthless banknotes. The
state printing presses worked round the clock in order to keep
pace with demand, and when state paper supplies ran out, paper

rolls intended for printing books were impounded from the publishing firm of Ullstein.

The collapse of the currency was accompanied by a breakdown in the traditional values and norms of a society accustomed to order. Confidence in the democratically elected politicians' ability to govern rapidly disappeared. Matthias Erzberger, who had signed the declaration of capitulation, Hugo Haase, leader of the Independent Socialists, and finally even Foreign Minister Walter Rathenau became the victims of right-wing assassins. Rathenau, who had previously served as Minister for Reconstruction, attempted to meet the demands of the victorious powers for reparations payments to the very limits of feasibility, but was held personally responsible for the political and economic chaos. His opponents derided him as a Jew and even described him as one of the 'Elders of Zion'. The fact that for two years, between 1914 and 1915, Rathenhau had built up the department for military supplies no longer interested anyone. A defamatory verse referring to Walther Rathenhau as a 'gottverdammte Judensau' (a goddamned pig of a Jew) and urging his assassination was doing the rounds in the pubs of Berlin.

On 24 June 1922 the demand became tragic reality. As Rathenhau was on his way from his home in the Grunewald to the Foreign Ministry two young men hurled a hand grenade into his open car. That Rathenhau of all people – the man who described himself as 'German of Jewish abstraction' and had proclaimed that 'the German nation is with him, Germany is his Fatherland and his faith is the German religion which towers above all other religions' – should have been killed by anti-Semitically motivated assassins was a true irony of fate. Although the Levy family in Polzin were by no means Rathenhau supporters, the day of his murder became a day of family mourning, for the sister of the Foreign Minister was married to Moritz Gottschalk's son, who worked as an electrical engineer at AEG. Ernst attended the funeral as the family representative.

In the early 1920s, there were many who once again sought to attribute the alleged failures of the establishment to Jewish intrigues. At the time Germany was swarming with political adventurers, and one of them, Adolf Hitler, was instilling into his followers the idea that the salvation of Germany depended on the eradication of the 'Jewish pestilence'. Anti-Semitism was again gaining ground, finally even reaching the remotest areas. Superficially, the facts seem to confirm the claims of the far right – that Rosa Luxemburg and Karl Liebknecht, followed by the first Soviet Ambassador, Adolf Joffe, and the Polish revolutionary, Herschel Grynspan, had attempted to unleash a revolution in Germany. They were all Jews. In the major German banks too, Jews occupied positions of authority, particularly at the Deutsche Bank and the Dresdner Bank. Leading department stores such as Wertheim, Tietz, Schocken, and Israel were also Jewish owned. Jews like Mosse and Ullstein headed publishing houses and the press. Max Reinhardt, Bruno Walter, and Oskar Straus were celebrated stage successes, and Albert Einstein, Fritz Haber, and Otto Meyerhof were distinguished academics. The demagogues of the new right used these prominent figures to highlight Jewish supremacy.

In Polzin life continued as usual. The thunder of the approaching storm was just a distant rumble. Leo's chief concern was the energetic expansion of the limeworks at Gramentz, as this was closest to his love of chemistry. But he was also involved with other aspects of the firm. Anyone doing business with him soon came to realize that he was upright, conscientious, and correct, but also unyielding. He was respected for being straight, but feared for his hardness. He had many acquaintances but his friends could be counted on the fingers of one hand. When Siegfried once taunted him by saying that in dealing with his fellow men he turned them into enemies and adversaries, Leo had replied likewise in jest: 'God protect me from my friends, I can handle my enemies on my own.' Yet Leo had distinct problems in distinguishing between friends and foes and, in the confusion of events, he did not recognize the writing on the wall. In his view the representatives of racial ideology did not constitute a threat, whereas those Jews who advocated a national rebirth in Palestine did.

Under British military rule since 1918, in 1923 Palestine was placed under the control of the British Mandate by the League of

Nations, and the Zionists were hopeful that the central principles of the 1917 Balfour Declaration would be enacted. At the time London had promised:

> His Majesty's Government is favourably disposed towards the establishment of a national homeland for the Jewish people in Palestine, and will endeavour to facilitate the implementation of this plan to the best of its ability, with the express proviso that nothing shall be done to interfere with the civil and religious rights of those non-Jewish communities already living in Palestine, or adversely affect the political status of Jews living in any other country.

Leo did not like the sound of this at all. 'You can't make an omelette without breaking an egg,' he grumbled. 'Germany is and remains the national homeland of the German Jews. In my view anything else damages our rights and our loyalty.'

'You really are the alter ego of our late father,' Siegfried mocked. 'You repeat his views like a scratchy gramophone record.'

'Is it such a disgrace to repeat something that is not only true and relevant, but that also exactly reflects one's own views?'

'Not mine, dear brother.'

'Well, why don't you emigrate there to drain the swamps and catch malaria?'

Siegfried burst out laughing. 'You know perfectly well why. I love my comforts and good food, and don't have the slightest desire to sink into a malarial fever. Apart from that, the stock exchange is holier to me than the holy sites of Palestine.'

'So at least you have one positive quality,' said Leo mockingly.

'Which is?'

'Honesty!'

'But only in moments of weakness, and only when the two of us are on our own. But seriously, though, do you really believe that it's possible to halt the flow of history? That we can bend the inevitable to our personal desires?'

'I don't quite understand what you mean.'

'Oh, really, Leo! You understand perfectly well. All nations strive for independence. Why do you object to it only in the case of Zionism?'

'Because all other nations base their sovereignty on the tradition of their fathers, whereas the Zionists ignore the roots of Judaism. The second in command of the movement is married to a goya. And if you believe that a mixed marriage is in accordance with Jewish tradition, then there is simply no point in our discussing it any further. Continue the conversation with Rudolf. He'll understand you.'

'Now don't get angry, Leo. I had no intention of recruiting you to the Zionist cause. Basically I was simply questioning the logic of your vehement disapproval. Every time I visit Berlin I break out in goose pimples. We are wealthy, intelligent, enlightened, and support the consolidation of Germany – and all the same we have to ingratiate ourselves and beg the Germans to tolerate our presence. Isn't that rather absurd?'

'You spend too much time in Berlin. That's all.'

'Things aren't much different in Stettin. Can't you face up to these issues like an adult? You sit in your room here and block your ears to the rantings of the racial fanatics. You persuade yourself that what you don't hear doesn't exist.'

'I am not in the least naive, Sigi. But what does racial ideology amount to after all? Extremists and lunatics insisting that biology counts for more than anything else. The Marxists tried to do the same with the economy. And where are they today? The revolution has devoured their children. And what happened in the past? Haven't there been endless attempts to curtail our equal rights as citizens? We are here. You are here. I am here. And Germany is here. Do you happen to be afraid of historical developments?'

Siegfried made a dismissive gesture with his hand. 'You're shooting at a defenceless individual. I don't want to argue about ideology. Let's have a ceasefire.'

'Right,' Leo gave in, 'but no Versailles Treaty.'

'No Versailles Treaty,' agreed Siegfried. 'Come on, let's go and have a coffee at Zell's.'

Café Zell was the meeting place for Polzin's high society. Karl Zell had the finest pastries in town, the best beer in the region, and always greeted his patrons warmly. The café was located beside the artificial lake in the spa park, and in the summer it was pleasant to sit outside. As the brothers arrived Herr Finkelstein came towards them. He had recently opened a kosher *pension*, and was now putting himself out to be pleasant to everyone.

'Have you heard the latest?' he asked, visibly excited. 'No? A young Darmstadt banker has been appointed the Reich fiscal commissar and president of the Reichsbank, and has announced that the exchange rate for the mark has sunk to four dollars twenty cents.'

'You see?' grinned Leo. 'Everything is going back to what it was.'

This new arrival from Darmstadt was only thirty-six years old, and in those days was considered a financial genius. His name was Hjalmar Horace Greeley Schacht. Twenty years later, a psychologist who investigated him at the war crimes trial (Schacht had served the Nazis until 1944) found him to have an IQ of 143, way above that of the other defendants. But back to 1923. The newly appointed fiscal commissar was allotted an office that had previously been a boxroom for cleaning materials. Based in this tiny room, he pushed through a painful financial operation – he turned off the tap for the profitable state credits unrelated to currency and halted the printing presses that were spewing out banknotes with twelve noughts on. In this way he sawed off the branch on which the speculators were perched and caused innumerable firms to go bankrupt, including conglomerates that had grown fat as a result of inflation. The result was mass unemployment. So although Germany escaped from the turmoil of inflation in November 1923, at the same time this was to prove the springboard for a far more dangerous form of lunacy.

The republic was proclaimed on 9 November. The mayor of Polzin urged the town's inhabitants to decorate their houses with the national flag. There were very few who did so. In the conservative heartland of Pomerania the democratic constitution of the Weimar Republic was not exactly considered a brilliant achievement of the German spirit. 'This is not our celebration,' was Leo's reply to one of his employees who asked whether he should hoist the flag outside the firm's offices. As it was a democratic national holiday, the extreme right in Munich did not celebrate 9 November either, but many flags were put out there – bearing swastikas. Hundreds of demonstrators marched through the streets. The previous evening in the beer cellar Hitler had called for a 'national revolution' and attempted a putsch by the right. That night the army and the Bavarian regional police were mobilized against the rebels. But although Hitler lost this round, on the following morning he summoned his supporters to 'march on the General Headquarters'. The gathering soon moved towards the Odeon Square in the centre of the town. Curious passers-by lined the route of the march, and watched the events from the pavements. The conspicuous figure of Rudolf Levy was among the onlookers. He too had stopped as the procession came into view. By now a balding man of forty-seven – or to put it more charitably, a man with a high forehead and glasses – he absently observed those on the march. He wore a light suit, a yellow bow-tie, and a broad-brimmed hat, indicating that he had just that morning returned from the sunny French Riviera. There he had committed to canvas the colours of the Bay of Sanary, near Toulon – blue clouds and turquoise-coloured sea, trees a delicate green, lush grassy meadows and flowers in every colour of the rainbow. Now he shuddered.

The stormtroopers struck up marching songs, but Rudolf was not fully aware of what was going on around him. Munich had a magical attraction for him, second only to Paris, his favourite city. It was here on the banks of the Isar that the twentieth century had begun for him with a painful failure at the Academy of Fine Arts – he had painted and submitted a portrait and a drawing of a nude in an 'unacademic fashion'. This had been twenty-three years ago, and yet he remembered it as if it were only yesterday. Some time later he had knocked timidly at the door of Professor Heinrich von Zügel and asked if he could be taken on as one of his students. Zügel looked more like a traditional forester than an artist, and was famous at the time as a painter of animals. Zügel

asked him into his studio. Every single canvas showed an enormous donkey. To Rudolf it seemed as if the donkey was waggling
its ears and laughing at him. Even before Zügel accepted him as a
student Rudolf knew that he had landed in the wrong place. And
sure enough, it did not take long for Zügel to criticize his work –
the first cow Rudolf drew was too small and the landscape in the
background was 'too big'… There was no getting away from it,
Rudolf was passionate about landscape, not cows.

Meanwhile the marchers had passed by and disappeared round
the next corner. The singing eventually faded away, and the
onlookers dispersed. Rudolf wondered what time it was, and
drew out a gold fob watch from his waistcoat pocket. He intended to take the fast train to Berlin that evening, for he had an
appointment the following day with Alfred Flechtheim, a gallery
owner. The connection with Flechtheim went back to pre-war
days. The gallery owner from Düsseldorf had taken to him, had
exhibited his work and, even before he had sold his first painting,
had handed him a not inconsiderable sum as an advance. Such
generosity was not unfounded. Flechtheim, an experienced art
dealer and collector, had confidence in Rudolf's talent and considered that by supporting him now he was investing in the
future. Over the years their working relationship had grown, and
Flechtheim now paid him a regular monthly salary. When these
modest monthly payments were insufficient for Rudolf to manage
on, he would find other work. At this very moment he had an
edition of Stendhal's *Le Rouge et le Noir* in his briefcase, which a
major Berlin publishing house had commissioned him to
translate.

In the early 1920s Berlin was awash with Dadaists, Cubists,
and Futurists. Many who made history, and other artists who
subsequently sank into obscurity, would meet in the coffee houses
of Berlin. A regular at the Romanisches Café was Johannes
Bader, a protagonist of the Dada movement, who was in possession of a medical certificate, so that later on he could not be held
responsible for his actions. George Grosz, whose pictures hit out
at the materialism and militarism of the age, frequented the
Monopol. Käthe Kollwitz, known for her drawings of poverty

and war, Wassily Kandinsky, and Paul Klee – later to be professors at the Bauhaus – and a clique of younger artists, sculptors, and poets who attached themselves to them, lent the city its particular flair. Rudolf had easily found his place in this glittering circle, although he was neither a rebel, nor pushy, nor did he bandy words about or even produce the fashionable revolutionary paintings required at the time. Artistic Bohemia was his natural setting. In 1921 he had exhibited alongside Hans Purrman, Max Pechstein, and others in the Berlin Free Secession.

About a year earlier the postman had brought him a letter sent by recorded delivery from Stettin. Dr Marcuse had sent him a copy of his uncle Bernhard's will and added a few lines of his own. Rudolf read the letter and the will, laughed, and threw both into the waste-paper basket. Once again the family was concerned for the salvation of its Jewish souls. Had they still not realized that for him Cézanne and Matisse were more important than the *Shulchan Aruch*, and that colours meant more to him than any prayer? As far as he was concerned, the Temple had not been destroyed anyway, for what mattered to him was not that it had been built of Lebanese cedarwood, but that the stories born of the power of the imagination had survived.

Rudolf grinned at Bernhard's restrictive clause. His stubborn uncle was still trying to influence his way of life from beyond the grave. He had largely escaped the critical eyes of Bernhard and Henriette, but his marriage to Genia had obviously not remained a secret. Eugenie Schindler, the daughter of well-to-do farmers from Geislitz in Upper Hessen, had come to Munich at the age of seventeen to study photography. In 1919 she met Rudolf, twenty years her senior, and fell under the spell of his charm and his intellect. Their relationship was anathema to both families. Genia's parents were firmly opposed to their daughter being involved with a Jew. In Polzin it was seen – from a different angle – as a betrayal of all the values and norms considered sacred to the family for generations. Eugenie was effectively regarded as a prostitute who had seduced a naive man, a dreamer, remote from reality. Neither those in Geislitz nor in Polzin understood the nature of the relationship between the two. When they decided in

November that year to marry, Eugenie was twenty-four. She was a skinny young woman with narrow shoulders, protruding collarbones, and large, staring eyes – a far cry from the bewitching young girls in the clubs and cafés of Paris, Berlin, and Munich. Yet it was not a matter of physical attraction but a deep intellectual affinity which created the bond between them. Sometimes as they sat drinking coffee with cognac in their favourite café, Rudolf's friends and acquaintances would look at Genia with undisguised curiosity and wonder what this fragile young creature could possibly see in the ageing artist, who had not had his first solo show until 1922. Rudolf and Genia were totally oblivious to these stares, for they were always deep in conversation about God and the world. And if they did discuss material matters, it would mostly be about the adventures of the creative life in a gruesome world. Only those who were very close to Rudolf were aware that the most important piece of furniture in their home was the table, at which they sat and talked, and not their marital bed. The couple's wedding in December 1919 was a very modest affair. As expected, their families boycotted the wedding. Paul was the only one to send his brother a telegram of congratulations and Siegfried rang to wish the couple *Mazal Tov*.

Accompanied by a number of friends, led by the painters Roda Roda, Rosenfeld, Alfred Flechtheim, and Oskar Kokoschka, Rudolf and Genia went straight from the registry office to gamble at the Casino Kleist, just to prove that fortune was still smiling on them. In the space of one hour Rudolf lost all the money he had on him at roulette. As they left the dimly lit gaming room, Rudolf placed his arm around Genia's narrow shoulders and laughed. 'We really couldn't have chosen a casino with a more appropriate name. After all, wasn't it Kleist who sent his character Michael Kohlhaas in search of justice, and then ended up by ruining and murdering his protagonist? And what was it that Kleist did to himself, as his Henriette lay on her sickbed ...?'

Indeed, all Heinrich von Kleist's characters allowed their fellow men to influence them to commit the most abhorrent deeds. He himself committed suicide on the banks of Berlin's

Wannsee lake on the very spot where 130 years later Heydrich was to set in motion the 'Final Solution to the Jewish Question', on 20 January 1942. Was this innocent visit to the casino on their wedding night an omen and a warning? Not at all. Losing the money meant nothing to them. They took a taxi home, for the first time as a married couple.

'We're probably the first couple in the world in no hurry to leap into the marital bed,' laughed Rudolf.

Genia squeezed his hand understandingly, saying, 'That is true liberation.'

Rudolf had discovered true liberation back in 1897 when he came to Munich for the first time. Later on in Paris he had revelled in it to excess. He used to send his father in Danzig and his uncle in Polzin non-committal postcards from the South of France, where he would follow in Cézanne's footsteps to capture the beauty of Sanary and Cassis on canvas. And although rumours about his way of life reached even Pomerania, they would be lightly swept aside. 'Our Rudolf? No, impossible. That can't be so.'

Only the regulars at the Café du Dôme on the Boulevard Montparnasse knew the truth. Rudolf broke with all convention, and not just where religion was concerned. In his endless search for the ultimate experience he also discovered love between men.

The Café du Dôme was a small and smoky place opposite an imposing Catholic church. The café was under the all-embracing dominance of André, the nimble waiter. The artists treated him with true reverence, and not just for his skill as a waiter. In their hour of need, André would act as their banker. He was always prepared to provide a few francs to someone short of cash 'till the end of the week', and it goes without saying that some of these weeks were very long.

The tables were set out along the walls. A low partition divided the room. One half housed the American bohemians, the other was occupied by the Germans and the Austrians. No one ever tried to cross the demarcation line. France stayed outside on the terrace. Within a very short space of time Rudolf had become the uncrowned king of the German-speaking group. Those who may not have been enchanted by his paintings admired the ease with which he recited Virgil, in fluent Latin, needless to say. But apart from his artist friends such as Hans Purrmann and Jules Pascin, Rudolf would constantly be in the company of some youth or other, who would gaze at him in adoration, ready to fulfil his every wish. Peter Weigel was one of these young men.

From his home town of Düsseldorf, Peter Weigel had ended up in Paris. The relationship between the two had begun the moment they had set eyes on each other. On Sunday they had a Pernod together, and on Monday Peter moved into Rudolf Levy's studio on the place de Clichy in Montmartre. The artist and his admirer got on like a house on fire, until the day that Gertrude Stein and her brother Leo, the art collector and patron, appeared on the scene at the Café du Dôme.

'And what do you think of Picasso?' asked Gertrude Stein, after she had looked at a few of Rudolf's watercolours.

'Picasso? I've heard of him. But I've never set eyes on the man or any of his works.'

'Well, you simply have to meet him,' insisted Leo Stein. 'He is enchanting, and I predict a great career for him.'

'He will have to be successful, and do you know why? I've acquired two of his paintings. The Stein family is not one to throw its money out of the window,' joked Gertrude.

'Come to the Lapin Agile tonight,' urged Leo Stein. 'What, you don't know it? It's one of the most amazing establishments in the whole of Paris. How can you have missed it? The whole Picasso gang is in and out of there all the time.'

Rudolf hesitated. Hans Purrmann, sitting at the next table, had been listening to the conversation, and answered for him. 'Of course we'll come. All of us.'

That same night the German artists and their French colleagues had a great time together. Picasso, a dark-skinned Spaniard, small in stature, impatient by nature and dressed like a workman, appeared accompanied by Fernande Olivier, his latest conquest, and a whole delegation of friends and admirers. Rudolf had brought Peter Weigel along. But as he set out for home at two in the morning, completely drunk, the beautiful Peter was no longer at his side. Rudolf found the empty studio depressing and within a few days he returned to his former haunt on the Boulevard Montparnasse. There he learned that someone from the 'Picasso gang' had taken Weigel over, had rented a room for him in a house that had once been a huge laundry and was now divided up into many studios, preferably let out to artists. Picasso himself had occupied the room at one time. Mutual friends said that Peter had taken to drugs. He was smoking hashish, and even injecting cocaine.

'Please keep an eye on him,' Rudolf asked Manolo, the sculptor. But the attention of his friend did nothing to help.

One day, as Rudolf was drinking coffee as usual at the Café du Dôme he was called to the telephone. Manolo's agitated voice came from the receiver, saying: 'He's hanged himself from the window. I'm so sorry.'

The funeral of the young suicide turned into a veritable procession of the Paris artist community. Behind the coffin, his head bowed, walked Rudolf Levy arm in arm with Picasso. Père Fred, landlord of the Lapin Agile, dressed in a white jacket, and Picasso were in the second row, followed by Purrmann and Manolo, Pascin, Derain, Wilhelm Uhde (who had just bought a Blue Period Picasso, *The Blue Room*), and many, many others. Of course there were also no end of models, negresses, and prostitutes, and it is hardly surprising that in his memoirs Purrmann declared, 'It was hard to remain serious'. And instead of dispersing at the cemetery gates, Picasso suggested going back to Gertrude Stein's salon to console themselves with a glass of calvados and the latest gossip. Gertrude Stein was around thirty and American by birth. She had spent her childhood in Vienna and was completely captivated by European culture. She had settled in Paris in 1903 and held open house for young artists. She and her brother Leo had a keen business sense. Gertrude bought paintings by Picasso, Georges Braque, and Matisse, long before they were discovered by the professional art market.

Rudolf Levy got to know Matisse in 1905 at the time of the third Salon in Paris, when the latter's *Woman with Hat* threw the critics into a turmoil. The critics could not stomach the lush colours of Matisse's portraits and landscapes, and one of them even likened his works to anarchists' bombs. Another disparagingly called him and his followers 'les fauves' – the wild ones – thereby unintentionally giving members of the new movement their name: Fauvists. The critics tore Matisse to shreds, but Gertrude and Leo bought his *Woman with Hat*. In so doing they displayed a healthy instinct for investment, for just a few years later the museums of Europe and America were fighting for his work.

It was Gertrude Stein, too, who persuaded Matisse to set up a students' workshop 'to establish the new style'. But Matisse hesitated. 'I've no wish to raise a generation of imitators,' he declared. But in the end he allowed himself to be talked round, and in 1908 he opened the studio in the rue de Sèvres. Rudolf soon became one of his students. At peak times Matisse had as many as eighty students, and he soon moved the studio to the former convent of Sacré Coeur in the Boulevard des Invalides. One day a week they would paint, on another they would have specialized tours of the Paris museums. Matisse loathed having to lecture to students who did not understand him, and soon lost patience, preferring the south of Spain to the lessons in his studio. On his recommendation the students chose Rudolf to head the studio. But Rudolf lacked the ability, and he probably did not have Matisse's knowledge and experience either, so the atelier closed down in 1912. Although Rudolf only worked alongside Matisse for a short while, he continued to be influenced by his style for the rest of his life. 'I've come to understand,' he wrote to one of his young friends, 'that colour is not just an adjunct to depicting a subject. Colour lives and exists for itself, and can influence the observer by its own power.' Some time later Picasso attempted to direct Rudolf's attention towards abstract painting, which was considered the natural continuation of this stylistic trend. But Rudolf was sceptical. 'I recoil from abstract painting. The coldness that it radiates on to its surroundings makes me afraid of losing all human feeling.'

In 1911 and 1912 several of Rudolf's works were exhibited in Amsterdam's Stedelijk Museum. A few years later a landscape was shown in the Armory Show in New York. His brother Paul, who was still living in Damascus and laying railway tracks to Mecca, continued to send him a modest monthly sum, but for the first time in his life Rudolf's income was enough to live a normal life, without having to think twice about every penny he spent. His financial position was finally assured when sixteen of his paintings, along with other pictures by the Café du Dôme group, were exhibited in Flechtheim's Düsseldorf gallery. The exhibition had been meant to travel to Berlin and other cities in Germany, but the outbreak of war wrecked these plans. The war also put an end to the gatherings of the German artists' clique at the Café du Dôme. Most of them packed their bags and returned home to enlist, as did Rudolf. A sense of national duty overrode all other feelings, just as if he had never had a cosmopolitan outlook on life. When he appeared before the medical board in Danzig he was declared fit for duty with a fighting unit.

'Good God,' he said to himself, as he stood on the pavement in Munich on 9 November 1923, 'is this the Germany I was prepared to give my life for?'

He looked at his watch again and realized that unless he hurried he would miss his train to Berlin. It was only later he discovered that Ludendorff and Hitler had been arrested and that Hess and Göring had cleared off to Austria, but he attached no importance to this. He was not interested in politics. Genia was now living in a fine apartment in Küstriner Strasse in the Charlottenburg district of Berlin, where Rudolf had set up a studio for her. Until Hitler came to power Rudolf lived in the German capital, apart from a short two-year break when he followed his friend Herbert Schlüter to Paris. He had met Schlüter, a writer and intellectual, at the beginning of the twenties in Paris. Rudolf and Herbert shared the same sexual inclinations, and their friendship, apart from a short separation, was to last for more than twenty-one years, right up to Rudolf's arrest in Florence.

Rudolf soon became a key figure at the Berlin artists' balls. He felt at home in the bohemian nightspots and was also a welcome guest in the houses of rich patrons of the arts. From 1928 onwards he was even on the board and a jury member of the Berlin Secession, along with Charlotte Berend, George Grosz, Max Pechstein, Hans Purrmann, and others. There was one door, however, that was closed to him. On the Bismarck Promenade in Polzin he had become persona non grata. Not content with excluding him, Leo even forbade everyone around him from so much as uttering the rebellious family member's name. Siegfried and Lisbeth, who divided their time between Stettin and Berlin, ignored these orders. On the contrary, they even met Rudolf and Genia on a regular basis. Siegfried, who was fascinated by photography, loved going to see Genia at work in her studio, developing films and preparing prints, mainly photographs of paintings for art books and exhibition catalogues.

Siegfried and Leo directed the family business with great prudence. They would be on the phone every day, and neither took a business decision without consulting the other. There had never been a really serious difference between them. Both were out for lucrative deals, and the firm's annual balance sheets were proof that everything was in the best possible order.

Leo and Siegfried had no difficulty in paying out to Ernst, Ida, and Lina their due share of the business in accordance with the provisions of the will. Leo carried out every single stipulation of the testament to the last detail, not deviating from it by one iota. As ever, the business was run on conservative and inflexible lines. Yet despite maintaining the old-established traditions, every trading year ended in profit, exceeding the family's needs. Siegfried invested the surplus in shares and securities, ensuring that it was spread widely – a little heavy industry, a bit of banking and insurance companies plus some foreign currency – that was his formula.

On his visits to Polzin there were two subjects that Siegfried avoided at all costs: ethics and politics, for there was no common ground between the brothers in either. Siegfried felt threatened by the subversiveness of the far right, and viewed the mounting activities of these circles with alarm. For Leo, on the other hand, Adolf Hitler was no more than an 'idiot with a moustache', as he called him, and just a passing phenomenon. But after the 'idiot' had given an aggressive speech in Stettin, Siegfried did bring up the subject.

'Anyone who has read *Mein Kampf* simply cannot dismiss it as unimportant.'

'You shouldn't read such trash,' declared Leo heatedly. 'This whole racial ideology is nothing but a sad joke, and will soon be forgotten. I would never read books like *Mein Kampf* or have them in the house.'

'You once said exactly the same about Herzl's *Jewish State*,' objected Siegfried.

'How can you even mention those two books in the same breath?' asked Lisbeth who had been following the conversation.

'I'm not comparing them at all,' replied Siegfried, 'and yet they are like two ends of a stick. They will never meet, and yet, at least according to Leo's philosophy, they cannot be separated.'

'I've never thought of that,' said Leo, thoughtfully. 'But any stick can be broken in two.'

This awkward conversation was soon forgotten. Siegfried took leave of his brother with an affectionate handshake, and drove back to Stettin.

In addition to the family business, he had other ventures of his own. He used one of the rooms in the apartment as an office. Lisbeth, who loved entertaining, would host receptions. Siegfried and Lisbeth were just as discriminating as Leo and Else in their choice of acquaintances, but compared with their relatives in Polzin, they did not filter to the same extent, allowing a few to slip through the social net.

Unlike Leo, Siegfried and Lisbeth not only knew how to make money, they also enjoyed spending it. They loved travelling and went abroad often, visiting Sweden and Spain, and taking holidays in Italy and even in Lapland in the far north of Finland. Siegfried was never without his small Leica, and Lisbeth arranged the scenes he captured on film in numerous albums that were kept in the sitting room of their apartment. Many of the photographs show her in clothes from well-known Berlin and Paris couture houses. Leo disapproved of their way of life, but refrained from making any outright comments. When his daughter Eva

Else Levy, née Frensdorf, and Leo Levy, 1926.

turned fourteen and it was decided to send her to the high school in Stettin, he firmly rejected the idea of her going to live in his brother's home. 'I don't want her soaking up that secular atmosphere, I don't want her eating Lisbeth's cooking, which may well be very tasty, but is certainly not kosher. Nor do I want my daughter sniffing my sister-in-law's French perfumes. We shall find somewhere for her to stay with other members of the family who keep a thoroughly Jewish home. After all, we do have such relatives.' Siegfried was not offended.

Eva had been at the school for two years when a Nazi was appointed as her class teacher. The teacher set his class an essay to write about their family tree. They were told to go into details of dominant traits such as hair and eye colour, and to name the country of origin of their forefathers. His intention was all too obvious. When Eva paid a short visit to Polzin at the weekend, she told her father her troubles. 'What on earth shall I write, Papa?' she asked.

'Don't worry, my dear,' he reassured her. 'Jews have been living in this region for centuries. You can cite historic documents to prove it. Why don't you go and look in the town archive?'

Eva acted on her father's advice. She found a document dated 12 January 1325. This granted special rights to Jordan the Jew as well as his descendants in gratitude for loyal services rendered to the town. Jordan and his descendants were exempted from additional taxes; he was obliged to pay only the same forty thaler a year that was imposed on other citizens of the town of Stettin. The first document mentioning the Levy family dated from the early nineteenth century, when a proper Jewish community was founded in Stettin and was officially recognized. A member of the Levy family had donated a generous sum towards the building of the first synagogue, and had secured a seat during religious services for life for the sum of one hundred thaler. When the synagogue was broken into in 1848, the chairman of the community, Louis Levy, had offered a reward for catching the burglar. On 14 June a notice was attached to the synagogue gates reading: 'The stolen candlesticks have been returned. The thieves were apprehended after two days and handed over to the custodians of the law. Bernau the goldsmith, who helped to catch them, has been paid the stated reward.'

Eva put as much effort into her essay as if she were challenging not just one national socialist teacher, but trying to defeat the entire racial ideology. When she had handed in her essay the teacher could not conceal his anger. The names of her forebears appeared in 300-year-old civic registers of the city of Hanover, and according to Eva's description all members of the family had blue eyes, blond hair, and were strong and tall in stature – they could hardly have looked more 'Aryan' in appearance.

But even her 'Aryan' racial features did not help the Levy family, as Nazi ideology took an even stronger hold. Eventually Eva had to leave the high school. Her father began worrying about her future. Although originally totally opposed to the Zionist ideal, for the first time in his life it occurred to him to send her and her older sister to the Jewish 'national homeland' in Palestine, at least until feelings had calmed down. Like his Jewish neighbours in Polzin , Dr Leo Levy took the view that eventually common sense would prevail, and that people like Adolf Hitler would remain marginal figures in history. All the same he could no longer close his eyes to what was going on around him.

Pomerania had always been unswervingly conservative and Prussian-nationalist, and the left had never gained a foothold there. In the Reichstag elections on 5 March 1933, some two months after Hitler had been declared Chancellor of the Reich, despite its terror tactics and obstructing the other parties on a massive scale, the NSDAP (National Socialist German Workers' Party) had not succeeded in gaining an overall majority. In Pomerania, however, they received 56.3 per cent of all votes legally cast.

Some two weeks later Hitler disposed of the Reichstag by means of the Enabling Act. Parliament dismissed itself by suspending the constitutional legislative process and handing legislation over to the government. The 'idiot with the moustache' had become the all-powerful dictator. His henchmen rapidly seized all state and public institutions and declared war on the 'enemies of the regime', first and foremost socialists and Jews.

Up to this time hatred of the Jews had been a recurring phenomenon, but never institutionalized by the state. Four hundred years earlier Martin Luther had demanded that Germany rid herself of the Jews, confiscate their money and jewels, break into their homes and destroy them, house them in stables like gypsies, and set fire to their houses of worship, for 'they complain without respite about us to God'. The philosopher, Friedrich Wilhelm Nietzsche, had put forward the notion of the master race, and had maintained that the coming century would provide a verdict on the fate of the Jews of Europe. The Jews would either set themselves up as the rulers of Europe, or be made slaves by Europe, just as their fathers and forefathers had served as slaves in Egypt.

But all the slanders, persecutions and bloody pogroms of the past were to pale into insignificance in comparison with what European Jewry was to suffer through highly organized means, put into effect by law during the Third Reich. Members of the Levy household heard the rumble of thunder heralding the storm, without understanding that they heralded the end.

In 1933 the family gathered in Bad Polzin on Passover for the traditional Seder night. Ernst brought his wife and daughters.

Siegfried and Lisbeth were conspicuous by their absence. They wished to spend the festival as far away as possible from this homeland that did not want them. As Leo sat down at the table in Polzin, Siegfried and his wife were on their way to the South of France. They wrote home on 15 April. Two weeks before, Rudolf had separated from Genia and he left the Reich on 1 April, this time for good. He met Siegfried and Lisbeth in Nice. Their niece, Sanna, daughter of Paul and Ida, was also with them. They spent a few exhilarating days together. The pleasant sunshine of the French Riviera helped them forget what was going on at home. After this short holiday, Siegfried travelled to Switzerland on business. Sanna left for Rome, and Rudolf for Rapallo, to meet Oskar Kokoschka. His future was uncertain. He missed Genia and Herbert, who had stayed behind in Berlin, and had no idea where fate would land him. Only one thing was absolutely certain. He swore he would not return to Germany, as long as the Nazis remained in power. Only a month had passed since his departure, but his name had already been struck off the list of board members of the Berlin Secession. The following appeared in the German press:

> The Berlin Secession has been added to the numerous cultural organizations to have undergone a radical change in favour of the national socialist renewal programme. The consciously German strengths within it, suppressed for many a long year by the Jewish element, have now regained the upper hand. Jews have been excluded from the organization, and at the General Meeting of 2 May, the Berlin Secession was founded anew.

At the constituting assembly of this newly established organization, Emil von Hauth, the new president, outlined its future in the following words:

> We intend to construct the Secession on entirely new foundations. We wish to be a raiding party of German art, following on from the great tradition of the Berlin Secession. We artists

are obliged to recognize the consequences of the new state ideal with regard to the future, and to move in that direction. The Secession undertakes to gather the creative powers of all German landscapes and peoples and to express their diversity and variety. The founding of the Secession was initially a declaration of war on the reactionary, fossilized, academic, imitative attitude to art of what was then the official Germany. The Berlin Secession herewith assumes responsibility for contributing, through the serious work of its members, to the clarification of what German art will in future stand for.

As Leo sat at the head of the table during the festive meal, he felt like the captain steering his family's ship through safe waters, waters that in his view had been defined for ever by previous generations.

The next morning an unknown person threw a rotten egg into the basement room of the house in the Bismarck Promenade, occupied by Victor, the schoolteacher of religion. Bernhard had given his room to the scholar, who had come to Polzin from Eastern Europe and had taken over the teaching of Jewish religious studies. Leo detested the *Ostjude*, but out of respect for his father, he did not put an end to the arrangement. He also continued to pay him a salary so that he could meet his daily needs without difficulty and devote all his attention to his teaching.

At midday Victor came to the family apartment and whispered something in Leo's ear. Leo excused himself to his relatives, took his coat, pinning his military medal to the lapel, and strode out into the spa park. The Café Zell now had a notice pinned to the door that read: 'Jews enter this place at their own risk.'

Leo read the words over and over again. With a sudden movement, he pushed open the door and mounted the three steps leading into the main area, where a few bored customers were seated. Taken aback, they looked at him over their beer mugs with curious glances. They were probably hoping that at last something interesting would happen. Zell, the proprietor, was busy tidying up the counter, and pretended he had not seen the customer. Leo went up to him and greeted him.

Leo Levy in Bad Polzin, 1930.

'Good day, Dr Levy,' replied Karl Zell and laid aside the cloth. 'There's no more cake left. May I bring you a beer?'

'Thank you, no. On Pesach, both flour and beer are forbidden.'

'Yes, of course. Well perhaps some gut-rot?'

'Pardon?' Leo had no idea what the landlord was referring to. Zell explained, laughing. 'I mean a small brandy.'

'Oh, no, my friend. I didn't come to drink.'

'If you want to pray, you've come to the wrong place,' put in one of the customers insolently, and took a hefty swallow from his mug. Everyone burst out laughing. Leo said nothing, but did not seem unduly worried.

The landlord shrugged his shoulders, as if to indicate that he wasn't responsible for his guests, and asked: 'Well, then, Doctor, what is it you want?'

'I should like to find out what risks I run if I come in here,' said Leo, pointing at the notice on the door behind him.

'Oh that?' said Zell dismissively. 'That doesn't mean a thing, Dr Levy. Some of the local stormtrooper group came here yesterday, and asked me to put it on the door.'

'Do you belong to the stormtroopers?'

'No. But who am I, to pick a fight with that lot?'

'I understand. I understand you completely,' retorted Leo with unexpected vehemence. 'But if you ever need credit on special terms, you had better go to someone else.'

'I would have done so anyway, Doctor,' replied the landlord in a huff, adding, 'and anyway there's no knowing how much longer you'll have any money left to lend.'

The beer-drinkers snarled in agreement.

Leo said no more, and turning on his heel left the room with measured strides. He could feel the looks of those present piercing his back, but no one got up, and no one said anything. He went down the three steps to the door. His first inclination was to slam it shut, but thinking better of it, he closed it quietly and carefully. He was thoroughly pleased with himself.

That evening he told Ernst what had happened. His older brother always reacted rather slowly, and this time, too, a few seconds went by before he said anything.

'Leo, do you really think that you have defeated the NSDAP?' And after another minute's pause, he added: 'Did you know that the Reich Ministry of Justice has rescinded my son-in-law's appointment?'

Ernst's son-in-law was a lawyer, and in the last days of the Weimar Republic he had been made a judge. Everyone had predicted a rapid rise for him. But now after only four months in office he had been dismissed. On 7 April 1933 the 'Law of restoration of civil service with tenure' had been passed, removing all Jews from state office.

However, it was not this severe blow that induced Ernst to take stock. On 10 May, on his way home from his office, he became aware of a strange atmosphere in the streets of Berlin. Thousands of students had gathered on the boulevard of Unter den Linden and in the university forecourt for a torchlight procession. In view of his earlier experiences, Ernst hurried to get out of the area as quickly as possible. The next morning he discovered that the rabid mob had burned close on 20,000 books on a huge pyre. In addition to the works of Thomas and Heinrich Mann, Stefan and Arnold Zweig, the frenzied students had also consigned to the flames books by Albert Einstein and Marcel Proust, Erich Maria Remarque and Emile Zola, Jack London, Arthur Schnitzler, Lion Feuchtwanger, and H. G. Wells. There had not been a sight such as this since the burning of the Talmud in front of the Cathedral of Notre Dame in Paris on 3 March 1241. Now the German Students Union had declared war on all works that allegedly represented 'a pollution of German thought', and consequently on every printed word that did not accord with the national socialist ideology. This act was more abhorrent to Ernst than any anti-Semitic act of violence. He summoned his eldest daughter Thea and her husband. 'I'm afraid there is no future for us in this country,' he said.

Ernst, who never took important decisions without weighing them up at great length, instructed them to pack their suitcases the very same month. He bought first-class passages for them on the liner *Champollion*, which sailed from Marseilles for Haifa. Sixty-one years after Ascher Levy had visited the Holy Land, one of his descendants was once again on the way there, but this time not as spokesman for the poor and destitute, but as a refugee. 'Have no fear,' Ernst comforted them, 'it won't be long before we follow you.' And indeed in September 1933, Ernst and Käthe gave up their apartment, and moved into a Jewish *pension* in the Schlüter Strasse district. All that now remained was to arrange the transfer of their money from Berlin to *Eretz Israel*.

When Hitler was appointed Reich Chancellor, there were

Ernst Levy, Berlin, 1931.

approximately 500,000 Jews in Germany whose assets amounted
to a total of approximately 12 billion marks, a sum that was of
interest to the Reich as well as to the Zionists. On 9 April,
Arthur Ruppin, one of Tel Aviv's founding fathers, wrote in his
diary: 'If the German government were to permit the Jews to take
their money, or a part of it, out with them, then several thousand
of them could set up as farmers in Palestine.' This was essentially
the starting point for a large-scale, complex, and daring transfer
action, to be known as the *Ha'avarah* agreement.

The idea took shape when Gad Machnes and Sam Cohen met
in a modest Tel Aviv apartment. They were both major shareholders in the agricultural society, Hanotea, and owned orange

groves and land near Natanya. Following this meeting Sam Cohen travelled to Berlin. To his great surprise he was immediately admitted for talks in the Reich Ministry of Trade and Industry. In the office of a senior civil servant, Hans Hartenstein, Cohen put forward his plans and arguments:

'The economy of the Reich is suffering from the worldwide boycott by Jews. German exports are in rapid decline. Apart from this the government of the Reich is interested in the emigration of the German Jews. The Hanoteah society is prepared to transfer Jewish assets to Palestine on the following basis: for the amount in Reichmarks that German Jews pay in banknotes to a society in Berlin, we shall purchase German goods to that value, in order to sell them on in *Eretz Israel* or other countries in the Middle East. We shall then pay out the proceeds to those emigrants who have left the Reich and settled in Palestine. Both sides will profit from this procedure. Nazi Germany will break the boycott and increase its exports. Potential emigrants will be given an incentive to leave, which is in line with your policy. And the actual emigrants will have means at their disposal to establish a life in their new homeland.'

On 25 May, Sam Cohen left the Ministry for Trade and Industry with a black sealskin briefcase clamped under his arm, which contained the authorization for the first transaction for the sum of 3 million marks. PALTREU (Palaestina Treuhandstelle or Palestine Trust), which was to co-ordinate matters in Germany, opened their offices in Meinekestrasse in Berlin. PALTREU was permitted to open special accounts at the A. E. Wasserman bank in Berlin, and at M. M. Warburg's in Hamburg.

Hartenstein, the senior civil servant, had not merely recognized the advantages of the *Ha'avarah* agreement, but had also succeeded in persuading the party, the state authorities, and the various security branches of these benefits. The idea also met with approval in the office of the Führer. The heads of the main national bank saw the economic aspects as the priority. Although the *Ha'avarah* agreement did not bring the treasury any foreign currency, it did provide improved marketing for German

products, which for a variety of reasons – including the worldwide
Jewish boycott of German goods – were not finding any buyers
abroad. The long-winded discussions were summed up in the cir-
cularized statement from the Minister of Trade and Industry as
follows:

> As a means of facilitating the emigration of German Jews to
> Palestine, the permitted sums may be allocated without
> making excessive demands on the currency reserves of the
> Reich Bank and at the same time German exports to Palestine
> can be increased; an agreement to this effect has been reached
> with the Jewish offices involved:
>
> Those emigrants, to whom the emigration advice centre has
> ratified sums over and above the minimum amount of 1000
> Palestine pounds allowed for entry to Palestine, as necessary
> and appropriate for the establishment of a new existence in
> Palestine, may, in accordance with this report, be permitted to
> deposit a sum exceeding 15,000 Reichmarks into a Special
> Account I at the Reichsbank, made payable to the Bank of the
> Temple Society Ltd, thereafter to be deposited with a Jewish
> trust to be set up in Palestine.
>
> This Special Account I, for which, together with the Special
> Account II referred to below, the sum of three million
> Reichmarks is to be earmarked in the first instance, will be
> managed by the Bank of Temple Society Ltd as a trust account
> for the above-mentioned Jewish trust association. The emi-
> grants will be paid out the equivalent of their deposit in
> Palestine pounds, according to the amounts resulting from the
> sales of German products in Palestine, by the Palestinian trust
> association in order and in proportion to the deposits made on
> the Special Account I [...]
>
> Another Special Account II for the Bank of the Temple
> Society Ltd has been set up with the Reichsbank. Currency
> control departments are permitted to accept deposits of up to
> 15,000 Reichmarks per person on this account (again made out
> to the German Jewish trust company in Palestine) from
> German subjects of the Jewish race who are not intending to

emigrate at present, but wish to purchase a residence in Palestine.

If a person who has not yet given up their domestic residence here, receives credit in Palestine pounds from deposited payments for goods sold in Palestine, in accordance with the implementation arrangements, this amount must be offered to the Reichsbank currency control. However, the Reichsbank is prepared to allow this credit to remain in the person's favour for up to six months, and to extend this period on application, if accompanied by a supporting document from the Palestine Agency in Berlin. Should such an internal resident wish to use the credit to purchase land in Palestine or use it for other investments, he must apply for permission from the currency control agency, producing supporting confirmation from the German General Consulate in Jerusalem as to the seriousness of the intended investment. Permission for use of the credit for purposes other than investment in Palestine cannot be granted...

Since the *Ha'avarah* agreement had now been established on a legal basis, and it was assumed that the initial sum of three million marks would very soon be exhausted, the Nazis feared that contact with the Hanotea private company would not be sufficiently rewarding for the interests of the Reich. Hartenstein, the senior civil servant, now demanded that the *Ha'avarah* agreement should be transferred to agencies representing the Jews on an official and worldwide basis. The German industrialists thought that by this means they would break the boycott, which had found renewed support, especially in England and the USA. This placed the Jewish world organizations in a dilemma. Should the boycott be upheld or would it be better to support this agreement and rescue tens of thousands of Jews as a result? This was the central issue debated at the Zionist Congress in Lucerne in 1935. The Congress delegates decided by a huge majority to place the *Ha'avarah* agreement under the supervision of the World Zionist Organization. This set in motion an incredible situation, placing the Jewish establishment in direct negotiations with the Nazis.

The *Ha'avarah* agreement continued to function without a break until the outbreak of the Second World War. The Nazis were quite prepared to continue the transactions after 1 September 1939, since Palestine, being a mandate territory of the British, was not involved in the war. But the British government took a different view and prohibited any contact between the *Yishuv* in *Eretz Israel* and Nazi Germany. As a result the accounts of the two Jewish banks, Wasserman and Warburg, retained a sum of over eighty million marks. For some inexplicable reason the Nazis did not confiscate this money, and it was restored to the original owners after the war.

Several tens of thousands of Jews from Germany took advantage of the services of the PALTREU, and excess funds rapidly accumulated. At the beginning of the 1930s there were just 200,000 Jews living in Palestine. The poor economic situation of the tiny *Yishuv* made it impossible for them to purchase goods to the value of several million marks. Consequently the Zionists were obliged to find additional outlets in other countries of the Middle East, a difficult and complicated matter, particularly in view of the pressure being applied by the German consulate general in Jerusalem. They had been opposed to the agreement from the outset and, because of the vociferous demands of the Arabs, had raised objections to any actions related to the immigration of more Jews. Yet the president of the Reichsbank, Hjalmar Schacht, firmly rejected this opposition. Even after Schacht and Hartenstein had been dismissed from the management of the bank in 1937, the Nazis stuck to the *Ha'avarah* agreement. But over the years the so-called *Ha'avarah* mark diminished in value. Since the German manufacturers involved in the agreement did not receive the premium, which was usually paid to the overseas purchasers of their products in foreign currency, PALTREU was forced to use part of the deposited funds to meet the balance of the difference. Originally the exchange rate for one Palestine pound had been twelve and a half Reichmarks: by 1939 it was forty Reichmarks.

Ernst signed a contract under the *Ha'avarah* agreement for 50,000 marks with a minimal loss of three per cent.

'Have you gone completely *meshugge?*' was Siegfried's heated reaction when he heard about it.

Leo wrote Ernst a reproachful, warning letter: 'You always were irresponsible, but I would never have believed you would go this far. You may well be a knowledgeable lawyer, but you know nothing about money or business. Why ever didn't you consult me before signing this nonsense?'

In the end faced with the entreaties of his brothers, Ernst cancelled the contract. A few months later he heard from friends in Palestine that Thea was seriously ill. But when he arrived in Tel Aviv this turned out to be completely untrue. Thea was not ill at all. 'I'm going back to Berlin,' he reassured her, 'and I shall try talking to Siegfried and Leo. Directly I've done so, I shall come back, and settle here for good.'

But Ernst Levy was not to return to Germany. During his stay in Tel Aviv he fell ill and, within days, he died at the age of only fifty-seven.

Leo kept his grief to himself. But when Else lit a memorial candle thirty days after the death of his brother, he sighed, saying: 'You see, emigration isn't the answer.'

'Hush, how can you say so,' Else warned, placing a finger on his lips.

Whereas Ernst had already given up his apartment in September 1933 and moved into the *pension*, Leo was still radiating confidence. He ignored the attempts of the new regime to seize part of the family property. Some time earlier the head of the limeworks in Gramentz, Herr Filbrandt, had informed him of a surprising visit from the leader of the local farmers' association, who had arrived from Köslin specifically to demand that the business be handed over to a non-Jewish trustee. Filbrandt had referred him to the head of the company in Polzin, and nothing was heard from him there. But Leo's optimism was short-lived; in his naivety he seriously believed that the worst of the troubles were now over. Even though the swastika flag was flying from the town hall; and the pharmacist on the market square had proclaimed that he would sell 'nothing to pig-Jews apart from poison'; and Brunnenstrasse had been ceremoniously renamed

Adolf Hitler Strasse; and a notice had been attached to the entrance to the spa park, which read, 'Dogs and Jews not admitted' – the new regime still did not have too much effect on everyday life. Farmers continued to sell their grain to the Levy firm and to buy the fertilizer produced at the Gramentz works. The estate owners who needed credit still came to the office of the company, although admittedly they did try to keep their visits secret and demanded more favourable conditions of repayment and interest. Every transaction was entered into the company account books with meticulous accuracy, and Leo believed that nothing could happen, so long as all sides observed the necessary order.

Since the incident at the Café Zell, he made a point of always wearing his military medal in public. In addition, he had tried to obtain an official document certifying that he had fought at the front, for former front-line soldiers were treated better than 'ordinary Jews'. At the beginning of November, the Reich Representation of German Jews issued a statement in support of Hitler's foreign policy. Siegfried laughed out loud at this, but not Leo. He read every word thoroughly:

'Along with the entire German nation, as citizens of the state we Jews are also called upon to cast our vote in favour of the external policy of the government of the Reich. It is intended to promote Germany's equal place among the nations, the reconciliation among nations, and the pacification of the world. Despite everything that we have had to experience, the vote of the German Jews can only be Yes.'

The Jewish press regarded this as an expression of loyalty to the Fatherland, regardless of which government might be in power. The front-page comment of the 3 November issue of the *Jüdische Rundschau*, the paper that publicized the official announcements of the Representatives, read:

'The desire of every German Jew must be to produce a clarification of the Jewish position in the state, so that in these times of tension and decision there can be no doubt as to the entitlement of the Jewish citizens of this country to participate in the exercise of civic rights.'

Letter from the Mayor of Polzin asking Leo Levy to support him in the elections.

However, wishful thinking and reality were two very different matters. Not long after, the house of Levy received the first blow. It was a damp and misty day, typical for the time of year. The hills around Polzin created a kind of basin that trapped cloud and fog. Work was going on as usual in the offices. At about five in the afternoon, a black Mercedes stopped in front of the house at 14 Adolf Hitler Strasse. A driver in stormtrooper uniform opened the rear door. 'This is it,' he said and pointed to the company offices. Leo was just studying the estimated prices that had arrived that morning from the Gramentz factory, when a frightened employee showed the guests into his office without knocking beforehand.

'What's the meaning of this? I gave instructions…' said Leo angrily. But as he looked up and saw the uniforms, he fell silent.

'Are you Leo Levy?' asked a stout man in an olive-green Loden coat.

'I am Doc-tor Leo Levy,' he replied, stressing his title.

Uninvited, the unknown visitor pulled up a chair and sat down, as if to demonstrate his authority.

His companion first placed his hat on the table, and then introduced the visitor: 'You have the honour of addressing Herr Blödorn, leader of the regional farmers from the National Socialist farmers' union.'

'My pleasure,' said Leo stretching out his hand. The latter did not respond.

'I doubt it really will be your pleasure, Levy,' began Blödorn. 'I have come to discuss business.'

'We are always pleased to be of service to our customers, in accordance with the tradition of our company, which, incidentally, has existed since 1841.'

'Well, it's high time you cleared off then,' burst out the companion, who had not introduced himself so far.

Blödorn silenced him with a wave of his hand and asked, 'Have you read the new law, Levy?'

'New laws are passed every day. Which one is the gentleman referring to?'

'To the Reich inherited estate law.'

'No I haven't had the time to deal with it yet.'

'I expect you're too busy raking in the money all the time, are you?'

'We pay taxes on every penny that we earn, my good sir. We have nothing to hide.'

'From now on you'll pay one Reichmark for every penny you earn,' laughed Blödorn sarcastically, unbuttoning his coat and stretching out his legs. 'Warm in here,' he remarked. 'You're not short of firewood for heating, are you?'

'We have sawmills. The excess…'

'I know,' Blödorn cut him short. 'First of all read the law,' he said and threw a thin leaflet at him. Leo caught it, read it through silently, and turned pale. The edict issued by the Reich Ministry for Food and Agriculture classified property up to 125 hectares in size in use for agriculture and forestry as hereditary estates. The proprietor of an hereditary estate must possess German Reich nationality and be of 'German or equivalent racial descent'.

The Aryan family tree had to go back as far as 1 January 1800. Henceforth such estates were absolutely not for sale and could not be mortgaged. Debts owed by them could not be enforced.

'Have you finished?'

Leo nodded. 'Yes,' he said quietly.

'And have you understood what it says?'

'Yes.'

'That means, Levy, that you have to renounce ownership of the Neu Buslar estate. An official assessor will set the value, and we shall pay you legal compensation. After all, we are under the rule of law and do not rob citizens of the Reich. You are still a citizen of the German state, aren't you?'

'As far as I know, yes.'

'And there's something else I must remind you Levys,' said Blödorn. 'From today all mortgages taken out by farmers on their property are null and void. So you cannot call in their debts.'

'This law does not state that it has retrospective power,' observed Leo.

'Are you a lawyer or a property owner?' was Blödorn's cynical response.

His companion gave a malicious laugh.

'Of course none of this is relevant if you can prove you belong to the Aryan race.'

Leo simply ignored the remark. Blödorn continued, 'I give you three days to draw up a detailed list of every mortgage, all land, every agricultural property you own. I shall be back at the end of the week to complete the transaction. And as for the farmers who owe you money, you'll have to fight it out with them. I advise you to be moderate and lenient.'

The two men left the office. Leo went over to the window and watched until the car had disappeared around the corner. Then he sank heavily into his armchair and picked up the leaflet again. The language was full of qualifying clauses and was not entirely comprehensible. Finally he went home.

Once the house had fallen silent and Else had said goodnight to him, he dialled Heinrich Marcuse's telephone number in Stettin and asked him for advice. The old-established lawyer had to admit that he was equally powerless. 'I am a Jew, just like you, my good friend. In all dealings with Nazi officials, I shall always draw the short straw. They not only have the law on their side, they also have the power. But all is not lost. I advise you to approach Zubke, a lawyer in Köslin. Zubke is one hundred per cent Aryan and a cunning advocate, and he's not above accepting Jewish money, either. For a good fee, he'll certainly be prepared to get you off the hook.'

Farmers were delighted with the new legislation. Furthermore, the regime saw to it that the prices of agricultural products were raised and that farmers working their own land gained increased respect. The Nazi promotion of 'Blut und Boden' (blood and soil) was quite intentional and their extravagant propaganda declared the farmers to be the 'life blood of the German nation'. In the countryside the Nazis became increasingly popular. In his *Memoirs*, Albert Speer recalls a memorable car journey taken with Hitler: 'All over the countryside the farmers dropped their implements, the women waved, it was a triumphal drive. As the car sped along, Hitler leaned back to me and called out, "There's only one other German who's been honoured this way before – and that was Luther! When he rode through the land the people came streaming from afar to greet him. Like me, today!"'

In truth 1525 was the one and only time in their history when the German peasants rose up against the princes in revolt against the heavy burdens imposed on them. At the time Martin Luther had advocated harsh and violent treatment for these 'mad dogs', as he called the poor rebels ... But the historic parallels now being drawn were extravagantly inventive. Where a Jewish businessman and a German farmer were concerned, the equation was quite simple – the farmer did not need to pay his debts, and the Jew had to keep quiet. Leo realized that the firm would not be able to weather these conditions – they jeopardized its liquidity and its very existence. The new law very soon affected everyday existence, too. People were no longer the first to greet Leo, no one raised their hat or spoke to him in the street. A brief letter from the mayor informed him that he was no longer included as one of the town dignitaries. An atmosphere of social exclusion surrounded the family.

Zubke the lawyer charged a horrendous fee, but he was worth the money. He had a lot of experience in dealing with representatives of the regime. At this stage the government was still concerned to give its expulsion policy the appearance of legality, and therefore cloaked it in a mantle of ministerial decrees. Skilful jurists, 'Aryans' such as Zubke, navigated their clients through the paragraphs, searching for loopholes, and were frequently able to achieve at least partial success.

When the Nazis then sought to requisition the limeworks in Gramentz, for Leo and Siegfried it seemed obvious that the thing to do was to approach the legal chambers in Köslin once again. Siegfried, who had just returned from yet another of his trips abroad, simply regarded it as a financial issue. But for Leo it meant far more. The Gramentz works had been his inspiration; he had built them up and had tinkered around for months on end in order to achieve the most effective way of converting lime into fertilizer. His heart cried out to prevent the enforced sale. He felt that the loss of the Gramentz works would seal the fate of the family firm – to lose their most recent project would cut the roots of the family business that stretched back to the middle of the nineteenth century.

It was Sunday, 4 February 1934. After attending church Zubke the lawyer set out in his little Opel for Grünwald. The final chapter in the limeworks affair took place in the house of the National Socialist regional farmers' leader, Klix. Zubke had brought reinforcements. Leo Levy and Filbrandt, the works manager, accompanied him to Grünwald, plus another lawyer by the name of Bayer, from Neustettin. Klix received them pleasantly. His wife had prepared coffee and cake, and Klix took out some home-brewed kirsch from the sideboard. An uninformed onlooker might have concluded this to be a Sunday get-together of old friends. In actual fact it was a fight with no holds barred. The following day Leo sent Siegfried a summary of the course that the conversation had taken.

To start with Klix weighed in quite heavily by addressing Zubke and expressing surprise that he had agreed to represent us. Then he turned to me, saying he could actually have had me arrested long ago for antisocial conduct. In answer to my question as to what my antisocial conduct consisted of, he began by saying – as he had already done on the phone to Filbrandt a few days ago – that we had cut wages by thirty per cent but hadn't reduced the price of the lime at all. I immediately showed him the wages book to prove that we had lowered the wages paid from 1931 to 1932 by about fifteen per cent to the 1927 level, in strict accordance with the emergency decree of 31 December, and at the same time we had also reduced the price of lime to 110 Reichmarks. But Klix didn't seem to be interested in any of this; even though he himself had got lime at the lower price, he maintained that we had charged him the old price.

Then he started going on about the reduction in hours, on which I put him right by pointing out that we had followed the recommendations of the new government, which was repeatedly calling for shorter working hours in order to prevent laying off increasing numbers of the workforce. We had been obliged to cut their hours because of the drop in orders – as a result of the attempted boycott – in order to hold out at least until Christmas without shutting down.

In between Klix then mentioned – probably to frighten us – that young Dennig had been put under preventive detention for antisocial behaviour, and during the first half-hour there were repeated heated exchanges, as I constantly corrected him as best I could whenever he said something that was incorrect.

Klix then began to read out the letter from an agricultural society to Blödorn, the leader of the regional farmers, which he had already told Filbrandt about at the time back in December. This said that the limeworks should be put into other hands, so that the farmers could get the lime marl they desperately needed from the Gramentz works. Then he read out parts of a letter sent him by Moritz-Kalkberge, an engineer, in which Moritz-Kalkberge cited figures that were obviously very different from the ones he had quoted when he visited Gramentz and spoke to me. It is obvious from the letter that Moritz-Kalkberge – the prospective buyer trotted out by the government – intends to side with Klix in order to force us down to the lowest possible price. Whereas Moritz-Kalkberge assessed the value of the plant at 75,000 Reichmarks in the presence of myself and Filbrandt on 22 December, he apparently wrote to Klix with the figure of 40,000–50,000 Reichmarks.

We then began to go through the contract with the government, verifying the amounts of lime we have sold since 1928 and the money paid over this period (partly by asking Herr Frick over the telephone). I also told them how much profit Gramentz had made, approximately 10,000 marks per year over the past two years. The preceding year had shown a loss of approximately 4000 Reichmarks from the security procedures etc. The years before that, approximately 10,000–22,000. From 1930 onwards the turnover dropped by about half compared with previous years, as a result of agricultural difficulties, and of course profits also dropped accordingly [...]

Then we went back into the office, where once again political discussion cropped up, including the alleged justification for boycotting the Jews, since world Jewry was boycotting German goods, as was clear from the latest export figures. I said that we were by no means obliged to stick to the agreement, since there were a large number of firm existing agreements that went back several years, and it was likely that in any case the economic situation would improve. Klix maintained that he had such a strong grip on the estate farmers that if he gave the order for no one to buy from us, none of them would dare to do so. The fact that he had refrained from giving direct instructions until now was only out of regard for our workers.

But if we set too high a price, making it impossible to take over the lease, he would then issue strict instructions prohibiting buying from us, and we would then either be forced to close down very soon, or we would be working without any profit.

Both Zubke and I repeatedly referred to the various ministerial decrees, for example the one issued by Minister Frick a few days ago. To this Klix responded that he had no wish to do anything illegal, but that in accordance with the recognized principle of 'Blut and Boden' affirmed by the new state, he had the right, as leader of the farmers, to forbid purchase from non-Aryan firms.

In the end Klix insisted on our submitting a precise figure, at which I asked when the payment was likely to be made. Klix instantly replied that everything could be paid out right away in cash. I then went to another room with Zubke, where we reached the conclusion that if the amount were to be paid in cash, our final price would be 90,000 Reichmarks for the factory, and that the supplies of ready lime marl, tips of unprocessed lime, coal, as well as other factory materials, had to be taken over at their current value. It would be advisable to fix the handover date for 1 March...

At the end of the month outside workers appeared in Gramentz and took down the sign bearing the family name that had been put up years ago. It read: 'Imperial Province of Gramentz – Ascher Levy Lime Works'. The official contracts had been signed two days earlier. The works were transferred to the new owners for the sum of 75,000 Reichmarks. And, as in the case of Neu Buslar, once again the Levy brothers were satisfied with the outcome of the sale from a business point of view. Yet for all the pain it caused Leo, there is an almost incidental detail. He gave instructions for the sign to be loaded on to a small truck and brought to the sawmill at Kollatz. There it was cut up into kindling, and as the saw blades tore through the wood, for Leo it was as if they cutting into his own flesh. It was clear to him that every one of the other firms of the family business would soon go the way of Gramentz. The railway administration had already informed him that the sidings linking the Kollatz sawmill with the state railway network were to be shut down and dismantled. Closing down this stretch of track meant that transfer to and from the sawmill was no longer possible, bringing production to a standstill.

'What are you going to do with your pay-out?' asked Siegfried, on a weekend visit to Polzin with Lisbeth.

'For the time being I've paid it in to my bank account,' said Leo.

'How can you be so naive?' said his brother angrily. 'First they've taken Gramentz from us, next thing they'll grab our bank accounts.'

'You're exaggerating, as usual... And what are you doing with your money?'

Siegfried lowered his voice. 'Why don't you try to move your money abroad, where it will be secure?'

'Like Ernst? Every transfer abroad attracts huge taxes nowadays. I'm not so *meshugge* as to throw a third of my money out of the window.'

'There are other ways.'

'What do you mean by that?' asked Leo with a touch of suspicion in his tone. 'I do hope you're not doing anything that's against the present regulations?'

'Forget it, I didn't say a thing.' Siegfried shrugged his shoulders and fell silent. The brothers were never to bring up the subject again.

Outwardly nothing had changed. The office opened and closed at the usual time just as before. Leo and Siegfried had long telephone conversations, and gave each other advice on every matter, yet there were fewer and fewer important deals requiring consultation. Siegfried travelled abroad more and more, without telling his brother the reason for these trips. The business did not suffer from his absence. All that remained of the many different enterprises were the sawmills, and even these were not working to capacity. The railway administration found itself unable to provide trucks suitable for transporting timber. Leo was angered by the decision, for after all not only was it against the public interest, but it was also illegal. There was no decree empowering the regional director of the railways to dispute the right of Jewish-owned sawmills to transport their products to their customers. Leo sent a letter of protest to Köslin without ever receiving a reply.

Since his work on the Hejaz railway had come to an end, his cousin Paul was now a railway official in Stettin, and had worked his way up over the years to deputy chief engineer. With no other alternative open to him, Leo now turned to him for help. 'Do you happen to have forgotten that I am a Jew?' Paul asked him, when they spoke on the telephone. 'My days with the Reich Railways are numbered as it is, and there is certainly no one here who would be interested in my opinion.'

Paul Levy was to continue working for the Reich Railways for one more year. Those of his Jewish colleagues who had not served during the First World War, and who consequently were not classified as 'front line soldiers', had already been dismissed without severance pay during 1934. For the time being, at least, Paul was protected by his wartime army service. He had returned from the Russian front with a war wound and had twice been awarded the Iron Cross. The administration of the Reich Railways in Stettin opposed his early dismissal, since they could not find a replacement for an engineer with his wide-ranging technical experience. When Paul Levy read an article on the front page of the *Völkischer Beobachter* on 2 October 1935, urging the immediate dismissal of any Jews still employed by the Reich Railways, he realized that his hour too had come.

The Nuremberg Laws have already had practical results in so far that they provided the Deputy Director General S. A. Oberführer Kleinmann with the possibility of disregarding any opposition, and of immediately issuing instructions by telegraph to remove all Jews still occupying leading positions with the Reich Railways.

Now in the year 1935, more than two years after the change of leadership, we learn that there were still some thirty Jews in senior positions with the German Reich Railways, and we ask ourselves why action was taken only as a result of state pressure, and not through individual initiative?

When Paul was summoned to see the director of the Reich Railways in Stettin, he saw that an edition of the party journal lay open on the latter's desk. The conversation was brief. The director clearly felt uncomfortable about what he was doing, but Paul knew that nothing on earth would change the outcome of the interview.

'Your employment terminates today at four o'clock sharp,' announced the director and asked him to show in his successor. Then he added, 'The state has taken your army service into consideration. We are not sending you home empty-handed. Paragraph Four in the decree of 15 November states that "officials who fought at the front for the German Reich or its allies will receive the full salary they are entitled to as superannuation until retirement age." We shall have to see what happens when you reach retirement age, when the time comes.' *

In Bad Polzin the news of Paul's dismissal barely raised an eyebrow. The straitjacket was being tightened with terrifying speed, and meanwhile blows were raining down so frequently that they were regarded as almost normal. The control of timber transportation had long since dropped from being topmost priority. Since the firm had had to give up their property, particularly the vast forest areas, they had become hostages in the hands of those dealers who distributed the material. From time to time timber was offered for sale, or forests were released for felling by public tender, as was customary in this business.

Leo would not give up his legal entitlement to participate in the process. Immaculately dressed, with his Iron Cross prominent on his lapel, he would drive out to the small towns and villages to inspect the timber with an expert eye, and assess the price he was prepared to pay. Sometimes his would be the best offer, and yet he never got the order. More and more people preferred not to do business with Jews. 'Your co-religionists abroad are boycotting

---

*In 1941 Paul Levy was deported to the Piaski concentration camp near Lublin in eastern Poland and was moved to Majdanek in 1943, where he met his death.

German products,' they taunted him. 'So now it's our turn to boycott the Jewish businesses in our country.' In vain he explained that he, Dr Leo Levy, was a German citizen, just like them. His words fell on deaf ears.

The damage to the firm was massive. But what pained Leo far more was the increasing curtailment of his rights and the visible change in the behaviour of those around him. He was hurt and outraged. Worst of all was to be helpless in the face of all these machinations.

The employees of the firm in Bad Polzin and the senior workers at the factories had always treated Leo with respect. Most of them came from the nearby region, and were known to the firm of Ascher Levy from childhood. The fact that 'the Levys were here before we were born' had contributed in no small way to the prestige of the firm. To be employed by the firm of Ascher Levy in Polzin was regarded as something special. Employees of the firm had benefited equally from people's respect as well as from advantageous credit in the shops, as no one doubted their trustworthiness. The Levys made considerable demands on their staff, even though Ascher and Bernhard and Leo after them had never been excessively generous: the salaries paid by the firm had always been in line with those paid by other companies. Yet people did not regard this as miserly, but respected it as business prudence. It was not done to be extravagant with money in Pomerania.

Leo had always maintained a certain distance towards his staff, not from arrogance, but because he was convinced that everyone should know their place. However, this did not prevent him from discussing everyday issues or world events with his employees from time to time. They shared a common regret for times gone by under the Kaiser and the Weimar Republic. In short, a certain understanding had existed between employer and employees.

But even this relationship had begun to crumble. Political life does not tolerate a vacuum. Over the past years the place of the National Germans had been taken over by the NSDAP. And as the government began to undermine the economic foundation of the firm, and so call its existence into question, even the most loyal and long-serving of the employees realized that it was no longer advisable to hitch their own future to that of the Levys.

Leo was considered an inflexible person. Only those nearest to him knew that this hard, cool-headed man was highly sensitive to atmospheric changes. Mostly he acted as if he had not noticed the whispering behind his back and the averted gaze of passers-by in the street, but when Siegfried next came to Polzin for the weekend, he burst out: 'It looks as if we can't even rely on our employees any longer. There's no doubt that some of them are informers.'

'Are you surprised, Leo? They only want to save their skins. They can see very well which side their bread is buttered. Don't you know who's the last to leave the sinking ship? It's the captain, Leo, all on his own, the captain.'

'I'm surprised, all the same. Can they really not see that Hitler is just a passing phenomenon? In a hundred years' time no one will even remember his name.'

'Don't worry,' said Siegfried mockingly, 'in a hundred years they'll have changed their minds, and everything will be as it used to be.'

Leo was not amused. 'Can you never be serious about anything?' he asked.

'Quite the contrary, my dear brother. That was just gallows humour. You know the story of the Jew who goes to the rabbi, and complains about the hopeless situation he's in. He keeps going to the rabbi and weeping. But the latter keeps sending him away. Until finally one day the Jew goes to the rabbi and roars with laughter. At that the rabbi finally realizes how bad things really are for him…That's how it goes. Let's see what else this Herr Hitler has up his sleeve for the Jews, to make sure he gets a mention in the history books.'

The so-called Nuremberg Laws were proclaimed on 15 September 1935 – the 'Law for the Protection of German blood and German honour' and the 'Reich Citizenship Law'. For the first time in modern history a man's worth was defined in terms of the blood coursing through his veins and those of his forebears. These laws were the quintessential expression of the national socialist racial ideology. The 'Reich Citizenship Law' stripped the Jews of their civil rights. Henceforth Jews could only be subjects of the state. The 'Law for the Protection of German blood and German honour' prohibited marriages as well as extramarital sexual relations between Jews and 'Citizens of the Reich', namely 'Aryans'. These decrees were broadcast over the radio and printed in all the newspapers.

Leo listened to the special broadcast on the radio. The words stripping away what was dearest to him etched themselves deep into his heart. In dramatic tones the radio announcer declared: 'Only a citizen of the Reich, being entitled to full political rights, is permitted to cast a vote on political issues, and to occupy public office ... A Jew cannot be a citizen of the Reich.' Leo switched off the radio, went over to the bookcase, and took down a book with a dark leather binding from the shelves. It was the eleventh volume of *History of the Jews from Ancient Times to the Present*. On the title page, yellowed over the years, was the dedication that its author, Professor Heinrich Graetz, had written to his grandfather. Leo read aloud from the foreword: 'I am more fortunate than my forebears. I can conclude [the *History of the Jews*] with a joyful feeling, knowing that the Jewish people has at last found not only justice and freedom in civilized lands, but has also gained a certain recognition ...'

Else had seen her husband retreat to his room, and had also heard the voice on the radio. She followed him anxiously, but froze in bewilderment at the door. Leo raised the book above his head, and then hurled it to the floor with all his force. It was only then that Else broke out of her stupor and threw herself into his arms in despair. 'Leo, oh Leo,' she stammered, 'what will become of us now?'

In the two years since Hitler had seized power, some 25,000 Jews had found a fairly simple answer to this question. They left the Fatherland, where they had become an undesirable presence. Three of Leo's own daughters had gone. Eva was in Holland on *Hachsharah* to prepare for emigration to *Eretz Israel*. Hannah was in Lithuania at an ORT school, training in practical agriculture. There she was drawn to the Zionist ideal, and finally decided to emigrate to *Eretz Israel* as well. Margarete had found a job as a teacher in London, and it was obvious to everyone that she did not intend to return. After the death of Ernst, Leo had gone to Palestine on a brief visit to see his niece, Thea. He observed 'the national homeland' with a critical eye, and did not feel in any way drawn to the country that struck him as backward compared with Germany, light years away from being a cultural centre, and essentially Oriental. Many of his acquaintances were already living in Tel Aviv or in one of the agricultural settlements. He listened to their experiences, fully understood their motives, but he himself was not inclined to emigrate – neither to Palestine nor anywhere else. To have done so would have meant abandoning all the ideals that had driven him from childhood. He would have let his father and grandfather down, betrayed their philosophy of life and, possibly for the first time in his life, been untrue to himself. 'For me, emigration would amount to moral suicide,' he said to Else. 'We shall stay here – no one can escape their destiny, no matter where they go.'

The Last Painting

The Berlin–Zurich express via Nuremberg and Ulm was running twenty minutes late. 'I don't known what's the matter with me, but I'm feeling very edgy about the whole business,' said Lisbeth without looking directly at her husband. Siegfried did not respond. Buried in the sports pages of the morning paper, he was leaning back, sunk in the soft upholstery of the second-class compartment. The couple never travelled third class, with its hard wooden benches and passengers stinking of beer and tobacco. First class, on the other hand, was just for snobs and spendthrifts. And because there were very few people who bought the most expensive tickets, to do so inevitably meant attracting attention. It was August 1936 and by this time it was advisable to take every little detail and its possible effects into consideration – especially since Siegfried and Lisbeth's current mission was not without its dangers.

Lisbeth was standing at the open window, carefully observing the bustle of activity in the railway station. The platforms were packed. Porters all in the same work uniforms were rushing to and fro, and seemingly endless streams of people were making for the underpasses. A group of boys accompanied by an adult had lined up alongside the train and were singing a patriotic song. The outer walls of the central building were draped with flags and banners.

A few days earlier the Olympic torch had been lit in the new Berlin stadium. The hustle and bustle at the station was a product of the Games. The Olympic Games were an important propaganda tool for the Nazi regime, offering an opportunity to demonstrate to the world the 'achievements' of the Third Reich and its 'love of freedom'. Discreet orders had seen to it that all

notices stating 'Jews unwelcome' or 'Jews and dogs keep out' disappeared as if by magic. Previously these were displayed at the
entrances to public parks, cinemas, theatres, and swimming
baths, and in some cases even at the entry to certain towns. The
press had toned down its anti-Semitic utterances, and articles
about the superiority of the Nordic race stayed in editors' desk
drawers until the Olympic flame had been put out. Germany put
on the air of a calm and contented land to its visitors from abroad,
with its population rallying round the exalted figure of Adolf
Hitler.

It was little more than five months since the German
Wehrmacht had occupied the demilitarized Rhineland. Three
months later Benito Mussolini, Hitler's future ally, completed his
occupation of Abyssinia. The Nazis' support of General Franco,
who had unleashed civil war in Spain, was an open secret.
Furthermore, the race laws and confiscation orders were in full
force. And so visitors from abroad, especially the British and
Americans, were impressed by this apparently peaceful country,
governed by law and order. Or perhaps it was just more
comfortable for visitors to see only what they wanted to see?

'This is also our greatest hour,' Siegfried had said. 'Let's enjoy
it to the full.'

Lisbeth recalled these words of her husband as two helmeted
policemen advanced with measured steps towards their train,
which had been delayed. They stopped at the open door of their
carriage. One of the cops looked at the white notice attached next
to the door, and said aloud to his colleague, 'All right for some,
eh? On their way to Zurich, they are...' and leaned his hand
against the notice. An icy shudder ran down Lisbeth's spine. Just
before they had got on the train, Siegfried had inserted a thick
white envelope between the carriage and the notice, securing it
with sticky tape. Lisbeth had bought the tape two days before
from a pharmacy near their apartment. The chemist had asked
her, 'We have wide and narrow tape. Which would you like?' In
her agitation she was quite confused. Panic-stricken, she thought
the chemist knew exactly what the tape was going to be used for.
And now that the cops showed no sign of moving on, she could

not control herself any longer. Leaning over to her husband, she took the paper from his hand. This time panic showed on her face.

'What's happened?' he asked.

'Police,' she whispered. 'Two cops right next to the...you know, next to...' She pointed towards the door.

'Calm down, Lies,' he said to her gently and got up reluctantly. 'Let's see what's going on.'

The cops looked up as Siegfried's round face leaned out of the window.

Like all the Levys, Siegfried had no Semitic features. His blond hair and blue eyes would have defied the most experienced, thorough racial examination. Many years ago Leo had told him of an amusing incident during his student days at Heidelberg. One of the professors had been lecturing on the differences in physiognomy of European peoples. When someone asked him what an Aryan looked like, without hesitation he had pointed at Leo, saying, 'Like this student.' The entire class had roared with laughter, for all Leo's fellow students knew he was Jewish.

The two cops gave Siegfried a smile, and he smiled back.

'Off on holiday?' asked the cop who was leaning against the sign.

'We haven't even moved so far,' joked Siegfried, holding up his thumb and forefinger. 'I'm afraid this train isn't going to win any medals.'

'Never give up hope,' replied the cop. He was in high spirits. 'We'll be getting enough medals at the stadium.'

A whistle blast sounded from the other end of the platform. A hoarse voice ordered all the doors to be closed.

'There you are, sir. All's well that ends well,' laughed the cop, and saluted Siegfried by shooting his arm out.

The train moved off slowly, as if reluctant to desert the mighty glass and steel structure of the railway station. They passed the tangle of intersecting lines, and had soon left the city centre behind. The train picked up speed.

Siegfried closed the window and turned back to his paper. Lisbeth looked across at him. She took a shiny silver and mother-of-pearl powder compact from her handbag. Although they were alone in the compartment, they did not exchange a single word. Lisbeth powdered her face, Siegfried buried himself once more in his paper. Suddenly he burst out laughing. Lisbeth looked up from her mirror.

'I know. Very understandable after all that excitement.'

'No, my dear, it's nothing to do with excitement. I've just read that a black athlete has won four gold medals.' Siegfried was almost choking with laughter. 'Just imagine, a poor black from Alabama. A member of an inferior race, what a blow for the Nordic race ... incredible ... inconceivable. What I would give to have seen the expression on Hitler's face.'

'I'd give far more never to have to see his face.'

The train arrived in Zurich early the next morning. Passport control at the frontier had gone smoothly, and once on Swiss soil Lisbeth's nervousness evaporated.

The platform was filled with lively toing and froing. Siegfried removed the envelope he had inserted behind the destination notice on the train, without anyone noticing. Next morning about an hour after the financial institutions had opened, he was standing at the counter in his bank. The broad smile with which the employee greeted him indicated that Siegfried was no stranger here.

'How much is it this time?' he asked.

Siegfried pushed a bundle of securities and cash across to him. 'Sixty thousand,' he said.

'For deposit on your account, as usual?'

'Yes, as usual.'

The employee made out a receipt, and handed Siegfried a copy. 'Have a pleasant stay.'

'With money in your pocket, any stay is pleasant,' joked Siegfried. 'Goodbye until next time.'

'Goodbye, sir.' The bank employee arranged the papers in his drawer, and gave Siegfried a friendly nod.

Since the Nuremberg Laws had been issued, with repressive measures intensifying against Jewish businesses, Siegfried and

Lisbeth had been smuggling their money abroad. Siegfried was the wealthiest of the Levy brothers. Besides his income from the family business in Bad Polzin and Stettin, he had amassed a sizeable fortune from financial dealings of his own, mostly by buying and selling shares on the stock market. When government officials in Stettin started taking an interest in his operations, he had finally moved to Berlin, where he hoped to preserve a certain anonymity in the big city. The couple lived in a spacious apartment in the attractive district of Charlottenburg, very close to the Olympic Stadium, and Siegfried continued doing business from there. Dealers soon found their way to his new residence and offered their services to transfer money safely abroad. Hundred of ideas were put forward, complicated and cunning schemes, but the simplest were by far the most effective.

Siegfried's acquaintances made use of an ingenious scheme. They placed advertisements in the classified section of the *Völkischer Beobachter*, of all places, with the following text:

'Businessman with foreign connections seeks secretary with good knowledge of languages as companion on business trips in Europe and America. Serious applications only to be addressed to the Berlin offices of the paper, Box No. 2336.'

Thousands of young Germans dreamed of travelling in the wide world, and so it was no surprise when the advertising section of the *Völkischer Beobachter* was absolutely flooded with letters addressed to Box No. 2336. Three weeks later the advertiser wrote in saying he had been obliged to travel unexpectedly to Switzerland on business, and asked for all the replies to the advertisement received so far to be forwarded there. The bundle of applications was parcelled up into a large packet and sent on to Basle. It did not occur to the German customs to inspect a package with the sender named as the *Völkischer Beobachter*, and so it reached the addressee unopened. Only very few people in the know were aware that most of the letters sent to Box No. 2336 actually came from the person who had placed the advertisement, and that each of these envelopes contained two fifty-dollar bills. Altogether nearly $100,000 left the country by these means, before the advertiser himself finally turned his back on his inhospitable homeland.

Siegfried was aware of this ruse, but preferred to act off his own bat, without anyone else knowing or being involved. He frequently commuted between Berlin and Zurich. His passport, made out by the Stettin chief of police, was valid up to 1941, and did not as yet have the large 'J' stamped on it, which was soon to appear on the passports of all Jewish travellers. Every time he travelled to Switzerland, he took some of his securities with him, and stuffed them behind the notice outside his carriage that indicated its destination. Even if the Nazis had found the bundle, he would not have been in any danger. None of the securities was made out in his name; they were all stamped to the effect that they were owned by the holder.

When Siegfried and Lisbeth returned from Switzerland after the Olympic Games had ended, they spent several weeks with the family in Bad Polzin. In the space of just one year much had changed there. Max Kröning, mayor of the town and director of the spa since 1927, had soon realized which way the wind was blowing. The town administration had even presented the Luisenbad, the fine assembly rooms, as a gift to the Führer. Leo knew the mayor very well. When Kröning had first put himself up as a candidate in Polzin ten years earlier, he had still been registered as a resident of Schloppe. He had not hesitated to write to Leo at the time, to ask for a letter of recommendation. Leo, who never threw even the smallest scrap of paper away, no matter how insignificant, had kept this letter. 'Dear Doctor Levy', Kröning had written on 15 December 1926, extolling his own virtues and expressing his hope that he could count on Leo's support for his candidacy. Yet now he found himself unable even to grant 'dear Doctor Levy' the time for a short discussion. And a sign hung outside the new town administrative offices, now housed in the premises of the *pension* formerly owned by Herr Finkelstein, that read, 'Jews unwelcome'.

Once a week the Brownshirts assembled in the beer cellar of the Hotel Preussischer Hof in the market square. Leo could no more have entered the place than the Café Zell, as he had once done, without running into trouble. Recent events had shown beyond doubt the role that money played in a person's standing.

The regime had stripped the Levys of most of their property, and they now had the feeling they were naked in the jungle. If Leo took a walk through the streets of Polzin, he was ignored. The Iron Cross on his overcoat lapel had long since ceased to open doors for him. The new race laws admittedly made exceptions for those who had served at the front, but this counted for nothing in business. His daughter Eva had voluntarily left the Stettin high school, although she would have been entitled to continue study-ing there because her father had served at the front, when other Jewish students had long since had to move to institutions set up by the Jewish communities.

Only one Jewish girl still attended the elementary school in Polzin, and she was also the daughter of a 'privileged' person. Her father, Georg Zander, had not only been a front-line combatant, but in addition he was married to a 100-per-cent Aryan. According to the Nuremberg Laws, she was therefore a *Mischling* (of mixed racial origin), and for that reason was not expelled from the school. Years later when these dark days lay far behind her, she described how

> those two years among these German children etched them-
> selves onto my memory as a seemingly never-ending night-
> mare. Girls that I had grown up with tormented and kicked
> me, made fun of me, and prevented me from taking an active
> part in school lessons. I pleaded with my father to take me
> away from this hell, but he insisted on not giving in. 'You are
> entitled to a German education, and there is no reason to give
> this up just on account of a few undisciplined pupils,' he would
> respond to my repeated entreaties.

Of all people, it was the Reich Minister for Education who released the girl from her suffering. In a decree issued at Easter 1936, he insisted on the setting up of schools for Jewish pupils. On this subject, he stated:

> One of the chief preconditions for all successful educational
> objectives is racial harmony between teachers and pupils.

Children of Jewish origin interfere with the homogeneity of the classroom community and constitute a severe obstacle to carrying out the national socialist education of youth in schools throughout the country.

The sample surveys carried out on my instructions in various areas of Prussia have shown that state schools are still being attended in not inconsiderable numbers by Jewish girls and boys [...] This creates profound constraints on the development of the national socialist school system [...]

The setting up of public and private Jewish schools in certain places may have resulted in a certain degree of separation for those Jewish schoolchildren who belong to the Mosaic faith. However, distinction according to religion is not sufficient for a national socialist school system. The creation of national socialist classroom communities as the foundation for youth education based on the German philosophy of nationhood can only be achieved by a clear distinction according to the racial identity of children. From the school year beginning in 1936, I therefore intend to implement a preferably total racial separation of schoolchildren throughout the Reich.

In July 1937 this decree was extended to include children of mixed race, such as Zander's daughter. The directive of the Reich Minister for Education was eagerly implemented without delay by the Office of Racial Policy of the NSDAP, and the schools of Bad Polzin finally became *judenrein* (unadulterated by Jews).

Georg Zander and Leo Levy had grown very close in recent times. The drastic drop in business meant that both had a lot of time on their hands. They would have long conversations about what was happening in Germany, and take advantage of fine weather on a Sunday to go for long walks with all the family. The men would wear bright shirts and green riding breeches, and the women pretty flowery dresses.

So it was on this occasion. As usual Else had prepared a picnic basket with sandwiches and several kinds of dessert. At the time when Lisbeth was still living in Polzin, they used to place a cherry or plum kernel in one of the dessert dishes. 'Whoever finds the stone gets a wish,' was a standard joke. Now Else still continued the family tradition. The destination for their Sunday outing was the Luisenbad. Situated in the park were the Assembly Rooms adorned with baroque and gothic towers, like one of the Bavarian fairy-tale castles. Apparently the young Bismarck used to bring his mistresses here in the middle of the last century, to dance and drink champagne with them in the great hall, its walls lined with crystal mirrors. But much water had flowed under the bridges of Pomerania since then, and the place had taken on more of a commonplace character, and yet there was still a romantic feel to it. Lina Levy had once begged to celebrate her wedding to Karl Hamburger the lawyer here. It had been a magnificent wedding. But now they found the path leading to the Luisenbad suddenly barred with barbed wire. The approach road, too, carried a small sign saying 'Entry prohibited' and that trespassers would be fined. Below was the resplendent insignia of the SS. A hiker explained that the Führer had handed the building over to the SS and that they in turn had set up a home for single mothers there, provided that the women were pregnant by 'racially pure Aryans'. Disappointed, they returned home from their outing. Later that evening, the telephone rang in the Levy house. Leo picked up the receiver. 'It's for you, Siegfried. Dr Boling from Berlin is on the line.'

Boling was a lawyer who looked after Siegfried's many interests. He was a party member of the NSDAP and even occupied some office in the Chamber of the Judiciary. From time to time he would take on some transactions, which, although not entirely correct, nevertheless promised a handsome profit. That evening he also had a tempting offer to present him with. Siegfried chose not to be informed of the details. Walls might have ears, and telephone lines even more so. The two arranged to meet in a café on the Potsdamer Platz in the centre of Berlin.

'Tomorrow evening at seven,' said Siegfried into the mouthpiece.

'Fine, seven on the dot,' the lawyer confirmed.

When Siegfried arrived at the chosen place, he was surprised to find a third man present.

'May I introduce Herr Krieger?' said Boling, indicating the stranger. 'Herr Klinger has come specially from Hamburg.'

'Pleased to meet you. Levy is my name.' Siegfried reached out his hand and Herr Krieger shook it warmly.

It was only then that Siegfried noticed the round party member's badge on the man's lapel. Boling followed his glance and said reassuringly, 'Don't worry. We can speak openly in front of Herr Klinger. We've known each other for many years.'

'Well, if you say so ...'

'What would you like to drink, gentlemen? I suggest tea, they don't serve proper coffee here,' said Boling and, without waiting for an answer, placed the order with the waiter. 'Herr Krieger and his wife Martha own a charming property in Switzerland. Where did you say it was again?'

'In Bisone, Canton Ticino. Tessin, if you prefer the German name. It's a wonderful area. Lovely climate. Quiet neighbours, mostly Italians ...'

'Certainly,' the lawyer interrupted him. 'But Herr Levy has no intention of settling in Bisone. We're just discussing an investment here. To be precise, an exchange.'

'An exchange? I beg your pardon? Well, actually I wouldn't mind ... After all, I have every confidence in you.'

Siegfried looked at the guest from Hamburg thoughtfully. Somehow the way he spoke was curious, even suspicious. But Boling had already placed an extract from the Swiss land register on the table.

'Herr Krieger is prepared to dispose of the estate,' he explained. 'It strikes me as a splendid opportunity for the two of you, gentlemen.'

Siegfried examined the land registry entry.

'The papers are all correct. I've gone through the documents with a colleague from Lugano, Dr Valdo Riva. The plot is well situated. Maybe not the very best position, but after all, these days we cannot be too choosy, can we?'

'How much?' asked Siegfried and took a sip of hot tea.

'Two hundred thousand marks.'

'Payment to be made how?'

'Cash.'

'Is there an official valuation?'

'Yes,' Boling hastened to answer. 'The property is worth approximately ninety thousand. The valuation dates from this month. Are you interested?' Boling pushed the paper across to him.

Siegfried ran his eye over it. 'You must realize that the price is somewhat excessive?'

'Herr Krieger and his wife might be open to offer, isn't that so?' Boling threw the visitor from Hamburg a questioning glance.

'I shall have to consult with my wife. The property actually comes from her parents. A wedding present, you understand, Herr Levy...'

'I understand.'

Boling grinned. 'You won't find a better way of transferring your money to Switzerland, Herr Levy.'

Now it was Siegfried's turn to laugh. Boling continued: 'I'm prepared to do everything necessary. Riva, the lawyer, will deal with signing it over to your name. You know him, don't you?'

'We have had some business dealings with him from time to time in the past.'

'Good. Well, I shall stand surety for both sides. You will both pay the fee in equal parts. Five thousand Reichmarks each. You can see that in these circumstances this is by no means an excessive sum. Herr Levy will hand over the purchase price to me; I shall pass it to Herr and Frau Krieger the moment I have news from Switzerland that the transfer to your name has gone through. What do you say, Herr Levy?'

'I say – one hundred and forty thousand marks.'

'The Kriegers are taking an enormous risk...'

'So am I.'

'This twisted Jewish logic,' thundered Krieger. 'You are an obstinate race. I am beginning to understand why you're hated... This discussion is not at all to my taste. I've never learned how to haggle. But my wife and I will agree to a compromise of one hundred and fifty thousand, on condition you pay in cash, and right away. And that is final. One hundred and fifty thousand.'

'Done,' said Siegfried, the word slipping out unintentionally. 'It's a deal.'

'I should like you to bring the money to my office tomorrow evening, after my secretary has left. About half past seven. You remember the address?'

'Certainly.'

The men shook hands. Siegfried paid the bill, leaving a twenty-pfennig tip for the waiter. Krieger and Boling left first. Siegfried went to collect his hat from the cloakroom, and only as he reached the door did he notice the sign, saying 'Jews unwelcome'.

By the end of 1936 Siegfried and Lisbeth had succeeded in transferring altogether 300,000 marks to Switzerland – including the deal with Krieger – in cash or in securities. In 1937 they took a trip to the United States and smuggled approximately $100,000 in their luggage. In March 1938 they went to the British Embassy in Berlin to apply for an entry visa for Palestine.

'For how long?' asked the clerk in the consular section.

'Two weeks,' said Lisbeth.

'Fine,' replied the clerk and added, 'I have to inform you that we are exercising the strictest controls on travel to Palestine. We have to be on the alert for illegal immigration.'

'Don't worry,' laughed Lisbeth. 'We haven't the slightest intention of settling in Asia. Here, let me show you, we've brought the official receipt for tourist currency with us.' The clerk nodded, stamped their passports with the visa, and entered the numbers 72905 and 72906 with his signature below.

The *Vulcania* dropped anchor in the Bay of Haifa on 7 April 1938. Beside the two Levys there were about a dozen immigrant families from Germany on deck. On the quayside porters were waiting for them along with curious bystanders. 'The *Yekkes* are coming!' cried Hanoch, the kiosk owner, and hastened to spread delicacies from his kitchen on the counter. Traders, estate agents, and property speculators jostled them the length of the ship's gangway, and offered their services in a dialect that the new arrivals could barely understand. The impression made by the well-dressed German immigrants, some of whom were even

Receipt for 150,000 Marks paid by Siegfried Levy to solicitor Boling, 6 May 1938.

wearing cork pith helmets, was the embodiment of European foolishness. The Zionist pioneers who were cultivating the land had brought their own intellectual luggage with them but much to the amazement of the customs officials, these new arrivals were trailing collections of rare butterflies, leather-bound Escoffier cookbooks, heavy encyclopaedias, double basses in enormous cases, and ladies' round hatboxes.

Most of them knew almost nothing about the country they had arrived in. Although the Zionist press and the Palestine Office in Berlin supplied applicants with up-to-date information, most of the new arrivals were convinced that in Palestine they would encounter creatures, known as *Ostjuden*, who lived either on kibbutzim or in provincial towns built on the Eastern European model. Others regarded this journey as an interim evil – they were going to stay just until the hatred dispersed and the Hitler regime collapsed like a house of cards, when it would once again be possible to return home.

At that time his neighbours on the Panorama Boulevard on

Mount Carmel were filled with suspicion when engineer Joseph
Loewy used to clamber up on to the roof of his house and spend
hours with his eye glued to an enormous telescope. 'What's this
land speculator snooping about for?' they asked each other.
Joseph Loewy had already come unstuck twice before with his
land speculations, and his failures had not exactly enhanced his
reputation. But he simply paid no attention to their comments,
and through his telescope observed the busy harbour with its
throngs of new arrivals from Germany. Then he would direct the
lens at the northern end of the Bay of Haifa towards Acre and
even further north. Then he did a sum in his head and came to
the conclusion that two plus two could certainly come to more
than four.

In March 1934 a certain Alfred Tuani, a rich Arab from Beirut,
had taken a trip to the Riviera to broaden his horizons. However,
in Monte Carlo he had fallen under the spell of the game of
roulette. When he had exhausted his funds, he found himself
compelled to sell his property between Acre and Rosh Hanikra.
Joseph Loewy the engineer had his eye on this area. His idea was
plain and simple – buy the land, settle immigrants from Germany
there, and in so doing perform a good, patriotic service, which
would not be without a healthy profit. The development section
of the Jewish Agency in Jerusalem considered Loewy's idea completely unrealistic. 'Which of these doctors, professors, or
company directors will want to take up agriculture and, what's
more, in an area where there are no Jews?' they asked him. But
Loewy was known for being stubborn. On 15 May the sales
contract was signed in the solicitor's office of Jean Gadali. The
Tuani family property was signed over to a holding company set
up by Joseph Loewy, the agronomist Dr Selig Eugen Soskin, and
five other gentlemen who wished to remain anonymous. The
purchasers paid 4000 Palestine pounds as an initial instalment on
34,000 Palestine pounds, the total cost of the land. The same day
the new company, by the name of Little Nahariya Holding
Company, was set up in the house of the Carmelites.

At a later date it was a common joke that 'Nahariya will
remain for ever German'. Several hundred German families who

came to Palestine took up Joseph Loewy's offer and bought plots in Nahariya and the surrounding areas. Within a few years there was a story doing the rounds about a child of new immigrants, who had spied a strangely clad figure in a black caftan. The child had apparently run home, shouting, 'Papa, Papa, there's a Jew from Palestine who's come to see us!' And up to the time of the establishment of the state, Nahariya was indeed a very strange place, a kind of enclave that kept to the German language, German customs, and a German sense of order. News of this German settlement in the Levant even reached as far as Baghdad. In May 1948 Iraqi airplanes flew over Nahariya dropping leaflets in German that said: 'Break off relations with the Zionists and no harm will come to you…'

In April 1938 Lisbeth and Siegfried walked down the gangway of the *Vulcania* surrounded by swarms of Arab boys distributing seductively worded leaflets. 'Nahariya – new settlement in the north, where fruit trees flourish and it is easy to set up an agricultural business, to bring you a good income,' ran the enticing text. The Little Nahariya Holding Company made the following offers: 5000 square metres for 885 Palestine pounds, 7000 square metres for 1240 Palestine pounds, and 9000 square metres for 1640 Palestine pounds. Construction of a modest residence cost an additional 600 Palestine pounds. Nahariya appeared on no official map, for the settlement institutions, led by the Jewish National Fund, did not recognize the purchase of Arab land by 'private initiative', nor did it believe that a middle-class settlement on agrarian economic lines could succeed.

Siegfried scanned the brochure thrust into his hand by a barefoot Arab boy, and threw it away. Not for an instant would it have crossed his mind to stay in this backward, underdeveloped country. He had travelled here with his wife in order to meet members of the family, to make some excursions to Galilee, and to visit Jerusalem, all at breakneck speed, as they still wanted to catch the *Roma*, a luxury liner, before it left Haifa harbour for Naples.

The darkest predictions of the Jewish Agency and the Jewish National Fund were soon to prove well founded. Only twenty-five per cent of the 'capitalist' immigrants from Germany were prepared to live in agricultural settlements, most preferring to take up private accommodation, or at best to settle on land that had been purchased from private funds.

Twenty-five men and three women, all of them doctors, plus ten lawyers did take up the challenge and settled in Ramot Hashavim in the Sharon Valley. Their plots of land were too small for them to feed themselves from the agricultural products they could grow. But such trifles did not deter the doctor-farmers. They set up an agricultural co-operative and brought over from America an expert in raising chickens to advise them.

Curious visitors came from far and wide to Ramot Hashavim to gape at these 'chicken *Yekkes*'. In the daytime they worked in the chicken coops, and in the evenings they would read Heine or listen to classical music. The Sharon Valley echoed with laughter, and Ramot Hashavim was mockingly referred to as 'Cock-a-doodle-doo'. But for all their scorn, what their neighbours failed to realize was that the German doctors, aided by foreign expertise, had laid the foundations for modern chicken-rearing in Palestine.

The great wave of immigration from Central Europe had changed the towns and villages of Palestine to no small degree. The immigrants brought 'revolutionary' ideas with them – attractive shop window displays, a different culture of living and eating, a new architectural style, based in the main on the ideas of the Bauhaus, as well as modern medical and research methods.

Siegfried and Lisbeth were unable to carry out their intended tour of Palestine. It was a time of major unrest in the country. The clashes between the *Yishuv* and the Arab population erupted into violence. The front page of a German-language newspaper reported bloody massacres.

'I'm not so crazy as to go touring in a battlefield,' said Lisbeth indignantly.

The Palestine of the thirties did not appeal to her at all. How can people live like this? she wondered silently about her nieces, Ernst and Leo's daughters. Palestine was underdeveloped and limped along hundreds of years behind Europe. She found the dirt in the towns and in the Arab villages disgusting, whereas the arrogance of the well-off simply made her smile in mild derision. She could not identify in the slightest with the *Yishuv*. The Zionist ideal and the pioneering concept did not belong to her world. Her impressions were merely visual, not emotional. She absorbed nothing other than what met her eye, so that despite the brilliant sunshine everything appeared to her as black and white.

After the two weeks had passed, the couple took leave of the family as planned and set off once again for home in Berlin. They had originally intended to spend quite some time in Italy on the way home. Lisbeth had been looking forward to being at the Hotel Positano, where she had stayed in the past, with its wonderful view over the Bay of Salerno. But political developments compelled them to cut short their journey.

However, they did reach Amalfi, where they met Rudolf. He had come across specially from Ischia, where he had been living for some months. It was five years since Siegfried and Rudolf had last seen each other. Rudolf moved about for ever in search of sun-drenched landscapes and like-minded friends. He would really have liked to have stayed on in Calla Ratiada, a small village on the island of Majorca, where he had felt very much at ease. Many German artists who had fled from the Nazi terror had found refuge there. The outbreak of the Spanish Civil War in 1936, and the refusal of the police to extend residence permits on the island, meant that the community of artists had dispersed in all directions. Even before he was obliged to leave the island, he had officially separated from his wife. Genia had asked to meet him in Marseilles and he had agreed. They were always going to remain friends, but there was no longer any reason to maintain the relationship on an official level. Also, the regime was not exactly favourably inclined towards 'Aryan' women married to Jews. Genia had not asked outright for their marriage to be dissolved, but Rudolf had understood and agreed to a divorce. He had returned to Majorca feeling that he had done the right thing. However, he kept quiet about it; Herbert Schlüter was the only one he wrote to, saying, 'No one knows better than you that my marriage was totally inappropriate right from the start.'

As he talked to Lisbeth and Siegfried, the conversation turned on the latest events. They were sitting in a small Italian taverna, one of those tiny restaurants where the pasta always tasted delicious. It had to be approached across a roof, since it was built on a slope. They spoke about the Anschluss. Just one month earlier, Austria had forfeited its sovereignty. Following many intrigues accompanied by pressure and acts of violence, the country had been annexed to the Third Reich. The Austrian Chancellor, Kurt Schuschnigg, had been placed under house arrest in harsh and humiliating conditions. In all, 800,000 schillings were extorted from the Jewish community, when in the course of a house search of the Israelitische Kultusgemeinde (the Jewish religious community) the Nazis had discovered receipts showing that the community had contributed this amount in support of Schuschnigg. Adolf Eichmann announced his intention to set up a branch of the Central Office for Jewish Emigration in Vienna. All this did not bode well.

'I feel we ought to postpone our return to Germany for a while,' said Siegfried.

Rudolf nodded. 'I think that would be very wise.'

'What about you?' asked Lisbeth. 'Will you return to Ischia?'

'Probably,' answered Rudolf.

'We should stay in Switzerland over the summer,' said Siegfried and turned to his wife. 'What do you think?'

'You know I love good chocolate more than anything,' she laughed in reply.

'That will finally give us a chance to have a look at what we bought from that Herr Krieger.'

'I much prefer the Zurich shop windows or the hotels in Lugano. What is there to see on that estate? It's only a little patch of land.'

'True, it may be just a little patch of land, but it is on Swiss soil, and it belongs to us.'

'All right, then what about this as a compromise. We go to Bisone and look at the property, but we'll stay in Lugano.'

'Fine, Lies. After all, compromise is what marriage is all about. So, agreed. Bisone and Lugano.'

'I meant Lugano and Bisone.'

Both of them burst out laughing, as if they'd just solved their only care in the world. Rudolf looked at them sceptically, took a sip of wine, and then joined in their laughter. Now it was the waiter's turn to look at the three German diners in surprise. 'These Germans, they own the whole world,' he said to the chef, who had leaned out through the hatch to see what was going on.

The *pension* in Lugano at 4 Via Braganzone was a Mediterranean-style villa built in the twenties. It was in a quiet spot, at a distance from the main street that winds its way up the mountain. For the time being the couple took two rooms on the first floor. The windows looked out on the lake, and the little resort lay spread out below them. There was a small balcony in front of their bedroom. Right from the start Lisbeth felt comfortable. In the evening, when she had let down the shutters, she felt sheltered and secure, as if all worries and threats were banned from these four walls. She loved stretching out on the velvet-covered sofa and reading by the light of a table lamp. Every evening Siegfried was glued to the radio. In the mornings he would visit the cafés along the front, striking up an acquaintance with other refugees who had also found a temporary haven in Switzerland. They would sit together drinking Campari and soda, discussing the same subject for hours on end: when would they be able to return home?

News from Germany was far from reassuring. At least once a week Siegfried would telephone his brother in Bad Polzin. He rang his lawyer in Berlin every fortnight. 'I want to obey all the regulations, so that I don't run into trouble when I return to Germany,' he explained to his lawyer, Herr Boling.

'When do you intend to come?' asked the lawyer.

'When everything has calmed down,' replied Siegfried.

'I don't quite understand you,' said Boling and hung up. It was common knowledge in Berlin that the Gestapo listened in to all international telephone calls.

During the summer ever more Jewish refugees streamed into Switzerland from Austria. Only two weeks after the Anschluss, the Swiss government instructed the border police to intensify

*The pension in Lugano, the first stop where Siegfried and Lisbeth
stayed after leaving Germany.*

passport controls. Neutral Switzerland was only too happy to
receive refugees who deposited money and gold bars with Swiss
banks, but what they did not want was to be a refuge for less well-
endowed victims of persecution. The official reasons were simple
– a wave of immigration would lead to an increase in unemployment, and the unemployed would in turn be a drain on state

welfare. Yet tighter passport control in no way solved the problem. All Austrian citizens received Third Reich passports, and the holders of such passports could enter Switzerland freely without a visa. The border police had difficulty in distinguishing between welcome tourists and undesirable refugees. Essentially the Swiss officials took the view – quite correctly – that most of the Jews who came were refugees, and the non-Jews were tourists. But how were they to distinguish between Jews and goyim? This was the question troubling Heinrich Rothmund, head of the Swiss police, who was also in command of its aliens' section. Hoping to find a solution he decided to approach the German Consul in Berne.

The archives of the National Socialist Foreign Ministry contain a letter from the German Ambassador in Berne, dated 24 June 1938. For the benefit of his superiors in the Wilhelmstrasse, he bluntly records: 'I had a discussion with Rothmund. He said that Switzerland has just as little interest in the Jews as does Germany, and requested that direct contact be made with our police in Vienna.' Two months later the Swiss Ambassador in London announced that Switzerland had protested 'against a Judaization of the state' and insisted that the Nazis should block the escape routes for Jewish citizens of the Reich. This pronouncement was conveyed to Berlin with the aid of a senior German diplomat in London, Theodor Kordt. Soon after, Kappeler, the Swiss chargé d'affaires in Berlin, came up with an original idea – perhaps the German authorities would be so kind as to mark in some way the passports held by Jews, so that they could instantly be identified at border crossings?

This conversation was kept strictly secret. At the end of September Rothmund travelled to Berlin and was most warmly received by the Ministry of the Interior as well as by the Gestapo. A secret agreement was signed on 29 September, that from 5 October 1938 onwards passports held by Jews should be stamped with a 'J' no less than two centimetres high. From then on the Swiss authorities would only grant entry to those with passports marked in this way if they could produce residence permits from the appropriate Swiss authorities or authorizations certifying that

Switzerland had no objection to their passing through on the way to some other destination.

Of course Leo Levy did not have the slightest idea of what was being secretly planned. When he applied for a new passport at the end of August, the agreement had not yet come into force. His passport was issued without a problem. Eva had completed her training in Holland, and was now about to emigrate to Palestine. Her father had decided to accompany her as far as Trieste. It was not a pleasure trip for either of them. 'To tell you the truth, Papa, emigrating to Palestine is somewhat contrary to my philosophy of life,' said the young girl, as Else was packing her cases for her.

'To have a philosophy of life, you must first see something of the world,' pronounced Leo with fatherly gravity.

He realized he was being evasive. Emigration to the land of Zionism was now the only solution left, a demonstrable fact that only a simpleton could question. And Leo was no fool, even if he could not summon up the strength to act on this conclusion himself. He, the captain, would remain on the sinking ship. True, he would no longer be on the bridge but in one of the dark recesses of the hold. But at least he would have the feeling that he had done his duty. For the girls, well, of course that was another matter. There was no future for them in the Third Reich; worse still, they didn't even have a present there. All the turmoil warranted emigration. When he had accompanied Eva to the secretary of the Stettin branch of the Palestine Office at 6 Prinz Albert Strasse to see to the issue of a certificate, or entry permit, for her, there had been a conspicuous stack of the *Jüdischer Rundschau*, the mouthpiece of the Zionist Association in Germany, lying in the waiting room. The headlines proclaimed, 'Columbia closes its doors to immigrants'; 'Visas required for Cuba'; 'Paraguay considering restrictions on immigration'; 'Brazil – will only reunite families'… Hard as he found it to accept the truth, the numbers of desperate people seeking to escape the trap were constantly on the increase; and the more people there were trying to get away, the fewer doors were left open to them.

'You'd do better to send your daughter to China,' an old acquaintance had whispered to him. He too had travelled from

Bad Polzin to Stettin, and made contact with a travel agency that had hired a large passenger ship about to leave for Shanghai, as Shanghai's constitution permitted refugees from anywhere in the world to immigrate there. 'If you prefer Shanghai, I'll gladly give you the address,' the man had offered. But the mere idea that this would take Eva away to the other side of the world to a sinful city, only known to him from the stories of Pearl Buck – the very thought was intolerable to Leo. Given the circumstances, Tel Aviv seemed the lesser evil.

On 15 September 1938 Eva and Leo boarded the Berlin–Trieste express train. This was the same day that the British prime minister Neville Chamberlain set out on his fateful journey. Chamberlain drove to the Berghof at Berchtesgaden to meet Adolf Hitler and appease him. The Anschluss of Austria had merely served to increase the Nazis' territorial appetite, and now they had their eyes on the Sudetenland.

Two days earlier there had been a special session of the French cabinet. France had undertaken to stand by Czechoslovakia, in the event that another country should threaten its sovereignty and independence. But now the cabinet was divided – should they adhere to the contractual agreement even if this meant war with the Reich? A feverish debate went on all day long. By the evening a solution had been found – they would approach Chamberlain, ask him to meet Hitler and satisfy his appetite through some kind of agreement which the Western European public could accept. Officials of the French Foreign Ministry spent two hours tearing through the capital before they were finally able to track down the British Ambassador, Sir Eric Phipps, who was attending the Opéra Comique. The same night a telegram was dispatched to London.

At the Nuremberg rally in the presence of thousands of supporters, Göring had threatened: 'We know it is intolerable that this tiny scrap of a tribe – no one knows where they came from – should be constantly molesting and suppressing a civilized people... But we know that it is not these absurd wretches. What's behind it is Moscow, the eternal Jewish Bolshevik claque, they're the real culprits.' By now Chamberlain was on his way to

Berchtesgaden to appease Hitler. Afterwards he was to go on to
Bad Godesberg, and finally at the end of September to the infa-
mous Munich conference. The price for the surrender of the
Sudetenland was peace for Europe. No one asked, 'How long for?'

Even before the ink had dried on the Munich agreement, Eva
set out for Palestine. Leo stood on the quayside of the harbour at
Trieste, waving as the ship drew away until it had disappeared
from sight. He hurried back to the hotel, packed his bags, and
ordered a taxi to the station. The train to Lugano went by way of
Venice, Vicenza, Verona, and Bergamo.

'I'm only here for a day or two,' he said on arrival in Lugano.

'What's the hurry, Leo?' asked Lisbeth in surprise. 'Why don't
you take advantage of your stay to relax a bit? There are plenty of
rooms available here, and in view of everything that's going on in
Germany you could really do with a holiday.'

'Anyway – why go back at all?' added Siegfried. 'Give Else a
call... this is a marvellous house.'

'My house is in Polzin.'

'You're just in love with your four walls. But there's nothing
left there for you apart from those walls.'

'It's not the four walls I value, it's principles.'

'Who do you think you are? Galileo Galilei?'

'I'm Leo Levy.'

'So? Whether you live here or anywhere else, won't you still be
Leo Levy?'

'That's just the trouble with you, Sigi. You've never understood
me. And do you know why? Because you've never been guided by
any principles. A man without principles is a man without roots.'

'Both of us have experience in this area. We both know all too
well what happens to a tree. Never mind how deep down its roots
go, the tree still gets felled and sawn up into beams, poles, and
wood shavings.'

'But man is not a tree.'

'That's exactly what I meant. A man doesn't stay like a block of
wood in a place where the earth is burning.'

Leo hung his head. 'Maybe you're right,' he said. 'Now that
Eva has left Germany as well, things no longer look as simple and

straightforward as they did. And yet...no, Siegfried, I cannot suddenly deny my entire life.'

'You're absolutely right. I never will understand you properly. Reality changes, the regime changes, your surroundings change – and only you alone, Doctor Leo Levy, son of Bernhard Levy, grandson of Ascher Levy, great-grandson of Jäckel, you alone must stay like a rock in the surf, you are the only one forbidden to deviate from principles, even if their foundations have already been shaken long ago.'

'I won't argue with you, Sigi. You know what arguments are like between brothers? It's a tug of war. Each pulls with all his might, each in his own direction. But if I suddenly let go, then you fall over...That's from the *Mishnayot*...I bet you've never read them.'

Siegfried laughed. 'You're incorrigible.'

'That's exactly what I think of you.'

'For once you agree on something,' said Lisbeth in relief, and they all laughed.

Three days later Leo asked his brother to accompany him to the railway station. They drove in an open carriage along the boulevard that followed the contours of the lake. The summer was nearly over. The mountain peaks that rose above the lake were shrouded in thin wafts of mist. A white pleasure steamer moved across the water, with a few tourists standing on the deck. 'Look, Leo, how beautiful it is here. How calm and quiet!' Leo nodded, and asked if it was much further to the station.

'If everything goes according to plan, then I'll still be in time for the night train from Zurich to Berlin,' said Leo, as they reached the station. And then he added casually, 'And you, Siegfried?'

'Me? What do you mean?'

'Come on, Siegfried, you know perfectly well what I mean!'

Siegfried sighed and laid a hand on his brother's shoulder. 'No, Leo, there's not much hope. But you can come and visit us any time here in Switzerland. It's the kind of country I like, that can consider itself lucky. No war for hundreds of years. It seems as if nothing will ever upset it, and apart from avalanches in the Alps even natural catastrophes don't happen here. At times when Europe was in need, it was a safe haven. Here is where the Calvinists fled when they were being persecuted by the Catholics. And here is where... Yes, at the present time this is the right place to settle. And do you know what I particularly like?' Siegfried grinned like a schoolboy. 'Women don't have the vote in Switzerland!'

Leo kept silent. He did not share his brother's sense of humour.

Siegfried took his hand from Leo's shoulder, pulled his wallet from his pocket and, in a note of genuine concern, he asked, 'Maybe you could do with...'

'No, no, thanks. I'm not short of money.'

'I know, but just for the journey...'

'You know what a methodical person I am. I've thought of everything.'

'In that case, I have a favour to ask. Ida wrote to us that she's planning to take a trip to Italy.'

'Right. I believe she won't be using her return ticket either.'

'Ida doesn't need a ticket. She's driving. Sometimes I have to ask myself what kind of world we're living in. On the one hand there's the Anschluss, the rape of the Sudetenland, restrictions against the Jews, the Nuremberg Laws, seizure of private proper-ty – what have you. And on the other hand, here we are, sur-rounded by this magnificent scenery, and there's Ida driving to the sun in her sports car, just as if nothing untoward is going on.'

'You see, it isn't all as black as you make out. What do you want from her?'

'Ask her to bring us Lisbeth's family photo albums. The ones we left in Bad Polzin – they're on the bottom shelf...'

'I know. In father's old bookcase.'

'That's right. And something else. If it's all the same to you, Leo, I'd like to have great-grandfather Jäckel's silver candlesticks as a memento. They would be a kind of symbolic connection with home.'

'But you just said that your home is here, in Switzerland... All right, all right. Let's not start arguing again. I won't forget to send you the albums and the candlesticks. But I'm warning you, Siegfried. You're getting sentimental in your old age.'

'That's the way I like you, Leo. Fewer principles and more humour.'

The brothers embraced.

'Give Else our love … I hope everything will turn out all right.'

'Never fear. While there's life, there's hope. Hope only vanishes once you're dead. That's from the *Jerusalem Talmud*. Goodbye.'

'Goodbye, Leo.'

On the homeward journey, Leo stopped off in Berlin where his youngest daughter, Ruth, was living. He had made an arrangement to meet his wife there and to visit a dealer who was going to find a buyer for the sawmills in Kollatz. He returned to Bad Polzin on 7 November. When he left Lugano the sun had been shining, but in Polzin it was chilly, and everything looked grey and sad. He couldn't get over the difference between the two worlds. A huge banner emblazoned with the words 'Strength through joy' now hung over the name of the station when he arrived. In recent years convalescent homes had been set up all over Germany, offering workers from the Ruhr and other industrial centres the chance of short holidays. Their presence changed the atmosphere in the town. Bad Polzin had become common and vulgar. At times the residents felt like strangers in their own town.

The evening of his return, Leo switched on the table light and sat down to write a letter to his other daughters. Although Margarete was now in England, and Hannah and Eva were living in Palestine, he had the habit of addressing his letters to all three daughters as if they were living in the same place. Then he would send a separate copy to London.

Dear Hannah, Eva, and Margarete,

We returned home from Berlin today, I via Stettin at six o'clock, and Mummy just now at eight. What was special about this visit was that yesterday we signed the contract for the sale of Kollatz – the last of our businesses. The buyer is a Herr Micheli from Baumgarten in East Prussia, a somewhat older man (about forty-seven) and, as far as one could judge, very suitable for the Kollatz works. Now we still have to wait for the various authorizations necessary, which will probably take about two months, and only then can it be handed over. Even though this won't make a complete pensioner of me, retirement is not far off, and the questions this raises are enough to keep me awake in the wee small hours.

Your card of the third, dear Margarete, reached us in Berlin. And today Mummy spoke to Frau Epstein in person and received the jumper. Frau E. had had no idea that you are the daughter of your parents. If she had, she would have done much more for you. Why on earth you don't say who you are when you meet people, I really can't understand. You must surely all have come to realize how right and necessary it is to take advantage of the connections available to you through your parents! ...

We were very puzzled by the mention of 'marriage to an Englishman' in your card. After all, you know that in matters of this kind we abide by the good old Jewish values, that marriage and family form the basis of our entire existence, and constitute far too sacred an institution to be disparaged as experiments – regardless of practical, political considerations, however important these may seem ...

Next morning Leo went to the firm's offices as usual. In the lobby he found three employees engrossed in a newspaper.

'Haven't you anything better to do?' he rebuked them. Leo could not tolerate idleness.

'We haven't had a single client all week,' replied Franz, the bookkeeper's assistant.

'That's still no excuse for reading the paper in office hours,' Leo shouted at them angrily. The employee folded up the *Pomeranian News* and apologized.

The fact that Franz, the firm's only 'Aryan' employee, had apologized pacified Leo, demonstrating to all those present who was boss. Leo went into his office, shut the door behind him, went over to his desk, and was about to go through the post, when he noticed a copy of the same newspaper lying conspicuously on top. Someone must have placed it there intentionally. A huge banner headline proclaimed: 'German Diplomat assassinated in Paris. Embassy secretary Ernst von Rath shot by Jew.' Ernst von Rath was neither a national socialist nor an anti-Semite – quite the reverse. Some time ago the Gestapo had latched on to him as he was suspected of not being a supporter of the new regime. He had been shot in error. A young Jew called Herschel Grynszpan had intended to shoot the German Ambassador to France, to draw attention to the deportation of thousands of Jews of Polish origin who had been living in Germany for many years, some of whom had even been born in Germany. Grynszpan's parents and siblings were among those who had been expelled and detained at the Polish–German frontier. The seventeen-year-old student had mistakenly shot the wrong man. Naturally this made no difference to the storm of indignation that erupted in Germany. The German press immediately attacked its own Jews. It was not just the *Pomeranian News* that cried out for collective retaliation.

Leo opened out the newspaper, smoothed down the fold with his hand, brooded for a moment, then stood up and called out: 'Franz!'

'Yes, sir?' The employee looked at him, without getting up from his chair.

'Was it you who put the newspaper in my office?'

'I've already apologized for reading the paper. Now I apologize for entering your office without permission. I did it because I thought you'd want to know what's going on. After all, it's not every day that one of my countrymen is murdered by a Jew.'

Leo could barely contain his fury. With considerable effort he remained calm as he told Franz, 'You can collect your salary at the end of the month. Until then I don't wish to see you here any more.'

'We're certain to see each other again,' replied the employee through gritted teeth, and left the building, slamming the doors behind him.

A day later, just before midnight on 9 November, Franz was

standing beside an Opel-Blitz lorry parked in the inner courtyard
of the 'Lebensborn' Home in the Luisenbad. About two dozen
hefty men had been ordered to assemble here. They were all
wearing stormtrooper brown shirts and broad swastika armbands.
Very few people were aware that Franz had joined the party. He
had kept this secret, as his deeply religious mother hated Hitler
ever since the latter had attacked the Church. An additional
reason may well have been that her husband had left her for a
woman twenty years younger who was active in the Nazi Workers'
Front. Franz had secretly been a loyal and dedicated servant of the
NSDAP for the past four years. His instructions were to provide
regular information about what was going on at the firm of Ascher
Levy, and he had carried out this task to the satisfaction of his
superiors. He had eavesdropped on a conversation between Leo
and Siegfried and had passed on the contents. In addition he had
informed the Gestapo in Köslin about the doings of the Polzin
Jews from time to time. As he stood by the lorry in the Luisenbad,
he wondered what the reason for this gathering might be. He was
soon to find out, and just before he got into the vehicle the local
leader of the NSDAP came towards him and said in a loud voice,
'Tonight you will have your revenge.'

It was a chilly night; the sky was clear and bright with stars.
Leo had closed the office at eight in the evening and gone home.
Else had prepared a light supper, just chicken and vegetables.
'You've got to be a bit careful what you eat,' she smiled. 'I don't
want a husband with a paunch.'

After supper the couple went to their bedroom. 'I'm tired,' said
Leo, switching off the light. He fell asleep and had a strange
dream. He was climbing a mountain, puffing and sweating, but
the greater his efforts, the further the mountain peak receded. A
herd of cattle was grazing just below the peak. The sound of the
cow-bells around their necks sounded like machine-gun fire,
getting louder and then quieter. All the time he kept on climbing.
Suddenly he felt a hand touch him ... The movement was so real
that he woke with a start. The dream still had a hold on him, as
half asleep he heard his wife saying, 'Leo, Leo, I think the
telephone's ringing.'

The alarm in Else's voice shook him into wakefulness. The telephone was ringing ceaselessly in the adjoining room. 'Just a minute,' he mumbled as he went across to the living room, without switching on the light. He held on to his pyjama trousers with his left hand, groping his way with his right hand, to avoid bumping into the furniture. The telephone did not stop ringing.

'Hallo,' he said softly into the receiver. 'Who is it?'

'Zander.'

'Zander? For God's sake, do you know what time it is?'

'Quarter past four. I'm very sorry, but this can't wait.'

By now, Leo was wide awake.

'What's happened?'

Zander lowered his voice. 'Nazi hordes have seized the town.'

'I don't understand what you mean. It's all quiet here.'

'They're dragging Jews out of their homes, looting shops, and smashing windows.'

'Let me go and have a look.' Leo crossed to the window, pulled the curtain aside and looked down. There was not a soul about in the street. 'I don't see anything. Are sure you haven't just had a bad dream?'

'I'm afraid not, it's absolutely true. At this very moment they're in the house opposite. Don't you hear the shouting?'

'Why don't you call the police?' asked Leo. 'A gang of hooligans can't just be allowed go on the rampage.'

'I'm afraid there's no point in calling the police. The whole thing looks like a pogrom to me, and those taking part seem to be under police protection. Herr Abramson rang me half an hour ago. The synagogue in Stettin is in flames. Apparently they've also set fire to our sailing and tennis club pavilions.'

'Merciful God,' muttered Leo, 'I don't know what to say.'

'Better not say anything, Herr Levy. Just bolt and barricade your apartment – and pray.'

'Thank you,' stammered Leo and replaced the receiver. He stood rooted to the spot, unable to think straight. A total vacuum spread through his innermost being. It was as if the ground had suddenly been wrenched away from under his feet. He looked down. Only then did he notice that he was standing barefoot on the polished parquet floor. He dragged himself to the nearest armchair and dropped into it.

'Who was on the phone?' called Else from the bedroom.

'Zander. I'll tell you right away.' At that moment he heard a din on the street. A car pulled up, and men were speaking in loud voices. He wanted to go over to the window again, but his body was overtaken by a strange heaviness, and he simply could not get up. He was still sitting in the armchair when he heard the tramp of boots on the staircase, and the next moment there was a hammering on the door of the apartment.

As Else opened the door, she spotted three men. She recognized Franz. The other two were unknown to her, young men in their twenties. They were in high spirits, and oozed self-confidence. 'Out of the way,' yelled one of the intruders. Else wanted to ask Franz what was going on, but Franz, whom she had always known as an obliging and modest employee, roughly pushed her aside. She was forced against the wall as the uninvited guests stormed past her into the apartment.

'I promised you I'd be back before the month was out, old boy. Now you know, we National Socialists always keep our promises,' said Franz mockingly, giving the armchair in which Leo was sitting a kick.

Leo did not react. He looked at his attacker in bewilderment, as if he had no idea what was going on around him.

Franz turned to his comrades. 'Well, who's going to volunteer?'

'Me,' said one of the intruders, and pulled out his pistol.

Only now did Leo leap to his feet. In a fraction of a second, he came to his senses. He saw the pistol aimed at his head.

'This is against the law … you have no right!' he yelled. We shall never know what else he was going to say. His attacker pulled the trigger twice. Leo's hands went to his face, as if to escape the inevitable, then he fell to the floor. Else threw herself over her husband; she knew that he had stopped breathing for ever.

'Nice work,' grinned the murderer, and stuck the pistol back in its holster.

'Now let's take a good look round,' said Franz coldly. 'These Levys have been stashing money away for the last hundred years. It's high time it went back to its owners.'

Bent protectively over her husband's body, Else watched help-lessly as the three men tipped out the contents of cupboards and drawers and rummaged through them. When they finally left the house, she crept to the telephone and dialled Georg Zander's number. There was no answer. At this very moment, Herr Zander, who was a highly respected cattle-feed dealer among the farmers and owners of smallholdings throughout the entire region, was being dragged off to the assembly point in the town. His civil rights, granted by the Fatherland, and the desperate protests of his wife (who had been born in the region and was easily able to demonstrate her 'Aryan' origins back to the third generation, as stipulated by the Nazi racial laws) were to no avail. After ransacking his apartment, the SA barbarians threw him on to a lorry like a sack of potatoes. There he found himself in the company of about twenty other Jews, who had similarly been dragged from their homes, beaten, and pushed on to the floor of the grey Opel lorry. By midday all men of Jewish origin were held in the local police station. Towards evening they were once again bundled into a lorry and driven away to an unknown destination.

At midday, Else range Zubke, the lawyer. 'I'm afraid it's beyond my power to help you,' he informed her. 'I cannot bring the dead back to life. And as far as the material damage is concerned, I suggest you approach your insurance company.'

The following night the chief of police of Bad Polzin instruct-ed four Jews to make their way to the Levy house under cover of darkness and 'bury the corpse as quickly as possible and without fuss or bother'. However, when they turned up at the house in the Adolf Hitler Strasse, Else told them, 'You've come for nothing. We buried him immediately after the catastrophe.' It didn't occur to anyone to check what she said. The Polzin police had their hands full with getting those they had arrested to Köslin, whence – so they were told – they would be taken to the Oranienburg concentration camp.

Else had lied. Covered with a sheet, the body of her husband lay on the sofa in the drawing room. Else informed her daughter, Ruth, who was still in Berlin waiting for the necessary emigration papers. A few hours later she arrived in Polzin. Even though she was only seventeen, she made the arrangements for the burial. Two Christian gravediggers had prepared the grave.

'How sad that there's no one to say Kaddish for him,' sobbed Else. Now, as she stood by the grave, she could not contain her tears any longer.

The gravedigger, who was familiar with the Jewish ritual, shrugged his shoulders. 'I don't know your Kaddish, but I don't mind praying for the salvation of his soul. He wasn't a friendly person, but he was straight. May he rest in peace,' he said and knelt down on the freshly dug earth.

Apart from Else and Ruth, there was no one present. But even before Leo Levy was buried, mother and daughter had sat down and written letters to the daughters of the Levy family who had succeeded in leaving Germany.

Dear All Three of You!

I hope that by now you will have had our telegram [wrote Ruth]. Yours reached us by phone from Gerda. I'll write down the contents anyway, just in case ours didn't reach you: 'Dad gone away, am healthy and composed. At home with Ruth. Still unsure what to do. Apply for certificate for Ruth too. Mummy.'

You'll gather from this that so far Mummy is all right. She manages to sleep and is in good health. I arrived here on Thursday evening. Daddy was collected at eleven o'clock. The Kollatz people arrived with horses on Friday afternoon, and then we brought Daddy to the old house. Yesterday Daddy was put in the right coffin (he had been in another one before), and we hope to put him to rest tomorrow. Mummy is over there at the moment and, I believe, is writing to you as well... For the time being there's nothing more to be done, except wait. You can imagine the number of questions that are surfacing, but they can't be answered for the moment... Daddy's funeral won't be what you might imagine, but that can't be helped. There won't be any outsiders, at best one or two gentlemen from Stettin ... I don't know what to tell you. Warmest greetings and Shalom – Ruth.

Lisbeth and Siegfried were sitting in a café on the square in Lugano, having afternoon coffee. The previous evening Siegfried had made a call to Bad Polzin. Since then the catastrophe that had taken place there had hung over them. Lisbeth sipped her white coffee and said, almost casually, 'Now that Leo is no longer with us, you're the last male in the Levy line.'

'Yes, you're right,' nodded Siegfried. 'But what makes you say so?'

'Nothing ... no reason.'

'Lisbeth, we've really known each other long enough ... You've never once said something for "no reason".'

'I was thinking what would have happened if you had married another woman ... I mean, a woman who could have borne you children. You know very well what I mean.'

'Yes, if I had married another woman, I would have twelve sons by now, enough for a football team with a goalkeeper in reserve.'

'You can't just shrug it off with your jokes. I know how important this is.'

'Important for whom?'

'For the family. For the line to continue.'

'I thought we dealt with this long ago?'

'But things are different now. Sometimes old cases are opened up again, even if the files have long since gathered dust.'

'I am over sixty. What do you want me to do? Shall I divorce, and marry a younger woman who will bear me a son? Or should I make do with an illegitimate son? The Italian chambermaid in our *pension* isn't bad looking. A friendly brunette. What do you think?'

'You won't be serious.'

'If there were an appropriate solution, then it would make sense to talk about it. But, as it is ... What's the point of picking at old sores?'

'Ha! Caught you!' Lisbeth raised her head, and looked him in the eyes. 'Even you refer to solutions and old sores. Even you have the feeling that the family tree is about to die out. That all the efforts invested over generations will have been in vain. That there's no one left to carry on.'

'Now just a moment, calm down. The fact that Leo has been murdered doesn't change anything... What I'm trying to say is that it makes no difference, positive or negative, to the way things are. After all, it is hardly credible that Else would have got pregnant again and brought a son into the world. If you believe in the Talmud, then all right, that did happen in Sarah's case. But nowadays things like that just don't happen. And as far as we're concerned, we need to worry about the present, perhaps about tomorrow as well, but certainly not about future generations. Apart from which, have I ever complained about you, even in the very slightest?'

'I know, Siegfried. But sometimes I get so depressed. Other women might creep into a dark corner and weep. Tears can bring relief. But it's not my style to cry my eyes out. For me it helps to talk about it. Please, don't be angry with me.'

'It wouldn't even occur to me to be angry with you.' He placed his hand on hers and stroked it gently.

'Poor Leo. I often used to tease him for being so conventional, with his concern to carry out the letter of the law, and his blind faith in the principles of justice... I never really felt close to him, but just now of all times, now that he is no longer alive, I miss him as if someone very dear to me had gone. Perhaps we can at least manage to persuade Else and Ruth to join us here?'

'Don't you remember? When I telephoned them yesterday evening, Else told me that she had sold up the business, and was going to Tel Aviv with Ruth. After this tragedy, they treated her decently at the Palestine Office in Stettin. Apparently they will be getting their certificates shortly.'

'Leo had to be murdered for them to take the first step. What a price to pay...'

The offices of Valdo Riva, the lawyer, were on the opposite side of the square on the second floor of an old house with a

Renaissance façade, and vast rooms and ceilings with ornamental wood carvings. Lisbeth and Siegfried went to see him the same day. He received them in his office, furnished with antique pieces, which was plunged in semi-darkness. Seated behind an enormous, richly carved desk, he greeted them as usual in a friendly way. However, this time the purpose of their visit was not financial business. The Levys had come because they were concerned about their future residence in Switzerland. Following the introduction of obligatory identification on passports belonging to German Jews, the previous unmarked passports they held were no longer valid. Siegfried and Lisbeth now faced the alternative of either travelling to Berlin to have their passports appropriately marked, or applying for temporary permission to remain in Switzerland. Travelling to Germany would be fraught with danger, with every likelihood that they would not be granted permission to re-enter Switzerland on their return.

'Signore Riva,' said Siegfried, 'we have to obtain these residents' permits, no matter what the price.'

The lawyer nodded sympathetically. 'Did you bring the bank receipt with you?' he asked in fluent German.

Here in Canton Tessin, south of the Alps, the official administrative language was Italian. Valdo Riva, a young, dynamic lawyer, dealt with a lot of German clients because he spoke perfect German. Siegfried handed him a letter from the head of the Schweizerische Bankgesellschaft in Zurich, confirming that there was a total of 60,000 Swiss francs in his account. Signore Riva glanced at the document, gave a satisfied smile, and promised to take on the case. In a detailed and well-reasoned letter, he requested the Justice Department and the Berne Police to grant Herr Levy and his wife permission to remain in Lugano. 'Apart from the liquid funds confirmed by the enclosed bank receipt, the couple own a property in Bisone, valued at 46,000 Swiss francs. They are childless, and own other properties in Germany, and are therefore financially secure and do not need to find jobs in Switzerland. There is no danger whatsoever that they will be a burden on welfare provision ...'

Two weeks later Siegfried had to present himself at the aliens' police station in Bellinzona, capital of the canton. A serious-looking officer passed a yellow booklet across to him, a kind of pass that was issued to foreigners temporarily living in Switzerland. 'Your application has been granted,' he pronounced. 'You have permission to remain in our canton until 1 September 1939. As you see, sir, Switzerland was and remains a byword for hospitality.'

On the night of 31 August to 1 September 1939 – a Friday – Lisbeth packed their cases. A taxi had been ordered for seven in the morning. The express train for Genoa via Milan left at eight o'clock. They were going to travel onwards to Nice the following day, where at the recommendation of friends they had reserved a room in the Hotel Windsor.

The day before their expulsion from Switzerland was a day of great tension throughout Europe. Following the seizure of Austria and Czechoslovakia, Poland was the next item on the menu of the Third Reich, even though Poland had military allies in Great Britain and France. An attack on Poland would produce a decisive – namely, military – reaction from the two allies. This meant another world war. The world at large wanted to see a check put on Hitler's greed. The statesmen had finally come to realize that even surrendering Poland would not ensure lasting peace in Europe.

The night that Lisbeth was packing her suitcases was when the army supreme command opened the documents held in secret for the operation known as 'Operation WEISS'. After faking a Polish attack on the German broadcasting station at Gleiwitz in the German–Polish border region, ostensibly giving them good reason, German planes set out at dawn, bombing Polish cities, bridges, and airports. Tank units and motorized infantry crossed the border points, and using heavy artillery the destroyer *Schleswig Holstein* set alight the munitions dump on the Westerplatte, near Danzig. The ferocity of the attack was such that the defeat of the Polish army was just a matter of time.

Just as Siegfried and Lisbeth were about to leave the *pension* in Lugano the telephone rang. Rudolf was on the line. News of the attack in the east had got him out of bed.

'Have you heard the news?' he shouted into the receiver. 'What are you going to do? What on earth is going to happen to our relatives?'

'We're leaving Switzerland,' replied Siegfried and asked where Rudolf was calling from.

Rudolf was on the island of Procida, but offered to meet his relatives somewhere. Siegfried suggested the resort of Bordighera on the Riviera di Ponente. The two arranged a rendezvous in a small café by the beach.

'Isn't fate ironic,' said Rudolf, as they sat at the table together. 'Three generations of Levys fought against the French. And now you're seeking shelter from the Germans in France.'

'I never could stand the idea of war,' said Lisbeth. 'And what about you, Rudi? Where will you end up?'

'Don't worry. I live like a butterfly, I flit from flower to flower. And as far as I know, they never aim cannons at butterflies.'

'That's no answer.'

'For the time being, I'll stay in Italy,' Rudolf answered, serious this time. 'Maybe I'll go back to Ischia or to my friends in Rome. I always did have a soft spot for that city.'

'I've heard that Mussolini is also in the mood for war. Maybe...'

'I don't like to wish misfortune on anyone. I have no enemies. As long as nature exists, and the sun rises, I enjoy the pleasures of life, no matter where I happen to be.'

'I envy you,' sighed Lisbeth. 'If only I were like you...'

'What a blessing that the Almighty didn't create us all from the same mould, that really would be boring. I derive my greatest satisfactions from those very differences. Imagine if the world around you were just black and white with no shades in between, and no colours!'

'You're a poet, Rudolf. We are made of flesh and blood. You called yourself a "butterfly" – a butterfly that flits from flower to flower. Unlike us, who flounder reluctantly from place to place, and don't even notice the flowers on the way. Consider yourself lucky.'

It was time to say goodbye. 'When do we see you again?' The cousins shook hands.

'Only God knows.'

Lisbeth stood on tiptoe, kissed Rudolf on the cheek, and whispered in his ear, 'Watch out for the hunters' nets, my little butterfly.'

In truth Rudolf was by no means as carefree as he pretended to be, even though he had no notion of the horrors in wait for mankind. He was like someone caught in a shower of rain while out for a stroll, trying to avoid the raindrops without really worrying about the bad weather ahead. From Bordighera he went back for a short time to the Hotel Savoia on the island of Procida, where he spent the last summer months before the outbreak of war. His room had, in his own words, 'a view of the entire bay, Capri, Vesuvius, Cap Misenum, Torregaveta, Ischia, and all the rest in one sweep of the eye'. Soon after, he moved on, first to Ischia, then to Rome, and then he journeyed back north to Genoa. By now he was no longer travelling in search of breathtaking scenery but on the lookout for a means of escape. The Italians refused to extend his residence permit. He faced deportation on 25 November. He had no experience of dealing with officialdom, on top of which he had no money. In growing desperation he aimed at emigration, but the list of countries still accepting refugees was getting shorter day by day.

All his hopes now rested on Erik Charell, a theatre director and choreographer he had befriended, who had fled immediately after Hitler seized power and who had taken Rudolf in as a guest in New York in October 1936. The two had travelled all over the United States together and had even paid a visit to the Hollywood Dream Factory. Now Rudolf appealed to Charell for help. There was absolutely no chance of arranging immigration to the USA, explained Erik, but a few days later a telegram arrived from him saying: 'Trying to get entry permit for Chile stop costs three hundred dollars stop must pay another three hundred dollars deposit stop can you raise fare by boat Genoa–Chile with help of Genia or other friends stop wire back stop Erik.' But Rudolf was too proud to turn to Genia, and replies from other friends were not forthcoming. He could not raise the money.

His attempts to get a visa for Ecuador were equally unsuccessful.

To return to Germany would have amounted to suicide. Contact with family members in the eye of the storm raging in Central Europe gradually diminished. His brother Paul, who had moved from Stettin to Berlin after his dismissal from the services of the Reichsbahn, continued to send him small sums of money, although due to the existing currency restrictions they were often quite tiny amounts. Sometimes ten, another time twenty marks. Genia sent him friendly words of encouragement, but her relationship with another man was no longer a secret in artistic circles. However, she and Rudolf had been separated for so long that this now meant nothing to him. Herbert Schlüter had long ago replaced her in his affections. This scrawny-looking man with angular features and a calm temperament was currently in Florence, so this was to be Rudolf's next destination.

In December 1940 he arrived on the banks of the Arno, and found himself in a spacious room on the fifth floor of a dark, gloomy house on the Piazza Santo Spirito. He rented this from a plump and friendly Italian woman, who ruled the house with an iron hand – a familiar phenomenon in artistic circles. He liked the place, even though his room was extremely sparsely furnished. Apart from a double bed, an oak wardrobe, and a desk with two chairs, there was nothing else in it. Yet its very emptiness appealed to him, for it left enough space to set up an easel. From his window he had a direct view of the church of Santo Spirito, which he painted in brilliant colours.

The Pension Bandini was on the top floor of the Palazzo Guadagni, an ancient palace that had seen better days. 'A luxury stable,' was how Rudolf thought of it at first, as he heaved his cases up the broad, dilapidated staircase. And yet Herbert's recommendation had met his needs exactly. There were several German intellectuals and artists living under Signora Bandini's roof, all of whom for various reasons had chosen to live beyond the frontiers of the Third Reich. Despite the Berlin–Rome Axis, the regime was not in the least interested in them. The Italian police did not bother them, or worry about the validity of their residence permits. It was as if this beautiful city was being watched over by successors of the Medici, the one-time generous patrons of the arts, and not by the fascists. This may also have been why the residents talked so little about politics when they sat in the lounge of the *pension*, and so much about the fine arts.

Two old friends, Heinz Battke and Kurt Craemer, provided Rudolf with company at that time. Later Craemer recalled those days:

> His change of address was certainly not permitted under the law, and it was only the sympathetic leniency of the official on duty in the Office for Aliens Department that stopped Rudolf being sent back to Rome. When Karli Sohn-Rethel then bumped into us, a normal atmosphere gradually re-established itself. We worked all through the day, and met in the evenings by the fireside – the winter turned very cold. For Rudolf Levy the new apartment at last offered a certain degree of security, for the first time in years. He felt protected in our company, so that external events and problems, especially financial ones, were easier to put up with, as there were trusted friends on hand.
>
> Our rooms, which had for so long looked like temporary accommodation, gradually began to assume the appearance of studios again. I myself hadn't worked for more than a year, and Rudolf for almost two. It had been a long time since any of us had been in a situation where we could wander in and out of rooms in the same house, and take a discreet look at what was being produced...For me and for the younger people, who were in and out of the house and who took part in this contact and interaction, Rudolf Levy's disciplined manner of dividing up the day and his regular, flowing output were an important influence. He would devote certain periods daily to drawing from memory. The pile of papers that he filled every day, placed on the left-hand side of his meticulously tidy desk, grew visibly. Rudolf's habit was to write on each sheet in his beautiful, neat handwriting, making each one look like a letter by attaching colourful postage stamps, preferably from exotic countries. As he put it, he needed this kind of presentation for his manuscript, so that he did not lose the immediacy of

writing in a letter-like form. Indeed, the visual aspect alone of each sheet had an immediate appeal. When he went out, he used to hide the manuscript somewhere that only my mother knew about. When friends were searching for this manuscript after his death, we sent a drawing of the place with precise instructions to Florence, but sadly nothing could be found...

In the meantime, in this atmosphere of apparent calm, Rudolf still held on to his paintbrush. Practically every fortnight he would take a finished painting from his easel. Some would be sold, thus easing his financial straits. Others he kept back to decorate his room, such as a portrait of Schlüter and a landscape with narcissi.

Just as in the good old days of the Café du Dôme, the German artists settled on a regular meeting place. At the Café Giubbe Rosse on the Pizza della Repubblica, Rudolf displayed his mastery at chess, among other things. Battke's mother invited him to spend the summer months in Vallombrosa. But he missed his friends, and after just one month he was back in his room in the Pension Bandini. This was the only place where he felt calm and secure, even though the news from Germany was ominous. In February 1943 Rudolf informed his brother Paul in Berlin that he was suffering from kidney disease, and intended to remain in Florence for the time being. His letter was returned unopened, the envelope bearing a brief note: 'Addressee unknown at 54 Nestor Street. Jew.'

In Florence Rudolf had also met up again with Hans Purrmann, his companion in the bohemian days of Paris and Berlin. Purrmann had come to Florence in 1935 to direct the Villa Romana, a private foundation that exhibited the works of German artists and which from 1939 had close connections with the German regime. The paths of Purrmann and Levy had often crossed and then separated, and their friendship had also had its frequent ups and downs. Purrmann was not exactly popular among the exiled community staying at the Palazzo Guadagni, and when he put on an exhibition of his own paintings, he did not receive a single word of encouragment from these refugees. Rudolf too did not bother

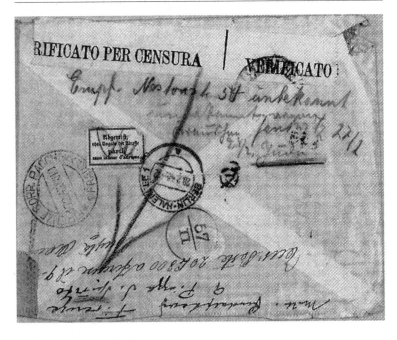

'Addressee unknown – Jew'.

with this exhibition. During the entire time that they were both in Florence, between 1940 and 1943, Purrmann did not once visit the Pension Bandini, and Rudolf did not set foot in the Villa Romana either, which is not to say that they didn't meet. They avoided each other only in public, although not because the other artists shunned Purrmann. Unlike Rudolf Levy, who ignored the danger because he was simply unaware of it, Purrmann knew only too well that Florence was swarming with Gestapo informers, exposing them both to danger. Consequently he made sure that they were never seen together. After all, Purrmann represented an institution that was more or less under the aegis of the German Reich, and Rudolf Levy was a Jew.

Leo Stein too had moved from Paris to Florence. He resided in an old, luxurious villa in the Settignano quarter of the town, overlooking the Arno. Once a week Hans and Rudolf would sit together on the balcony of this house, drinking wine and enjoying the view. The whole of Florence lay at their feet.

'Beautiful surroundings like these are enough to make all fears and worries disappear,' said Rudolf.

'Nero set fire to Rome, when it was at its height,' replied Purrmann.

For the moment it looked as if fortune was smiling on Rudolf. On 10 July 1943 the Allied Forces landed in southern Italy. Two weeks later the fascist high command woke from its slumber and turned against the Duce. Italy had had enough of war and of Hitler, its Axis partner. Benito Mussolini was summoned to see the King and arrested. In a lorry disguised as an ambulance, the Duce was brought to his place of imprisonment, first in a filthy police station in Rome, later on the island of Ponza, and finally to Gran Sasso in the Abruzzi mountains. Marshal Badoglio was appointed prime minister. Happy crowds thronged the streets of Florence, chanting, 'Hitler is kaput! Viva Italia!' In the lounge of the Pension Bandini glasses were clinked in celebration.

But by the beginning of September the tables had turned. On 3 September, Badoglio signed a ceasefire with the Allies, which was announced five days later. Hitler's response was to send the Wehrmacht marching into Italy. On 9 September, one day after the Nazis entered Florence, Purrmann telephoned Friedrich Kriegbaum, head of the German Art Historical Institute, whose offices were in the same house as the Pension Bandini. Purrmann yelled down the receiver, 'Go right away and tell Levy to disappear!' Kriegbaum did as he was asked, but Rudolf bluntly refused to follow this advice. He acted like an obstinate little boy, replying, 'My conscience is clear. There is absolutely no reason for me to hide.' Kriegbaum returned to the empty premises of the Institute, packed his belongings, ordered a car, and took the shortest possible route to the railway station. He was aware that not all his doings would find favour with the new ruler of northern Italy.

Three days earlier, on the evening of 6 September, Mario Carito, an officer in the upper echelons of the Italian security police, who had already succeeded in making his mark in the city, parked his car next to the building at 20 Via del Bardi. Swastikas adorned the gateway of the house, as well as the shield of the

German consulate. In the pouring rain, Carito looked up at the windows. The lights were on. He jumped across the puddles, crossed the pavement, and rang the bell. The consul's secretary recognized him immediately. 'What on earth brings you here so late at night?' Carito left her standing without a word, and went straight into the office of the consul. Dr Gerhard Wolf had previously been the Foreign Office representative in Warsaw and in the Vatican, and had the status of a full-ranking diplomat. He had already served his government at the consulate in Florence for two years, and by virtue of his position enjoyed excellent relations with the local security police.

'Good evening, Commander. Has something happened…? You're wet through. Won't you take off your coat?'

'Thank you, but I'm in a hurry.' Carito sat down. Drops of water were running down his uniform. 'I have to discuss an important top secret operation with you.'

'Even the toilet paper we're issued with here is stamped "top secret",' joked Wolf.

Carito ignored the quip and went on: 'Tonight a special unit will move in here to round up the Jews. We wish to eradicate the vermin from the city thoroughly and with the utmost speed.'

'Vermin? That would seem to be more a matter for the Public Health Department,' replied Wolf, maintaining his jocular tone and making a note in his jotter on the desk in front of him.

'I don't regard this as a joking matter,' was the officer's sharp retort.

'I didn't mean to upset you, Commander. It's just my way. The consulate will of course implement any orders it is issued with. How can I help you?'

'We need a list of all Jews holding a passport of the Reich. Also those who have not registered with the consulate and have no valid residence permits.'

Dr Wolf became serious. 'I cannot promise…I mean to say, we are not in possession of exact figures of illegal residents.'

'I rely on your skills and your loyalty.' Carito was now deliberately putting on the pressure. 'I need names and addresses. Any information you can lay your hands on.'

'I shall try my best,' said Wolf, giving way. 'My secretary will assemble the information by about midday tomorrow. When does the operation begin?'

'On 9 November.'

The consul stood up and stretched out his hand to say goodbye. Carito, however, responded with the customary fascist salute. 'Thank you. I knew you wouldn't disappoint me,' he said brusquely and left.

Dr Wolf waited until he heard the car starting up. Then he went back to his desk and dialled a number in Florence. 'Hallo,' he whispered into the receiver, 'Signora Combarti? It's good you're at home. Please inform Rudolf Levy right away that he must leave town immediately...No, I can't give you any details, but it's a matter of life and death...'

Signora Combarti, the owner of an exclusive art gallery, had been acting for some time as a go-between for the consul and a number of artists living in Florence. This warning was also delivered to Rudolf in good time but on this occasion too he took no notice. Heinz Battke's pleas that he should go and hide at his mother's house in Vallombrosa likewise fell on deaf ears. The most Rudolf was prepared to do was to hand over twenty of his most recent paintings to Battke. On the morning of 10 November, he could maintain that he had been unbelievably lucky, for his name had not been on the list that the consul had had drawn up, and on the first night of the wave of arrests the police had overlooked him. The next morning he sat calmly drinking coffee with his neighbours. A little later he was back at his easel, putting the finishing touches to his *Self-portrait with Glasses*.

With each day that passed the Gestapo intensified their search for Jews who had gone underground. Not a week went by when they didn't discover someone, who would then be deported to the Carpi transit camp near Modena. No one ever returned from there, and no one knew what happened to the detainees. For the first time, even Rudolf Levy began to be seriously concerned for his safety. At the beginning of December, he unburdened himself to his friend, Schlüter, who was back in Berlin.

...Up until now my outlook has always been optimistic, but now I am slowly beginning to foresee terrible things ahead. Will I be an old man before it will be possible to board an express train for Paris or anywhere again...I'm really living like a prisoner. And yet I have to be grateful that things aren't any worse for me. My paintings are still selling quite well, even though I have put up the prices in line with the current circumstances. I have also taken over your former room with the Lodoli woman and sometimes sleep there for a change. You see life has become expensive. The evenings are really terribly long and monotonous, and for me the blackout is one of the most dreadful aspects of the war. Does away with all enjoyment...

It was only now that Rudolf gave in to the insistence of another friend, Max Krell, and agreed to spend the nights in the latter's apartment. But no power on earth could keep him indoors all the time. He would leave at dawn and stroll around town. At about midday he would seek out the company of fellow artists, who continued to meet in the cafés, even though it was common knowledge that public meeting places were under constant surveillance by both Italian and German secret agents. In the afternoon he would return to his studio in the Pension Bandini and paint. He was now concentrating wholly on still lifes – yet another painting of flowers in a yellow vase. He loved yellow: the colour of the sun.

We shall never know how the henchmen got on to him. About a week before Christmas 1943, in the early hours of the morning, Signora Bandini informed him that Corsini, the art dealer, would be coming to see him at eleven o'clock to purchase another, possibly two more, of his paintings. Accordingly, Rudolf strolled from Krell's apartment to the Piazza Santo Spirito and entered the dark stairway of the Palazzo Guadagni. As he reached the fifth storey, he noticed two men standing beside the entrance to the *pension*. He asked them to let him pass, but they blocked his way. Even before they said anything, he realized that he had walked into a trap. One of the men drew some kind of pass from his pocket, pushed it under Rudolf's nose, and said coldly: 'State Secret Police. The game of hide and seek is over. Don't even try...'

'I've no intention of running away,' Rudolf replied coolly.

One of the policemen rang the doorbell. Signora Bandini opened the door and shrieked something in Italian. She was ordered to step aside, and the two men accompanied Rudolf into his room to carry out a search. Terrified and completely beside herself, she offered to make them all some coffee. 'Not a bad idea,' said one of the Gestapo men. Signora Bandini went into the kitchen, but by the time she returned with the coffee cups on a tray, Rudolf's room was already empty. The footsteps on the stairway continued to echo in her ears, long after the butterfly catchers had disappeared with the catch in their net.

After Lisbeth and Siegfried had said goodbye to Rudolf in September 1939, room no. 35 of the Hotel Windsor in the rue Valpozzo in Nice became their temporary home. It was a grey five-storey building, whose appearance reflected its architect's lack of inspiration, but Lisbeth enjoyed its comfort and, above all, the view. Her window looked out over a small garden with several trees and three tall palms. She also liked the hotel's location, far from the bustle of the harbour but near the seafront. There were a few other German refugees apart from the Levy couple living in the hotel, both Jews and non-Jews. In the evenings they would all sit together in the bar, immediately next to the entrance. They drank brandy, played cards, and competed in predicting the future. On the whole there was a yawning gap between their expectations and reality. The war in the east was over, Poland having surrendered after engaging in fighting that was hopeless from the outset, but had nevertheless lasted seventeen days. The country was divided up between Soviet Russia and Nazi Germany. In the west, not a single shot had yet been fired, but there was a sense of expectancy, filled with tense anxiety and profound distrust.

Although Lisbeth and Siegfried were now refugees who could not return to their home in Germany, in France they were regarded as subjects of an enemy state whose army was threatening the existence of the Third Republic. The mere presence of swastika stamps on their passports produced hostile reactions.

The date of 9 November is repeatedly associated with terror. In 1923, 9 November found Rudolf Levy standing in Munich, witness to Hitler's first attempt to seize power. On the night of 9–10 November 1938, Leo Levy was shot in his own home, thereby bringing to an end the history of the Levy family on German soil. Exactly one year later, on 9 November 1939, two French policemen knocked on the door of room 35 at the Hotel Windsor and ordered Siegfried to take a warm overcoat with him and follow them.

'What have I done? Where are you taking me?' asked Siegfried.

'To the Fort Carré internment camp,' said one of the policemen, adding sarcastically, 'You, madame, may stay in bed. We French consider bed the most appropriate place for the weaker sex.'

Lisbeth was aghast. Scarcely had the door closed behind her husband than she rushed downstairs to the hotel proprietor's office. Monsieur Alfred Cafiero, a hotelier to his fingertips, knew how to be of service to his guests. 'Don't worry, madame,' he reassured Lisbeth. 'I know a doctor who will concoct a miraculous certificate that is sure to let your husband go free. Given the circumstances, we can claim that he has gone down with leprosy or the plague, or he might even be nine months pregnant. Doctor Delair can produce the right answer to any problem. In any case he's saving up to transfer his practice to Casablanca. He's been dreaming of those brilliant white houses in North Africa for years on end – and he's always just short of the last few thousand francs.'

Dr Delair's practice was less than thirty paces from the hotel. The doctor was not in the least surprised by Lisbeth's request. When Monsieur Cafiero gave him a nod, he sat down at a desk with many drawers, and began to write in a clear hand:

I, the undersigned, Dr Delair, formerly departmental head of the Chardon-Lagache Hospital in Paris, and chief doctor at the British Hartford Hospital, cardiologist and specialist, hereby certify that I have examined Siegfried Levy, [...]. From an electrocardiographic examination, I have established that he is suffering from a chronic bronchial infection with sclerotic elements in the pleura, clearly indicating a debilitation of the cardiac musculature and the likelihood of an impending cardiac arrest, making hospital admission imperative.

'That should convince them,' he laughed and wrote his signature below. 'I know the lieutenant of Fort Carré, Dupuy. He has great respect for medical specialities and patients with heart conditions. His father died of a heart attack recently. He was a good man...Now let's go to the Préfecture, to have my signature authenticated. We could have it done by a notary, but I've found that a police stamp on medical certificates carries more weight. An unholy alliance, but in these circumstances, what can you do? But before we go, perhaps...'

Lisbeth opened her purse. 'How much, monsieur le docteur?'

Cafiero placed his hand over the purse. 'Not now. I know the tariff, madame. We shall simply add the amount to your weekly hotel bill. That's the way we always do it.'

'How odd...but, as you wish, gentlemen.'

'You must understand, madame, everyone wants their slice of the cake.'

'Obviously this is what makes the world goes round.' She smiled as she stretched out her hand to the doctor. Dr Delair shook it warmly.

Siegfried Levy had grown accustomed to the pleasures of a comfortable life, and so it was hardly surprising that life in the internment camp was not at all to his taste. The prisoners slept in the dormitories of an abandoned barracks, on three-tiered wooden bunks without pillows. The food had no flavour and, to make matters worse, was served in rusty metal bowls. The chilly autumn temperature and the thin, rough blanket were equally trying. By bribing one of the guards he was able to make contact with Lisbeth. Anxiously he followed her attempts to get him released. At last the day came, on 18 December. Lieutenant

Dupuy in person led him to the gate. Outside a taxi was waiting.

Nice was already decked out for the coming festival. A Christmas tree was set up in the entrance hall of the hotel. In their room Lisbeth kindled the Chanukah candles, as the beginning of this eight-day festival that year coincided with Christmas. In spite of the war, on 31 December there were New Year's Eve balls in almost all the hotels, as if to say, 'Eat, drink, and be merry, for tomorrow we die.' All offices remained closed until Epiphany, on 6 January. Directly they reopened, Siegfried began doing the rounds, seeking out the authorities. Tirelessly, he went from one office to another, for the couple desperately needed a French residence permit; without it he was bound to be rearrested. By now their tourist visas were completely useless. France was absolutely flooded with illegal immigrants and political refugees. Siegfried and Lisbeth claimed to be tourists, but given the current situation they were regarded as spies or saboteurs. The stack of authorizations, identity papers, and documents required for presentation to the authorities grew daily, and they had to dig deep into their pockets for every piece of paper stamped with an authorization. In addition three of the hotel's long-term residents had to testify to the Levys' loyalty towards France. The commander of the La Mila internment camp, responsible for 'Jewish Affairs' in the South of France, ordered Siegfried to present himself for a medical examination at the police headquarters in Aix-en-Provence. The order was dropped only after Dr Peaudeleu, medical officer and forensic doctor at the High Court, was kind enough to confirm Dr Delair's diagnosis. Lisbeth and Siegfried finally received a residence permit in the second half of January 1940, allowing them to remain in France for a year. 'I get the impression,' said Siegfried to his wife, when he returned to the hotel with the coveted permit, 'that in these crazy times, a scrap of paper like this is worth far more than a human life.'

But the really bad times were yet to come. In the summer of 1940 the beaches of the Riviera did not fill up with holiday visitors, the exquisite hotels in Cannes were depressingly empty, and it was only refugees on the run from Germany who saved

Monsieur Cafiero from bankruptcy. The German high command launched an offensive in the west with 143 highly trained and well-armed divisions, ignoring the neutrality of Belgium, Luxembourg, and the Netherlands. The French defensive positions collapsed like a house of cards. Within six weeks the 'Frog' army was defeated. One dramatic event followed another – on 10 June, Italy entered the war against France. On 12 June the French government fled from Paris to Tours and, a few days later, from Tours to Bordeaux. On 14 June, there were swastika flags flying from the Eiffel Tower. On 16 June, Prime Minister Reynaud resigned, to be succeeded by the aged Marshal Pétain. The next day members of the German Pioneer Corps, using pneumatic drills, tore down the walls surrounding the museum at Compiègne, and dragged out the old railway carriage in which the armistice had been signed in 1918. That day the former German Kaiser sent Hitler a greetings telegram from his exile at Doorn in Holland: 'Under the profound impression made by the spread of arms through France, I congratulate you and the entire German Wehrmacht on the great God-given victory, in the words of Kaiser Wilhelm: "What a change, by the grace of God…"' The German dictator had the telegram placed in the archives, even though in his opinion it was not divine providence but his own personal skill as commander-in-chief that was responsible. At any rate, the French delegates were obliged to witness the ceasefire being dictated in the same forest clearing and in the same carriage as in 1918. But this time Adolf Hitler was enthroned on the seat once occupied by Marshal Foch. The tables had been turned.

Foreign newspapers reported the events in every detail. Siegfried bought them from the kiosk beside the hotel, and a full hour later he was still immersed in them. The aroma of fresh coffee permeated the dining room. A pretty waitress wove her way among the tables, and the head waiter kept an eagle eye open to ensure that the guests were served in order of rank. The diners spoke softly among themselves; the air was filled with a curious humming, drowned out from time to time by the clatter of a tea-spoon or a fork against porcelain. In short there was the everyday background noise typical of an upper middle-class hotel in an exquisite location, from which the rest of the world with its persecutions, battles, and political manoeuvrings seemed excluded. But this apparent calm was misleading – the news indicated bad times ahead.

At the age of eighty-four, Philippe Pétain had been appointed governmental head of 'independent' France, which had been set up with the agreement of the Nazis during the surrender negotiations. On 9 July, parliament assembled in Vichy, to discuss the future of France, just as if they had the power to exert any influence. Hitler's only reason for agreeing to the existence of an 'independent' France was in order to prevent a government in exile based in London or North America. But anyone with an ounce of sense knew that if the present situation were to change – if Hitler were able to (or was compelled to) renounce collaboration with Pétain – the Wehrmacht would come marching into south-eastern France, and put an end to the farce of 'independent' France.

Vichy France was rather like a dilapidated canoe tossing about on stormy seas, easy prey for pirates. The foreign consulates adopted the role of rescue boats in this scenario. Thousands upon thousands of hapless passengers – refugees from Nazi-occupied territories as well as those made homeless by Franco's Spain – were all trying to get aboard these boats to escape from drowning. Scheming racketeers, with contacts in foreign agencies and the local security authorities, demanded huge amounts in currency in return for their services, payable on the spot, of course. The exchange rate for the dollar on the black market soared to sixty francs. Anyone who wanted to save his skin was held to ransom. Whoever did not have the ready cash was not worth the effort.

The law of the jungle and the constantly changing regulations gave rise to totally absurd situations. Thus, refugees who were able to prove they were intending to leave southern France were permitted to stay. This produced a new kind of service industry. The applications for visas to distant countries exceeded the demand for bread and meat. A stamp in your passport from the consulates of Paraguay, Cuba, Siam, or any other exotic state was the necessary prerequisite for a residence permit from the police. But you needed more than stamps to set out from Nice or Marseilles on the journey overseas. Before leaving, a refugee had to obtain dozens of different, bizarre certificates, proving that he did not suffer from any infectious diseases, that he did not wish to join the army, that he had no debts, that he was in possession of all his mental faculties and, to cap it all, that after leaving France he would in no way undermine the status of the country and its good reputation in the world. However, in occupied, intimidated Europe, just getting a birth certificate was almost as difficult as crossing the Red Sea had been of old. Obtaining all the necessary documents was a labour of Sisyphus.

The Café Roma and Aux Brûleurs des Loups in Marseilles became nerve centres for this document market. Siegfried would go there once a fortnight, in order to keep up with developments and pick up unofficial information that was not published in the censored newspapers. Waiters became speculators, and barmen sold diluted drinks along with the latest shipping news. Clients would discuss the latest gossip with profound and desperate concentration. Every now and again rumours would go the rounds about passages still available on passenger ships bound for Tangier or the Fiji Isles in the Pacific. With equal regularity 'official news' of the impending occupation by the Wehrmacht 'next week' or 'next month' would strike terror in the hearts of the café regulars. Discouraged and impoverished people would hang about for hours on the Quai des Belges in the hope of stealing aboard one of the fishing boats about to set sail, maybe reaching North Africa by this means.

There was not a single empty page left in the passports of the Levys. Siegfried had acquired entry visas for Spain, Portugal and, as a last resort, Bangkok and Siam. Impatiently he waited for a reply from Francis Maclaren Withey, the deputy United States Consul in Nice. About a month earlier the man had declared that Siegfried stood a 'very good' chance of getting an entry permit to the United States. But the wheels of bureaucracy were grinding slowly, and the coveted permission had still not arrived. The local police were threatening to declare his residence permit invalid, as

he had not officially registered to emigrate. Once again Siegfried
travelled to Marseilles, and for $500 he received a certificate from
a major shipping company, stating that he had been granted two
passages for Havana. By means of this certificate he was able to
avert their deportation to Germany for a further two months.

'Havana? Where on earth is that?' asked Monsieur Cafiero,
when he saw the certificate.

'For me, my friend,' answered Siegfried, 'it's a stop between
Marseilles and New York. But the atlas is unlikely to confirm my
reasoning.'

Cafiero laughed. 'Atlas? What can atlases tell us these days?!
No matter how fast they change, they still don't keep up with the
present. The strangest map I've ever seen was a year-old map of
France. When I looked at it, I didn't know whether to laugh or
cry.'

Two months later Siegfried was forced to buy another certificate for a sea passage. A new certificate was due every few
months, as the consuls, aware that there was easy profit to be
made, kept shortening the validity of such documents. On 21
September 1940 the first decree was issued, obliging Jews to register. Officials of the Vichy regime did exercise leniency towards
French people of the Mosaic faith, but not towards Jews who
were not born in France and who did not hold French citizenship. The latter were pursued remorselessly. Lisbeth and
Siegfried were aware of the noose growing ever tighter around
their necks. Although they wished neither to hear nor see it,
those letters that still reached them from Berlin proved what fate
befell a Jew who fell into the hands of the Nazis. As early as
February 1940 the Jews of Stettin had been put into cattle trucks
and deported. Bulldozers tore down the synagogue building and
razed it to the ground. The Reich Organization of the Jews in
Germany was presented with the bill for carrying out the work.
The ancient Torah scrolls, in their embroidered velvet mantles
and adorned with precious silver crowns, were taken by the
Gestapo, 'for safe keeping' as they put it, to a place in Hamburg.
There were no Jews left in Bad Polzin either. The firm of Ascher
Levy had been liquidated, and those branches of the business that

had not been seized up to the time of the Reich Kristallnacht were taken over by a new Nazi institution – Allgemeine Treuhandstelle (ALTREU).

Representatives of the Guaranty Trust Co. in New York did all they could to speed up procedures at the immigration offices. In the spring Siegfried gave instructions for the bulk of his assets, still deposited in Swiss bank accounts, to be transferred to this financial institute. Even before Consul Withey could inform him that his application had been successful, a telegram from Siegfried's New York lawyer was delivered to the Hotel Windsor: 'Visa number 18163, within the German quota, being sent to Nice this week stop Have booked second-class cabin on Excalibur stop Departure Lisbon 23 August stop US Consul advised to give preferential treatment stop Welcome to the US...'

But their delight was short-lived. The *Excalibur* weighed anchor without the Levys aboard. The American immigration officials took more than half a year to deal with the Levy file. And even when Siegfried was summoned to the consulate on 17 January, and the deputy consul entered the immigration certificate into his passport and that of his wife, they had still not overcome all the hurdles. In the meantime new laws had again been issued, and no one could leave France without an exit permit.

A sour-faced officer grimly inspected Siegfried's application for this permission, and handed it back, saying: 'I regret, monsieur, that you must first give me a certificate from your representative in Aix-en-Provence.'

'Representative? Who represents me in Aix-en-Provence?'

'I'm referring to the embassy of the Third Reich, monsieur. We can no longer issue refugees of German origin with exit visas, without this embassy's permission.'

'What on earth do you want of me?' asked Siegfried in mounting anger. 'Don't you welcome the prospect of getting rid of a refugee like me, a member of an inferior race?'

'Monsieur,' replied the officer heatedly, 'I don't have the time to argue with you. You can see that there are hundreds of people waiting here. Come back when you have the permission. *Au revoir.*'

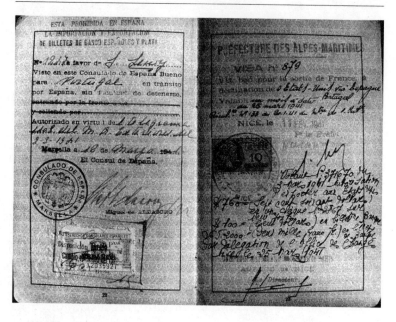

30-day visa to Portugal.

It was anything but easy to surmount this last obstacle on the route to a safe haven. The German embassy in Aix-en-Provence was obviously not interested in yet another two refugees. However, their interest was aroused by the couple's assets. Siegfried explained in vain that he had no property left in Germany, that everything had either been sold or confiscated. He had to appear repeatedly for lengthy questioning, until a compromise was finally reached. Lisbeth and Siegfried received the written permission in exchange for the property in Bisone.

Siegfried did not wish to remain in France a day longer than necessary. Who knew what further requirements could be imposed? Apart from this, their exit visas were only valid until 25 March. The couple took leave of the hotel proprietor, Monsieur Cafiero, and their other acquaintances lodging there, and on 13 March 1941 they crossed the Spanish border on their way to Portugal. They reached Lisbon on 4 April, and at the beginning of May, finally aboard the passenger ship *Nafar*, they cast a last look at the rapidly disappearing coastline of Europe.

Siegfried's certificate of naturalization, issued by the American Department of Justice, 26 November 1946.

'Strange,' said Siegfried and he turned to Lisbeth, who was standing on deck beside him, leaning against the railing, 'I would never have thought I'd be able to leave Europe without a parting pang. I always thought there is no life beyond Europe. As it turns out the very opposite is true.'

Epilogue: The Living and the Dead

The *Nafar* docked in New York in the second half of May 1941. Friends waiting for Lisbeth and Siegfried brought them straight to the flat they had rented for them in Forest Hills.

By now the war in Europe and its terrors lay far behind them. When they read in the newspapers that the United States had entered the war, it all seemed extremely remote, even to them. It had taken them very little time to shake off the old continent, although they did not manage to put down roots in their new home. Siegfried did not find an occupation, but the money that he had managed to transfer from Germany to Switzerland provided them with an easy, untroubled life. When Siegfried died in 1955, there was nothing to keep Lisbeth in the USA. Most of her nieces lived in Israel, and she desperately missed the family. She died at the ripe old age of ninety-two in a residential home near Tel Aviv. The executors of her estate were not interested in the various documents, letters, and photographs stored in a suitcase in one of her wardrobes, and that is how it found its way to the flea market in Jaffa.

Siegfried had two brothers – Ernst Levy, the lawyer, who died of a sudden illness in 1934 during his visit to Palestine, and Leo Levy, who was murdered in Bad Polzin during the rioting of Kristallnacht. His widow, Else, had the following text engraved on his tombstone: 'Here lies Leo Levy, who died an honest death, for he led an honest life.'

She emigrated to *Eretz Israel* shortly after her husband was murdered, and died there in 1943. Käthe, Ernst Levy's widow, also lived in Israel until she died. Siegfried's cousins, Paul Levy the railway engineer, and the artist, Rudolf Levy, both fell victim to the Nazis. Paul perished in a concentration camp. Rudolf Levy was last heard of on a transport to the camp at Carpi, near Modena.

Since the descendants of Bernhard and Julius Levy were not blessed with sons, that spells the end of the Levy family. The firm of Ascher Levy in Bad Polzin no longer exists. The heirs – all women – were not interested in reviving the family business. None of the descendants of the Levy family wanted to return to Germany and settle there. The only one of the family whose name may remain in the common memory is probably Rudolf Levy, who enriched German culture with his paintings. Two of them were presented as a gift to Golda Meir by the German Chancellor Willi Brandt, when he came on a state visit to Israel. Genia and her second husband Heinrich Koppold spared neither money nor effort in scouring the whole of Europe in search of his work, in order to catalogue it. Genia began this task on the day that the International Red Cross informed her that her first husband's name was not among those to have survived the Holocaust. She dedicated herself to this undertaking up to the time of her death in Munich in 1953. Furthermore it is worth noting that the Galeria Firenze was the first to seize the initiative by putting on a show of his paintings after the war. Frau Susanne Thesing of Munich devoted her thesis to the artist, and in 1990 published a well-documented monograph on him.

Bernhard's daughter Lina and her husband Karl Hamburger lost their lives in Theresienstadt. Their only son Alfred managed to escape. Today he is a pensioner in New York. Ida, the second daughter, married again after her divorce from Paul Levy. Her second husband, Otto Feldman, was a Jewish art dealer, originally from Czechoslovakia. They divided their time between Bad Polzin, Berlin, and Paris. Ida had a daughter, Susanna, known as Sanna, by her first marriage. In the late summer of 1938 mother and daughter went on a holiday to southern Europe, and it was this that saved their lives. Ida died in the United States of America at the age of ninety-one. Sanna married a non-Jewish German and still runs a bookshop today in Los Angeles.

Leo Levy had four daughters – Hannah, Eva, Margarete, and Ruth. All four managed to escape Nazi Germany in time.

Hannah and Eva are both still alive in Israel, where they have their own families. Hannah Slijper, the widow of a Dutchman, lives in a little house surrounded by a wonderful garden full of flowers in Ramat Hasharon, not far from Tel Aviv. She was immensely helpful in reconstructing the Levy family history. Her entire life was spent in carrying out the *Hachsharah* ideal. Up to the time of her husband's death she managed a small farm in the co-operative village of Beit Yitzchak.

Margarete Levy left Germany a year before the night of the pogroms, and went to a boarding school in London. In England she married a non-Jewish art historian, Klaus E. Hinrichsen, who had left Germany in 1939. The couple own a pretty little house in Highgate, in North London. He earned a living working in the pharmaceutical industry. Margarete started a toyshop, specializing in wooden and educational toys, which became well known beyond the confines of Highgate. Her two children grew up into true-blue Brits.

At the time her father was murdered, Ruth was only seventeen years old. Since she was still legally under age, her name had to be entered on her mother's visa. Both arrived in Tel Aviv in 1939. Ruth got married in 1953 to a man who was born in Berlin, and the two of them emigrated to the United States of America, where they settled on the West Coast. By a tragic coincidence, their only son was killed in a car accident on the very day that had come to have a fateful significance for the Levy family – 9 November.

Ernst Levy also had four daughters – Thea, Marianne, Brigitta, and Gabriele. All four were able to get out of Germany before the Second World War broke out, and emigrated to Palestine. Each of them married and started families there, bringing sons and daughters into the world. It is worth emphasizing that almost all the women in the Levy family survived because they emigrated to Palestine in time, where they took an active part in the Zionist development of the country. Thus they were involved in the very region of all places that previous generations of the Levy family had so strongly disapproved of. Today Gabriele Bradmann lives with her husband in Givatayim. Thea

Löwenthal married a bank employee, and Brigitta Wolfsohn's husband was a lawyer and notary, who is no longer alive. Marianne Lewin is the only one who returned to religious observance, and observes the mitzvot. She will continue to wait for the Messiah to come until the day she dies.

Glossary

ADAR – A month in the Jewish calendar.

ALLIANCE ISRAÉLITE – In full, the Alliance Israélite Universelle, the first modern international Jewish organization, established in 1860, with headquarters in Paris. The formation of the Alliance Israélite was influenced by the ideological trends and political events of the second half of the nineteenth century. Its objectives and activities were wide ranging: representing political interests on the diplomatic stage, providing assistance to new immigrants to Palestine and, above all, providing education and vocational training.

ASHKENAZIM – The name of an unknown Biblical nation, which is used in Hebrew literature to denote Germany and German Jews. Jewish families who fled from Germany from the twelfth century onwards to southern Europe or to the Orient added 'Ashkenazi' to their own names to indicate their origin. In today's parlance 'Ashkenazim' stands for Western Jewry. See its opposite: Sephardim.

BAKSHEESH – Persian. 1. Alms, tip. 2. Bribe.

BAR KOCHBA REBELLION – When Roman Emperor Hadrian proposed to build a new city on the site of Jerusalem, including a temple to Jupiter, it triggered a Jewish rebellion of surprising intensity led by Simon Bar Kochba.

BAR MITZVAH – Hebrew. 'Son of God's commandment'. At the age of thirteen, a boy is elevated to this status, when he is called up for the first time to read from the Torah with the other men in the synagogue.

BRUCHIM HABAIM – Hebrew. Literally: 'Blessed be those who come'.

B'SHANAH HABA'A BEYERUSHALAYIM – Hebrew. 'Next year in Jerusalem'. A traditional blessing, symbolizing the Jews' longing for Jerusalem since the destruction of the Temple.

BURIAL RITE – In Judaism burial must take place within twenty-four hours of death. The funeral may be slightly delayed only to permit absent close family members to arrive.

CANTOR – Also known by the Hebrew term, *chazan*. A person who leads the worshippers in prayer during services in the synagogue, and who should also have strong religious beliefs, as a role model for the community.

CHABAD GROUP – A populist grouping of Chassidism, stressing permanent communication with God and intense emotion and spiritual concentration at prayer.

CHACHAM – Hebrew pl. *Chachamim*, the Wise One(s).

CHALLAH – Hebrew. Plaited, usually sweetish white bread, over which a blessing is recited at the beginning of the meal on the Sabbath and festivals, after which it is then shared out among all those present.

CHALUKAH – Hebrew. 'Distribution'. Term denoting the traditional financial support of Jewish inhabitants of *Eretz Israel* by their co-religionists in the Diaspora. Since the eighteenth century, *chalukah* in the broader sense has meant the organized form of financial contributions and the institutions responsible; the *chalukah* system was abolished when the State of Israel was established in 1948.

CHANUKAH – Eight-day festival of lights in commemoration of the re-dedication of the Temple following the Maccabean uprising against Antiochus IV Epiphanes (165 BCE). A post-Biblical festival.

CHASSIDISM – A variety of religious-mystical movements within Judaism that arose from the twelfth century onwards; in the eighteenth century Chassidism spread predominantly through Eastern Europe and today is represented worldwide by the Lubavitch movement. Its followers emphasize the emotions in religion and the revelation of nature as against belief in the law. They reject all modern phenomena and lead a very spiritual life, totally dedicated to the service of God and the study of the religious scriptures. See also *Chabad* group.

CHOVEVEI ZION – Hebrew. 'Friends of Zion'. The name adopted by amalgamated groups in Russia and Rumania, Western Europe, and the USA, which are regarded as the forerunners of political Zionism. They promoted the return of the Jewish people dispersed throughout the Diaspora.

CITY WALLS – From the period when Jerusalem was settled by the Jebusites, and its subsequent conquest by King David, it was repeatedly fortified over time, depending on the geographical conditions and population density. The city walls, as they stand today, were built by Suleiman the Magnificent during his rule over the city (1520–66). With the expansion of Jerusalem during the nineteenth century, the term 'city walls' changed to the 'walls of the Old City'.

CONSERVATIVE JUDAISM – This developed to distinguish itself from Reform Judaism, which went too far in the view of some rabbis. Followers did, however, favour a change in attitude towards ritual and the observance of certain laws, yet wished to preserve the Jewish traditions. Unlike Reform Judaism, the followers of Conservative Judaism were pro-Zionist from the outset.

DIVORCE – Divorce is not only permitted by Jewish law, it is actually favoured where a marriage is regarded as irretrievably broken down. If a woman has been unable to bear children, Orthodox rabbis will even advise divorce.

DRAGOMAN – Turkish. 'Interpreter'. An interpreter in the Middle East, especially from Arabic, Turkish, and Persian countries.

'ELDER OF ZION' – A reference to the alleged *Protocols of the Elders of Zion*, revealed as a forgery long before 1933, but exploited to this day for anti-Semitic purposes.

ELIJAH – A prophet, miracle-worker, and servant of God (2 Kings 1:3); a prophesier and precursor of the Messiah; a deliverer and comforter in times of need, whose presence is awaited on Seder night at Pesach.

ERETZ ISRAEL – Hebrew. Land of Israel, Land of the Fathers, also known as 'Zion'.

EXPULSION OF THE JEWS FROM SPAIN – In 1492 those Jews who refused to convert to Christianity were driven out of Spain and Portugal. See Sephardim.

FEZ – Turkish. A flat-topped, conical felt cap worn in Muslim countries.

GEMARA – Hebrew, 'completion'. A text based on the rabbinical discussions of the Mishnah. The Talmud consists of the Torah and the Mishnah together.

GERMAN COLONY – A name still in use today for the residential districts founded in the middle of the nineteenth century by the Pietistic Templars in Jerusalem, Haifa, and elsewhere.

GOY, GOYA, GOYIM – Hebrew. A term for all peoples other than the Jewish people; also used to denote non-Jew.

HACHSHARAH – Hebrew, 'preparation'. Training mainly for young people who needed to be prepared in practical ways for emigration to *Eretz Israel*. *Hachsharah* became increasingly widespread in the Jewish youth movements in Europe from the beginning of the twentieth century onwards, but in Germany only after Hitler seized power. The youth movements would mostly lease farms, horticultural nurseries, or similar concerns, where young people were trained not only as farmers, cattle breeders, domestic workers, and managers, but also as blacksmiths, cobblers, etc.

HALACHAH – Religious legal code.

HOLY SCRIPTURES – All texts that contain the history of the Jewish people, and the religious precepts, rules of conduct, and their interpretations. The Torah alone is *the* Holy Scripture.

JEWISH AGENCY – In Hebrew, *Sochnut*. An international, non-state institution with headquarters in Jerusalem, the executive of the World Zionist Organization. The aims of the Jewish Agency are to help Jews from all over the world when they settle in Israel and to promote the development of the land.

JEWISH CALENDAR – The Jewish calendar follows the moon. Consequently a new day begins in the evening, and the months are counted according to the cycles of the moon. As a rule, one year has twelve such months or 354 days. The Jewish year is therefore on average twelve days shorter than the solar year. In order that the religious festivals in the year are observed at the right time, a thirteenth month is inserted into the Jewish calendar. There are seven Jewish leap years in a cycle of nineteen years. The calculation of the Jewish calendar years begins with the assumed date of the Creation in 3760 BCE. By this reckoning the Christian year 2002 is equivalent to the Jewish year 5762.

The months (beginning with the New Year) are: Ellul/Tishri – September; Tishri/Cheshvan – October; Cheshvan/Kislev – November; Kislev/Tevet – December; Tevet/Shvat – January; Shvat/Adar – February; Adar/Adar Sheni (II)/Nissan – March; Nissan/Iyar – April; Iyar/Sivan – May; Sivan/Tammuz – June; Tammuz/Av – July; Av/Ellul – August.

JEWISH NATIONAL FUND – In Hebrew, *Keren Kayemet L'Yisrael*, and usually abbreviated to JNF. The Jewish National Fund of the World Zionist Organization for land purchase and development in *Eretz Israel*, founded at the 5th Zionist Congress held in Basle, in 1901.

JEWISH QUARTER – Inside the walls of the Old City (see 'City walls') of Jerusalem, there are four distinct residential quarters – the Armenian, the Christian, the Muslim, and the Jewish quarter.

KABBALAH – Hebrew, 'tradition'. The teaching and texts of Jewish medieval mysticism, dealing with the supposedly secret mystical meaning of the Old Testament and the Talmudic religious laws. The expulsion of the Jews from Spain and Portugal (1492) turned Kabbalism into a popular movement. The later sixteenth-century form of Kabbalism gave rise to Chassidism.

KADDISH – Hebrew, 'sanctification'. The Kaddish is a prayer in praise of God, recited during a religious service and by mourners, but not, as is often mistakenly assumed, a prayer for the souls of the dead.

KADI – Arabic, a religious judge in Muslim countries.

KASHRUT – Hebrew. The Jewish dietary laws, laying down those foods that are permitted and those that are prohibited, but also prescribing the methods of food preparation. Observing *kashrut* means having two separate sets of table- and kitchen-ware, one for milk and one for meat dishes. *Kashrut* also includes the laws of ritual slaughter.

KIBBUTZ/KIBBUTZIM – Hebrew, 'collection'. A voluntary agricultural collective in Palestine/Israel; work is unpaid in exchange for provision for the family members.

KOHELET – Hebrew name for Ecclesiastes, sometimes incorrectly described as the Book of King Solomon, since the author refers to himself as 'Son of David, King of Jerusalem'. Historians have traced linguistic evidence that rules out the likelihood that the book was by Solomon. The Hebrew in which this book is written is one of the latest developmental stages of Biblical Hebrew.

KOLELIM – Hebrew, pl. (sing., *Kolel*). A community of Jews in the old *Yishuv* in *Eretz Israel*, all originating from the same country.

KOSHER – Hebrew, *Kasher*, meaning 'proper', 'right'; in accordance with the ritual dietary laws.

MAIMONIDES – Rabbi Moshe ben Maimon (1135–1204), religious philosopher and theologian, the leading Jewish teacher of law in the Middle Ages. As a philosopher, he also influenced Aristotelian-inclined Christian scholasticism.

MAZEL TOV – Yiddish, 'congratulations'.

MEGILLE – Yiddish (Hebrew, *Megillah*). The Book of Esther in the Apocrypha section of the Bible, read aloud on Purim, which tells the story of how Queen Esther saved the Jews of the Persian kingdom.

MEIR BA'AL HANES – The 'wonder rabbi'. From the sixteenth century onwards, charity boxes in memory of this rabbi were an important and highly effective method of collecting money for the Jewish community living in *Eretz Israel*.

MEMORIAL CANDLE – During the week of mourning (*Shivah*) following the death of a close relative, a memorial candle is lit in memory of the deceased. It is lit again thirty days later, as well as every year on the anniversary of the death, known in Judaism as the *Yahrzeit*.

MESHUGGE – Yiddish, 'mad', 'crazy, abnormal'.

MINYAN – Hebrew, a quorum of ten adult men required for a service worshipping God.

MISHNA – Hebrew, 'copy'; an interpretation of the orally transmitted Torah, written down c. CE 200. The Mishnah and the Torah together form the Talmud.

MISHNAYOT – The Mishnah is subdivided into six orders. Each order generally consists of sixty-three tractates. Each tractate is divided into chapters, which again contain a series of individual teachings and are sometimes referred to as the Mishnah (pl. Mishnayot).

MITZVA/MITZVOT – Hebrew, sing. mitzva, pl. mitzvot; a term used to denote the laws and prohibitions in Judaism, altogether 613 articles of faith, 365 of which are prohibitions and 248 laws.

MOHEL – Hebrew, 'person who performs circumcision'. A God-fearing man, who performs the ceremony of circumcision on a boy, eight days after birth, as a symbol of his acceptance into the covenant with God.

MORNING PRAYER – The Jewish law prescribes three daily prayers: *Shacharit* – morning prayer, *Mincha* – afternoon prayer, and *Ma'ariv* – evening prayer. There are additional prayers for religious festivals and *Shabbat*.

ORT – Russian, abbreviation of Obshchestvo Rasprostranenya Turda sredi Yevreyev – Jewish Association for Craft and Agriculture, originally a private initiative to improve the situation of Russian Jews under Tsar Alexander II. There are now ORT schools and training centres all over the world. The first international ORT organization was founded in Berlin in 1921.

ORTHODOX JUDAISM – The term first appeared in 1795 and became established in the nineteenth century to distinguish itself from Reform Judaism. The Orthodox regard themselves as the preservers of the authentic Jewish religion. They observe all the written and unwritten laws, and attach particular importance to the *Halacha* and the *Shulchan Aruch*.

PALESTINE OFFICE – The departments affiliated to the World Zionist Organization, offering on-the-spot advice and assistance to those wishing to emigrate.

PESACH – seven-day festival, commemorating the liberation from slavery in Egypt. The *Haggadah*, which tells the story of the Exodus from Egypt, is read on the first evening – Seder night. A special meal is prepared; a cup of wine for the prophet, Elijah, is placed on the table and an empty place is left for him; for according to popular belief the herald of the Messiah could appear on this particular evening, when the scattered people of Israel are gathered together.

PURIM – The 'feast of lots' recalls Queen Esther, who foiled the intended mass murder of the Jews in the Kingdom of Persia, by revealing to King Ahasuerus that she herself was Jewish. Purim is a joyful festival, with a tradition of wearing fancy dress.

REFORM JUDAISM – In the middle of the nineteenth century eman-cipation caused religious traditions to be questioned, particularly in the German-speaking areas. The outstanding personality in this movement was Rabbi Abraham Geiger, who is regarded to this day as the actual founder of the movement. He rejected the concept of revelation from an academic standpoint, declared that a return to *Eretz Israel* was pointless, and reduced the Torah to a 'source of ethics'. Accordingly the Talmud and the *Shulchan Aruch* are no longer regarded as binding, and with emancipation, the Messianic hope was considered to have been fulfilled. Reform Judaism was later to find a firm foothold in the USA.

REICHSVERTRETUNG DER DEUTSCHEN JUDEN (REICH REPRE-SENTATION OF GERMAN JEWS) – Later: *Reichsvereinigung der Juden in Deutschland* (Reich Organization of the Jews in Germany). Umbrella organization of the major Jewish organizations and com-munities from 1933 onwards, headed by the highly respected Rabbi Leo Baeck. The work of the *Reichsvertretung* consisted in the main of co-ordinating the activities of the Jewish organizations for the fol-lowing relief activities: preparation for and implementing emigra-tion; change of career; education and training; financial aid; welfare work. It had no political influence. In 1939 the national socialist authorities changed the name of the *Reichsvertretung* to *Reichsvereinigung der Juden in Deutschland* (Reich Organization of the Jews in Germany).* From then on it was under the power of the national socialist authorities and was controlled by them, and its practical work was exploited to serve the aims of the Reich.

ROSH CHODESH – Hebrew, 'beginning of a new month', which is marked by special prayers.

ROYAL TOMBS – One of the most interesting burial sites in Palestine/Israel, which was long thought to contain the tombs of the Jewish kings. In actual fact these cave tombs were installed only by Queen Helene of Adiabene (Mesopotamia).

SABBATH CANDLES – At the beginning of the *Shabbat* or of a festival, the woman of the house traditionally lights two candles and recites a blessing over them.

SANHEDRIN – Hebrew, in Greek *Synedrion*; 'assembly' of the Supreme Judicial Council of the Jews in Greek and Roman times.

SARACENS – A term used in antiquity to denote the Arabs in the north-western part of Arabia and the Sinai peninsula. It was used in the Middle Ages for all Arabs and then all Muslims in the Mediterranean region, particularly those fighting the Crusaders.

SEDER NIGHT – See Pesach.

SEPHARDIM – Spanish-Portuguese Jews and their descendants, who, after the expulsion from Spain and Portugal in 1492, dispersed throughout the entire Mediterranean region and the Orient, as far as the Far East. In current parlance Sephardim refers to Jews from Oriental countries, as distinct from Ashkenazim.

SHABBAT – The appointed day of rest in Judaism is also a day of spiritual retreat. Religious Jews do not work on *Shabbat*, with the definition of 'work' being somewhat variously interpreted. Fires are not permitted to be lit, and only a specified distance is allowed to be walked, so that nowadays religious Jews will not use electrical equipment, including electric light or transport, on *Shabbat*.

SHIDDUCH – A match of two partners for marriage.

* From then on the Jews were classified by the Nazis as subjects of the German Reich.

SHIVA – Hebrew, 'seven', the seven-day mourning period following a death.

SHULCHAN ARUCH – Hebrew, 'prepared table', a legal code compiled by Josef Karo in the sixteenth century, which is still observed today by religious Jews.

TALMUD – 'Encyclopedia of learning', completed c. CE 200, consisting of the Mishnah and the Gemara. There are two *Talmudim*: the *Jerusalem Talmud* (compiled in the Land of Israel) and the *Babylonian Talmud* (written during the Babylonian exile). The *Jerusalem Talmud* is different in structure, shorter, more concise, and occasionally more puzzling, as well as concentrating more on legal issues.

TANACH – Hebrew, an abbreviation for the Holy Scriptures, from the three words *Torah*, *Neviim* (Books of the Prophets), and *Ketuvim* (body of texts – Psalms, Book of Job, etc.).

TEMPLE – The first Jerusalem Temple was built by King Solomon in c. 960 BCE, and was destroyed by Nebuchadnezzar in 587 BCE, followed by the Babylonian exile of the Jews. In the reign of King Cyrus, some of them returned to Jerusalem and began building another Temple. In CE 70 the Second Temple was destroyed by the Romans. The 'destruction of the Temple' refers to these events.

TISHA B'AV – The ninth day of the month of Av; a day of fasting in memory of the destruction of the Temple.

TORAH – Hebrew, 'instruction, teaching' – in the narrower sense, the Scroll of the Pentateuch, containing the Five Books of Moses, which are kept in the synagogue. In the wider sense, Torah means the learning contained in the Holy Scriptures.

TOWER OF DAVID – Also known as the Citadel by the Tower of David; the former palace of Herod the Great, beside the Jaffa Gate in the Old City of Jerusalem, from which the Tower of David is visible from afar.

TREIFE – Yiddish, a term from the codex of the Jewish dietary laws (see *kashrut*), originally denoting an animal barred from consumption, because it was sick or wounded, but in the wider sense everything that is not kosher.

WAILING WALL – The Western Wall, Judaism's holiest site. The sole surviving part of the Temple, destroyed by the Romans in CE 70, where to this day Jews still pray and weep, and push scraps of paper bearing entreaties to God between chinks in the masonry.

WEDDING CANOPY (*CHUPPA*) – The bridal couple exchange vows under the canopy; the bride receives a ring as a symbol of the union, and the bridegroom stamps on a glass, in memory of the destruction of the Temple.

WORLD ZIONIST ORGANIZATION – Established in 1897 during the First Zionist Congress in Basle as the umbrella organization for the world Zionist movement, over the years it spawned an ever-increasing number of committees, bodies and subsidiary organizations. Essentially it represents every brand of party political activity.

YEKKES – Yiddish, sing. *Yekke*, an affectionately mocking term for immigrants from Germany, which allegedly derives from the fact that even in Palestine's hot climate, they did not take off their jackets.

YERUSHALAYIM – Hebrew for Jerusalem.

YISHUV – Hebrew, a term for the settlement of Jews in *Eretz Israel*. There is a distinction between the old *Yishuv* – the pre-Zionist settlement – and the new *Yishuv*, which formed the nucleus of the State of Israel.

YONTEF – The Yiddish version of the Hebrew *Yom Tov*, meaning 'religious festival'.

ZIONISM – The concept of political Zionism was formulated by Theodor Herzl at the end of the nineteenth century, in his book, *Der Judenstaat* (*The Jewish State*), the first call for the establishment of a Jewish state in *Eritz Israel*.

ZIONIST ASSOCIATION IN GERMANY – The umbrella organization of all Zionists in Germany was founded in October 1897. In 1902 the Zionists in Germany established the weekly publication *Jüdische Rundschau*, which was to become their mouthpiece. During the Weimar Republic, membership of the Association reached its peak with 35,000 supporters. Once the Nazis came to power, the activities of the Association were mainly assisting emigration and *Hachsharah*. After the issue of the so-called Nuremberg Laws in 1935, the Association was subjected to numerous restrictions, and in 1938 it was closed down by the Nazis.